Run for the Diamonds

Run for the Diamonds

100 Years of Footracing in Berwick, Pennsylvania

MARK WILL-WEBER

BREAKAWAY BOOKS
HALCOTTSVILLE, NEW YORK
2008

Run for the Diamonds: 100 Years of Footracing in Berwick, Pennsylvania
Copyright 2008 by Mark Will-Weber

ISBN: 978-1-891369-78-0
Library of Congress Control Number: 2008934821

Published by Breakaway Books
P.O. Box 24
Halcottsville, NY 12438
www.breakawaybooks.com

FIRST EDITION

Contents

ACKNOWLEDGMENTS

Writing this book was a bit like running the Berwick course—only longer! I did, however, have some great "teammates" en route—so many that I fear I cannot acknowledge all of them, but here are a few front runners.

First and foremost, Run for the Diamonds race director Margaret Livsey, who spent numerous hours collecting information and contacts for me. In addition, a nod of thanks to Berwick Marathon Association members Bill and Bev Bull, Bill Hower Jr., Bob Eveland, and Lanny Conner, who were generous with their collections of race information and/or inspiring stories. Freddi Carlip of *The Runner's Gazette* deserves an assist as a source, especially in regard to the great H. Browning Ross. A special thank-you to John Sabatino of Harry's Sports in Berwick, for sharing his uncle J. Howard Remley's (who fired the starting pistol for many a great Berwick races) captivating special collection of old photos. Speaking of photos, the last quarter century at Berwick has been well captured by shooters Clay Shaw and Karen Mitchell.

Stephanie Miller (Moravian College) deserves much thanks for her help in the early stages of race research, while my friends Adam Bean and Carla Thomas Lindenmuth answered the call to read some of the early chapters and gave me back encouragement. Along the encouragement line, much love to my parents, Jack and Trudy Weber, for their constant support.

For help with valuable research, Barb Landis (and her crack staff) of the Cumberland Historical Society in Carlisle, Pennsylvania, and the volunteers at the Berwick Historical Society, rose to the call. A nod across the waters to Finland is due to Dr. Ossi Viita, an author-researcher for the Finnish Sports Archives, for his correspondence and insights on Hannes Kolehmainen and Ville Ritola.

From the thanks-for-your-patience department there is my ever-steady publisher, editor, and friend Garth Battista of Breakaway Books. . . . And my family: wife Sally and daughter Jordy, who learned more than perhaps they wanted to know about Louis Tewanima as I held court at the dinner table.

SOURCES

The primary sources for this book came from a variety of publications and interviews. Those included old newspaper clippings from the *Berwick Enterprise* and the *Bloomsburg Morning Press*, the *New York Times* historical archives, *Collier's* magazine, numerous Berwick Marathon race programs (including a good starting point from Dan Spadoni's articles on the event . . . ditto, Maxim Furek) and race stories from *The Runner's Gazette*. Books that provided valuable background support include (but are not limited to) *Marathon* by Clarence DeMar, *Flying Finns* by Matti Hannus, *Young at Heart: The Story of Johnny Kelley* by Frederick Lewis and Dick Johnson, *Boston: The Canadian Story* by David Blaikie, and *Ellison "Tarzan" Brown: The Narragansett Indian Who Twice Won the Boston Marathon* by Michael Ward, to name a few.

Preface

Not all the mysteries of the Berwick Marathon (aka The Run for the Diamonds) can be solved. That's just the way it is. I know because I just spent the better part of two years finding out. For example:

In the late fall of 1944, the US Army had crossed the Siegfried line into Germany and was pushing toward the Rhine River. Among those khaki-clad troops was Rudyard Sloane, a young lieutenant from Berwick, Pennsylvania. As the *Berwick Enterprise* noted in late November of that year:

> Lt. Sloane was moving along German lines in a recently captured village. In a conversation with another army officer, the officer asked Sloane where he was from.
>
> Sloane replied, "Oh, you wouldn't know this town of mine. It's just a little town in Pennsylvania called Berwick . . ."
>
> To which the officer answered, "I wouldn't know it, eh? Look at this . . . I won this ring in a marathon race there one time."

Sloane wrote home to Berwick about the strange coincidence but was unable to remember the other officer's name—or perhaps he simply had neglected to get it to begin with. However, at the time of Sloane's letter, race director Chiv MacCrea (who was getting ready to conduct the 1944 race) surmised that the man with the prize diamond ring was most likely Peter Olexy, the former Penn State cross-country captain who had won the Berwick Marathon in a blinding snowstorm in 1938.

But it turned out *not* to be Pete Olexy (who did serve in World War II, but not in Germany). In fact, as I write this in July 2008, I don't know—for sure—who that officer with the ring might have been. I may find out some day; I may not. The Berwick race is stingy when it comes to revealing *all* its secrets; some remain elusive.

Nevertheless, I love that story concerning Lieutenant Sloane, the mystery officer, and the Berwick Marathon ring. Maybe I love it more because it is—essentially—an orphan. It was what I came to call a "nugget." By that I mean a find—that glittering piece of gold twinkling enticingly in the battered tin pan after you've sifted through hours upon hours of silt, pebbles, and river-bottom muck. You could argue, of course, that this particular nugget was fool's gold.

But we can easily picture young Lieutenant Sloane—the Berwick native—wide-eyed after seeing that ring, an unusual coincidence. The odds of such a chance meeting—in a war zone—were nothing short of astounding, and perhaps he saw its appearance as an omen of good fortune.

The Run for the Diamonds—the traditional 9-mile race that for most of its nearly 100 years was known as the Berwick Marathon—is still one of our sport's best kept secrets. But knowing the legacy of the race can only enhance our knowledge and appreciation for the history of long-distance running—and for that the Berwick race is a veritable treasure chest.

For many of us, *reading* about the Berwick race would be something of a passive investment. For those of us who run the race, it is worth asking "Why?" The course is borderline brutal and the weather sometimes inhospitable. Then there's the Thanksgiving Day date, which can prove problematic, if not for us, then for those preparing the holiday feast back at home.

Well, the feel of this race is completely genuine and rather unique. In an age of flat 5Ks with ridiculous entry fees, racing at Berwick has all the truth and texture of some grand master's priceless painting discovered in the mahogany-paneled study of a country manor. The history of it . . . the challenge of it . . . the tradition of it . . . cannot be counterfeited.

Berwick is arguably the fourth oldest continuous footrace in America. Particularly in its first half century, Berwick attracted many of the same runners who made the Boston Marathon famous. And then there are those famous Berwick diamonds—a unique prize, though extremely difficult (for most of us) to win.

Of course, running is a perfect metaphor for higher struggle. When we race—*really* race—we confront certain fears. We joust a little bit with pain—or at least its mild-mannered cousin, discomfort. (A coach I know used to yell: "Get out of your comfort zone!" at his runners; and by that, I think, he meant—conversely—"acquaint yourself with discomfort.") Racing at Berwick, we learn things about ourselves. We get knocked around . . . and sometimes—on those rare splendid occasions—we break through.

Writing a history of the Berwick Marathon—the Run for the Diamonds—is a humbling experience, not unlike laboring up "the Hill." (Think of the myth of Sisyphus.) There is the nagging suspicion that *nothing* you write will completely measure up to Berwick's rich history.

But I hope I have come close. It was a multifaceted journey that was simultaneously daunting and fascinating—the first "locals" and what the race meant (and still means) to them . . . the moccasin-clad Carlisle Indians . . . the Canadians . . . the fantastic Flying Finns . . . More than thirty Olympians, more than a dozen US Cross-Country champions, plus a large handful of Boston Marathon champions, have all competed at Berwick.

Where do you *start* a story like that?

For me, the story started with the image—a vaguely haunting one—of Louis Tewanima, the fleet little Hopi who would become the Berwick Marathon's first great champion. The US 5th Cavalry had only weeks before snatched Tewanima from his Hopi homeland and sentenced him to a stint at the faraway place called the Carlisle Indian School.

I can picture him, then, on a train rocking east . . . somber and stoic, a captive clad in a faded castoff cavalry uniform. He really knew next to nothing about where he was headed or what exactly would happen to him once he arrived. All the running—the two Olympics, three Berwick victories, races at Madison Square Garden—well, those experiences (like his eventual return home to Arizona's high desert) were all shrouded in the fog of the future.

Mark Will-Weber
July 2008

1

Before Berwick

I
How Tewanima—the Hopi Olympian—arrived at Carlisle

It would not be an exaggeration to say that the first major star of the Berwick Marathon was a prisoner of war. His name was Louis Tewanima and—in addition to winning the Berwick race three times—he twice represented the United States in the Olympic Games, winning a silver medal in the 10,000 meters in 1912.

Life offers strange twists for some of us, and this how Louis Tewanima ended up in Pennsylvania—far from his Hopi homeland in the arid Arizona high desert of mesas, canyons, and plateaus.

On October 19, 1906, troops H and K of the United States 5th Cavalry trotted out from Fort Wingate, New Mexico, and headed west into Arizona's high desert country. They ambled through the sprawling lands of the Navajo tribe, bound for the "island" of the Navajo's smaller, encircled neighbors known as the Hopi.

The horse soldiers looked virtually the same as their predecessors of previous frontier decades: equipped with wide-brimmed hats, canteens, carbines and revolvers, leather boots and saddles, bugles and regimental flags. Their snorting, sure-footed horses were still one of the most practical means of travel in this rugged, arid terrain of old Indian trails and boulder-strewn arroyos—though arguably mules were even better. Arizona was still a semi-wild territory: Geronimo, the infamous Apache war chief, and his band had been subdued less than two decades before, and statehood status was still six years away.

Once the troopers left Fort Wingate (near present-day Gallup, New Mexico), their shelter consisted of standard-issue pup tents. In the mornings and evenings, the soldiers warmed themselves near crackling fires fueled by dry piñon branches. Autumn in the high desert typically meant hard-frost mornings and perhaps even snow falling in the higher elevations, such as the peaks of the San Francisco Mountains looming to the west.

But just two days out, the troopers were confronted by several inches of snow—the near-blizzard conditions enough to warrant a two-day layover at the St. Michaels Mission. A Franciscan brother named Simeon Schwemberger recorded their brief stay with photographs, the officers breaking out their heavy, knee-length coats and some bemused expressions in response to the untimely fall of snowflakes.

Once the weather returned to more fall-like conditions, the cavalry column again set out at a steady clip, direction due west. In a matter of days they sighted a trio of distinctive mesas—jutting out like the huge stone fingers of some mythical giant—on the top of which the remote Hopi villages stood perched.

The troopers were led by two experienced officers, Captain Lucius Roy Holbrook and First Lieutenant J. H. Lewis—the former a West Point graduate and a much-decorated career soldier. In the early stages of a rising military career, Holbrook had already won the Silver Star for Gallantry during the Spanish-American War against insurgent forces in the Philippine Islands.

As requested by Indian agent Reuben Perry, the cavalry was on a mission—one blessed at the highest levels of the US government, including President Theodore Roosevelt—to subdue renegade members of the Hopi tribe, specifically those situated near the village of Oraibi on Third Mesa and the newly settled village of Hotevilla.

What was their crime against the government? These particular Hopis adamantly refused to send their children to the reservation schools. Certain factions of the tribe resisted mandatory education by whites—whom they called the *Pahana*—because the process seemed to go sword-in-scabbard with eradicating Hopi cultural traditions. For example, young Hopi boys were forced to cut their shoulder-length hair, learn English (and speak it exclusively at the school or face humiliation and punishment), and worship Jesus Christ and the one true Christian God.

The Hopis—with few exceptions—had no intention of ceasing to worship the plethora of spirits of their surrounding natural world, such as Masauwu (god of the earth and guardian of the dead), Tawa (the sun god), and the life-giving Spider Woman. Some *Pahana* even looked askance at the traditional "snake dance" conducted by the Hopi—a ritual that the mesa dwellers believed helped bring sacred rains to their perpetually parched environment.

By twentieth-century white American standards, the Hopi life was bleak. The tribe scraped out a living in the arid conditions, herding sheep, hunting small game such as jackrabbits, and coaxing corn, beans, and melons from the harsh, draught-prone land. A recent wave of smallpox had decimated the population, estimated at less than two thousand people in the early 1900s. Nevertheless, the beleaguered Hopi did not wish to be constricted by the larger Navajo Nation or assimilated by the *Pahana*.

Although rarely violent in terms of armed resistance (the word *Hopi* translates loosely to "the peaceful people"), the Hopi were bitterly divided on the issue of mandatory schooling. The Hopi who bowed to the decree—no matter how reluctantly—were dubbed friendlies by the US authorities. Conversely, those Hopi who refused to send their children to the *Pahana* schools were branded as hostiles. In fact, the US government had previously dealt harshly with the so-called hostiles and in 1894 shipped off nineteen Hopi leaders to serve time at Alcatraz Prison—the infamous rock in San Francisco Bay—for refusing to snap to attention on the education issue.

The two Hopi factions had squabbled in recent years, but in September 1906 their feud seemed to simmer with the potential of real violence. The friendlies attempted to evict hostiles from the Oraibi village, resulting in several physical confrontations—with the hostiles eventually leaving and founding a new village at nearby Hotevilla. Government officials, however, feared a cycle of revenge and increased violence if they did not intervene with a show of military force—and, of course, a reaffirmation of mandatory schooling for all Hopi youth.

When the troopers of the 5th Cavalry arrived at the Hopi mesas on October 27, they soon rounded up the dissidents—identified by Agent Perry. Perry wore a suit, white shirt, and tie for the occasion—in contrast with the dusty, motley attire of the Hopi.

Among the band of hostiles was a young man named Louis Tewanima, who originally came from the Second Mesa village of Shungopavi. In all likelihood, Tewanima was already in his twenties in 1906 and possibly closer to thirty, but his small size and gaunt frame (about five foot three, 110 pounds) may have made him appear younger than his true age to his captors. The military report concerning this particular mission describes Tewanima at the time of his capture as "skinny, emaciated, beligerent [sic]."

Photo courtesy of Northern Arizona University

Against Their Will: The 5th US Cavalry rounding up so-called Hopi "hostiles"—including Tewanima—in Arizona Territory, 1906.

Regardless, the diminutive but feisty Tewanima was among the captured Hopi men during this expedition and taken—obviously against his own will. At St. Michaels, Schwemberger again brought out his camera, snapping a group picture of the downtrodden Hopi hostiles. Soon after, the troopers and captives arrived back at Fort Wingate. Imprisoned there for weeks, Tewanima "chose" to be sent to the Carlisle Indian School in Pennsylvania, rather than face a sentence of hard labor on chain gangs required to maintain area roads. As they awaited their fateful transportation to the East, no doubt the Hopi prisoners heard the *Pahana* soldiers celebrating Christmas and, days later, welcoming in the New Year of 1907.

In late January, Tewanima—along with ten other young Hopi men under the custody of Lieutenant Lewis—was loaded onto a train and chugged off to Carlisle. Founded in 1879 by a former frontier 10th US Cavalry officer, Colonel Richard Henry Pratt, the institution continued to reflect Pratt's philosophy (he retired in 1904) concerning Native Americans and his infamous catchphrase, "Kill the Indian, save the man." Translation: Stamp out the Indian language, culture, and religion, for the purpose of recasting them, as closely as possible, in the mold of white Americans—hardworking Christian citizens.

As Pratt once shared with a group of ministers he addressed: "In Indian civilization I am a Baptist, because I believe in immersing the Indians in our civilization and when we get them under holding them there until they are thoroughly soaked." That thorough soaking included some basic education, music, learning viable trades (tailoring and blacksmithing, for example), and—arguably what the Carlisle Indian School eventually became most famous for—the pursuit of athletic excellence.

One can only imagine the consternation of the captured Hopi men as the train steamed east across the Mississippi, bound for an unknown destination some 2,500 miles away, tucked deep in the heartland of the *Pahana*. They arrived in Carlisle, Pennsylvania, on January 26, 1907 and stood outside the hard winter grounds and barracks of their new "home." In technical terms, they—and all the other Native Americans from dozens of different tribes across the land already at Carlisle—were wards of the nation.

A New York newspaper account later described the rag-tag contingent of young Hopi men—clothed haphazardly in the faded remnants of castoff US army uniforms, and looking quite wild with their straggled, shoulder-length hair—as a group of "sun worshippers and pagans."

According to the *New York American:*

> When these savages [the Hopi] arrived at the Carlisle Indian School they would have nothing to do with the other students and began to live their lives apart. As they could speak no English, they expressed their thoughts by gestures and garbled language . . .

Even Tewanima's eventual mentor—the famed Carlisle coach Glenn "Pop" Warner—spoke to the untamed appearance of the Hopi Indians only recently arrived from Arizona. In a 1931 article for *Collier's* magazine, Warner remembered the Hopi bunch as "a wild-looking lot, with their long hair, huge earrings, and furtive eyes, not one of them ever having been away from his reservation before . . ."

Life, of course, is nothing if not random circumstance laced with the occasional odd irony—the tumultuous turn of events that has us down one day, up the next. And so it was for Tewanima. Just one year and six months after his unceremonious arrival at Carlisle, the little Hopi—clad in a running vest displaying the US Olympic team shield—appeared in much more regal surroundings. On July 24, 1908, Louis Tewanima stood in front of England's Windsor Castle—where members of the British royal family were among the thousands of spectators—and toed the starting line for the 1908 Olympic Marathon.

II
The 1908 Olympic Marathon in London

The 1908 Olympic Marathon in London is one of the most important events in the history of footracing for two reasons. The first is the drama surrounding the Italian runner Dorando Pietri's historic collapse in the White City Stadium; the second, that the course was significantly lengthened (by more than a full mile) and, for the first time, became 26.2 miles. Ironically, the former occurrence might not have happened but for the latter.

The first modern Olympic Marathon—staged from the Greek village of Marathon to the white-marbled Olympic Stadium in downtown Athens in 1896—was actually just short of 25 miles in distance. Had the Olympic Marathon in London been of a similar distance, then arguably Dorando Pietri would have finished first rather handily and the subsequent controversy most likely avoided.

The lengthening of the course for the 1908 Olympic Marathon came strictly out of a regard for royal convenience. It was decided that the race should start near the apartments of Windsor Castle—perfect for royal viewing of the start—and finish at the White City Stadium in Shepherd's Bush. The distance was 26 miles, but once again consideration of the royals came into play and it was agreed the race course would continue on for another 385 yards on the White City track so that the race would finish right in front of the Royal Box.

Convenience for the royals, however, resulted in Dorando's infamous unraveling—though most certainly the warm, humid conditions on July 24, 1908, played an equally critical role in the Italian runner's near-fatal collapse.

The first to suffer from the oppressive temperatures were the British entrants themselves. British runners Fred Lord and Jack Price surged into the lead in the early miles. But by 10 miles Lord had wilted in the devilishly deceiving conditions, and Price, too, saw his nearly half-minute lead at halfway quickly disintegrate. In addition, one of the pre-race favorites—the Canadian Indian Tom Longboat, 1907 Boston Marathon champion—had stunningly dropped out before 20 miles.

After taking the lead late in the race, Dorando arrived weary and disoriented in the packed stadium. He fell five times upon entering White City Stadium, and finally alarmed officials pulled him to his feet and helped him across the finish line.

In the words of Sir Arthur Conan Doyle (author of the famed Sherlock Holmes stories) who witnessed Dorando's stagger-and-stumble plight over the final 300-plus yards: "It is horrible, yet fascinating, this struggle between a set purpose and an utterly exhausted frame."

Meanwhile, Johnny Hayes—the persistent little Irish American who had followed a more patiently paced strategy in the warm conditions—passed South Africa's Charles Hefferon just outside the stadium, then charged onto the track in firm command of second. Soon after he crossed the finish line, the American contingent filed a protest on the grounds that Dorando quite likely would have never have completed the course without assistance. Dorando was disqualified (although the following day, Queen Alexandria presented him with a special cup to acknowledge his courageous effort) and Hayes was declared the champion in a time of 2 hours, 55 minutes, 18.4 seconds. Hefferon held on for second, while American Joe Forshaw took third.

Since the London Olympic Games were marred by constant bickering between the host British and the American team (heavily laced with Irish American athletes), there were some suggestions that the finish-line officials were quick to assist Dorando partly to prevent an American from winning the race.

In their defense, the British finish-line officials said in an official report: "It was impossible to leave [Dorando] there, for it looked like he might die in the very presence of the Queen."

The US marathoners might have displayed even *more* domination in the London Olympic Marathon had their Hopi runner Louis Tewanima been 100 percent healthy. However, he went to the starting line with "bad feet." Training methods were still in the experimental stages, and the American coach Mike Murphy opted to do something that would be unlikely today: After they arrived in England and just days before the race, he had his marathon charges run a 15-mile time trial in Brighton. In that time trial, Tewanima bettered *all* his American teammates—including Hayes—but came out of it slightly injured.

According to an article in the *Carlisle Arrow* (the Carlisle Indian School's publication) edition of September 11, 1908, Tewanima suffered some ill effects from the time trial: "Lewis Tewanima came in 9th in the marathon race, which was considered the most important event of all the contests. The distance was 26½ miles and 58 of the world's best runners competed and it was a great performance for Tewanima—who up to about a year ago, had never worn a running shoe and was suffering from sore feet and bad knees—to come in among the first ten . . ."

Whether "bad feet" meant something serious, like an Achilles tendon strain, or simple blisters, is unknown, but the marathon racing shoes of the day were typically made of stiff and heavy black leather.

Nevertheless, Tewanima persevered and still proved to be competitive in his first full whirl against international competition. Along with his teammates, Tewanima helped carry Hayes around the stadium on a small massage table in celebration of the New Yorker's winning performance— no doubt amid a nearly palpable atmosphere of British bitterness.

Hayes's Hurrah: Johnny Hayes is carried in triumph by his teammates after winning the 1908 Olympic Marathon, as Louis Tewanima (middle) puts his shoulder to the task.

In addition to setting up a several semi-lucrative professional rematches between Hayes and Dorando in both 1908 and 1909 (the most grueling being 26 miles on the tiny board track of Madison Square Garden, probably run through a haze of spectator cigar smoke), the drama of the Olympic race in London set off a tremendous wave of interest in marathon racing around the world.

The drama of the London Olympic Marathon also infected at least several individuals with marathon fever in Berwick, Pennsylvania—a small manufacturing and farming town perched on a bluff above the Susquehanna River.

III
Brainstorming in Berwick

A sports enthusiast and sometimes football referee, Chiverton N. MacCrea of Berwick closely followed the exploits of the US Olympic team competing in London in 1908. Newspapers across the land gave the Games coverage, including the famous marathon won by Hayes after Dorando's marathon meltdown. The subsequent marathon rematches in the Olympic aftermath also received lots of ink on the sporting pages—the primary source of athletic information in decades long before ESPN or *Sports Illustrated* came on the scene.

Around this time, "Chiv" MacCrea struck up a friendship with Canadian Alfred E. Domville, who had come to Berwick to work a management job at the American Car & Foundry (AFC) plant that was manufacturing steel railroad cars in the midst of boom demand. A former resident of Hamilton, Ontario, Domville was quite familiar with the famous Around-the-Bay 30K (about 18.8 miles) race in that town—an event that started on Christmas Day in 1894 from Billy Carrol's cigar store.

According to a historical booklet published in 1936 to celebrate Berwick's sesquicentennial, Domville was "the moving spirit" behind staging a marathon event in his new place of residence "because of his knowledge of the long-established marathon at Hamilton." In addition, Domville's early involvement readily explains the Canadian connection to the Berwick race.

MacCrea and Domville took vigorous Sunday walks together around Berwick's surrounding hills, presumably for fitness, conversation, and camaraderie. It is likely that during these walks Domville spoke to MacCrea concerning the popularity of Hamilton's Around the Bay Race.

For Domville and MacCrea, it seemed a small jump to this clear, simple thought: Why not a marathon footrace in Berwick?

And so Domville and MacCrea's "Berwick brainstorm" began to take shape. They soon found a prominent ally in Professor James Sigman, a Lafayette College graduate and principal of Berwick High School, where he also served as football and track coach. In the late summer of 1908, the men met at the Old Reliance Fire Hall, located in "a fine brick building" on Mulberry Street.

The trio began to mull over the actual particulars of what a footrace in Berwick might entail. They considered—but then ruled out—a route that would have started at the YMCA, crossed the bridge into Nescopeck, heading downriver toward Mifflinville, crossing the bridge into that town, then returning to Berwick on what is today Route 11. Fearing potential problems with the D L&W railroad lines that ran along the riverbank, they opted for something else. (This was not just an idle concern given that much of the 1907 Boston Marathon field—won by Tom Longboat—had been cut off—with only the top few runners slipping by before the untimely interruption of a slow-moving freight train.)

They settled upon a layout that Domville and MacCrea had covered on their walks on the outskirts of Berwick. It was a roller-coaster route of more than 9 miles (or so they thought at the time) and would present a formidable challenge to all those who ventured to run it.

Photo courtesy Harry's Sports

C. N. "Chiv" MacCrea
"In Charge of Race."

THE COURSE

The course in 1908 was essentially the same one that runners take on today: out Market Street, right on Summerhill Avenue (and the first mile marker); then down to Foundryville, where the runners cross a small bridge at around 2 miles.

After crossing the bridge at Foundryville, the course goes dramatically up—the infamous (about 1.6 to 1.7 miles long) quad-and-lung-punishing climb to Summer Hill. Maxim Furek, a regional writer and runner, waxed eloquent on the ascent in a 1987 article for a local publication.

> "The Hill" is a separate and unique part of the race. It is a time warp where novice runners, unprepared, find themselves alone and abandoned . . . a space continuum where veteran striders, fine-tuned and confident, ride their horses recklessly up the steep grade before suddenly hitting the wall. It is a price one pays for disrespecting "The Hill."

Passing the Summer Hill churches (around 5K), the runners catch a short reprieve—a stretch of flat, a quick down, followed by a short but noticeable up called Hosler's Hill in those early races. After the earlier major climb, Hosler's Hill is nothing if not insult to injury.

Off the top of Hosler's Hill, the steep downhill plunge (about half a mile in length) stretches out just before the halfway mark. The early race reports inevitably refer to the Carlisle Indian runners bursting forth with loud "war whoops" as they flew hell-for-leather (literally, as they were clad in deerskin moccasins) on the layout's biggest descent—their arms stretched out before them as if they were prepared to meet their makers in the event something went awry.

Then, as today, runners had to negotiate the sharp left turn followed by the wave-like grades of small hills (mostly downs) through Kachinka's Hollow and past the 5-mile point.

At around 6 miles, the Martzville Church marked the horizon, where the course soon turned left onto Martzville Road (there would have been no Berwick Golf Club for those earliest runners to use as a landmark, since it did not open until 1920), heading back to Berwick and its Market Street finish.

The course differed from the present-day route in one important way. In pre-World War I Berwick, the roads were essentially unpaved and strewn with stones, prone to mud or frozen ruts from both wagons and what was then a recently arrived mode of transportation—the "horseless carriage" known as the automobile. Within a few years, automobiles would go from being a novelty to something of a nuisance on the course, kicking up dust, or simply narrowing passages; a headache for both runners and organizers.

When it was all mapped out, the course looks somewhat like the shape of an arrowhead or a pointy leaf. Depending upon the bounds of your imagination—perhaps one could argue that it is shaped like a butterfly net or a hangman's noose.

The race founders believed the layout to be approximately 9½ miles in length. Before the course became ingrained in history, there was some occasional banter about stretching it out to a full 10 miles. When roads were graded or slightly rerouted, it's possible the course actually lost a small amount of distance. There were years when the course was advertised as 15K (9.3 miles) in length, but it is accepted today to be very close—give or take a few feet—to 9 miles.

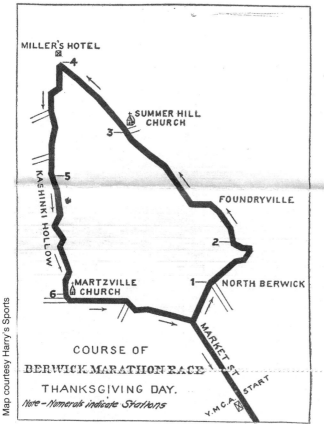

A map of the course from the 1927 race application.

Map courtesy Harry's Sports

The course still has a rural feel to it, but certainly the route is far less country-like than it was in its first half century. For example, there are a few references to hunters coming in through the fields—taking a break to stand with their rifles and watch the runners go by—during those races of yesteryear.

Naming the race the Berwick Marathon never warranted a second thought among the founding fathers; the term *marathon* was used quite loosely in its earliest interpretations and generally meant *any* long event, not just 26-mile races. Word went out to the local young men who might have the stamina and audacity to meet the challenge of running through the Briar Creek Hills.

And so it started—like most grand undertakings—with a simple daydream. The daydream infected others, like a mild fever. The fever begat a plan and a course map.

On Thanksgiving Day 1908, the race took the big leap—from a daydream to toe-the-line reality.

Ready, Set, Go! A century of racing in Berwick, Pennsylvania, is about to begin as A. E. Domville (left) raises his pistol. Notice some of the thirteen runners opting for the sprinter's start.

Photo courtesy of Harry's Sports

2

"A Great Race Superbly Run"

I
The Inaugural Race
1st Berwick Marathon, November 26, 1908

In the weeks prior to the Marathon, there were odd sightings—very likely ones never witnessed before in the town's history—of athletic young men jogging with serious purpose in the bucolic hills just beyond Berwick.

These were the local lads—from late teens to perhaps thirty years of age on the high end—who had no doubt shown that they were fleet of foot and steely of mind in other athletic endeavors. One of them, Clyde Hicks, had recently won the local tennis championship (and an $8 Spalding racket for his efforts); we can only imagine the rude transition from that sport's fancy footwork and finesse to the pure unadulterated grit of charging up Foundryville Hill.

If we close our eyes and try to picture them, perhaps we come up with fellows in running vests and thigh-length togs, ambling over rocky and rutty roads in clunky black leather shoes, their brows furrowed in deep concentration, the slightly older men maybe dreaming of cold draft beers, slurping foam off their mustaches or even—God forbid—a good cigar. By today's standards, they would have known little about training methods—no six-ounce racing flats, no energy gel packs, no beeping black plastic running watches or high-tech heart monitors, no lightweight running clothes to protect against chafing, no injury-prevention guides in *Runner's World* magazine. Most of their training was based on trial and error and individual preferences.

Nevertheless, more than a dozen men were willing to sally forth into this relatively unknown territory of marathon running and even post an entry fee of 50 cents for the dubious privilege of toeing the start line. The entry blank also clearly outlined various rules, such as absolutely no "pacemakers" on the course and a reminder that a runner should be 8 feet ahead before cutting in on a fellow competitor.

The rewards probably seemed well worth all the rules and stipulations and even the half-buck entry fee. The Berwick Marathon awards gleamed enticingly in Housenick's storefront window downtown, before a backdrop of college and high school pennants—a handsome silver loving cup for the winner (donated by Domville), a solid gold medal for second, a solid silver medal for third, and a solid bronze medal for fourth (all donated by Professor Sigman). In addition, there were "three handsome coat sweaters" offered as "team prizes." As the *Berwick Enterprise* newspaper noted, "The prizes are all handsome ones and the display has been attracting much attention."

One can only imagine how those awards—and the obvious glory that would go along with winning one of them—would have fired the imagination of these rookie runners. The general populace, on the other hand, was not above looking for other reasons to make this inaugural footrace more compelling to watch.

The same article remarked: "Interest in the race which will start promptly at 9:30 AM is increasing and there is already much betting on the favorites of the twelve or more entrants."

In addition, aficionados of sport could take in a special holiday showing at Berwick's Lyric Theater: "All Day, The Famous 'Marathon' at London: Showing the entire race, including Dorando falling and being helped over the line by English officials—Hays [sic], the American winning."

All this buildup contributed to the pre-race excitement of the first Berwick Marathon, contested on Thanksgiving Day—an added attraction to what for Berwickians was already a festive holiday that would culminate with the afternoon football game against Slatington ("Gentlemen 25 cents; Ladies 10 cents . . . Presentation of Marathon Prizes during intermission").

Race day morning dawned cloudy and mild, good running conditions by any measure, but especially so since it was late fall in north central Pennsylvania. Thirteen intrepid runners lined up on the unpaved thoroughfare of Market Street, near the YMCA They arrived at the starting line to much fanfare: Crisply played notes from the thirty-six-piece Berwick Cornet Band resounded from the YMCA porch. By 9 A.M., "a mass of humanity" pushed at the perimeter of the roped-off square at Second and Third streets and Market, with two dozen Berwick fire police attempting to keep the most rambunctious ones at bay.

Handlers removed blankets—meant to keep their runners warm until the last few minutes—and draped them across their shoulders. A large banner behind the line was strung across Market, trumpeting both the race and the upcoming football game to be played in the afternoon. A pair of fans climbed a telephone pole for an unobstructed view of the start.

Five minutes before the gun, a bugle call sounded and each entrant was introduced by announcer James Hughes. If you were looking for proof of the sheer innocence and pure amateur nature of this event—a great un-known for virtually all of the young men—then a study of the picture shows several of the runners opting for the only recently introduced "sprinter's start." What purpose that crouch start might have served against more than 9 miles of distance racing—and the copious glop of a muddy Market Street—we can only guess.

Regardless, a pistol shot from the lifted right hand of the Canadian en-thusiast Domville—a bowler hat on his head—sent the runners scurrying off toward Foundryville. The first Berwick Marathon was away.

Wearing the blue and white of the Rangers Hose and Ladder fire com-pany, Harry L. Williams took an early lead. With the race being such a nov-elty, none of the thirteen entries was totally discounted, but some thought that Williams—a native of Carbondale (near Scranton) but recently a res-ident of Berwick—ranked a co-favorite, along with Conway Paden. But Con Paden turned his ankle virtually at the start, and by the 2-mile post in Foundryville—the climb up to Summer Hill looming ahead—he was forced to drop out. A doctor pronounced Paden's injury a severe ankle sprain. (Several days after Thanksgiving, the *Bloomsburg Morning Press*'s "Berwick Department" column dutifully updated that "The condition of Conway Paden, the marathon runner, was not improved yesterday"—so his ankle sprain must have been the real deal.)

Williams churned on ahead, lengthening his lead. According to news-paper reports of the day, "He gained up the long Foundryville hill until at the turning point at Miller's Hotel he had a lead of a half mile." Meanwhile, Robert Eshleman—a Berwick High School junior and honor roll stu-dent—raced into second, and behind him, Earnest Hicks, Clyde Hicks, and Clarence Hock jostled back and forth for the third, fourth, and fifth spots. The trio was followed by the remainder of the field, then the race ref-eree Brit Seely trailing the runners on horseback, kicking up puffs of dust or clumps of mud. Along the route, periodic reports by telephone updated officials back at the finish, whereupon Hughes bellowed the race develop-ments through a megaphone for spectators to ponder.

Williams maintained his lead through Kachinka's Hollow, no doubt dodging the muddy spots as best he could. Spectators from nearby farm-houses cheered him as he churned on to Martzville, turned the corner and headed for home. As he arrived back in Berwick, thousands of spectators lined Market Street—predictably thick down the homestretch. "The road of the winners was a narrow line, through crowds of people for a quarter mile or more," reported the *Berwick Enterprise,* "augmented by thousands after the start."

In fact, the paper proclaimed this bulging throng to be the largest to ever witness a sporting event in Columbia County. "As to the crowd there must have been 15,000 people. At every farm house and crossroads there were dozens of people cheering the runners."

Even assuming crowd tallies to be slightly embellished, Williams nonetheless was "loudly cheered" as he raced in to break the finish line tape stretched across by Professor Sigman and Chiv MacCrea. His time was 59 minutes, 37 seconds. It was approximately 3 minutes more before young Bob Eshleman finished, claiming runner-up honors to the pre-race co-favorite. Clyde Hicks, the recently crowned town tennis champ—who had fired in a surge coming out of Kachinka's Hollow—crossed the line third, while Hock held off Earnest Hicks by about 30 yards to secure fourth place.

Following the top racers were: Arthur Bower (6th), Roy Bowman (7th), J. C. Yingling (8th), Erwin Becker (9th), Drew Gingher (10th), and Victor Brocious (11th), the last taking just over 1 hour and 8 minutes to complete the run. Along with Paden, Arthur Lowry failed to finish. (Lowry had been forewarned by his physician not to even try and perhaps once he stared Summer Hill in the face he concurred with that sage advice.) A four-teenth entrant, John Cox, had failed to appear at the starting line.

According to one report, not long after Williams crossed the finish line, an outrageous rumor swept the crowd at wildfire speed, the gist of it being that the front-runner had received—or, more accurately put, reached out for—illegal assistance.

As noted in the *Berwick Enterprise:*

> Charges were brought that the winner had been assisted by grasping the back of a buggy, however, when the charges were formally aired, they were entirely disproved and the town set-tled back to await the second race.

Had there been any true attempts at shenanigans, then Brit Seely—the horse-sitting referee of the footrace—obviously was a key man to

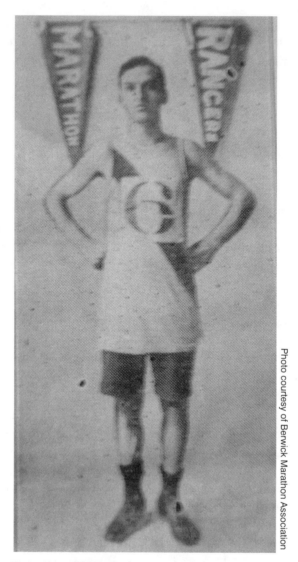

Photo courtesy of Berwick Marathon Association

First Flight: Harry Williams won the 1908 Berwick Marathon—despite outrageous rumors (proven false) that he held on to the back of a buggy up the Foundryville Hill. As the pennant acknowledges, Williams represented the Rangers Hose and Ladder Company.

provide testimony. A former captain of the Dickinson College football team and also one of the first men in Berwick to play organized basketball for the YMCA team, Seely undoubtedly carried some clout in town when it came to anything that involved the sacred conduct of all things athletic. And Seely promptly proclaimed, "It was a great race, fair and won on its merits."

Perhaps surprisingly to some of the curious observers (particularly those who might have watched Dorando's five falls captured on film at the Lyric), the runners finished the race virtually unscathed. Nobody died à la Pheidippides—the ancient Athenian messenger of Greek marathon myth, his alleged last words of "Rejoice, we conquer!" still fresh on his patriotic lips. As a precautionary measure, most of the Berwick runners retired for an immediate rest. But, in fact, some of the finishers looked surprisingly jubilant and energetic (runner's high?) when they arrived back at Market Street.

The newspaper account noted that 10th place finisher Drew Gingher looked as bright as new paint on a barn. "Gingher finished one of the freshest, and while he did not get a prize, he came in for some of the most enthusiastic cheering. He gave his friends a better race than they expected and was one of the few who did not go to bed directly after finishing."

By the afternoon, presumably after some short naps and a nourishing lunch, the runners were in attendance of the football game (well, it *was* Berwick, Pennsylvania, and, yes, football was big even then, dating back to the tail end of the previous century), where they received their awards. Williams (who along with Hicks and Bowman won the team prize for Rangers, and thus the "three handsome coat jackets") was asked to make a short speech, a request to which he readily complied. Berwick beat Slatington on the gridiron in "a spectacular game" and—on the heels of the great Marathon race—no doubt the town's unbridled jubilance was elevated to even more dizzying heights.

And so the inaugural Berwick Marathon was history. Domville and MacCrea's brainstorm had combusted into reality and struck the hearts of the locals with all the power of a thunderbolt tossed from the very heights of Mount Olympus by the immortal Zeus himself. Fifteen thousand spectators! A local man who could run over 9-plus hilly miles in less than 1 hour!

"It was a great race, superbly run, perfectly arranged and exciting an interest that augurs well for the future when the race is thrown open to county entrants," beamed the write-up in the *Berwick Enterprise.*

Among the crowd that day was a young Berwick High School girl named Ruth. In the late 1930s—on the thirtieth anniversary of the first Berwick Marathon—Ruth Follmer penned a first-person article for the *Berwick Enterprise* (titled: "Berwick in the Making") on what some of those early races—particularly the inaugural one—were like.

The consensus of opinion in the high school crowd was that it seemed a rather pretentious undertaking but, since Berwickians were ever ready to take a chance, why not? It would provide a local rivalry at least, and Thanksgiving Day was a long day until time for the afternoon football game to begin. The Marathon race would fill in those dull hours perfectly. If Chiv MacCrea wanted to kid himself about the race ever becoming a national event why should we attempt to disillusion him? Let him dream on!

Regardless of *where* the Berwick race was headed in terms of importance, there was little doubt that it had already indelibly etched its presence on the imaginations of the locals. Just a few days after the Thanksgiving race, a bunch of clerks and stock boys at the Berwick Store Company (a pre-Wal-Mart enterprise that claimed it had "everything for everybody") launched into a spirited debate about who among themselves might possess the most mercurial magic. As the *Bloomsburg Morning Post* reported on December 4, 1908, under the headline "Exciting Race On Market Street":

An exciting race took place on Market Street last evening. Ever since the Marathon race on Thanksgiving Day, four young men from the Berwick Store Company have been disputing their relative speed and endurance and finally decided to run a race to show which was the best.

Plans were well laid and 200 people were on hand last evening at six o'clock when Fred Sheesholtz who acted as starter gave the word to go. Taking part were Harry Sherrington, Ed Rough, C. M. Lamon, and Clark Rubb. The course was out to Fourteenth Street where Carl McClure was stationed to see that every man touched the crossing and returned.

Rough won by a lead of a square over Herrington, Lamon was third and Bubb failed to show up at the finish. The distance was one and a quarter miles, the time 7 and 1/4 minutes and the purse $4.00.

So enthusiasm of one and all—including Berwick Marathon wannabes—was obviously running hot following that first Thanksgiving Day race in 1908.

Of course, they had no way of envisioning that future Berwick Marathons would reach far beyond rural Columbia County; no way of knowing that "the Indians were coming" (and soon!) and "Flying Finns" and New York City hotshots from organized metropolitan athletic clubs and dozens of die-hard Canadians and Olympic-class runners, not to mention—eventually!—women who would run fast enough to have beaten Harry L. Williams literally by a mile.

But on Thanksgiving Day, 1908, in Berwick, Pennsylvania, there was one certainty: These were the days of innocence and good feeling. Amid the festivities and celebrations, something like the mass slaughter of the Great War—hovering horrifically in the not-so-distant future—could not have been predicted or even imagined.

The Famous Berwick Diamonds

The famous Berwick Diamonds were not initially part of the prizes in those first few years of the Marathon. Instead, the runners received mostly cups, medals, or watches.

But even before the First World War, the diamonds did come on the scene. Soon they were an enticing prize that brought in runners. The Berwick Marathon Association somehow got the US Amateur Athletic Union (AAU) to agree to waive its usual stipulation that prizes could not be worth more than $35.

Many of the diamonds were donated by the most influential or prominent families (such as the Crispins and later the Wise family, of Wise Potato Chip fame) in town—chiefly high management from the American Car & Foundry (ACF) operation. Given the overflow crowds the race attracted (sometimes an estimated twenty-thousand-plus in those early years), it did not take long before the regional politicians got in on the prize-donating act. It was not uncommon for congressional candidates to donate a diamond or watch to the Berwick Marathon prize list.

PRIZES
19th Annual Berwick Marathon
To be awarded as follows:

First Prize	Diamond Ring
Second Prize	Diamond Ring
Third Prize	Diamond Ring
Fourth Prize	Diamond Ring
Fifth Prize	Diamond Ring
Sixth Prize	Diamond Ring
First Local Prize	Gold Strap Watch
Second Local Prize	Silver Cup
Special Prize	Silver Cup

to the Runner breaking the Course Record of 47 Min. 57 3-5 Sec. held by Wm. Ritola, 1922

State Prize	Silver Cup

Courtesy of Harry's Sports

Berwick Booty: For those early footraces, the enticing diamond prizes all but twinkle on the race application. This is from the 1928 Berwick Marathon application.

Betting On Berwick

Betting on the Berwick Marathon (and later on, even the Run for the Diamonds) certainly did happen. In fact, betting on the runners—alluded to openly in the local newspapers prior to the inaugural event in 1908—probably was partially responsible for some of those twenty-thousand-plus crowds who swarmed into Berwick in those early years. In subsequent years, the newspapers openly talked about "favorites" and "dark horses" and "upsetting the dope" . . . all thinly veiled references to some structured wagering.

Although it certainly is less organized now, one probably could get a small wager on the Berwick race even today. (Some locals assure me that this could be arranged.) That some betting continued into the so-called modern era can be assumed from two somewhat humorous stories.

Sometime in the 1970s, a contingent of Canadians came down to run. It just so happened this was one of their very rare off years—meaning, they were not in killer racing shape, like they had been the year before. In fact, a number of the Maple Leaf lads even stayed at the Berwick Hotel bar a bit later than normal the night before this particular Berwick Marathon.

The next morning, a waitress at the hotel informed the Canadians that she had "won some money" betting on them the year before. Good guys that they were, the Canadians immediately said that they hoped she hadn't bet on them this time around . . . The waitress assured them that she hadn't. "Oh, no . . . Not this year. I talked to the bartender first."

Two-time race winner Budd Coates recalls one year in which—at the last minute—he decided not to run the race because of a slow-healing injury. Nevertheless, he traveled to Berwick to watch his wife, Ellen, run. After the start, he was walking around the finish-line area and he overheard two local men debating who might win.

"I'm betting on that Budd Coates guy . . . He could win it!" said one of the locals.

"I don't think betting on Coates is such a great idea," said Budd Coates.

"Yeah? Why not?"

"Because I'm Budd Coates, and I'm not running today," said Budd Coates.

Bringing in the Stars

Although the diamonds and the challenge of the course certainly were an incentive for attracting top-notch runners in those early years, it stands to reason that expense money also played a part.

Berwick Marathon Association member Dan Spadoni addressed that very issue in an article published in the 1982 race program ("The Berwick Marathon—1909-1941—The Formative Years"). Spadoni—whose work served as a good starting point and overview for this book—writes about under-the-table payments to runners in those early years, noting:

> This practice was contrary to the amateur running rules at the time. As such, it was never mentioned in the press, at least not locally, but there is evidence that members of the Berwick Marathon Booster Association actually went door-to-door collecting money for runners' travel expenses (they came by car or train). It's been reported that many individuals gave $5 or $10, an imposing sum of money in those days. But this should come as no surprise, especially if one considers the local popularity of the race and the pride of the community that hosted it. Local industry, especially the ACF, most likely contributed a large sum, too.

Even as early as the prewar years, with elite New York City runners such as Harry Smith, Willie Kramer, and Hannes Kolehmainen, expense money—legitimate for sure, and perhaps with a sweetener added in—was very likely a necessarily operating cost. If you wanted to conduct a great race—and the Berwick Marathon Association did—then you had to bring in "the horses" (in fact, the thoroughbreds) of the sport. However, those exchanges of expense money could sometimes go awry, as Harry Smith (1912 Berwick champ) would one day learn.

3

Tewanima's Triple

Photo courtesy of The Library of Congress

Big Hit: Whether it was New York (above) or Berwick, the Carlisle Indian runners always seemed to gather a curious crowd.

I
"Me Run Fast Good!"

If the inaugural Berwick Marathon left promoters, townspeople, gamblers, and runners anxious for expansion to a countywide race, then 1909 provided them with an unexpected express ride to the next level. For the second edition of the Berwick race, the promoters (specifically Chiv Mac-Crea) reached far *beyond* local—right past regional—and promptly landed one of the best long-distance runners in the world.

The big catch was none other than Louis Tewanima, the tiny Hopi runner, now in his second year at the Carlisle Indian School. Chiv MacCrea—perhaps due to his part-time vocation as football referee—had a personal connection to "Pop" Warner, the nationally renowned football coach at Carlisle. In addition to his duties as football coach and director of athletics, Warner also served as the Carlisle track coach and sometime traveling companion (when it didn't interfere with gridiron games) when his charges were invited to competitions.

As an oft-repeated, well-documented story goes, Tewanima—just months after his arrival at Carlisle in the winter of 1907—approached Warner and asked to try out for track. Warner, no doubt more used to the classic football-type physiques—young men who could readily meet the explosive demands of sprinting and hurdling and throwing—was dubious that the scrawny-looking Hopi could make any meaningful contribution. However, according to a *Collier's* magazine article ("Red Menaces" October 31, 1931) that Warner later wrote, Tewanima vehemently persisted and said—in his limited, halting English: "Me run fast good. All Hopi run fast good!"

Although the diminutive Tewanima was never going to help Warner on the gridiron—even in those third-down, mile-to-go situations—Pop allowed him to try track, and the coach soon learned he had an ace for long distance track events. The addition of Tewanima dovetailed nicely with Warner's team. Pop already had an Olympic-caliber hurdler-jumper in Frank Mount Pleasant and—although he was just coming into his own—the mortal world's equivalent to a meteor in the athletically astounding Jim Thorpe, to dominate most of the nondistance events.

At any rate, Tewanima made rapid advancement and landed in the Olympic Marathon in London in 1908—the very event that got men like A. E. Domville and Chiv MacCrea excited enough to stage an endurance race in Berwick. After his ninth-place finish in London, Tewanima returned to the States and—as a US Olympic team member—was soon in demand by race promoters in New York. Along with other 1908 US Olympic squad members, Tewanima also briefly met President Teddy Roosevelt at Sagamore Hill—TR's "summer Whitehouse" on Long Island. It seems doubtful that Tewanima would have registered the full irony of the invitation: It was Roosevelt himself who had given Bureau of Indian Affairs Commissioner Francis Leupp the green light to send in the US 5th Cavalry to squelch the hostiles at the Oraibi pueblo less than two years before.

Back at school, Carlisle instructors were teaching the little Hopi the basics of the tailor trade. But Tewanima, with Warner acting as coach-agent, went off to races whenever they were arranged—and that seems to have been quite frequently.

In fact, on the very day Harry L. Williams was cruising to victory in the inaugural Berwick Marathon, Tewanima was racing in the Yonkers Marathon—a full marathon. According to a newspaper account of the race, "The course was about twenty-six miles, twenty-one being across country . . . ," the final 4 miles coming on the Empire City (horse racing) track.

Tewanima led the race from about 10 miles to 16 miles and was still in contention when the runners came back to the track. But extremely foggy conditions and officials of limited experience (it was only the second year for the event) may have derailed his best possible showing. James Crowley of the Irish American Athletic Club won in 2 hours, 49 minutes and change (over a hilly and muddy course), followed by Sam Mellor and Robert Fowler. Tewanima was given credit for fourth, but his handlers protested that his laps had been miscounted. According to a New York newspaper report:

> "Protests were repeatedly made that the scorers had not kept proper track of the laps and it was charged by representatives of the Carlisle Indian School that Tewanima had been obliged to run five times around the mile track, instead of four."

II
War Whoops on Market Street
2nd Berwick Marathon, November 25, 1909

Whether or not the 1908 Yonkers debacle left some bad feelings between Carlisle officials and the race promoters, the next Thanksgiving Day morning—a snowy and bitterly cold one in 1909—saw Tewanima on the starting line at Berwick. In addition, a number of his Carlisle teammates were with him, including a promising young teenager named Mitchell Arquette.

Harry Williams was back, but Tewanima's reputation already was such that nobody realistically talked of Williams defending his title.

The weather—spitting snow and sleet—was less than ideal for any man. A recent cold snap had left the unpaved roads frozen and snow-covered. Since there were often frozen ruts from wagons, or rocks of various sizes, the weather simply added to the danger of a runner turning an ankle.

It's doubtful, however, that the seven Carlisle Indian "student" runners were cowed by the conditions. Even the Hopi runners—Tewanima and Archie Quamala—were quite familiar with snow, not an uncommon occurrence in the high desert country of their native Arizona. Similarly, Mitchell Arquette—a muscle-toned Mohawk from the St. Regis reservation situated along the St. Lawrence River in extreme upstate New York, would have had plenty experience of slogging through snow.

Regardless, it is a matter of record that the Carlisle seven arrived at the starting line with much fanfare, projecting all the exuberance of warriors on the brink of some great adventure.

If the spectators reveled in the exotic presence of the Indians (for example, the band played an Indian march, drumming out a predictable tom-tom beat as the runners were introduced), there is at least some evidence that the Carlisle runners were not above hamming it up for the crowd: When the starting pistol sent the field of twenty-seven men off and running, the Indians—en masse—let loose with a much-spirited war whoop and caused some trepidation in at least one of their opponents. The local papers took delight in reporting that John Stookey (spelled *Stuckey* in the 1909 results, but *Stookey* in some newspaper articles)—an African American runner from the local area—immediately gave way and let the bellowing braves pass by. When the episode was rehashed in subsequent newspaper accounts over the years, Stookey inevitably is referred to (in the unflinching racist rhetoric of the day) as "the colored lad whom the Indians had frightened almost white . . ."

The Indian war whoop was a harbinger of how the race itself unfolded: the Carlisle team dominated. Tewanima and Arquette soon made it a race between themselves, before the Hopi standout pulled away in the last mile to win in 54 minutes, 16 seconds. Arquette finished 24 seconds later, and then it was several minutes until a pair of Pawnees—Water Hunt and Fred Pappan—slogged in through the snow. Don McQuaig, the first-ever Canadian entry and also a man from Domville's hometown of Hamilton, Ontario, finished 5th (58:21), while defending champion Williams managed to gamely trudge in for seventh—his time of 1 hour, 24 seconds not that far off his winning time from the year before when the weather conditions had been much better suited for fast running. Sandwiched between McQuaig and Williams was Peter Thomas (6th, 59:31), another Carlisle Indian School runner.

Though the temptation might have been for spectators to attribute the Indian domination to natural genetics for endurance running or their familiarity with their rugged day-to-day existence, there certainly were other factors at work that contributed to their success. The Indians were in top-notch racing shape, having just come off cross-country season. Their cross-country races involved some time trials among themselves (often handicapped races with the best runners starting last) and also a win over the University of Pennsylvania—coached by Olympic mentor Mike Murphy—at a meet held in Philadelphia at the Belmont Plateau in Fairmont Park. Murphy, in fact, was on the record as saying that, at the time, Tewanima was the best runner in the world when it came to races in the 10- to 15-mile range.

III
The Carlisle Indians Return
3rd Berwick Marathon, November 24, 1910

The Carlisle Indians—a big hit with the Berwick crowds in 1909—were back again in 1910. If anything, their drawing power had increased with the talk of their spine-tingling war whoops at the start and their astounding running prowess during the race itself.

Tewanima was considered even more formidable for the 1910 Berwick Marathon. He had another year of organized racing experience under his belt—keeping in mind that he had been essentially a rookie when he suddenly found himself in the Olympic Games in 1908—and also arrived at the starting line knowing what the Berwick course, including the winding climb up to Summer Hill, would be like.

The Berwick crowds seemed to be greatly intrigued by the Native American runners, though the prevailing myths—and volatile rhetoric of the age—also seemed to drum up some apprehension concerning their "guests" from Carlisle. Some accounts allude to the fact that the Indians were kept in their hotel rooms.

They stayed at the St. Charles Hotel, situated right next to the Nescopeck bridge and built on the site of Evan Owen's original homestead. (A Quaker from the Philadelphia area, Owen founded Berwick in 1786.) The St. Charles is long gone today, but it was considered quality lodging back in its time. On the eve of the race, the Indian runners were closely watched by their overseer—most likely Wallace Denny, the Carlisle Indian School athletic trainer. Denny was a loyal member of Pop Warner's inner circle. (When Warner left Carlisle and took the Stanford University football coaching position, he eventually brought Denny with him.) According to a small article that originally ran in the *Berwick Enterprise* (and was then republished in the 1990 Berwick race program):

> The local race secretary remembers well their appearance here and the color and excitement it added to the race. The Indians did not speak English, he recalls, and they had a disciplinarian with them by the name of Denny. He kept the Indian squad in check and had them under lock and key in a local hotel. He brought them out as a group and kept with them all the time they were in Berwick.

The impression, of course, is that the Indians were unleashed for race day, then hastened back to Carlisle soon after.

Whatever apprehensions their appearances seemed to drum up, the Carlisle Indian School runners were a major draw. A sample of the "pre-race promotional propaganda" of the day is quite evident in this local news article before one of the pre-World War I Berwick races: "The Indians are coming! Not the blood-thirsty, scalp-lifting redskins of yore, but Uncle Sam's protégés from the government Indian school at Carlisle . . ."

Today, it is impossible to not wince at these words so blatantly brimming with racism. But the popular culture and recent history of that American era—just three decades removed from the ill-fated Last Stand of George Armstrong Custer's 7th Cavalry at the Little Big Horn—remained fixated with the image of the Indian as a war-like heathen.

In fact, the region's own early frontier history was also steeped in incidents of Indian warfare, including an 18th-century massacre at nearby Sugarloaf, Pennsylvania. In "The Story of Berwick: 1786 to 1936" (a booklet put together to celebrate the town's sesquicentennial), the fate of some of its earliest would-be settlers was recorded in blunt fashion: "The first white family to settle at Nescopeck arrived before 1778. They were massacred."

Of course, sensationalized words concerning Native American runners were by no means limited to the backwaters of the nation; big-city newspapers were not in the least reluctant to refer to Indian runners as "redskin" or "copper-colored" in their write-ups.

Stereotypes aside, the spectators were clearly fascinated by the Carlisle Indian School runners—admittedly some more than others—as one can tell reading Berwick native Ruth Follmer's memories of those early races.

In a newspaper flashback called "Berwick in the Making," she wrote:

> It seems to me that there was a peculiar satisfaction in see-
> ing Indians win those early races. The skinny, narrow-chested
> Tewanima was nothing to attract feminine attention as he stood
> shivering in the cold wind, waving his long, thin arms, but he
> managed to do quite well for himself, you may recall. Arquette,
> one of his running mates, was a bronze Adonis compared to
> him. The High School girls all gazed at Arquette with the same
> intensity today's girls would gaze at Clark Gable, but he never
> even saw us!

Although Arquette may have scored points—unknowingly it appears—
with the local lasses in terms of pure masculine appeal, Tewanima once
again relegated Arquette to runner-up status in the 1910 edition of the
Berwick Marathon. However, the Mohawk runner obviously raced well,
and the conditions—warm and fair—brought out fast times.

The pair of Carlisle runners charged onto Market Street—with, according to some accounts, Arquette slightly ahead—before Tewanima
scooted by in the final half mile to post Berwick's first sub-50-minute performance in 49:56. Just 8 seconds later, Arquette finished, followed by
Philadelphia's Johnny Gallagher in third. Gallagher, representing the
Shanahan Catholic Club, clocked a very respectable 50:30. It was over two
minutes more until Gallagher's Shanahan teammate George McInerny
chugged across the line for fourth in 52:45, about 100 yards ahead of
Canadian George Adams.

Tewanima and Arquette competed against each other dozens and
dozens of times, with the little Hopi always leading the way. However,
there *was* some suggestion—completely unsubstantiated by any real evidence—that Arquette "acquiesced" to his more famous teammate in the
1910 Berwick Marathon. The story surfaced years later in a nostalgic column (penned by a sports columnist/wag identified only as "Uncle Jake")
in the local press:

> Arquette had the misfortune of attending Carlisle School
> when there was another great star, Tewanima. Arquette was a
> great runner in his own right but he was overshadowed by his
> teammate. Many an old-timer who saw the two Indian stars race
> contend in 1911 Arquette could have beaten Tewanima when he
> was leading him into Market Street on the home stretch by 100
> yards. Race fans say that Arquette slowed up to allow Tewan-

ima to pass. The answer to the unexpected turn in the race was never given. But those on the "inside" knew that the Indians were under strict discipline and if [Pop] Warner said that Tewanima should win, then he won.

If "Uncle Jake's" insider musings sound somewhat dubious or a bit befuddled, then well they should—because there are certainly some misstatements of fact at work in his column. First and foremost, Uncle Jake would have us believe the 1911 race between Tewanima and Arquette was the close one; but it wasn't. In fact, Arquette was more than a minute behind the Hopi star in the 1911 race—a distant third. The 1910 race—just 8 seconds—was the close one. And so the discerning reader might wonder: If Uncle Jake had the *year* incorrect concerning this alleged shady switch on the homestretch, then could Uncle Jake—just perhaps—have also been a bit off target on the facts in general? Without pure proof, we must assume that—like Harry Williams's alleged grabbing of the buggy in the inaugural race—what remains is most likely innuendo.

That said, a cynic might advance the theory that anything is possible with money on the line. And we *do* know that the average spectator on Berwick Marathon day didn't have to look too far to place a wager on a runner—and where that runner might place in the final results.

IV
Third Jewel in the Crown
4th Berwick Marathon, November 30, 1911

The Irish American lads from Philadelphia's Shanahan Catholic Club had gone head-to-head with the Carlisle Indian School runners, and although they would have lost in a team race (either using the classic cross-country "five men score" or the Berwick method of scoring three runners), they nonetheless performed well. However, none of the Philly runners returned for the 1911 (and fourth annual) Berwick Marathon. Whether it was the slog up Summer Hill or the tough competition from Tewanima and Arquette that deterred them, we can only guess.

No matter, the New York City-area runners came out in force for the first time in 1911. And although they certainly would have respected the ability of the Carlisle Indian School road warriors the New Yorkers would not have been awed by any preconceived mystique surrounding even the likes of Tewanima or Arquette—simply because the two factions had raced against each other a few times in New York area races.

Mike Ryan—a several-time veteran of the Boston Marathon (a race he would win in 1912)—had lots of experience, but, strange as it sounds, the Berwick distance was probably too *short* for him. But besides Ryan, men like Harry J. Smith of the Pastime Athletic Club, Fred Bellars of the New York Athletic Club, and Irish American Athletic Club runner Thomas Barden from Yonkers made a formidable force.

Bellars came to Berwick with an outstanding running résumé; he'd already notched three US national cross-country titles in 1907, 1908, and 1910. Smith—the captain of his club team—had placed third to Tewanima (but ahead of Arquette) in a field of a thousand runners in a New York "modified marathon" (12 miles or so) that finished at New York City Hall back in May. The affable redheaded Barden was still building his reputation, but he was destined to become a top-notch competitor at Berwick and an extremely popular one with the fans.

Whether you were a Carlisle Indian School runner or a seasoned New Yorker, cross-country experience was never a bad thing to have if you were a runner-up for the challenge of these early Berwick races. The roads were still unpaved, rocky, rutty, muddy, slippery, or sometimes chokingly dusty if the weather was dry. For the 1911 race, however, the roads were frozen rock-solid.

Tewanima responded to the "big city comp" by simply kicking his game up a notch. The diminutive Hopi scooted away to his best time in his three Berwick Marathon races, clocking 49 minutes, 34 seconds over the tundra-like surface. So convincing was his victory that the crowd had to wait a full 1 minute and 1 second before Bellars charged in for runner-up honors (2nd, 50:35), and the New Yorker needed a strong finish to hold off Arquette (3rd, 50:42) in the homestretch.

Smith—who would make the US Olympic team the following year—trudged in a distant fourth in 51:53, while Barden (6th) was sandwiched between two Carlisle runners—Washington Talyumptewa (5th) and Andrew Hermequatewa (7th). Talyumptewa and Hermequatewa were both Hopi men who, like Tewanima, were essentially prisoners of war when they were packed off to Carlisle against their will after the 5th Cavalry operation rounded up the hostiles back in 1906.

The competition was fierce, the route as tough as advertised (four of the twenty-two starters dropped out), but the Indian charges from Carlisle never shrank from the natural challenges of the weather, the course, or the New Yorkers.

After the 1911 race, the Carlisle squad would never be quite as formidable. The main reason may well have been Tewanima's return to Arizona after the 1912 Summer Olympic Games. Although the Carlisle Indian School would continue to send forth some good teams—and tough-running individuals such as Charles Peters in 1915 and Juan Pablo Routzo in 1916—its years of domination at the front were over.

Photo courtesy of Harry's Sports

Stone Cold Courage: Winter-like conditions greeted the runners in 1909—the first Berwick Marathon for the Carlisle Indians School runners led by Olympian Louis Tewanima.

V
The Bloody Footprints

The Carlisle Indian runners will always be remembered for their war whoops on Market Street, which seemingly continue to echo down the decades and enhance the history of those early races. But there is another anecdote that resonates in the Berwick story of those same Native American harriers—one that arguably is even more powerful and memorable.

Some of the early observers of the Berwick Marathon remember the

Indians racing in their leather moccasins, and ripping them to shreds on the hard, frozen ground— to such a degree that you could see their bloody footprints on Market Street as they labored to the finish line.

Most likely this was the 1909 race, in which case the footprints would have stood out on the snow-covered road. However, at least one account said it occurred in 1911—when the ground was also frozen solid and particularly rutty.

Regardless of which year this event happened, it serves as an exclamation point—a testimony to the Carlisle Indian runners, their tough-mindedness, and their ability to endure whatever the world threw at them.

4

Tewanima's Farewell

I
Berwick Stars Go Olympic

In July 1912, several runners who had displayed their talents (or one day would) on the rural roads, hills, and town streets of Berwick, Pennsylvania, were off to race in the Olympic Games in Stockholm, Sweden.

A veteran of the London Olympics and a man who had only gotten faster since then, Louis Tewanima was named to the 1912 US team without so much as a time trial. Tewanima also had the benefit of traveling in very familiar company: teammate Jim Thorpe—destined to be Team America's brightest star with gold-medal wins in both the decathlon and pentathlon events—and Coach "Pop" Warner, named to the coaching staff, were along for the ten-day voyage on the *Finland* bound for Sweden. These long trips by sea were somewhat dicey for the athletes; they had to avoid eating too much and the runners tried to maintain fitness by striding on a cork track that circled the ship's deck—less than an ideal training situation. Some of the athletes (Tewanima being one of them) suffered from seasickness.

Nevertheless, Tewanima displayed the experience of a veteran in the Stockholm Games. Entered in the 10,000-meter (6.2-mile) run, he wisely ran hard enough to qualify in the trial heats but resisted the urge to go all-out. An Associated Press report of the competition stated:

> The sensational event of the morning was the splendid race between Louis Tewanima the Indian, and L. Richardson of South Africa in the second heat of the 10,000-meter flat race in which 11 runners started . . .
>
> About the beginning of the last mile, Stenroos dropped back and Richardson pushed forward from 100 yards in the rear and took his place. The tall man in green and his little red brother were almost shoulder-to-shoulder for two laps. On the final circuit Richardson sprinted at a quarter-mile gait. Tewan-

ima once came to the front gamely, but Richardson won by a yard amid great enthusiasm.

The Indian walked freshly across the field afterward, but his opponent had to be helped away.

The weather for the Stockholm Olympic Games was extremely hot for the Scandinavian country, and distance runners suffered severely from its effects. Tewanima certainly displayed uncanny racing savvy by saving himself for the final (he was also again entered in the marathon, which would be the final event of the Games). In fact, it was hot enough that only eleven of the fifteen qualifiers started the race.

A huge favorite in the 10,000-meter final was Finnish star Johan "Hannes" Kolehmainen—a man whose name and prodigious distance running skills would become well known in Berwick, Pennsylvania, in the future. The first of several of his countrymen deemed worthy of the esteemed nickname "the Flying Finn," Kolehmainen lapped every runner in the field except Tewanima—who placed second for the silver medal in 32:06.6—and his fellow Finn Albin Stenroos (bronze, 32:21.8) en route to his winning performance of 31:20.8 despite the toasty conditions. Richardson, the South African whom Tewanima had pushed to the brink of collapse in the trial heat, did not place among the top five in the final.

No doubt worn down by his two 10,000-meter races, Tewanima was not among the front-runners in the marathon. The race was won by Ken McArthur of South Africa in 2:36:54 (about a minute ahead of his countryman Christian Gitsham), while Gaston Strobino of Patterson, New Jersey, put the Americans in the medals with a third-place effort of 2:38:42.

The conditions were so oppressive that a twenty-one-year-old Portuguese runner named Francisco Lazaro collapsed and eventually died from heat stroke. In one of sport's brutal ironies, it was said that while the South Africans McArthur and Gitsham celebrated and were toasted by fans in the streets of Stockholm, Lazaro tossed in a coma state in a room so close by that the revelries from below could be heard by those who attended him. Young Lazaro, feverish and on death's threshold, heard nothing. He died the next day in his small room. Said one bystander: "In his delirium, he seemed to still be struggling in the marathon."

Other Berwick participants who took part in the 1912 Olympic Games included Willie Kramer of New York (who was injured and "obliged to give up" after 4 hard miles of his 10,000-meter trial heat), the free-spirited Canadian Jimmy Duffy, who placed fifth in the marathon, and New York upstart Harry J. Smith, who managed fifteenth.

Another US Olympic marathoner at Stockholm who would one day race at Berwick was Clarence DeMar—the famous multi-time winner of the Boston Marathon. Writing his racing memoirs in 1937 (*Marathon, 1937*, by Stephen Daye Press, Brattleboro, Vermont) DeMar recalled that Olympic team coach Mike Murphy, while cautioning the runners not to drink too much "beer and milk" (interestingly, Murphy did not object to the lads drinking either milk or beer—just not *both* liquids while in training), also made special note to lecture Harry Smith to "stay away from those Swedish girls!"

Smith's interest in the Swedish sweeties perhaps was a diversion to take his mind off his real concern: a sore knee. The overzealous coaches—head coach Murphy was assisted by special marathon coach Johnny Hayes, the gold-medal winner in London—may well have contributed to Smith's nagging knee. According to DeMar and others, the coaches insisted on working the marathon squad too hard in the days leading up to the Olympic Games. For example, when the ship stopped in Antwerp, Belgium, en route to Stockholm, the coaches made the marathon team run some 20 miles around a hay field.

Regardless, the arduous training regimen and the diabolical heat wave combined to wilt US marathon expectations; none of the dozen Americans raced as well as anticipated, with the surprising exception of Strobino who landed a bronze medal behind the South Africans. (Tellingly, DeMar credited Strobino's great effort with being somewhat *ignored* by the coaches. Named late to the team when Sidney Hatch of Chicago declined his spot, Strobino was deemed by US officials to have no chance for a medal.)

As for Smith's Olympic marathon effort, the *New York Times* said: "Special mention should be made of the plucky Harry Smith of New York, who despite a sore knee, insisted on starting, and finished fifteenth."

II
Homeward Bound: Tewanima Leaves Carlisle

Upon returning to the States, the US team was once again feted and toasted. Thorpe, Tewanima, and Pop Warner in particular received victory parades and honors in New York City, Philadelphia, and Carlisle. An estimated crowd of five thousand turned out in Carlisle, and President Howard Taft sent a letter to be read in the team's honor.

Ironically, some pictures from that time show Tewanima—the Hopi who was taught the tailor's trade—decked out in a snazzy suit, as were Jim Thorpe and Pop Warner. Tewanima's suit was in stark contrast with the faded, raggedy, castoff military garb the Hopi "hostiles" had arrived wearing at Carlisle just five years before. The celebrations were festive, and you might argue the high-water mark of Thorpe's amateur career. (Sadly, Thorpe was later stripped of his Olympic honors and awards when it was learned he'd participated in sandlot baseball one summer and earned a meager amount of money.)

But Tewanima's time away from his native, wind-buffeted mesas in Arizona was running out. He was ready to return to Hopi country. He was lauded by Carlisle's superintendent Moses Friedman at the school's graduation ceremony in mid-August.

"[The Hopis] were ridiculed at first by the other students, it being a common habit of the aboriginal race," proclaimed Friedman. "But the newcomers persevered, until they were among the most respected and best-liked students in the school. The Hopis were absolutely converted to education and civilization. Where before they were sun worshipers and the snake dance was one of their principal ceremonies, they have all joined Christian churches.

"When these Hopi boys return home they will be leaders among their people and fight for both education and righteousness. Now, all speak English, all read and write, they are courteous, and are gentlemen. They have kept in continual touch with their people and already this influence has been noticeable in the Hopi country."

Friedman could not have been more wrong. Tewanima returned to the mesas and quickly re-embraced the Hopi way. If he had a reaction to arriving back in Arizona and finding his wife of six years before married to another man in the tribe, none is recorded. Tewanima eventually became a respected elder and medicine man in the tribe.

In his final days at Carlisle, Tewanima was his typical low-key self. If Jim Thorpe was somewhat used to the spotlight, Tewanima avoided it as best he could. On at least one occasion, Thorpe spoke at length about his Olympic accomplishments before an audience at the Carlisle School. In an oral history interview for the Cumberland Historical Society in 1981, Mrs. Luane Mangold remembers:

> They were at the stadium and people made speeches, and
> Jim Thorpe made a fairly lengthy speech . . . Lewis Tewanima

got up and said: 'Me too . . ."' and everybody applauded.

According to *Sports Illustrated* writer and author Lars Anderson (*Carlisle vs. Army: Jim Thorpe, Pop Warner, and the Forgotten Story of Football's Greatest Battle*, Random House), as the now megafamous athlete Jim Thorpe prepared for the 1912 Carlisle football season, the introverted Tewanima—the two-time Olympian and first big name to win the Berwick Marathon—prepared to leave the barrack ground that had been his place of residence for the last half decade. Anderson writes:

> Thorpe's fellow Olympian Tewanima left school for his old home on the reservation in Arizona. All the soft-spoken Hopi ever wanted in his life was to tend his herd of sheep, and before stepping on the train to head west, he gave most of his track medals away as presents. A few girls at Carlisle promptly used them as shoe buckles.

Although Tewanima generously gave away his medals before leaving Pennsylvania, one of the few items he kept was his Carlisle Indian School running singlet, with its large C stitched prominently on the chest. Although Tewanima participated in very few running events after his return to Arizona, he would sometimes show up at local village footraces. In an article published in the *Smithsonian Magazine* (2002, "Hopi Olympian Lewis Tewanima" by Patty Talahongva), the Olympic runner's great-great granddaughter Melania Honwytewa noted: "When there was a race, people would say, 'The big C is coming up!' because he would wear his Carlisle jersey."

The racing singlet with the big C would have been quite a familiar sight to those thousands of fans in the early days of the Berwick Marathon, too—conjuring up a mental snapshot of fleet little Tewanima spurting (pursued by the well-muscled, more athletic-looking Arquette) down Market Street toward the finish line, an image forever etched in the memories of all who witnessed it.

TEWANIMA OF CARLISLE

Photo courtesy of The Library of Congress

Tewanima's Trophies: Tewanima, the great Hopi runner, gave his medals away to schoolgirls who used them as shoe buckles. However, he kept his big C racing vest.

LOUIS TEWANIMA: Pride and Perseverance

As a boy, he had no coaching in any formal sense of the word, but Louis Tewanima emerged from an ancient culture in which running was part of the Hopi Way. Some Hopi religious *Kachina* rituals involve running; Hopi hunters also would run down game animals for food. They did this, for example, with dozens of boys and men forming a large, ever-constricting "noose" of perhaps a mile around and then flinging hunting sticks at flushed jackrabbits.

Running for a Hopi could also be sport and entertainment. Not only did Tewanima participate in races against other Hopis, but he was said to sometimes have run 60 miles to Winslow, Arizona, for the sheer, simple pleasure of watching trains rock by on the rails. Then he would run back again.

In addition to his silver medal in the Stockholm Olympic Games and his three Berwick Marathon victories, Louis Tewanima—the reluctant Carlisle Indian School recruit—ran dozens of other great races from 1907 to 1912.

Two of his most impressive performances came in New York City—an indoor 10-mile event and a modified marathon (just over 12 miles) that started near Fordham University in the Bronx and finished at New York City Hall in Manhattan.

Tewanima's indoor gem was run on the tiny board track in Madison Square Garden on January 25, 1909. Perhaps after his problem with the miscounted laps in the Yonkers Marathon two months prior, Tewanima was apprehensive about counting 10 miles' worth of circuits on the board oval. As Pop Warner remembered it in a 1931 article for *Collier's:*

> Once I took him over to New York for a ten-mile competition in Madison Square Garden, and after looking at the track, which was 10-laps to the mile, he turned to me and said: "Me afraid get mixed up go round and round. You tell me front man and I get him."
>
> Along the middle of the race I began to catch his eye and point out some runner who led him, and one by one he picked them up, finally finishing in a burst of speed that established a new [indoor] world's record.

Tewanima's main rival for the event was a Boston-based runner named Jimmy Lee, but Carlisle's star distance runner ran him down. His time of 54 minutes, 27 seconds was billed as a new indoor world record for the distance. The *New York Herald*—stooping to some of the typical racial rhetoric of the time—reported the finish like this:

> Louis Tewanima, an Indian from the Carlisle School, won the ten mile race at Madison Square Garden last night at the Carnival of Sports of the Pastime Club that met a crowd of 4,000 in a frenzy. When the tawny little aborigine sped down the home stretch and broke the tape half a lap before "Jimmy" Lee of Boston, the enthusiastic crowd surged down upon him and

bore him off on their shoulders. The ovation tendered to the red man was a tribute to one of the pluckiest exhibitions seen in an athletic contest in this vicinity in years.

One can only wonder what Tewanima—by most accounts, an introverted man of few words, especially in his early years in the land of the *Pahana*—thought of the impromptu victory shoulder ride. He also was awarded a large bronze statue of the wing-footed Mercury for his efforts. In addition, his Carlisle teammates John Corn and Mitchell Arquette (running one of his first races at age sixteen) placed fifth and ninth respectively in a field of fifty-six starters. (It is also worth wondering if Coach "Pop" Warner did not perhaps wager a few dollars on his Hopi star, since certainly there were bets to be taken on the race in the smoke-hazy arena.)

Although the race went amazingly well for Tewanima and his accompanying Carlisle protégés, their athletic successes were almost overshadowed by a near-fatal accident, as Pop Warner related:

> It came close to being a costly trip, however, for I put Tewanima and two other Hopi runners in a hotel room and forgot to tell them about the gas. As a consequence, they blew it out. But for an open window there would have been three dead Indians. As it was, they were unconscious when I found them the next morning and it was some time before we could bring them back to normal.

Tewanima's other major win in New York City was the so-called modified marathon sponsored by the *Evening Mail* newspaper on May 6, 1911. The *New York Times* account began with:

> Tewanima, a ward of the Nation and a student at the Carlisle Indian School, yesterday demonstrated the superiority of the red man as a foot runner over a cosmopolitan field which numbered nearly 1,000 athletes . . . in the so-called modified Marathon—the distance being twelve miles—under auspices of The Evening Mail. The copper-colored youngster negotiated the distance in 1 hour, 9 minutes and 16 seconds, being 1 minute and 21 seconds ahead of the second man, Frank Masterson, Mohawk A.C. Harry Smith was third in 1:11:10.

Tewanima arrived to a thunderous ovation at City Hall plaza, but—in a response typical of him—the quiet Hopi, according to newspaper reports, "took in the whole scene as a matter of course, and upon learning his time, grunted, shrugged his shoulders, and walked to the dressing room, weighed down somewhat by a massive cup, which was his winning portion."

There were other races, of course; perhaps by today's knowledge too many races and sometimes too close together to produce the very best results. For example, Tewanima won a 20-mile race in New Orleans (Joe Forshaw, Olympic Marathon bronze-medal winner in 1908, was among the men he beat there), and just a day after his return to Carlisle, he was shuttled off to Trenton, New Jersey, where he won a 10-mile race.

Tewanima also played a major role in one of the Carlisle Indian School's most storied athletic feats—the victories over Lafayette College's outstanding track and field teams with just a handful of Carlisle competitors. Depending upon the year (and the story), Carlisle—with Jim Thorpe, Frank Mount Pleasant, and Tewanima leading the charge—defeated a full squad of Leopards from Easton, Pennsylvania, with anywhere from three to six athletes.

After his final races in the East in the weeks immediately following his second-place effort in the Stockholm Olympic 10,000 meters, Tewanima returned to his true home—the high desert Hopi mesas of north-central Arizona. Despite the predictions of Carlisle Superintendent Moses Freidman and others spouting the "Indian Affairs" doctrine of the day, there is absolutely no evidence that Tewanima ever attempted to continue with the ways of the *Pahana* world—let alone sway other Hopi to embrace the culture of white America. Conversely, the facts indicate that he soon became an important man in the tribe—a practicing priest of his Hopi clan.

Tewanima's reputation for running continued to carry some weight and he sometimes showed up for low-key village races. In 1924, he won a 10-mile race in Gallup, New Mexico, not far from Fort Wingate where he was once held by the US Cavalry.

The white world, however, continued to reach out to Tewanima—though most definitely in a much more respectful manner than his first encounters.

In 1954, Tewanima was named to the "all-time" US Olympic Team and the Helms Foundation flew the Hopi priest to New York City—site of many of his outstanding races—and feted him. Probably well into his seventh decade of life at that time, the still-lively distance runner was asked the secrets of good health and—according to newspaper accounts—replied: "Eat good food . . . tend sheep . . . tend garden."

New York City wanted Tewanima to visit again—this time at the request of a somewhat new magazine called *Sports Illustrated*—in an effort to get former Olympians to raise funds for the 1956 US Olympic team that was bound for Australia and the Melbourne Games. *SI* publisher Harry Reilly wrote in "Memo from the Publisher":

> Only special circumstances prevented Louis Tewanima from being on hand last month when Sports Illustrated gathered some 30 team members of past and present US Olympic teams in New York for a press conference and an appearance on the Ed Sullivan Show . . . Tewanima received his Sports Illustrated invitation to come to New York at his native Hopi village . . . in northeast Arizona, to which he returned after the 1912 Olympics. Now 74, he directed a nephew to write a reply through a friend, Bill Close, a news and sports director of radio station KOY in Phoenix.

Close—who had accompanied Tewanima on his Helms Foundation trip two years before (Close grappled with airsickness during a bumpy flight, but Tewanima, his first time flying, sat calmly and puffed on several fat cigars)—then explained to Reilly that:

> Louis Tewanima is an antelope [clan member], high in the priesthood, and also is known as one of the wise men of the council. His responsibility is great and he feels it to such an extent that he must pass up this trip, although there is none he'd rather make. In Arizona, we are very proud of Louis Tewanima.

Tewanima occasionally took some short trips to Phoenix—about 300 miles away—riding in the back of a nephew's pickup truck. He was the first inductee to the Arizona Sports Hall of Fame there in 1957, receiving a standing ovation from the crowd. Perhaps more comfortable in his older years, Tewanima entertained the audience with some running anecdotes from his Hopi youth.

One of the last visitors from the *Pahana* world to track down Tewanima was *Wall Street Journal* reporter Edwin McDowell in 1968. McDowell found him well recovered from a bout of pneumonia that had plagued him the previous winter.

> When I visited him four months before his death, at his isolated pueblo on Second Mesa, high above the wind-swept Painted Desert region of northeastern Arizona, Tewanima—resplendent in red hairband, turquoise earrings, bright blouse and brown cotton pants—was still trim, erect and alert.

McDowell found a simple man, content to tend his sheep and grow melons, beans, corn, and peaches in his garden. His many trophies, cups, and medals were conspicuously absent, but McDowell spied an autographed picture of Glenn "Pop" Warner, his former coach. The *Wall Street Journal* writer surmised that Tewanima had "escaped the worst effects of the nation's paternalistic Indian policies, no doubt because his deep religious faith sustained him."

In mid-January 1969, Tewanima was returning from a religious ceremony in the dark. The former Olympian and antelope clan priest—perhaps mistaking some distant lights as a beacon from the village—took a wrong turn and fell off a sheer 70-foot cliff, plunging to his death. Villagers searched for him all night. After his fatal fall, he was buried within four days, as is the Hopi custom. The great Hopi runner is honored each September on the mesa—where he lived all but five of his estimated ninety-plus years—with the Louis Tewanima Memorial Runs.

5

The New Yorkers Take Charge

When the runners returned to Berwick in 1912 for the fifth running of the Marathon the lads from New York must have felt their chances for winning to be greatly improved. Much of that optimism could undoubtedly be traced to Louis Tewanima's departure for Arizona.

In their defense, these metropolitan front-runners were a tough and talented lot in their own right and by 1912 may have been prepared to take even the great Tewanima right to the wire—Berwick wasn't a race that they needed to win by default. Why were the New Yorkers so good? First and foremost, they benefited greatly from the intense rivalry among the various club teams—dozens of them in the metropolitan area—that made New York City a hotbed for distance racing in those early years of the twentieth century.

The clubs naturally created ample opportunities for New York area runners to race. Van Cortlandt Park in the Bronx was often the site of the national cross-country championships (although sometimes they were held on Philadelphia's Belmont Plateau), and Madison Square Garden, of course, hosted a multitude of indoor track events. In addition, New York races were sometimes conducted at the Polo Grounds or even in Yankee Stadium. Macombs Dam (next to Yankee Stadium) and Celtic Park on Long Island also were popular racing venues (as were various armories)— with still more racing opportunities across the river in New Jersey.

As it was—even without Tewanima—the competition among the New Yorkers themselves was intense enough to produce a new record at the 1912 Berwick Marathon, and the estimated twenty-five thousand spectators were treated to the fastest, deepest field (nineteen runners under an hour) in the short history of the race.

I
Harry in a Hurry: Smith Sets Sail
5th Berwick Marathon, November 28, 1912

Harry J. Smith of the Pastime Athletic Club was one of those rapidly improving New York runners. In addition to his third-place run in the

1911 modified Marathon won by Tewanima, Smith also rose to the challenge of long, multi-lap races inside the smoke-hazed confines of Madison Square Garden. Dominating a field of thirty-four starters, Smith won a 15-miler on the boards there in early December (just days after his fourth at the 1911 Berwick race) and drew high praise from the papers for his performance. As noted in the *New York Times* historical archives:

> Harry J. Smith, the Captain of the Pastime A.C., a much-improved runner, was the winner in a sterling time of 1:26:16, which establishes a new record for the distance . . . At thirteen miles the Pastime lad had a lead of twenty-five yards, which he increased with every circuit, coming through on the final lap like a real good runner and winning almost by himself.

However, running a tough marathon with an inflamed knee forced Smith to take some much-needed downtime after the Stockholm Olympics in July 1912. He had plenty of time to heal up, too, since the ship's journey in itself would have taken more than a week. By fall Smith was racing well. He captured the 10-mile national championship in New York in October, arriving in Berwick the next month with a good head of steam and confidence to burn. And judging from the way Smith took on the Berwick course, he also may have conjured up a race strategy: Be aggressive from the start and see what happens.

Although still a relatively new race, the Berwick Marathon already had a certain buzz about it. There was also an emerging theory on how to win it—to lead early, certainly at the top of Foundryville Hill, if not before. The newspapers were already reporting that the runner who led at these early checkpoints was certain to arrive first at the finish line. It was information that the runners themselves certainly would have heard bantered about and a strategy they would have mulled over.

In the fifth Berwick Marathon, Harry Smith took this win-from-the-front theory out for a road test. The weather was cool and clear, but the course conditions were deemed "very muddy in spots" and with some patches of snow, but—all in all—a good day to run fast.

As a special report to the *New York Times* noted:

> Smith took the lead from the start and maintained it throughout the grueling course. McNamara, Gallagher, Holden, McGuire, La Funa, Root, Bellars, and Sturgis trailed him for the first mile, with Smith gradually drawing away from the bunch . . .

By the time Smith reached Summer Hill, his lead had increased even more, and the pursuit pack may well have settled down to the task of racing for second, with J. J. McNamara, George Holden, the 1911 runner-up Fred Bellars, and Tom Barden jostling for position. They ran "the Hill" aggressively, and only Georgetown student John J. Gallagher—who came from Philadelphia—stayed close enough to reestablish contact.

Stated the *Times:*

> All the New York runners took the long hill in fine form, and it was there that they ran away from the remainder of the field. McNamara, Bellars, and Holden were separated by not more than 30 feet with Johnny Gallagher, the Philadelphia runner wearing Georgetown University colors, 100 yards behind.

But Gallagher must have paid a steep price for trying to hang with the gang from New York; the *Times* reported that "A mile from the finish [Gallagher] collapsed and fell into a ditch. Receiving prompt medical attention, he made a quick recovery, but was unable to finish."

The *Times* noted that Russell Springsteen (10th, 53:59) also had a rough Berwick: "Springsteen of Yonkers managed to finish, but collapsed soon after and is still under the physician's care."

Smith had no such worries. He blasted by the boisterous crowds on Market Street and came away with a new course record of 49:26.8—carving off 26 seconds from Tewanima's old mark. J. J. McNamara (2nd, 50:15) held off Holden (3rd, 50:31), Bellars (4th, 50:37) and Barden (50:45) in an incredible show of metropolitan might as the New Yorkers swept places first through fifth.

So dominant were the New Yorkers that it was nearly 2 minutes more before Philadelphia's Paul La Funa checked in (6th, 52:38), just ahead of two New England runners—Hugh Maquire of Rhode Island (7th, 52:59) and young Jimmy Henigan of Boston (8th, 53:16). It was the first time New Englanders had run at Berwick and the start of a storied tradition.

The Carlisle Indian School did have four entries, but without Tewanima and Arquette to lead the attack, they wallowed in the unaccustomed muck of the mid-pack—a curiosity still, but certainly not a factor. Their top finisher was Jesse Wakeman, a modest 11th place in 54:47.

On the local scene, Berwickians were pleased to see Bob Eshleman back in the Marathon fray. Four years from his start in the pioneer event, Eshleman ran about the same time he did for his second place behind Harry Williams in 1908—only this time, against such stellar competition, his

Big Apple Blitz: Record-setting Harry J. Smith was the first New Yorker to lead the charge at Berwick in the post-Tewanima era. Smith raced for both the Pastime Athletic Club and the Bronx Church House during his career, prior to his suspension for expense money violations.

place was a modest 22nd. The regional followers, however, had to take some pride in two sub-hour performances from a pair of Sunbury, Pennsylvania, high school runners, as William Bachman (18th, 58:48) and Rosten Kesty (19th, 59:30) displayed both grit and promise with their efforts.

II
New York, New York, Encore
6th Berwick Marathon, November 27, 1913

Had it not been before his time, Yankee catcher and quipster Yogi Berra might have described the sixth Berwick Marathon—at least in terms of New York domination—as "déjà vu all over again." If the Carlisle Indian School runners were no longer the fast kids on the Berwick block, then the confident—and now Berwick battle-tested—New Yorkers were only too happy to set the pace for the rest of the field.

On a cold day with light snow, the New York crew once again dominated the field—sweeping the top five slots—although the Carlisle Indian School squad, with six runners placing between sixth and 12th, ran a solid second.

The New York runners merely seemed to switch some places around, with defending champ Harry Smith—although he ran essentially the same time as his winning race the year before—dropping to third, and George Holden moving up one place to second. Russell Springsteen, who needed medical help after his 10th place finish in 1912, moved all the way up to fourth overall and dipped under 49:50. But it wasn't easy; this time Springsteen lost a shoe racing through Kachinka's Hollow, but ran the last half of the race without it—despite the snow. Tom Barden settled for fifth in 51:39, which was not a super race for him in terms of time, but nevertheless gave the metropolitan men another sweep of the first five places.

The winner, however, was a Berwick rookie—William J. "Willie" Kramer. But with three national cross-country titles (1909, 1911, and 1912) on his résumé, the Brooklyn man and Long Island Athletic Club runner had the right stuff for whatever the course had to throw at him. A bigger, more powerfully built runner than the typically slightly built harriers, Kramer followed Smith's successful game plan. He jumped to an early lead and simply added to it. And although there was some snow and the temperatures were cold, the roads were actually in good shape for running. For Kramer, it all added up to a new Berwick Marathon record. When Kramer broke the finish-line tape—his vest resplendent with the easy-to-recognize Cherry Diamond logo of his LIAC club team—the time was a sizzling 48 minutes, 33 seconds, eclipsing Smith's previous mark by nearly a full minute.

Mitchell Arquette was back for Carlisle, but—perhaps without Tewanima to train and race with—couldn't match his old form. Arquette could only muster seventh, one spot behind his teammate Robert Nash.

Canadian Jimmy Duffy, who had placed fifth in the Stockholm Olympic Marathon, had to settle for a modest eighth place at Berwick. The free-spirited Duffy—he allegedly asked for a cigarette and a beer shortly after winning the 1914 Boston Marathon—was definitely better at longer races. Nine miles just wasn't far enough for him. Duffy had twice won the Hamilton Around the Bay Race (the very event that had inspired the transplanted Domville to dream up a Marathon for Berwick), but that was slightly over 18 miles in length.

A slew of Carlisle Indian runners—Francis Oakes, John Razer, Carmalito Torres, and Mitchell Shongo—swept the next four spots, with a solid performance from Berwick's Harold Ridall in 13th, clocking 55 minutes, 57 seconds, a new record for locals and his place put him right in the middle of the field of twenty-six finishers.

WILLIAM J. KRAMER
CROSS COUNTRY KING

Photo courtesy of Harry's Sports

King William: Willie Kramer of the Long Island AC won three US cross-country titles and captured Berwick in his first (and only) race in a record 48:33. He rebounded from what some thought might be a career-ending injury at the 1912 Olympics.

III
Holden Holds Off Barden
7th Berwick Marathon, November 26, 1914

Despite Kramer's debut win at the 1913 Berwick Marathon, the importance of experience on the course was never to be underestimated. To have *heard* about the hills at Berwick—particular the arduous ascent up to Summer Hill—was one thing; to actually *run* it was another. Even at such an early time in the history of the Berwick race, runners most have asked themselves this obvious question: Is it purely coincidental that there are churches and graveyards situated at the top of such a hill?

Running the Berwick hill—actually more of a mountain—wasn't something a runner forgot while waiting for the pumpkin pie and whipped cream to digest later in the evening. The New Yorkers were well versed in the ups and downs of Berwick, the peculiar road surfaces that might confront them through Kachinka's Hollow, and the dig-deep grit that would be required for that final charge down Market Street. But first and foremost, there was "the Hill."

In the summer and fall of 1914, Tom Barden—the affable redhead and popular Irish American Athletic Club runner—decided to make a concerted effort to prepare specifically for the Berwick Marathon. And that meant hills. What Barden did—which seems obvious to us in our modern era—was seek out the nastiest hills he could find and make them part of his training regimen.

Barden was familiar with the Yonkers Marathon course. The Yonkers course had some challenging hills on it. Those Yonkers upgrades couldn't match the torturous length of the climb to Summer Hill, but they were tough enough to prep for the real thing. Like a knife subjected to the red-hot flames of the forge, Barden hoped to harden his racing body and steel himself for the Thanksgiving Day test. Dedication and determination! Tom Barden longed to improve upon his fourth-place best at Berwick.

As the New Yorkers continued to dominate the race, they seemed almost to be taking turns in the winner's circle. It wasn't planned. Most of them ran for different club teams and—although they enjoyed thrashing runners from other cities and states (especially Philadelphia, it seems)—they were also keen to outrun each other. Barden wanted it to be *his* turn, though admittedly he was a dark horse.

Although the New Yorkers once again were expected to dominate the top half a dozen positions, Berwick Marathon observers—men in the know like race director Chiv MacCrea—might have been leaning toward a Canadian entry in the days prior to the seventh running of the Thanksgiving Day classic.

The Maple Leaf men believed they had the man in hand to break up the Yankees when they brought Arthur Jamieson to the starting line. A Native Canadian runner from the Six Nations Reservation in Ontario, Jamieson came into town with a string of race victories and a glowing running résumé, as noted in the local news:

> Jamieson had the strongest following and his record of having won every race he has ever entered since joining fast company and the fact that he has smashed Canadian records galore the past year . . .

Some of those records had belonged to his famous Indian predecessor, Tom Longboat, the 1907 Boston Marathon champion. But with Longboat having turned professional (he had redeemed—somewhat—his infamous London Marathon collapse and DNF by winning some pro races over the Italian Dorando Pietri), Jamieson was now the great hope for the lads from the Great White North.

Of course, Jamieson had never run the Berwick course. But since Willie Kramer had won in 1913 without previously having run the hill or the course, perhaps the Canadians thought it wouldn't be so critical. Like Kramer, Jamieson was a proven talent—and, besides, hadn't Indian runners raced superbly at Berwick in the past? Jamieson, some thought, could well be a Canadian version of Louis Tewanima.

In addition to the hard-training Barden, the New Yorkers brought forth George Holden. The man who represented the Yonkers YMCA team did not have much room for improvement; he had already been second and third in previous Berwick Marathons. Holden was looking for a modest elevation—just one place better—as he toed the 1914 starting line.

Willie Kramer, Harry J. Smith, and Fred Bellars were not entered, which certainly improved Holden's and Barden's chances to take a shot at the winner's circle—though the overall result was that New York contingent was not as deep as in previous years.

The conditions were mild, but the course was muddy in spots, and parts of the Martzville Road had recently been filled in, leaving a loose, unstable running surface. Still, all signs pointed to a competitive run—if not a record one—as the pistol shot sent fifteen men hustling up Market Street,

Foundryville-bound.

Spectators knew they were in for a great race when Holden, Jamieson, and Nick Giannakopoulos—a Greek runner representing the Millrose Athletic Club of New York—were so close as they approached the summit at Summer Hill that it was if they "were running as one man across the road."

And although the course was muddy in places—particularly through the low-lying parts of Kachinka's Hollow—automobiles on the unpaved course (a constant problem in the early years) also caused headaches for the front-runners on the dry stretches. As the *Bloomsburg Morning Post* noted in its race write-up, these autos kicked up

> a dense cloud through which it was impossible to see more than a few hundred feet. Dust covered the forms of the runners and they had their mouths caked with it as most of them were breathing with their mouths open.

On the strength of some nice downhill running, Barden had charged all the way up to second place, right behind the race leader Holden, while Jamieson had fallen about 100 yards back, and Giannakopoulos and Springsteen jousted for the fourth and fifth spots. The course fought their best efforts.

> At the foot of the Martzsville hill the road from side-to-side had been filled in and the runners darted from one side of the road to the other slipping on stones or going over shoe top in the dirt.

Jamieson's trainers were concerned. If Jamieson was going to save the Canadians' Berwick bacon, then it was clear he needed to rally—and quickly—to reestablish contact with Holden and Barden. The trainers trotted after him on the Martzville Road

> with a bucket of water and a sponge. They sponged off his head and face, while he was given a drink from a bottle . . .
> Falling in behind the Indian they sought to spur him on . . .

But it was Barden who was bursting with resolve and running on the pure adrenaline of realizing that his best Berwick race ever was unfolding. He chased Holden all the way down Market Street, and only a burst of strength and speed from Holden allowed him to hold off the ever-popular Irish American Athletic Club runner. Holden clocked 50 minutes, 29 seconds—a scant 2 ticks ahead of Barden in the closest Berwick Marathon to date.

Photo courtesy of Harry's Sports

Main Man on Market: George Holden, Yonkers YMCA, takes first in the 1914 Berwick Marathon. In May 1918 Holden's ship—the USS *President Lincoln*—was torpedoed by a German U-boat off the coast of France. Holden was among the rescued.

Barden was as jubilant as a man who just misses winning could ever possibly be. "It's sticking at it that did it!" he exclaimed to reporters, revealing that he had purposely picked "the worst hills around New York to drill himself for the grueling climb up to Summer Hill."

Jamieson, arguably a pre-race favorite, had to settle for third (50:55), while Springsteen (4th, 51:11) pulled away from Giannakopoulos (5th, 51:45) in the last mile. Representing the Marion Athletic Club out of Bloomsburg, Arthur Letteer ran a very strong sixth in 52:55—9 seconds ahead of Frank Zuna, a man who would one day win the Boston

Marathon. Berwick's own Harold Ridall finished eighth in 54:18—more than 2 minutes ahead of another local, Elias Whitmire (9th, 56:45).

Although Jamieson's third place broke up the New York sweep of all the top prizes, the metropolitan men (even without Kramer, Smith, and Bellars) were still the guys in control.

The New Yorkers would be equally formidable in 1915, led by an Irish American Athletic Club runner—but this particular athlete would not have any traces of a brogue, and it's extremely unlikely that he would have known the words to "Danny Boy."

Tom Barden (28)—the winged fist of the Irish American Athletic Club on his vest—shadows Holden (of the Yonkers YMCA) in their 1-2 finish at the 1914 Berwick Marathon.

Photo courtesy of Harry's Sports

6

The First Flying Finn

I
Berwick Gets the Best

If there was one runner in the world that race director Chiv MacCrea would have immediately signed on—had MacCrea been given the equivalent of a first-round NFL draft pick—then that man certainly would have been one specific bricklayer living in New York City and running for the Irish American Athletic Club.

That man was neither Irish nor American. He came to New York City from Finland and he already had three Olympic gold medals to his name; he would win a fourth in the 1920 Antwerp Games to cap a glorious career. His name was Johan "Hannes" Kolehmainen, and he was arguably the best distance runner in the world for most of a decade.

Kolehmainen originally came from the town of Kuopio in the southeastern part of Finland. But he chose to emigrate to New York following his much-celebrated victories in Stockholm, partly for the economic and athletic opportunities that awaited him there. Kolehmainen was well informed on the opportunities in America because his older brother Wiljami was already living in the US and racing as a professional. That there was money to be made in America was quite evident; Wiljami had generously sent periodic payments to Finland to help support Hannes and another running Kolehmainen brother named Tatu, so they could train properly for the 1912 Olympic Games.

But in addition to simple advancement, it is quite possible that Kolehmainen also felt inclined to avoid an unstable political situation. The Finns—who officially had competed at the Stockholm Games as a Grand Duchy of Russia (an affiliation that virtually all Finns despised and none more than the Olympic athletes)—secured their own independence in 1917, but soon fell into class warfare among themselves. This turmoil permeated virtually all facets of Finnish life, even something as seemingly simple as which athletic club one joined. Eventually this tension erupted into a horrendously bloody civil war in 1918, between "Whites" (prosperous farmers and upper-crust bourgeois Finns) and "Reds" (socialist workers located in bigger towns and cities). But Kolehmainen—perhaps long sensing the inevitable—was already well established in America and avoided the bloodshed and brutality.

So those were the circumstances that brought Kolehmainen to New York. Once in New York (he also lived in other parts of the country, including Detroit and Philadelphia), he joined the Irish American Athletic Club (the Finns would later develop their own running club). His teammates would have told him of the important Berwick Marathon race. Tewanima, the slight but speedy Hopi, had helped provide the Berwick race with credibility; now Chiv MacCrea had landed the man—the "Flying Finn"—who had relegated the great Indian runner to second place in the Olympic 10,000-meter race and lapped most of his other rivals. In addition, Kolehmainen had won a historic 5000-meter race in Stockholm, and also placed first in the Olympic cross-country race (an event no longer conducted) while leading his fellow Finns to the team silver behind the Swedes. Understandably, Marathon fans in Berwick could hardly wait to see him race.

II
Kolehmainen Delivers
8th Berwick Marathon, November 25, 1915

The headlines were a ringing endorsement and the words so pregnant with praise that they seemed to suggest that everyone else would be racing for runner-up honors even before J. N. Harry squeezed the trigger on his starting pistol.

"World's Greatest Runner to Start" (and this was merely about the Finn's entry blank arriving in the mail) proclaimed the local newspaper headlines, followed by a gushing, unabashed admission of just how badly the Berwick Marathon Association wanted Hannes Kolehmainen to display his famous, rhythmic strides—and flash his equally famous smile—to the multitudes of Thanksgiving Day fans in Berwick.

> It is with great pleasure that the Marathon Association is able to announce that the world's greatest runner, Hannes Kohlemainen [sic], the "Flying Finn," will be a starter in the eighth annual Berwick Marathon . . . The letter received yesterday

> assuring the association that he will positively be here, brings to
> successful conclusion negotiations extending over . . . several
> months.

Those negotiations most likely involved meeting Kolehmainen's price on "expenses"—although the Amateur Athletic Union officials supposedly kept a vigilant watch on any such payments made for services rendered. It was a tightrope that the best runners of the day walked at their own peril, and it would have weighed heavily on the minds of the top entrants as they warmed up for the 1915 Berwick race.

That's because Harry J. Smith, the Olympian and 1912 Berwick Marathon champion—along with Abel Kiviat, team captain of the Irish American AC and an Olympic silver-medal winner at Stockholm in the 1500 meters—were declared ineligible by the AAU in October 1915. The pair allegedly demanded expenses above and beyond the allowable limit from the officials conducting a Schenectady, New York, track meet in September. Smith even enlisted his congressman to plead his case, but the charges stuck. In those days, being banned by the AAU was essentially a career-ending ruling, unless a runner could go pro. (Smith was eventually reinstated in the 1920s, but he never regained his old form.)

Whatever the enticements were that lured Kolehmainen to Berwick, the Marathon Association—with MacCrea at the forefront, of course— was elated to have him and not in the least bit shy to express it on the sporting pages, using the lavish language of the era, even if they misspelled the sports hero's name.

> Even more than Caruso to the musical world, Willard to the
> pugilistic, Ty Cobb to the base ball, is Kohlemainen [sic] to the
> running world. For while others must divide in a measure their
> honors with other claimants, Kohlemainen stands supreme the
> unquestioned champion of the world and the athletic marvel of
> all times.

The write-up went on to predict that—with "fair conditions"—the Flying Finn would "probably place a new mark on the course." Of course, when discussing Berwick conditions in those days, the meaning was dual—obviously the weather on race day, but also the conditions of the unpaved roads.

Race day weather was deemed "pleasant," while the route surface received a verdict of "muddy." To be more precise, the roads were glossed over in spots, particularly up Summer Hill, with "a slippery covering which melted frost had left."

As usual, the runners were introduced with great fanfare before the thousands clogging the Market Street start. When Charles Peters, a Chippewa from the Carlisle Indian School, came out to the bugle call, the Berwick band downshifted to a soft playing of the Indian march. The other runners soon followed. It was cold enough—and in contrast to the stuffy confines of the YMCA basement—that the entries ran some short striders off the line or pranced about in the street in an effort to stay warm in the cold fall air in those long minutes between introductions and the report of the gun. Kolehmainen, slight but well muscled, had a handkerchief tied to his head, and was easy to pick out.

Cruise Control: Hannes Kolehmainen (white kerchief, gloves), the first Flying Finn, is content to run with the front pack early in the 1915 Berwick Marathon. Others include: Tom Barden (leading by a step), Nick Giannakopoulos (behind Barden), Joe Schwartz (M on his vest), and the Carlisle Indian School's Charlie Peters (back right).

The reverberating pistol shot from starter J. N. Harry sent nineteen men off the line. They did not dawdle at the front, with the smooth-striding Kolehmainen passing the first mile in 4:42—pulling Tom Barden, right on the famous Finn's heels, along for the ride. By mile 2, Barden actually jumped briefly into the lead, perhaps willing himself to act on visions of a one-place improvement from his fabulous effort in the 1914 edition. As a newspaper account later noted: "It was the only time on the entire course that the winner was headed."

Some wag of a kibitzer in the crowd reportedly crowed: "The Finn can't do it! The hill tells it . . . !"

However, as if in answer to such nonsense, it was Kolehmainen who inched back into first as the runners began their slick-footed trek up to the Summer Hill churches. Greek native Nick Giannakopoulos, a sturdy-looking plow horse of a runner representing John Wanamaker's Millrose Athletic Club in New York, and crowd favorite Barden both responded to the move. Meantime, the top three put a progressively bigger gap on the rest of the field, all the way up the hill. The Berwick newspaper account stated bluntly: "The hill proved slippery and the running was hard."

On the subsequent plunging downhill, and the hard left turn for Kachinka's Hollow, Kolehmainen added a little bit more to his cushion. But perhaps even more telling than the Finn's small lead was his appearance in comparison with his rivals.

> All had a steady gait and maintained it. Kohlemainen [sic] appeared to be running at this best and the others were exerting every ounce of muscle and mental stamina. The Finn alone appeared fresh and was the only one to recognize the crowds that cheered or called. The other runners showed the effects of the grueling race.

In other words, Kolehmainen was—as coaches sometimes like to say—running "well within himself." Certainly he would have felt quite confident in his finishing kick, if in fact someone caught back up to him and it came down to a shoot-out on Market Street. After all, Kolehmainen had run down the fabulous Frenchman Jean Bouin in the 1912 Olympic 5000-meter final—a classic race—en route to a world record of 14:36.6.

The dual for second was actually more exciting. Giannakopoulos and Barden fought back and forth through the hollow and on the Martzville Road. At one point it looked like Barden had gapped his Greek opponent, but Giannakopoulos repassed the Irish American stalwart as they approached North Berwick.

> From this on running through a lane of people and automobiles, the order was the same. Kohlemainen about 150 yards ahead, Giannakopoulos and Barden running close. Some distance behind came Peters and following him Jamieson. [Philadelphia runner Joseph] Schwartz, Holden and Springsteen could not be seen.

As Kolehmainen fluidly strode for the finish line, a rolling wave of shouts swept ahead of him, sweeping through the thousands of spectators on Market Street like sizzling electricity as if supplied by Edison himself: "The Finn! The Flying Finn!"

Kolehmainen's winning time was 49:06—about half a minute off of Willie Kramer's 1913 course record that was clocked over near-perfect road conditions. Giannakopoulos launched a furious sprint down Market Street—more to distance himself from Barden than in any real hopes of snagging Kolehmainen—but it provided him with a second-place time (49:09) that made the race appear much closer than it actually was. Barden settled for third (49:45), and then it was 50 seconds more before the Carlisle Indian School runner Peters checked in for fourth. Jamieson, the Canadian star, finished a disappointing fifth (50:54), but more than a full minute ahead of Schwartz, the next man in sixth place. Arthur Letteer, now a resident of Berwick, finished 10th—chasing in the likes of Newark, New Jersey, runner (and future Boston Marathon champ) Frank Zuna (7th), defending champ Holden (far off form), and Russell Springsteen.

III
The Mudfest Marathon
9th Berwick Marathon, November 30, 1916

Kolehmainen's first Berwick Marathon experience must have been to his liking, because he was back again in 1916. Unfortunately for the Flying Finn, so were the poor road conditions, though the weather certainly seems one of those rare treats for late November in northeastern Pennsylvania—described as "mild and fair." In fact, the road conditions were so sloppy that the subheadline the day after the race trumpeted: "Champions of the East Again Fight Over the Grueling Course Through Mud Ankle Deep."

Although the headline may have slightly embellished, the course was certainly less than ideal, thanks to a steady Wednesday-night rain. However, the competition proved to be tight between the top three finishers, even if the footing was loose.

The unknown of the trio was Juan Pablo Routzo of the Carlisle Indian School, a Native American from the same desolate Southwest region as three-time Berwick champ Louis Tewanima. A Pueblo Indian, Routzo did not come into the race with the same reputation as the famous Hopi, so he definitely took the field by surprise.

Once again, the pace was swift, zipping through 2 miles in just over 10 minutes, or, as the sports write-up observed, close to the legal limit for mechanical vehicles in town.

> The pace set . . . shows the high speed of twelve miles per hour and gives an idea of the caliber of runners and the terrific pace that was set. An interesting comparison is the fact that fifteen miles per hour is the lawful rate for autos.

As he did in the 1915 race, Kolehmainen took control on the climb up to the Summer Hill churches, with only George Holden—no doubt determined to redeem himself for his lackluster performance the year before—and Routzo keeping contact. Even Tom Barden was slightly off the leaders.

Kolehmainen may not have been rattled, but when Routzo flew past him on the downhill toward Miller's Hotel and the sharp turn for Kachinka's Hollow, surely it must have caught the multi-time Olympic gold-medal winner's attention. The Finn, always cool under attack, reestablished his lead through the hollow where the footing was at its most precarious due to swaths of mud, and the powerful-running Holden passed Routzo and moved back into second place.

> It was a pretty sight this race . . . with the swift pace at which the runners were traveling and the mixture of red, white and blue in the running trunks and jerseys, with Rutzo [sic], the Indian, red; Kohlemainen [sic], the Finn, white, and Holden blue. It was a battle between Finn, redskin and white American and the Finn, without a peer, the fleetest man in the world today, showed out in the test.

Kolehmainen risked a glance back as he passed the 6-mile mark and made the turn onto the Martzville Road, Berwick-bound. But his sneak peek simply confirmed what he probably suspected—he needed to keep racing. Holden was pounding through the mud a mere 25 yards back, with the Pueblo Indian runner just a tick or two behind him. Kolehmainen worked the long downhill after the Martzville Church and added precious seconds to his lead.

Once the Finn reached Berwick and made the turn onto the final straightaway, he risked another look back—saw two men still racing in the distance—and, buoyed by the cheers of the enormous Thanksgiving-afternoon crowds (the race had gone off at about 2 PM), picked up his cadence and bore in on the finish line.

And the crowds were tremendous. The good weather (at least for watching) brought out an estimated twenty thousand fans. As the *Berwick Enterprise* observed:

> Long before two o'clock people were taking points of vantage along the ropes and from then on Market streetwas the converging point for lines of people coming in all directions. Trains, trolleys and automobiles brought more people from other towns than had ever before been here . . .
>
> Market Street was black with people and the usual crowds were massed at the start and finish . . . The route out Market was a line of people and automobiles and hundreds of automobiles had gone to points on the course where the winners could be seen in action.

Through this chute of people and autos, Holden charged in less than a half a minute behind, gamely pursued by Juan Pablo Routzo, his shadow, who gave it absolutely everything he had and "fell into the arms of his waiting trainer and had to be assisted to his dressing room."

The ever-popular Barden, who had chased Holden to his 1914 victory, had to settle for a distant fourth (50:52), nearly 2 minutes behind Routzo. It was the last Berwick Marathon for Barden—a man who had so often run near the front, but never first at the finish line. By 1917, he would be swept up in the Great War along with many others.

Some runners handled the muddy conditions better than others. The 1916 Boston Marathon winner Arthur Roth was a nonfactor in sixth. Surprisingly, Nick Giannakopoulos—the proven cross-country harrier—could only finish ninth, a far shout from his runner-up performance in 1915.

Back in 13th place—a lucky finish for him as it turned out—was Penn State student Carl Kahley. Kahley was the first Berwick finisher, and his time of 56:16 was fairly solid for a rookie. He also won a diamond pin valued at $50 for the honor of being first local finisher. Racing after a hard rain on unpaved roads was dirty work, but how could you not love it?

Road Warriors: While the Great War raged in Europe, Berwick had one more run before the event took a break. Kolehmainen (33) and Henigan (5th from left) were the favorites.

IV
A Battle of Smilers in Wartime
10th Berwick Marathon, November 29, 1917

In the spring of 1917, America entered World War I. It would be tempting to say something like "the shadow of war then descended upon the Berwick Marathon." But in fact, everyone—runners, organizers, citizen-fans—had been increasingly aware of its presence even back to 1914.

Followers and participants of the now-famous Thanksgiving Day race needed to look no farther than the absent Canadian contingent to bring on a sincere lump in the throat, or tears to their eyes. Gone were the likes of Jimmy Duffy and the Canadian Indian star Arthur Jamieson, both buried "over there." Only the memories of those fleet, game lads racing up and down the hills of Berwick, then charging down Market Street to the cheers of the festive crowd, remained.

In addition, the Yanks were now well in it. Tom Barden sent word to the race that he was now in the US Navy. Yonkers standout George Holden (also a navy man)—second just a year before and the 1914 champion—

wrote from France, noting how much he wished to be lining up for the race instead of serving in a war zone.

So it was against this somewhat somber backdrop that Kolehmainen arrived on the starting line in an attempt at a "hat trick"—three straight wins—to equal the triumphs of Tewanima. A shot of the 1917 starting line shows several American soldiers—in doughboy attire—standing tall behind the runners.

The field was on the small side—just thirteen finishers. For the second straight year, there were no Canadian runners in the race—for reasons obvious to anyone who was following world news. To make matters worse, the Carlisle Indian School team entered the race by telegraph on Wednesday but never arrived—much to the disappointment of "the Marathon Association and the crowd." Clinging to hope, the officials even delayed the start for forty-five minutes to wait for the train from Sunbury, thinking the Indians might show in the final minutes.

> During the wait for the Indians, a number of Company F men from Camp Meade drilled on Market Street and received the cheers and applause of the crowd as they marched. It was the usual great outpouring of thousands that witnessed the race at its various stages.

Nevertheless—despite the Carlisle Indians' mysterious no-show—the Flying Finn got all the competition he needed from one man: James Henigan from Boston and the Dorchester Athletic Club. Just like Kolehmainen, Henigan often *appeared* to be smiling as he ran, but it is also true that a few select runners simply have a grimace that looks like a grin to the noncombatants standing on the sidelines. Kolehmainen was sometimes referred to as "Smiling Hannes," and Henigan often was called "Smiling Jimmy." (Which was a moniker he probably preferred to another nickname of his—"Hinky.")

Keeping with the troubling times, the runners were sent down Market Street, not with a pistol shot but

> At the sound of the bursting bomb, [Boston's Clifford] Horne leaped forward and took the lead. The others were only a yard or two behind him and running in a bunch.

Shortly after the mile, Horne was passed and Otto Laakso of Brooklyn led down to Foundryville, shadowed by Kolehmainen and Henigan "one running in each wagon track, with Laakso three yards ahead."

But by the time they hit the hill, it was Kolehmainen and Henigan at the front. And the Irishman, stocky in build to the eye when compared with the slight, smooth-running Finn, was determined to improve on his debut Berwick back in 1912 when he finished eighth. They were together at the summit, past the Summer Hill churches, down the free fall to Miller's Hotel . . . banging the hard left . . . then back and forth—like a couple of prizefighters exchanging punch for punch—through Kachinka's Hollow.

At the Martzville church the Irishman and the Finn were still on even terms and were a quarter-mile ahead of Laakso, who continued to fall back as the men increased their pace . . . But through Martzville and on for a considerable distance beyond neither secured a permanent advantage.

Ah, but Kolehmainen always had the best hole card—a better kick. And in truth, it is quite possible—given the less-than-ideal conditions in all three of his Berwick races—that the Flying Finn never went completely full-throttle over the entire distance—despite the apparent closeness in times on paper. When they turned onto Market—approximately a mile to go—Kolehmainen went to his afterburners (someone who must have been clocking him in an auto claimed the Finn hit 18 miles per hour, equivalent to a 49.7-second 400-meter pace) and left Henigan to settle for a hard-fought second.

Kolehmainen hit the tape in 49:15—and 14 seconds later, or about 80 yards, Henigan charged in for runner-up honors. Laakso placed third (50:42), while early pace setter Horne (4th, 51:57) and Terry Halpin of New York (5th, 52:33) followed. After missing the 1916 race, Arthur Letteer was back and finished a respectable eighth (53:30) to secure the local prize.

Whether anyone knew it or not, another era had ended. Kolehmainen—who liked to relax the night before by shooting pool in Berwick's Acadia Club and often appeared just as cool winning the race the next day—would never again break the tape on Market Street. As for Henigan, he would be back again—and often enough to become a Berwick crowd favorite.

The Berwick Marathon Takes A Break

Not surprisingly, with the Americans joining the Great War in Europe, the Berwick Marathon was canceled in both 1918 and 1919. It is quite likely the cancellation also came about because Chiv MacCrea went to Buffalo to work—possibly at the American Car & Foundry plant there that was pumping out munitions for the Allied war effort. Both A. E. Domville and Professor James Sigman had moved from the Berwick area, and with MacCrea in upstate New York, there was no one to ride herd on the various tasks needed to conduct the Marathon. However, the race was still very much etched in the minds of the townspeople. When the war ended (and MacCrea returned to Berwick) it did not take much to rekindle interest in the event.

Photo courtesy of Harry's Sports

Stride for Stride: Jimmy Henigan (left) and Hannes Kolehmainen (33) battle over Berwick's stone-strewn roads in the Flying Finn's final appearance in 1917.

Back in the Running

Ritola Rocks Record: Ville Ritola shows his *sisu* (Finnish for "guts") as he fights through the pain barrier for his 1922 Berwick course record.

With the end of the Great War—and with the Roaring Twenties just revving up—America was back in full swing. The country was riding high upon a wave of pure unadulterated joy and looking to return to normal peacetime activities.

In Berwick, there was no question that jump-starting the Marathon footrace was on the celebratory agenda. Chiv MacCrea, who had briefly gone to Buffalo to work during the late war years, was back in town and again ready to run the show. (When the local newspapers listed the roster of race officials, it always read: "C. N. MacCrea, in charge of race.")

The newspapers trumpeted the race revival. It seemed only fitting to bring it back in this time of great joy, with lightness and hope once again prevailing over the forces of darkness and despair in the world. By early October, articles concerning the restart of the famous race were already appearing:

> Two years ago the race was discontinued owing to the war, but it is believed that the time is again ripe for resumption of the event which means a lot more to Berwick than the having of a crowd for the holiday ... The plans for the 11th annual race are now well along ...

Although the people of Berwick today still support their race with great enthusiasm, it is hard for us in modern times to truly comprehend just how much the Marathon had weaved its way into the fabric of the town's heart and soul in those early years. For example, after the 1916 race, the Reverend J. Ellis Bell even summoned the metaphor of the marathon to serve as the foundation of his sermon—delivered at the First Methodist Church on Market Street, virtually at the start and finish of the race, as noted in the local papers.

> Rev. J. Ellis Bell, pastor of the First Methodist church, commended the Berwick Marathon race in an eloquent sermon last evening on the theme "The Great Marathon Race." The pastor highly commended Berwick's great race and the importance of the event in the town's welfare.
>
> His text was "So run that ye may obtain." He applied the local race to the great Christian race to which every man, woman and child, he said, should be entered. He also emphasized the moral element of the local race to the great Christian race ... All the services on Sunday were unusually large in attendance ... The collection amounted to $38.56.

The temptation is to speculate if any of those who contributed to the church plate when it was passed might not have also won a few extra dollars betting on the Marathon on Thanksgiving Day.

Regardless of the race's moral merits, it was back in business as the 1920 Thanksgiving holiday approached. And not only were runners once again prepared to take on the challenging 9-mile-plus course, but the officials had somehow managed to attract a highly competitive field for the rejuvenated race.

As the lead paragraph in one of the pre-Marathon articles enthusiastically exclaimed:

> After a lapse of two years, Berwick will on Thursday hold the eleventh annual Berwick Marathon race, an event that will be marked with the classiest field of runners ever participating in that widely known event. For the first time in history, the

winner of the Boston Marathon, the intercollegiate champion,
and the junior national cross-country champion will meet.

The Boston Marathon champ was Peter Trivoulidas, a Greek living in
New York City and running for the Millrose Athletic Club. The junior
national cross-country champion was Ville Ritola ("William" or "Willie"
in most of the American papers), a Finnish carpenter living in New York
City. Even though he had only begun to race seriously in 1919, Ritola had
already shown promise. Nicknamed "the Wolf from Peraseinajoki" (*Pera-
seinajoen Susi* in Finnish . . . Peraseinajoki being Ritola's native village back
in Finland), Ritola was rapidly improving.

The intercollegiate champ—recent winner of the IC4A cross-country
title—was John Luther Romig. Captain of the Penn State team, Romig was
nicknamed "Blondy" and, although he was a dark horse, he was attracting
much local attention. Romig was, as the local papers gushed, a "Wapwallopen boy" and you simply *had* to be local—*really* local—to know of it.
Wapwallopen was—and still is—a blink-and-you-miss-it rural burg on
the other side of the Susquehanna, a few miles upriver from Nescopeck.

Ritola arrived just in time to continue the Finnish tradition at Berwick.
Three-time race winner Hannes Kolehmainen—having won a gold medal
in the Olympic Marathon that summer—was back in Finland and unable
to defend his Berwick title. However, Kolehmainen's Finnish American
wife—presumably still in the States—sent along a letter to Chiv MacCrea,
and this correspondence was printed in the local papers. Mrs.
Kolehmainen graciously wrote:

> I am sure Hannes would be very glad to compete in your
> Marathon this year, but he intends to remain abroad, for a while
> at least. It will be impossible for him to be present. I thank you
> and all your friends for the kind support you have given him,
> and hope your Marathon on Thanksgiving Day will prove a
> huge success.

Also back in Berwick after an absence of four years was George Holden,
a Marathon champion in 1914 and the runner-up in 1916. Judging from
his experiences in World War I, Holden may have been simply glad to paw
the starting line. As the local paper noted, "Nothing had been heard of
Holden since the close of the war, during which he served in the Navy. He
enlisted in 1917 and was one of the crew of the President Lincoln when
that transport was torpedoed off the coast of France." Even running the
Berwick Marathon in terrible weather conditions had to be better than

floating around in the frigid Atlantic Ocean waiting to be rescued.

In addition to the favorites—present and past—in the days leading up to the race, the *Berwick Enterprise* headline read: "Colored Runners In The Marathon."

> For the first time in the history of the Berwick Marathon col-
> ored runners will be among the competitors. Indian and prac-
> tically every nationality have been represented but it has been
> reserved for the 11th annual event to feature colored runners
> of national standing.

Although you could have argued that the Berwick Marathon had al-ready had an African American runner with John Stookey (or Stuckey) taking part in the 1909 Indian war-whoop incident, these runners were from the St. Christopher's club in New York City and were trained and ex-perienced runners. Four of the St. Christopher's runners were slated to run, but on race day only the two best men—Clifford Mitchell and Aaron Morris—actually trotted out to the starting line. As it turned out, they could hardly have picked a worse day in terms of weather and road con-ditions to run Berwick.

I

A Dark Horse Named Blondy
11th Berwick Marathon, November 25, 1920

Terrible just might have been an understatement when describing the weather conditions for the eleventh edition of the Berwick Marathon. The weather ranks up there with the all-time worst years—1909, 1938, and 1940 also come readily to mind—for Berwick races. According to the post-race assessments:

> There was mud ankle deep for several miles of the course,
> and during the greater part of the race, there was such heavy
> snow falling that it was impossible to see more than a hundred
> yards.

Whatever visibility problems there were, it didn't prevent the race spot-ters along the course from reporting that Romig—the local lad—held a very slim lead over Ritola at the Summer Hill churches. Already far back in third was Jimmy Henigan, and—judging from his occasional glances back—the Boston-area runner's hopes of moving up were far overshad-owed by his concerns of holding on to third. Behind the top three came two New York club runners—Arthur Hulsebosch of the Paulist AC and

James McGuinnes of the Mohawk AC—and they were jostling for position with Arthur Studenroth, Romig's Penn State teammate.

As the spotters reported back to the YMCA by telephone, race workers took the latest updates out to George Hoppes, the race announcer. As Ruth Follmer noted, reflecting on some of those early races years later in the *Berwick Enterprise,* the chain of reports from the course went something like this:

> Telephones at North Berwick, Foundryville, Evansville and Martzville relayed the latest "flash" bulletins to the Y.M.C.A, and thence to the spectators who lined Market Street. Not even a curb for them to stand on then. Slippery, slushy ground was the vantage point for the owners of the high-buttoned or laced shoes which were worn by the adventuresome feminine spectators of those early marathon races.
>
> The telephoned messages were given to the crowd from the Y.M.C.A. through a megaphone manned by the leather-lunged announcer, George Hoppes.

The partisan crowd in this particular 1920 mud-and-snow-fest became more and more excited from George Hoppes' announcements, as each one seemed to confirm that the "Wapwallopen boy" might come through with a victory. As the next day *Morning Post* write-up put it:

> The crowds went wild when it was reported from Foundryville that Romig was slightly in the lead at the Summer Hill churches the State College captain was nearly a hundred feet ahead and the joy of the crowd increased. Their voices could be heard for blocks. When the Wapwallopen boy was reported from the turn at the mountain as ahead, they went still wilder, and when he turned in Market street in the finish, their joy knew no bounds. Hats were thrown in the air and voices became hoarse with cheering. The band struck up a lively air, and Berwick saw a local man break the tape a winner for the first time since the first race was one that only had local participants.

Romig reportedly had gained a 60-yard lead over Ritola, charging toward North Berwick. Henigan was a distant third. By the time Romig turned onto Market—his long stride stretching out through the slop on the course—his lead had slightly increased. No doubt spurred on by the grand reception from the crowd and perhaps the realization that he was a mere

5 minutes or so away from cementing local-hero status, Romig finished nearly 100 yards ahead of the Finn.

The sloppy conditions were reflected in the times. Romig won in 50:51, with Ritola second in 51:02. Henigan settled for third in 52 minutes flat. Hulsebosch took fourth in 53:40, while Studenroth—who would make the 1924 US Olympic team in the cross-country team event—edged McGuinness for fifth by 1 second in 54:05.

Although Blondy Romig could have laid claim to both his first-place diamond and the local award, he graciously passed up the latter. That allowed Arthur Letteer (14th in 58:11) to corral the local laurels for slogging through the horrendous road conditions and the falling flakes of snow.

While it was the brutal weather and road conditions that understandably drew much of the attention, the competition was deep. For example, Holden—although not in top shape after his war years—finished 12th overall out of 15 finishers (four men dropped out). The St. Christopher runners, Mitchell and Moore placed 11th and 15th respectively. And relegated to also-ran status were *three* Boston Marathon champions—Henigan in a respectable third (who would finally win Boston in 1931),

The Upset Special: John Luther "Blondy" Romig, local lad from nearby Wapwallopen.

Trivoulidas (9th, Boston champ in 1920) and Frank Zuna (7th, who would win Boston in 1921).

Finish Lines: Blondy Romig placed 4th in the 5000 meters at the sweltering 1924 Paris Olympic Games, an event in which Finns Paavo Nurmi and Ville Ritola went 1-2. Fifth-place Berwick finisher Arthur Studenroth started the infamous 1928 Race Across America, but—along with most other entrants—did not finish the event.

II
Ritola "the Pup"
12th Berwick Marathon, November 24, 1921

As most runners will attest, dogs are not *necessarily* man's best friend—especially if that particular man happens to be huffing and puffing past what a particular dog deems to be his own territory. But everybody loves the right kind of dog story, and the 1921 Berwick Marathon (or was it 1922? See the disclaimer below) had a beauty when the 12th annual race was over.

The race itself—at least once the gun went off and Ville Ritola stormed into the lead—turned out to be a yawner. Only nine men finished. The course was muddy again, and only Ritola ran fairly fast—posting a commendable (but not record-setting) mark of 49:24 for the win. The Finnish star was nearly three-quarters of a mile ahead of Jimmy Henigan in second place (53:04). Frank Titterton of New York City took third (54:34), a big move up in the results from his eighth place the previous year. John Weber of Pittsburgh held off little Johnny Gray—an up-and-coming runner from Philadelphia—for fifth (55:24). In addition, Wapwallopen wonder John Romig—so unstoppable the year before in the storm—didn't have the right stuff on this particular day and had to settle for seventh (55:50) out of nine finishers.

The highlight of the day involved an unregistered runner who joined the race just after the official start. Not long after Ritola sped off down Market Street, he was joined by an unnumbered companion—a mongrel dog darted onto the course and began to run withthe Finn. Far ahead by the time he hit the two-mile mark, perhaps Ritola was glad for the company. As for the dog, perhaps he sensed something of a cousin in the runner who was nicknamed for *Canus lupus*—the wolf.

The persistent pup ran the rest of the way with Ritola—slightly ahead most of the time, in fact, and allegedly avoiding the muddiest spots with such accuracy that the Finnish star simply followed the dog's lead. If reports of the time are accurate, they crossed the finish line virtually together. The nondescript pooch was scooped up by Berwick High School runners, who promptly deemed him the new school sports mascot and gave the canine a new name—"Ritola"—in honor of the Berwick Marathon champion.

And here's the disclaimer—and the explanation for the disclaimer: Years after the alleged "Ritola the Pup" incident, the local papers often attributed the incident to the 1922 race when they did a nostalgic flashback piece on the most famous races. But they also made mention of the muddy course, and the course was *not* muddy in 1922 (in fact, it looks quite dry and dusty from the photos) and the quick route (along with a fast rival for the opening 2 miles), helped Ritola set a course record. The 1921 race was the muddy one and—and least in this writer's opinion—in all likelihood the run that included one special mutt prancing ahead through the mud.

Diamond Duel: Johnson (1, far left) and Ritola (10) ready to rock in their 1922 grudge match in Berwick.

III
The Grudge Match: Ritola vs. Johnson
13th Berwick Marathon, November 30, 1922

If the 1921 event lacked any truly competitive aspects, the 1922 Berwick Marathon had more than enough to make up for it. What today we might call "pre-race hype" began weeks before when Ville Ritola defeated R. Earl Johnson—an African American runner who represented the Edgar Thomson Steel Works located in Braddock, Pennsylvania. The race was the US 10-Mile Championship on the track in New York in late October. Johnson—the defending champion and also the reigning US cross-country champion—not only lost to Ritola, but was lapped in the process. One report said Johnson had experienced stomach trouble during the event. A top-notch runner in his own right, Johnson may have felt some humiliation at the thumping he received from the aggressive-running Finn.

At any rate, Johnson and Ritola exchanged harsh words after the race—a situation the *Berwick Enterprise* had no reservations bringing to light in the pre-race buildup prior to the 13th Berwick Marathon.

> It ordinarily would be a great privilege to see Johnson in a race, but back of his decision to come to Berwick is another story that makes his local appearance all the more interesting. Some weeks ago Johnson lost the National Ten Mile championship after holding it for three years, to his greatest rival, Ritola, at New York. After the race the men met in the dressing rooms. A heated argument occurred during which Johnson singling out Ritola said: "I am not going to Detroit this year, but I will be at Berwick and I will give you a beating over that course." Ritola answered that he would be there to see him do it.

Regardless of how Johnson's interest in coming to Berwick was ignited, Marathon officials were thrilled. Chiv MacCrea had been hoping to get Johnson to Berwick in previous years. MacCrea enlisted a Berwickian by the name of William F. Lowry Jr., who was apparently working in the Pittsburgh area to acquire steel for operations at Berwick's American Car & Foundry Company, to seal the deal. Lowry made sure that Johnson knew the race would pick up all expenses, and that sweet offer—along with Johnson's vow to seek revenge against his Finnish rival—must have turned the trick. Several days before Thanksgiving, Johnson's entry arrived in the mail, along with a short letter, the latter virtually beaming with civic pride from Berwick native son Lowry:

> Pittsburgh, Pa.   Nov. 19, 1922
> Mr. C. N. MacCrea, Sec.
> Berwick Marathon Assn.,
> Berwick, Pa.
>
> Your various communications have been duly received and to show you that I have not laid down on the job given me I am enclosing Earl Johnson's entry for 13th annual race. It gives me great pleasure to be of this service in obtaining Johnson.
>
> In talking with him yesterday I learned that he will run in "The National Cross Country Championship" at New York on the 25th. He will arrive in Berwick Tuesday following, his time of arriving I asked him to advise you later direct or through me.
>
> Regarding expenses I advanced him nothing. If I should please let me know and I will take care of it before he leaves. He was pleased to learn that full expenses would be taken care of.
>
> Now, I talked Berwick hospitality sky-ward and I trust that every courtesy will be accorded him and I am only sorry that I personally will not be in Berwick this year as I was last or I would look after him while there, but I am too busy trying to keep Berwick going with material. You will find him a likeable fellow in every respect. I also want you to realize that it has been through many of my personal friends that I was able to get him as they spoke to him knowing me as they do. . . . Mr. Hart-suff, superintendent of the Edgar Thompson [sic] Works, having been interviewed personally.
>
> Trusting that this race will be the greatest race yet and that my man Johnson will win.
>
> Yours truly,
> W. F. LOWRY, JR.

The much-ballyhooed Ritola-Johnson feud, and—for a much-welcomed change—both perfect weather *and* ideal road conditions, translated into great expectations for a fast race. Could Willie Kramer's 1913 record finally tumble? Many thought it would, but who would come away with the new mark if it did? Johnson or Ritola? Or might a third, less heralded harrier sneak in and steal their thunder with a blistering sprint to the finish down Market Street?

However Johnson's desire for revenge might have figured into the formula, Ritola—having already run the Berwick course twice, plus just days before relegating Johnson to a distant second in the US cross-country national race that Lowry made mention of in his letter to MacCrea—probably entered the race feeling quite confident.

Only eight men lined up on Market Street on race day, the crowd enjoying unusually mild temperatures. Once the gun went off, however, the pace was anything but mild, and it didn't take long for the competition to become a *mano-a-mano* affair between the co-favorites. Down to Foundryville they raced, Johnson—his racing vest sporting the name of Andrew Carnegie's steel mill—and Ritola, representing the Finnish American Athletic Club team. Perhaps fueled by their blatant animosity, Ritola and Johnson immediately locked on to a pace laced with intensity. Obviously, the race was to be a put-up-or-shut-up confrontation, hard from the get-go, and tactics be damned.

> The eight starters went out Market Street at a fast clip, so fast that the first mile was done in less than five minutes. Ritola and Johnson were slightly in the lead . . . Ritola and Johnson drew away from the others as they turned from Market street into Summer Hill Avenue . . .
>
> At Foundryville, Ritola had a slight lead, and when they started going up the hill, Ritola took a commanding lead . . . From then on it was simply a question of time, and a question of how the others would finish.

Johnson gained some ground back on the steep side of Hosler's Hill, but the Finn began to pull away again through the little rolling hills of Kachinka's Hollow. The ever-popular Jimmy Henigan and Ilmar Prim, another Finnish AC runner, battled for third—and sometimes pulled within 30 seconds or so of Johnson, but were unable to establish what coaches like to call "contact." Perhaps Henigan hoped that Ritola and Johnson—like the Kilkenny Cats of Irish legend—would destroy themselves in their competitive ferocity, and the ever-plucky Irishman might sneak in and snag the top diamond.

If so, then Henigan's thoughts were wishful thinking. The race simply became Ritola against the clock and—as noted in the post-race *Morning Press* write-up—"the long hair of the Finnish runner kept flying in the air considerably ahead of Johnston [sic]."

Spurred on by thick crowds, the Finn stayed in attack mode through Martzville and back to North Berwick. Perhaps he imagined Johnson just yards back, savoring revenge (what front-runner has not occasionally been both plagued and spurred by a simple case of late-race paranoia?), but that simply was not the reality.

In great physical shape and taking full advantage of the fast course, the Wolf from Peraseinajoki devoured the last mile. When he breasted the tape—engulfed by the cheers of thousands of fans—Willie Kramer's 1913 record was utterly shattered: 47 minutes, 56 minutes. And although it may have seemed as if Johnson had been thrashed, the Pittsburgh runner held it together enough that his runner-up effort of 48:36 was just 3 ticks off Kramer's old course mark. Henigan pulled away from Finnish runner Prim in proper fashion over the late miles, solidifying third place with a time of 48:55.

And so the great Berwick Marathon grudge match was over. Johnson had tried—and failed—to hang a payback beating on the ever-scrappy Ritola. No doubt his diamond award for second place brought Johnson some consolation, but the great runner from Pittsburgh never again raced at Berwick. In fact, neither did the Flying Wolf—but both men would meet again in the 1924 Paris Olympic Games, fighting it out over an arduous cross-country course along the Seine River on a sweltering day that wilted dozens of world-class runners and even sent some to the hospital.

Finish Lines: In the 1924 Olympic Games, Johnson finished third behind Paavo Nurmi and (probably much to his chagrin) Ville Ritola—but nevertheless landed a bronze medal. In addition to his running skills, Johnson managed an African American sandlot baseball team at the Edgar Thomson Works. Johnson also wrote sports articles about the city's best African American athletes for the *Pittsburgh Courier*.

Rocket Ritola: In a series of shots, Ritola and Johnson at the mile mark in North Berwick; the Finn breaks away near the Foundryville bridge; Ritola stretches out his lead in the hinterlands.

Photos courtesy of Harry's Sports

THE FLYING FINNS: Kolehmainen and Ritola

Hannes Kolehmainen

Hannes Kolehmainen already had three Olympic medals (golds in the 5000 and 10,000, and a team silver in the cross-country event) before he came to the USA. Those successes came in the 1912 Stockholm Games, but they were somewhat subdued for political reasons; technically the Finns were still a Grand Duchy controlled by czarist Russia. A persistent story (perhaps more legend than verified fact) is that Kolehmainen—having seen the Russian flag hoisted after one of his Stockholm victories—was said to have muttered: "I would almost rather not have won than see that flag up there . . ."

In New York, Kolehmainen practiced his bricklayer's trade and ran races when he wasn't working. Before he won his three Berwick Marathon crowns (1915 through 1917), Kolehmainen had won numerous races in New York City, including the US cross-country championship in 1914. In that era, the Irish American Athletic Club was certainly one of the most powerful in the city. That may explain how the Irish landed young Hannes—then in his early twenties—to run for them in the "winged fist" vest.

Behind his quiet, seemingly affable demeanor, Kolehmainen was a shrewd man who knew how to navigate the whirlpool waters of so-called amateur athletics of that era. Says Dr. Ossi Viita—an academic, author, and runner who wrote his doctoral dissertation on the hero-myth aura of Hannes Kolehmainen: "They [the Kolehmainen brothers] considered sports a job. They sold their running skills to competitive fields the same way they sold their masons' skills to construction sites."

As noted in his wife's letter to the Berwick Marathon Association in 1920, Kolehmainen had returned to Finland to prepare for the Antwerp Olympic Games. Older now—and arguably having missed his peak Olympic years because the 1916 Games were canceled due to World War I—Kolehmainen opted to move up to the marathon.

However, once again political controversy threatened to sabotage Kolehmainen's Olympic pursuits. Although the Whites had won the Finnish Civil War, there was still much post-conflict animosity and turmoil. The Finnish Workers' Sports Federation (TUL) vehemently opposed participation in the Antwerp Olympic Games.

Urged on by Wiljami, Hannes and his younger brother Tatu opted to compete. That decision did not come without a price. According to Dr. Viita, Kolehmainen and other Finns who defied the TUL ban were labeled as "scabs, renegades and traitors" by their working-class comrades both at home and abroad. For Kolehmainen, the toiling bricklayer, the remarks must have left some scars on his already much-conflicted psyche.

Considering the controversy Kolehmainen had to endure merely to compete, perhaps the marathon itself came as a welcome relief. For once the race was run in cool temperatures. Kolehmainen—always calculating and displaying great sense of pace—held back until halfway. Then he took control, en route to what was then a world-record time of 2:32:35—and the third Olympic gold medal of his career.

It was after the Olympic Marathon triumph that a Finnish sportswriter named Yrjo Halme conjured up the nickname "Smiling Hannes the Champion Runner"—insinuating that the grin was likely a reflection of Kolehmainen's natural modesty and affable personality. However, Dr. Viita puts forth the proposition that, in fact, Hannes's famous smile was actually well-honed gamesmanship—a ploy to emphasize to rival runners that he was never tired during—or even after—races. "Hannes did not show possible fatigue to fellow runners, but instead kept smiling and starting immediately giving comments to the press about how easy the competition had been—something the brothers had practiced with each other in their youth in Kuopio." (Today we might call this "getting in the other guy's head.")

After winning in Antwerp, Kolehmainen returned to Finland, not the States. He was widely acclaimed by the bourgeois businessmen for his Olympic triumphs; indeed, they gave the former bricklayer a farm. Perhaps the man used to the brisk pace of Brooklyn didn't adapt readily to rural life; he eventually moved to Helsinki and sold sporting goods.

Of course, nothing is truly free, and the establishment relished the chance to use "Smiling Hannes" for the greater good. During Prohibition, Kolehmainen—who shunned alcohol when in training—was something of the poster boy for abstinence.

In addition, Kolehmainen attempted to bring bourgeois and working-class factions in the Finnish sporting world closer together. Just as he displayed great patience in his training and racing, Kolehmainen kept to the task—even if he met with only marginal success. Prior to the 1952

Olympic Games, Kolehmainen toured Finland with other Finn stars of the past to drum up support for hosting the event in Helsinki.

Writes Dr. Viita: "Gradually, Kolehmainen started to be seen as a hero who crosses and unites social classes, even if his hometown activists still considered him a contested hero . . . Furthermore, the oldest activists never forgave him for switching to the bourgeois side of sport."

Regardless, Kolehmainen—even in recent decades and long after his death—rates hero status in Finland. In 1989, in recognition of the one hundredth anniversary of his birth, the Finnish government issued a Hannes Kolehmainen stamp depicting his 5000-meter win in Stockholm in which he nipped the French star Jean Bouin at the tape in a world record 14:36. And if you visit a small museum next to the Olympic Stadium in Helsinki—although it is certainly less prominent than the huge Nordic-style statue dedicated to Paavo Nurmi—you can find the ancient pair of spikes that Kolehmainen wore en route to victory in Stockholm.

Ville Ritola

By most accounts, Ville Ritola was usually an affable fellow. But he also had a stubborn I-won't-back-down streak. Growing up impoverished in Finland—the fourteenth born in a spillover family of seventeen children—he learned early in the game of life to fend for himself. According to the Finnish sportswriter Matti Hannus, young Ritola immigrated to New York City in 1919 and—in addition to his immigration papers—he was also sporting a black eye he apparently had incurred during some sort of altercation on the three-week-long voyage across the Atlantic.

Already seventeen when he left Finland, Ritola didn't take up running until several years after he arrived in New York. But the hollow-faced Finn from Peraseinajoki already knew how to endure hardships and persevere. In his book *Flying Finns,* Hannus writes:

> For the next several years, Ville "Willie" Ritola was searching for his own place in the puzzle of life. Doing odd jobs, often unemployed, he was traveling from one city to another in the dark carriages of [freight] trains—sometimes underneath them!—eating something or nothing. Not so seldom he was sleeping in cemeteries; they had the peace and security he was looking for.
>
> After only two years of elementary school, a young man did

not have many opportunities. But Ville Ritola—phenomenon out of the ordinary, both mentally and physically—kept the course of his life. He did not become a criminal; he became a brilliant carpenter, and later also a brilliant distance runner . . .

Ritola was twenty-three when he attempted his first real race in New York City in 1919, a road event across the city. He finished a modest—but nonetheless promising—thirty-third (out of 700 starters) in the event. A Finnish American Athletic Club official and a competitive racewalker named Vaino Noppa took Ritola under his wing and helped guide the future Olympian's early career. Later in the fall of 1920, the naturally talented Ritola won the junior US cross-country at Van Cortlandt Park in the Bronx and just days later entered his first Berwick Marathon race, in which he placed second to Penn State standout John "Blondy" Romig.

Hungry like a wolf, Ritola built upon these early glimpses of success. The scrawny-looking Finn lost a 5-mile US Championship race to the experienced R. Earl Johnson of Pittsburgh in 1921, but that was only by several seconds. Ritola was obviously getting better. In fact, Ritola soon became Johnson's archnemesis, purposely seeking the Pittsburgh runner out in a New York race and beating him

That rivalry perhaps reached its zenith in 1922, when Johnson was lapped by Ritola in the US 10-mile championship (contested on a track) and the next month ran away from Johnson at Berwick, despite the fact that the Pittsburgh star had predicted—to Ritola's face—that he would vanquish the Finn.

After that humbling experience in Berwick, Johnson was never really able to run at Ritola's level again—including the 1924 Paris Olympic Games when Johnson competed in the 10,000-meter race and the Olympic cross-country event. It wasn't that Johnson slowed down that much; Ritola just got stronger and faster.

In addition to his two Berwick Marathon victories and his runner-up finish to Romig in 1920, Ritola, of course, had many national and international triumphs. He also demonstrated fantastic range. He could run a world-class 5000, but he had the range to run a quality marathon (although it was not his best distance) as demonstrated by his runner-up effort behind Clarence DeMar at the 1922 Boston Marathon.

Track, road, or cross-country hill and dale, Ritola seemed equally adept over any racing surface. He won five national cross-country titles during the 1920s and—since he raced there frequently—was particularly tough on the famous Van Cortlandt Park layout in the Bronx.

The Wolf from Peraseinajoki performed quite well in both of his Olympic appearances. He won four gold medals in Paris in 1924—the 10,000 meters, the 3000-meter steeplechase, the 3000-meter team race, and the cross-country team race. In addition, he won silver medals in the 5000 (clocking 14:31.4—a mere two-tenths of a second behind Nurmi!) and the cross-country individual race.

By all accounts, the 1924 Olympic cross-country event was brutal. Only 15 men out of 38 starters completed the course, chiefly because the temperatures must have seemed like hell's own fires, hovering close to 100 degrees in the shade. Even the Finns had to wait for their third runner and scorer to virtually crawl across the line to notch their team gold. The race bordered on a death march—Sweden's talented Edvin Wide being a prime example, as he collapsed with heatstroke and ended up in the hospital.

Nurmi won—looking remarkably fresh considering he had won two track events (the 1500 and 5000-meter races) just two days before. Then Ritola finished—one spot ahead of his old rival Earl Johnson. Johnson ran a very gutsy race and landed a bronze medal in the cross-country event, but finishing behind his nemesis (Ritola had also lapped Johnson in the Olympic 10,000 meters, en route to first) might well have taken some of the joy out of placing third and leading the Americans to second behind the powerful Finns in the team standings.

In the years between the 1924 Olympics and the upcoming 1928 Olympics in Amsterdam, Ritola dominated races in New York City and also typically anywhere else he competed—the notable exception coming when Paavo Nurmi conducted his take-no-prisoners barnstorming tour of the US and won some fifty races in 1925.

However, one of Ritola's most fantastic races also came in 1925. The Wolf scorched a 14:23.2 clocking for 5000 meters in Madison Square Garden—an indoor world record that would last for four decades.

At the 1928 Olympic Games, Ritola ran his fastest 10,000 in 30:19.4, but Nurmi won by less than a second (30:18.8). The Finns left everyone else in the wake of their relentless pace, including bronze-medal winner Wide of Sweden, who was more than 40 seconds back in third.

Ritola *did* hold off Nurmi one time, winning the 1928 Olympic 5000-meter race by 2 seconds with a time of 14:38. Wide was third again, but this time quite close (14:41.2). Neither Ritola nor Nurmi was a natural steeplechase runner, and both came out of the 3000-meter steeplechase trials nursing some aches and pains. In the steeple finals, Ritola dropped out and Nurmi had to settle for second behind fellow Finn Toivo Loukola—though the latter needed to run a world record 9:21.8 for the event to secure the victory.

Ritola fell on hard times in his later years. Perhaps it was a combination of all his running and the life-draining labors on the docks of New York City, but he suffered from arthritis. When he returned to Finland in 1971, he was—financially, physically—broke. As Finnish sportswriter Matti Hannus so splendidly described him, Ritola was "a happy, good-natured, jovial and practical man, with more wealth in his soul than his bank account."

Fortunately, his onetime rival—and obviously a friend as well—the flinty, seemingly unsentimental Nurmi gave the "old Wolf" some much-needed financial assistance in those twilight years. A natural businessman, Nurmi had become quite wealthy. Nurmi—who is depicted on the Finnish 10-mark note and also honored with a compelling statue outside the Helsinki Olympic Stadium—died in 1973, but before he did, he saw to it that Ritola had enough to live on in relative comfort.

Ritola died in Helsinki in 1982, at the age of eighty-six. It was almost ten years after one of the last of the Flying Finns—the great Lasse Viren—appeared on the Olympic scene to carry on the tradition of Kolehmainen, Ritola, and Nurmi.

The Henigan Double

8

For some reason, the Irish American runners in those early Berwick Marathons always attracted great crowd support—enough so that it makes one consider how this support might have manifested itself had the race been staged on St. Patrick's Day instead of Thanksgiving.

The trend to back the Irish harriers may well have started with the likable Tom Barden, the Yonkers man with his easy-to-spot red hair. The newspapers of the day are full of references of how the Berwick crowds cheered loudly for Barden when he flew past on Market Street. Years later, the Berwick Marathon backers would lavish similar adulation upon Boston's Johnny Kelley.

But in those races just after World War I, another Beantown-area runner—Jimmy Henigan—was the Irish favorite. A newspaper of the day noted Henigan's Irish features were such that he "could not have denied his ethnic roots, even if he had wished to." Like Barden and Kelley, Henigan was a working-class guy who managed to beat himself into a quality runner of his era, almost always representing the Boston Dorchester Club. Sometimes he also was called "Hinky" Henigan. Like Kelley, who came after him, Henigan also earned his living at times in the florist trade.

Henigan lacked the natural talents of men like Hannes Kolehmainen, Ville Ritola, or Willie Kramer. He didn't have blazing, burn-down-the-house finishing speed and certainly lacked the flowing, efficient running style of a Kolehmainen. If Kolehmainen was a thoroughbred, then Henigan was more of an Irish potato field plow horse—but a good, diligent plow horse. He simply worked extremely hard and—to put it into the parlance of boxing—Jimmy Henigan "kept coming out for the rounds."

Coming out for the rounds might have been Jimmy Henigan's biggest strength. His Olympic races were fraught with disaster; he never sniffed an Olympic medal. He also experienced the sting of many setbacks and some heartbreaking "almosts" when it came to winning the big races. One of those crash-and-burn attempts came in the 1922 Boston Marathon, when—very late in the race—Jimmy went from looks-like-a-winner to a DNF as Clarence DeMar cruised by for one of his seven lifetime victories.

He had similarly flirted with—but never achieved—victory in his first half dozen attempts at the Berwick race. He had been a mere three seconds behind Hannes Kolehmainen—the best distance runner in the world—but really with almost no hope of outkicking the famous Finn. It was almost as if the barmaid of fate had poured a picturesque pint of Irish stout, placed it before Henigan, and then allowed him a tantalizing taste of the foam—only to yank the actual beer away before he could bring the full mug to his parched lips.

But Jimmy Henigan persevered, and eventually that elusive luck of the Irish weighed in on his side—both at Berwick *and* at Boston.

I
Henigan's Hurrah
14th Berwick Marathon, November 29, 1923

As runners lined up for the 1923 Berwick Marathon, the crowd broke into spirited applause as an unexpected "exhibition" entry—a slightly pudgy middle-aged man—was announced. Mixed in with the eighteen official starters was none other than Harry Williams, the point man in Berwick's pioneer race of fifteen years before. As noted in the *Bloomsburg Morning Press:*

> Harry Williams, winner of the first marathon in 1908, grown heavy with the years, was in running togs yesterday and got an ovation from the crowd when he was announced. He started with the runners with the intention of going only a short distance and dropped out after covering several blocks.

The out-of-shape Williams must have stood out in the field of serious racers—the latter trained down to bone, rope-like muscles, and hard-pumping hearts and lungs. Nevertheless, Williams's appearance spoke volumes concerning the esteem the race and its history projected in the town of Berwick. Even though it was still a relatively young event, clearly the Berwick Marathon already was built upon a firm base of tradition.

Nostalgia aside, the nineteen runners (if you counted Harry Williams) blitzed out Market Street, the weather "fine and mild" and the course conditions listed as "very good" in the official results. A trio of men established themselves at the front by mile 1—Ilmar Prim of the Finnish American Athletic Club, the ever-popular Henigan, and Philadelphia runner Johnny Gray. A few yards back in fourth was former Penn State runner Arthur

Studenroth, followed by the likes of marathon runner Frank Zuna, veteran New York runner Mike Dwyer of the Mohawk Athletic Club, and Penn State runner M. S. Wendler.

Henigan's major move came about 2 miles into the race. As a strength-oriented runner (as opposed to a blazing kicker), Henigan wisely cranked up the pace as soon as the leaders crossed the small concrete bridge down in Foundryville and began the quad-deadening climb up to the Summer Hill churches. He opened up a big lead there, swept down the slight descent right after the churches, and rolled his momentum up the second, smaller hill—often referred to in those early race write-ups as Hosler's Hill. When Henigan reached the top of Hosler's Hill, the fifth place runner had finally reached the top of Summer Hill—about half a mile behind.

Prim, the Finn, however, was not that far back. As Henigan charged down the steep descent and swung the hard left at Miller's Hotel and began to work through Kachinka's Hollow, the Finnish runner held second place and was perhaps 20 to 25 seconds behind, with Gray giving chase.

The checkers diligently relayed the numbers of the runners across a field to a farmhouse, whereupon they were phoned back to the finish line at Berwick. The announcers then informed the fans, allowing them to keep close tabs on the leaders as the race progressed beyond the halfway mark.

Prim gained little or nothing on Henigan as the runners churned through Martzville and headed toward Berwick. Gray, however, was gradually cutting into Prim's hold on second place. Gray was about 150 yards behind Prim after the turn at Miller's Hotel, but continued to chip away in the second part of the race "until at the finish he was less than 25 yards behind and finished much stronger than the Finn."

Henigan was never in serious trouble once he took the lead, a fact he ascertained with his frequent habit—one most coaches would have vehemently advised against—of looking back during his races to keep tabs on the competition.

But on this day, Smiling Jimmy's racing idiosyncrasies did nothing to harm his results. His surge on the Summer Hill ascent had provided him with far too much racing capital for his rivals to regain, and he simply rode a wave of adulation from marathon fans over the final mile.

> Jimmy had a good lead when he hit Market Street and he grinned almost ear to ear as he came between the solid ranks of humanity vociferously giving vent to their joy at his victory. He waved his hands in an answer to almost every shout, it seemed,

and that enabled Ilmar Prim, a Finn of New York, to close up some of the gap and finish second, about 100 yards back of the winner.

As if to put an exclamation point on his triumph, Henigan crossed the finish line and found enough breath to blurt out: "At last!"

Henigan's stubborn stick-to-itiveness had carried the day. His time of 48 minutes, 39 seconds was good—although no threat to Ville Ritola's record of the previous year. But Jimmy Henigan—in his seventh attempt—finally had his Berwick victory, much to the delight of the thousands of race spectators.

Behind Prim and Gray, Studenroth placed a distant fourth. He was followed by Zuna, Dwyer, and Wendler, to round out the top seven. Arthur Letteer—formerly of Berwick—spearheaded an Allentown, Pennsylvania, contingent of four runners, finishing 12th overall.

Was Henigan's big victory enough for him to call it a career? Some wondered.

Photo courtesy of Harry's Sports

Henigan's Legacy: Like Tom Barden and Johnny Kelley, Jimmy Henigan (8) was a popular Irish American racer at Berwick. He won titles in 1923-24 and often placed among the prizewinners. Here he races John Gray (12) at the 1926 Berwick.

He promised some years ago he would retire after he won the Berwick race and never before, but it remains to be seen if he is ready to quit. In those six years he has won a host of friends in Berwick, and his numerous races and good finishes won him the plaudits of the crowd and explained his almost-sighed "at last" when he finished.

II
Henigan Again Again
15th Berwick Marathon, November 27, 1924

Like many runners subjected to the extreme heat of Paris in the 1924 Olympic Games, Jimmy Henigan had most certainly *not* had a wonderful experience. In fact, he was one of the majority of runners forced to drop out of the cross-country event. Johnny Gray also dropped out—but his DNF came on the track in the 10,000 meters. At any rate, just a few months after their respective Olympic collapses, both Henigan and Gray were back at Berwick looking for redemption of sorts.

For Gray, that meant improving on his third-place finish the previous fall. For Henigan—despite his alleged considerations of hanging up his racing shoes—perhaps a Berwick title defense offered him some redemption for his Olympic flop. In addition, he would be racing on very friendly turf. A title defense would also serve to vault him into the company of other multiple Berwick winners, such as Tewanima, Kolehmainen, and Ritola.

For the second straight year—and perhaps to everyone's astonishment—the Berwick Marathon was run amid splendid weather and good road conditions. The crowd—much more predictable than the weather—was once again stupendous, the population of the town (if we include those around the course) swelling to an estimated three times its ten thousand denizens, according to the papers.

A crowd of thousands witnessed the event, many former Berwickians coming back for the day as usual, while hundreds from this part of the state went to the scene by automobile. Some autoists said they had driven more than 100 miles to see the start and finish . . .

At points of vantage along the course there were scores of machines parked, as always, while at other places residents of the vicinity watched from their porches and hunters looked on from the fields as the runners passed.

Like a superb baseball hurler with a favorite pitch, Henigan decided to go with a proven strategy—that being to blast the rigorously rising road up to the Summer Hill churches, gain a lead, and then hopefully add to it up Hosler's Hill and down the other side. Once again he had company—in fact, more men than the previous year—over the opening 2 miles, his main rivals being Gray, John Bell of Syracuse University, Ville Kyronen (yet another tough-running Finn), marathon man Albert Michelsen from Stamford, Connecticut, and a pair of New Yorkers—Frank Titterton and Allie Mack. In addition, the Boston Marathon star Clarence DeMar was back at Berwick, but—once again—would find the distance too short for his liking. (In fact, DeMar would be nipped by 1 second for eighth place by Jimmy O'Connor of New York.)

Gray pushed the pace and held a short lead through most of the opening 2 miles, only to be passed briefly by Bell as the leaders neared Foundryville. But just as in the 1923 race, Henigan ratcheted up the pressure once the course began to climb. His strategy paid off with similar dividends.

> From the start at the Y.M.C.A. to Foundryville it was anybody's race, but when the long, steep hill commenced, Henigan began pulling away, looking back frequently with a grin on his face. He increased his lead steadily up the hill and down the other side, leading there by nearly a quarter of a mile. Kyronen gained on him, however, toward the finish, but Henigan had plenty to spare.

Kyronen, in fact, had to charge from fourth place at halfway before he could even lay claim to the role of chief contender. He flew past both Bell and Michelsen on the rolling terrain through Kachinka's Hollow and then tried to set his aim on Henigan, scooting along ahead of him. Johnny Gray—a strong third the year before—was already out of the race, having suffered a strained tendon that forced him from the competition near the turn at Miller's Hotel.

There was little mystery left about who would win once Henigan arrived on Market Street, still looking strong.

> Henigan was about 200 yards ahead as he turned into Market Street, and there was little doubt of the outcome. He kept on with his easy stride, looking back frequently and smiling as

always. It was a great day for Jimmy, the idol of the crowd for a number of years, and cheers greeted him as he came to the tape, a winner, taking his rank with Tewanima, Kolehmainen, and Ritola.

Actually, the most compelling races were for also-ran spots. After Kyronen (2nd), Bell (3rd), and Michelsen (4th), Titterton launched a furious kick in the last 50 yards to steal the fifth place award from Mack. Also, in a demonstration of energetic youth versus wily veteran, Jimmy O'Connor nosed out the 37-year-old DeMar by a mere tick of the clock for eighth place in the field of 22 starters.

Finish Lines: Jimmy Henigan finally won the Boston Marathon in 1931. At age 40, he was the oldest competitor in the 1932 Olympic Marathon in Los Angeles.

Albert "Whitey" Michelsen was the first man to break 2:30 for a full marathon, clocking 2:29:01 at Port Chester, New York, in 1925 (six weeks before Berwick!)—a world record that stood for nearly a decade. At age 38, Michelsen placed seventh in the 1932 Olympic Marathon in Los Angeles. In the dubious training methods of the era, it was his fourth full marathon in five months.

III
Fast Fred vs. Smiling Jimmy
16th Berwick Marathon, November 26, 1925

Not only did Henigan not retire, but he was back again at Berwick in 1925, looking to score a rare triple.

He could not have been suffering from overconfidence, though, as he toed the line for the sixteenth running, because there was a new top gun on Market Street—a German-born runner living in New York City and racing for the famed Millrose Athletic Association. His name was Fred Wachsmuth, and in the years of 1924 and 1925 he beat virtually everyone he raced against with the exception of Ville Ritola—who was, after all, an Olympic champion and (along with Paavo Nurmi, his fellow Finn) ranked as co-favorite in terms of who the world's best long distance runner might be.

Wachsmuth served notice when he thrashed the field en route to winning the 1924 US national cross-country championship staged in New

York (he had won the junior cross-country event in '23), although it was an event that the defending champ Ritola—for whatever reasons—did not run that year. Among those Wachsmuth beat handily was Jimmy Henigan, so the Boston veteran was under no illusions concerning the young German's abilities. Wachsmuth also won various races around the New York metropolitan area in the same time period, and Henigan had seen the German's disappearing backside on several of those occasions.

So what could Henigan's strategy have been going into the Berwick race against the young stud who had often proved to be faster? He hoped to use his experience on the course—specifically his ability to hit the tongue-dragging climb up to Summer Hill for all it was worth—to perhaps relegate the Millrose man to runner-up status. The pre-race article in the *Bloomsburg Morning Press,* in fact, explored that very scenario, with the voice of a kibitzer weighing a gambler's picks:

> . . . the element of uncertainty enters. Jimmy Henigan has never defeated Fred Wachsmuth, although he has tried many times. But this is Wachsmuth's first time on the tricky and treacherous Berwick course. Race fans last night were wondering whether Henigan's knowledge of the course through his appearances since 1912—he finished eighth in that year—will be enough to end the jinx that has hovered over his meetings with Wachsmuth.

Whatever the order of finish, the one sure bet was the runners were going to get dirty. Gone were the perfect road conditions of the previous two years. The sixteen starters were greeted by a clear day with bright sun—which no doubt added to the glare off the snow dusting the roads and radiating cold from along the sides of the course.

Perhaps somewhat wary of the course, Wachsmuth was content to let others set the early pace. Whether it was nerves or confidence, William Meyers of Philadelphia's Shanahan Club bolted into an early lead and was "ten feet ahead of the field in the first block." But by the time the front-runners charged down to Foundryville, Ilmar Prim—the experienced Finn—had the lead, with Wachsmuth moving up from fourth in the early going to second at 2 miles. Still, all of the contenders were close—according to the newspaper reports, in fact, "the first seven men were bunched within thirty feet." And Jimmy Henigan was in that seven—his face no doubt etched with his trademark grin, or grimace.

But if the defending champ had any thoughts of surging to the front and hammering the hills again, those faded quickly: Wachsmuth pulled the trigger first, and began to churn his way up the slushy, windy, winter-like road. As the paper noted:

> Wachsmuth took the lead for the first time and began to show the wonderful power he possessed. His steady stride never faltered although he slipped frequently in the ice and snow, as did the others. He swept up the hill ahead of the field, increasing his lead almost inch by inch. Back of him, however, the positions changed rapidly and repeatedly . . . The runners were going at the rate of ten miles an hour on the steep grade, automobile speedometers showed.

Photo courtesy of Harry's Sports

Snow Go: Fred Wachsmuth (1) plows ahead with John Bell (12), Johnny Gray (7), Henigan (left), and Albert "Whitey" Michelsen (barely visible, right), but he's ready to hammer "the Hill" en route to the 1925 win.

The well-muscled German runner had carved out a 20-yard lead by the time he passed the Summer Hill churches. Henigan had gamely moved into a solid second at the top, but Wachsmuth's long strides increased his lead to 100 yards by the bottom of Hosler's Hill and the turn at Miller's Hotel. As the runners negotiated the dubious traction on the tight turn and through Kachinka's Hollow, it seemed unlikely that Henigan would catch the young Millrose man, but the Irishman also held an equally large lead over Prim in third. Meanwhile, having run both smart and tough on the killer hills, the grand old man of marathoning—none other than Clarence DeMar—was running strong in fourth, not far behind the Finn. As the *Berwick Enterprise* report put it: "The elderly man was running easily while the Finn seemed to be laboring along . . ."

Not only did Wachsmuth increase his lead throughout the final miles, but he never really pushed himself to the limit.

> **His long strides never faltered as he went quickly down the long lane to the finish, and he went to his dressing room without assistance. He was in remarkably good shape, and bore out the belief of many in the crowd and many sports writers as well that went down the Berwick course. The time he made was remarkable considering the condition of the course.**

Wachsmuth clocked 49 minutes, 54 seconds through the slop. He was nearly a full minute ahead of two-time defending champ Henigan, who trudged in second in 50:52. Running an amazingly great race in third was the 38-year-old DeMar (51:09), who had muscled past Prim with a mile to go and then beat the fourth-place Finn by 11 seconds.

In an unusual happening for the early Berwick races, the winner and runner-up were quoted directly in the *Berwick Enterprise*.

"Disappointed?" said Jimmy Henigan. "Yes, I'm disappointed. I wanted to win the worse kind of way, but I couldn't do it. He was too much for me. I couldn't keep his pace in the last three miles."

"I'm glad," said Wachsmuth. "I have heard a lot about this race, and I wanted to win it. That's why I came here today, I'm glad I won. It's one of the hardest courses I ever ran."

As for the Berwick fans, they knew a champion when they saw one, and they obviously were looking forward to what Wachsmuth might accomplish next in the sport. They loved Henigan—and cheered the plucky Irishman on vigorously as usual—but (perhaps because Wachsmuth was far ahead and running strong) also clapped for "the sturdy, fair German, who finished almost as fresh as he started."

There were many who saw Wachsmuth run who believe he will, in a few years, be the premier distance runner of the generation. None has fine form nor more stability, and none is coming along at a more rapid gait. Running fifteen races during the summer in all parts of continental Europe, he finished first in 12 of them and second in the other three.

Unfortunately, Wachsmuth would never get to add a long-lasting shine to his potentially brilliant running career. In early August 1926, the young German runner crushed his leg when he was thrown from his motorcycle in a near-fatal crash with a car near Saratoga, New York. Wachsmuth became the first of more than a few Berwick standouts to be involved in a serious wreck. Sadly, Fred Wachsmuth never raced again.

9

The Maple Leaf Leader

The Canadians had made their presence felt in those early years of the Berwick Marathon, but they were—understandably—slow to get back in the race after the devastating losses of World War I. Some of those Canadian men who raced at Berwick—Arthur Jamieson and Jimmy Duffy—had given their lives in the Great War, and the running community (the hub of which was Hamilton, Ontario) was understandably somber.

But in 1926, the Canadians came south with a small but solid squad led by a talented runner named Cliff Bricker. Bricker—who hailed from Galt, Ontario—was just 22 when he arrived in Berwick, and he'd only been racing seriously for three years. Despite being relatively new to the running game, Bricker had shown considerable promise early on: In only his second race—a 10-miler in 1924—he finished first.

Bricker had a long flowing stride with a pronounced kickback that one report claimed seemed to nearly bring his heel up to his shoulder with each fleet flick. In latter years, some of his Canadian teammates would remember him as "a loose-limbed antelope." Apparently Bricker's running form served him well on the flats and climbing the hills, but proved particularly effective—and devastatingly so to his rivals—on the downgrades.

I
Bricker Solid
17th Berwick Marathon, November 25, 1926

With 1925 winner Fred Wachsmuth out due to his career-ending motorcycle crash, the pre-race hype had the seventeenth annual Berwick Marathon up for grabs. With his vast experience on the course, two-time winner Jimmy Henigan certainly had his backers. But the Canadians must have liked young Cliff Bricker's chances to contend for a title or at least finish in the top five.

That Bricker was bound to be in the thick of it—and not just the mud on the course, but the thick of the race—was readily apparent. The 22-year-old Canadian took the lead just half a mile into the race, though it looked like rush hour by the time the runners reached Foundryville. The race sported its biggest field ever—twenty-four starters—and thirteen of those men were still very much in the running at the 2-mile mark. Among those was one of the favorites, Gonzelo Moreno from the US Panama Canal Zone—considered one of the pre-race contenders—but it was doubtful he had ever taken on anything like the climb looming before him. The temperatures were quite different from those of his home territory, too.

The air was chilly, and the puddles of water that pooled up in the fields alongside the course were mirrored with thin ice. But the runners continued to heat up to the task of racing, and the Canadian kid proved to be the prime engine.

Bricker gradually carved out a lead up the mountain, stringing out the baker's dozen that had been clustered together at the bottom, and at the Summer Hill churches held a lead of "a scant 20 yards." But he soon launched a spirited downhill attack from the top of Hosler's Hill that essentially blew open the race.

> Bricker, slender, colorful, running in tennis shoes, and with tremendous reserve strength, ran smoothly from the start. His long stride carried him swiftly over the ground and he made his greatest gains on the downgrade from the Summer Hill churches and into Miller's at the turn of the course.

In the second half of the race, Bricker's biggest challenge, in fact, was the footing and some cumbersome autos parked along the route. Kachinka's Hollow was—per usual—muddy; nothing unexpected there. But between Martzville and Berwick, as Bricker tried to solidify his lead en route to the finish, he encountered long stretches of loose stone—part of a project preparing the local roads for improvement—"which gave precarious footing."

Bricker quickly opted for a path alongside the rough road (as would most of the men behind him), but it meant weaving around some autos parked on it. The more attentive motorists quickly moved their machines onto the road, but some drivers were slow to figure out the race leader's intentions.

> It was on them that Bricker wasted his breath, precious as the finish neared. The runner shouted at them to give up the path and when the state troopers, preceding the runners by motorcycle, saw that Bricker was forsaking the road, they quickly got the machines out of the way.

Muddy track and cars in the way . . . Bricker was ready for anything on this day. The worst of it behind him, he stretched out his stride toward

Canadian Olympian Cliff Bricker (left, Galt) and the fur trapper Charlie Snell (Gladstone AC) placed first and third in 1926.

Photos courtesy of Harry's Sports

Berwick and the finish, occasionally glancing back to reaffirm what his adrenaline rush must have been relaying to his brain: In his rookie attempt, he was winning the Berwick Marathon. On Market Street, the crowd swept him along with their encouragement, and he raced in to breast the tape in a time of 49 minutes, 5 seconds—Canada's first Berwick champion after numerous attempts. It was more than a minute before Moreno, who survived the hills sufficiently to secure runner-up honors, crossed in 50:20. Third place went to Charlie Snell, another Canadian (50:49), just 3 ticks ahead of Henigan.

Next to finish were Frank Wendling of Buffalo (5th), marathoner Albert "Whitey" Michelsen (6th), William Meyer of Philadelphia (7th), Carl Koski of New York's Finnish American AC (8th), John Bell, representing St. Bonaventure College (9th), and a man once dubbed "Mr. De-Marathon"—the wily old veteran Clarence DeMar (10th).

Road Warriors: Carl Koski (13), New York Finn, is stalked by Albert "Whitey" Michelsen past the Summer Hill churches. Michelsen set a world record (2:29:01) for the full marathon in 1925—a mark that stood for nearly ten years.

II
Bricker Goes Quicker
18th Berwick Marathon, November 24, 1927

Returning to Berwick to defend his title, Cliff Bricker had added another year of experience and—by evidence of his fourth-place finish at Boston in his full marathon debut—had added even more endurance to his already proven speed. Bricker also had won the Canadian Olympic Marathon trials in July (gaining him a place of the Maple Leaf team for Amsterdam in 1928), beating—among others—1926 Boston Marathon winner Johnny Miles of Nova Scotia.

Miles was reported in much-ballyhooed pre-race write-ups to be coming for the 1927 Berwick Marathon, but—for whatever reasons—his appearance never actually materialized. As a native of the storm-battered, well-weathered Down East province of Nova Scotia, Mile might have enjoyed the Berwick weather—hard rain that eventually relented, but only somewhat, to a cold, dreary drizzle. Nevertheless, a record 38 runners toed the starting line at Market Street, another record for participants and—despite the conditions—an estimated 25,000 spectators braved the elements.

Photo courtesy of Berwick Marathon Association

Ready to Rock: Billy Cox (4), Penn State's IC4A harrier champ, bolted to an early lead. But Bricker (10, mid-line) proved quicker in the end. The big scoreboard first appeared in the late 1920s. Nobody knows what happened to it—yet another Berwick mystery.

Perhaps because he was coming off the collegiate cross-country season and used to running in foul weather, Penn State's Billy Cox hammered right to the front. It was an off-the-line impulse that would prove more courageous than smart, as the Nittany Lion leader ("his shock of hair and his huge figure distinguishable even though his number was not . . .") essentially served as a target for the Canadian ace. As the *Berwick Enterprise* report analyzed:

> It was Cox who set the pace and led the field out to Foundryville, but it was Bricker who killed off all opposition when it came to climbing the hill to the Summer Hill churches . . . Bricker has improved immensely in the year. He permitted someone else to set the pace that killed yesterday, and Bill Cox couldn't keep it up.

Bricker took control of the race up to Summer Hill, and Johnny Bell passed the IC4A harrier champ Cox and tried to follow the defending champ. But there was no staying with Bricker on the sharp downhill after Hosler's Hill and into the sharp turn at Miller's Hotel—the latter made all the more precarious by the slick, rainy conditions.

> . . . on the downgrades there was something of the Indian in

that mechanic from Gault, Ont. He flashed out with strides several feet long, arms waving and feet flying. He seemed at times almost ready to fall, so great was his momentum, but he kept his feet and kept gaining.

Then came the messy part—Kachinka's Hollow—where "the mud was several inches deep and the runners slid around considerably." But Bricker, though definitely slowed down by this stretch, suffered no serious slips, and those trailing him were unable to make up any distance through this virtual quagmire, either. He also resisted the urge to check on his pursuers—a dubious racing practice that he had succumbed to in his 1926 Berwick—and stayed firmly focused on the road unfolding before him.

In fact, if Bricker *had* looked back, he would have deduced that he had an approximate quarter-mile cushion as he made the turn into Martzville. With the muddy parts of the course behind him, the lanky Canadian began to reap the rewards of the newly improved road—the very same stretch that had caused him and others problems the year before when it was under construction. His long, powerful, flowing strides ate up the road en route to North Berwick. In addition to the still-falling rain, Bricker was soon washed over by waves of adulation reserved for the soon-to-be race winner.

> As Bricker came in Market Street with the same easy stride he had used when he went out, the crowd cheered wildly, and the last mile was through a narrow lane walled with cheering thousands. . . . He was a happy lad and he had reason to be.

Bricker broke the tape in 48:22—less than 26 seconds off Ritola's still-standing (but wobbling) record, despite the hellish slog ("The runners sloshed about in mud and water that in a few puddles reached ankle depth") through Kachinka's Hollow. "Had it not been for the mud," stated the *Berwick Enterprise* article, "Bricker in all probability would have set a new record for the course."

Behind the now two-time race winner, Bell ran his all-time-best Berwick race. He continued to pull away from the fast-starting Cox in the second half of the race and posted a very commendable 48:47 clocking—up seven spots from his 1926 placing. Cox, to his credit, hung on for third (50:20), but he had to keep digging all the way down Market Street as the next three men—Finnish runner Ove Andersen (4th, 50:24), Boston warhorse Jimmy Henigan (5th, 50:30), and the Hamilton Olympic Club's Harold

Webster (6th, 50:34)—all fought their way home within seconds of one another.

Then 50 seconds back in seventh came Lou Gregory, a St. Bonaventure College athlete, running his first of what would be many Berwick Marathons—including three times in the winners' circle. In this rainy debut, Gregory posted a modest 51:20. (On the trip back to college, Gregory was in a serious car crash that tossed him from the vehicle and over a hedge. For a few weeks there was some question whether he could recover to continue his running career, but those fears were soon put to rest.)

A further testimonial to the depth of field was Charles Snell, the fur trapper from Toronto, who fell from third the year before to ninth place—despite running nearly the same time that he did in the 1926 event.

The locals had some interesting marks in the race, starting with Bloomsburg Teachers College runner Allen Parr of nearby Mifflinville. Parr, beginning a long solid race record at Berwick, placed 14th in 54:54. Austin Dyer, just 14 years old, finished the challenging route in 1 hour and 9 minutes for 26th place—one spot ahead of the last runner. But in the mucky conditions, ten runners failed to finish.

The race also seemed to indicate that speed and relative youth would be served, as opposed to older specialists of the full marathons. As the *Berwick Enterprise* noted:

> It was a day of triumph for youth. Bricker, Bell and Cox headed the field. Then came the veterans Anderson [sic] and Henigan. Then more youth in the persons of Webster and (Frank) Wendling; then veteran Michelsen. Thus it was, all through the list of 27 finishers, youth first, and age second.

Finish Lines: Cliff Bricker placed 10th in the 1928 Olympic Marathon in Amsterdam and ninth in the 10,000 at Los Angeles in 1932. In 1927 he placed fourth in the Boston Marathon.

Billy Cox won a bronze medal in the 1924 Olympic Games in Paris as part of the US 3000-meter team race, a now defunct event.

Ove Andersen managed just fourth at Berwick, but in the 1928 Olympic Games in Amsterdam, the Finn snagged a bronze medal in the steeplechase.

Harold Webster went on to win the British Empire Games Marathon in London in 1934. The Hamilton Harriers host a 10-mile race—one of Canada's oldest events—every Boxing Day in his honor.

10

Brooklyn Boys in Berwick

If you were looking to handicap the Berwick Marathon in the good old days (and, apparently, a lot of people were), then checking out the fall cross-country results would have been a smart place to start. More than the pure marathon runners (men like Clarence DeMar or Frank Zuna or Albert Michaelson, who often found 9 miles simply "too short"), harriers who could run well in 6-mile cross-country typically adapted well to the Berwick race, which—considering weather and/or road conditions—could often take on characteristics similar to cross-country slogs.

Those scanning cross-country results in 1927 and 1928 would have encountered the name of Phillip Silverman, a top young runner for the Brooklyn Harriers Athletic Association. In November 1927, Silverman won the Metropolitan AAU junior cross-country title, charging into the lead around the quarter-mile mark and holding it for the entire 6-mile route around Van Cortlandt Park in the Bronx. Silverman spanked a field of 150 runners and—as stated in the *New York Times:* "Silverman ran a splendid race and was clocked in an exceptionally fine time of 31:33."

The club system in New York City and its surrounding environs was, as usual, producing some intense competition and featuring dozens of racing opportunities at the end of the so-called Roaring Twenties. Silverman was a product of that spirited racing environment. In addition to Silverman, a Jewish runner, the Brooklyn Harriers soon followed with a promising African American runner named August "Gus" Moore. In fact, both Silverman and Moore were good enough that they often competed in "handicap" competitions in the New York area—races in which they started from scratch and were forced to catch those less skilled runners who were spotted leads of sometimes a minute or more, depending on the distance.

Both Silverman and Moore were destined to race quite well in Berwick's Thanksgiving Day classic, but they would endure disappointments there, too.

Fast Phil: Silverman posed for a photo op at Berwick, while a buddy clowns with the Brooklyn Harrier jersey in the background.

I
Silverman Shines Like a Diamond
19th Berwick Marathon, November 29, 1928

Silverman was again enjoying a solid cross-country season in November 1928, but he certainly didn't come into the Berwick Marathon race as a favorite. At best, he would have been lumped in with a group of a dozen contenders—and previous veterans of the race (like Jimmy Henigan) would have been given a slight edge (and attracted more betting money) over obvious Berwick "rookies" like the Jewish kid from Brooklyn.

Silverman did, however, run a good race at Van Cortlandt Park just the Sunday prior to the Berwick race, finishing third in the Metropolitan Senior Cross-Country race, clocking a new personal best on the rolling route of 30:43. His Brooklyn Harrier teammate Gus Moore won it (30:28), no surprise given that Moore had won the US cross-country championship just the week before over the same course. But Silverman had battled Moore well for more than half of the Met championship, and was relegated to third at the tape when former Johns Hopkins star Verne Booth charged up to nip him by a mere second.

Perhaps in deference to the course and stories of the infamous Foundryville Hill, Silverman held back four days later in Berwick as a new record field of 41 runners headed up Market Street in mild, slightly cloudy conditions. The roads were dry and ready for fast running.

Almost on the snap of the starting pistol, Gonzalo Moreno, second behind Bricker (who had not returned to defend his back-to-back titles) in the 1926 race, bolted right to the front and scampered to a 15-yard lead before the runners made the right turn in North Berwick. But by the 2-mile mark—the base of Foundryville Hill—the man from the Panama Canal Zone had plenty of company, as noted by the *Berwick Enterprise:*

> When the field reached the lower end of Foundryville it was still anybody's race, for there were 20 men within the first hundred dred yards . . . Then Silverman stepped out and matched strides with [Ove] Anderson [sic]. The straggling began about half way up to Summer Hill, when behind the leaders the field began to stretch out. Part way up the hill the four leaders went with Silverman on the right, Henigan in the middle and Anderson on the left. They were abreast and occasionally spoke to each other. Moreno was about three yards behind at that stage.

Soon after reaching the top, Moreno fell back to seventh. Silverman applied steady pressure from the front, up Hosler's Hill and plunging down to the curve at Miller's Hotel and all through Kachinka's Hollow. A strained tendon at the bottom of the big downhill put Lou Gregory out of the race; a car took the upstate New York runner—a man destined for better days at Berwick—to the finish.

Silverman's work gained him a mere 50 yards as he swung onto the Martzville Road and began to take on the final 2-miles-plus back to Berwick. Behind him Jimmy Henigan plugged along, followed closely by

Andersen, Canadian runners Billy Reynolds and Charlie Snell, and Buffalo's Frank Wendling. The Berwick crowds, of course, recognized and loved the Irish Bostonian and began to lend their voices in support.

From Martzville home, the crowd cheered Henigan, who was recognized by thousands who urged him to catch Silverman, but the fleet-footed Brooklyn lad was not to be caught, and the cheering only served to spur him on. He increased his lead steadily to the finish.

The Quicksilver Kid: When Phil Silverman galloped down Market Street to upset the favorites in 1928, few in the massive crowd knew who he was.

Photo courtesy of Harry's Sports

The Brooklyn runner opened up his long stride down Market Street and by the finish—where he arrived in 49 minutes, 50 seconds—he was a full minute ahead of the popular Henigan. Henigan, in fact, repulsed a late kick from Andersen by a mere second. Andersen had proven track speed—his bronze-medal effort in the 1928 Olympic steeplechase that summer having provided the Finns with a much-vaunted 1-2-3 sweep of that event—so Henigan did well to hold him off.

After that, Wendling (5th, 51:17) was sandwiched between the two Canadians, Reynolds (4th, 51:03) and Snell (6th, 51:31), while the early leader Moreno struggled home for seventh (51:46).

It was a huge win for young Silverman and probably sent many Berwick Marathon fans scrambling for their programs to verify the results and figure out just who this kid from Brooklyn might be. As the newspaper put it: "Silverman was not figured by many to have more than an outside chance in the race . . ."

The local charge was once again led by Bloomsburg Teachers College runner and Mifflinville resident Allen Parr. Parr was in the thick of the second pack and finished the race in a commendable 11th place in a new personal-best time of 52:25. Among those Parr relegated to places behind him was Booth, the former Johns Hopkins standout who had snagged Silverman at the line in cross-country just the previous Sunday. As the news write-up stated: "Verne Booth, who dared wear No. 13, finished in that position . . ."

II
Gus Moore's Berwick Debut
20th Berwick Marathon, November 28, 1929

Just a month after the historic Wall Street crash of 1929, the denizens of Berwick were nonetheless prepared to celebrate Thanksgiving in their usual manner, and that meant (in addition to church services) the traditional good stuff: turkey and all the trimmings, football and, of course, the Marathon.

Perhaps Phil Silverman talked up the Turkey Day race in Berwick, because the 20th edition of the classic footrace saw a second runner with a Brooklyn Harrier connection—August "Gus" Moore. Moore had been a schoolboy star at Boys High in Brooklyn; he briefly attended St. Bonaventure College in upstate New York, but then transferred to the University of Pittsburgh. It was from Pittsburgh in late November that Moore sent in his entry for Berwick, and it instantly made pre-race news in the local papers. In the "Berwick Department" of the *Bloomsburg Morning Press* it was reported:

> The caliber of the field for the Berwick Marathon Thanksgiving afternoon was raised yesterday when Gus Moore, famous Pittsburgh Negro marathoner and holder of the senior national cross-country title, telegraphed his entry for the race.

Of course, Moore wasn't really a marathon runner in the sense of competing in 26-mile races. But he was definitely one of the top American runners in the late 1920s, copping the US title in cross-country in both 1928 and 1929. He also had deadly finishing speed compared with most of the era's distance men, as exemplified by a textbook race he ran for Boys High at the 1926 Penn Relays (before a crowd of 20,000 fans), as detailed in an article titled "Special to the *New York Times*":

> Gus Moore, sterling miler of Boys' High School, Brooklyn, supplied one of the greatest thrills of the day when he pulled [his] team to victory in the interscholastic medley relay championship race . . . Moore was credited with a 4:27 1-5 anchor mile.
>
> The speedy little negro runner started almost last in the field of ten schools sixty yards back of the leaders on the final mile leg, but went away at a clip which enabled him to pick up on his rivals until half a lap from the finish he was fourth. Then Moore electrified the crowd with a closing burst of speed, which carried him to the front.

If the field—bolstered by the much-heralded Moore—was top-notch for the 20th running of the Berwick Marathon, the weather certainly was not. The lead paragraph of the race write-up in the *Bloomsburg Morning Press* summed up the horrendous racing conditions and continued to lace in references to them throughout.

> Over ice, through snow and in the face of a biting wind that chilled the bones to the very marrow, Gus Moore, University of Pittsburgh negro, the national senior cross-country champion, yesterday won the 20th annual Berwick marathon from a field of 31 starters in 49 minutes, 42 seconds.

How bad was the weather? Well . . . how about *this* bad!

> The weather and course conditions were among the worst in

the history of the race. Ice coated the hill from Foundryville up to Summer Hill to such an extent that many automobiles were stuck there. The word reached the starting point before the runners went away and the start was delayed for 45 minutes before highway patrolmen and state troopers could clear the way.

Over the years, cars on the course usually proved to be a nuisance for both runners and race officials. However, except for the 45-minute delay, the traffic on the course actually *helped* the runners for once, since they had crushed down the snow in spots that had drifted over. The intrepid runners tried to follow the tire tracks wherever they could, ducking their heads in an attempt to both watch their footing and to seek some relief from the whipping wind that made the below-freezing temperatures all the more frigid.

Moore took the lead early and held it for most of the race. Perhaps because of his college racing season, Moore opted to wear spikes—though one wonders if even spikes had much positive effect in such horrendous weather conditions. After slipping and sliding up and down the hills, slogging through Kachinka's Hollow, the leaders emerged onto Martzville Road. Moore held about a 100-yard lead on the pursuit pack (which, given the conditions, was a considerable cushion). Penn State's Dick Detwiler plowed along in second, but just ahead of Canadians Billy Reynolds and Wilf McClusky, and another Nittany Lion runner, Captain Radcliffe. Jimmy Henigan, as usual, was in the mix, too.

Amazingly, Moore held together enough to break 50 minutes. His winning time of 49 minutes, 42 seconds was only 12 seconds slower than Silverman's victorious effort the year before when the conditions were quite excellent for racing.

In something of a backhanded compliment, the *Bloomsburg Morning Press* allowed that

> The Penn State runners sprang the biggest surprise of the day. No one figured them strongly, although some had confidence that they were capable of a better showing than they made Monday in the intercollegiate cross-country.
>
> Detwiler held second position constantly from the end of the second mile, and those who expected momentarily to see him dropping back were doomed to disappointment.

For runners from the Berwick region, Allen Parr of Mifflinville again set the pace. Finishing 13th (just one place in front of Boston Marathon legend Clarence DeMar) in a time of 54:03, Parr was less than a minute behind a trio of experienced Canadian runners, including Charlie Snell, the fur trapper, who could only snare 11th on this frigid day. It was Parr's third "local" win in as many years.

Ironically, the only runner *not* to finish, despite the winter-like conditions, was the defending champion Phil Silverman. The Brooklyn Harrier star dropped out at the base of Foundryville Hill, feeling ill. It must have been a bitter disappointment for Silverman; just days before the race he had—according to the *Bloomsburg Morning Post*—"sent word that he would make a determined effort to break the course record set by Willie Ritola in 1922."

Of course—given the cold and slippery conditions on Thanksgiving Day in 1929—a new course record would have required something that had yet to be invented: a snowmobile. And beating Gus Moore—Silverman's Brooklyn Harrier teammate—would have, on this particular day, been as difficult a feat as staying *on* one's feet. Moore had beaten Silverman quite convincingly in cross-country races earlier in the month back at Van Cortlandt Park in the Bronx, and it would have taken a flawless race on Silverman's part to have upstaged the reigning American cross-country king at Berwick.

Mercurial Moore: August "Gus" Moore was one of the best long-distance runners in the country in the late 1920s. He won two U.S. cross-country titles (1928-29), in addition to his Berwick Marathon victory.

III
Dueling with Detwiler: See Dick Run
21st Berwick Marathon, November 27, 1930

Whether it was the now infamous weather of the 1929 Berwick race, or just a hunch that conditions would be similarly dismal for the 1930 event, one store in town ran this advertisement in the days just prior to the Marathon: "Be Comfortable While Watching the Race: Get into one of the good overcoats we are showing . . . $12.95 at Heicklen's new store."

Once again the course was icy and a belligerent wind beat through the gaps and hollows, making the runners work that much harder.

That was the bad news. The *good* news was the field was again of top quality and the race promised to be competitive, if not fast in terms of the clock. Gus Moore was back to defend his title, and the 1929 runner-up Dick Detwiler was ready to race, too. As noted in the *Berwick Enterprise:*

> Thirty-six starters came to the tape as the bugle brought them from the dressing room for a brief announcement to the crowd and to dance in the cold air as the full list was awaited. Some of the runners were clothed for the keen cold with flannels to their ankles while others were in the short running trunks in defying the bitter wind. The photographers got in their work and the crack of starter [Jack] Harry's pistol sent off one of the largest and best fields the Marathon has assembled.

Perhaps as a hint that he was on the verge of his best race, it was none other than Bloomsburg Teachers College runner Allen Parr who grabbed the early lead out Market Street, straight into the wind. The top contenders, meanwhile, seemed content to run in a bunch, a few yards back.

By the time the runners started up Foundryville Hill, however, the race began to look something like a rerun of the 1929 edition, with Moore taking the lead and Penn State's Detwiler determined to keep close. Parr and Lou Gregory followed just a few yards back; that pair was chased by the veteran Jimmy Henigan, Canadian hope Wilf McCluskey, and Scottish-born James McDade.

> The trying run up the steep grade saw each runner exerting every ounce and the changes of place came frequent but as the result of the propelling force of their best that put them there rather than an urge to be leading. It carried first Moore, then Detwiler, then Gregory a few places in front . . . It was a fasci-

nating test. Seven runners were within one hundred feet and remained there all the way up the grade, changing position but fighting together and refusing to give the gaps that usually thin out the line and readily predict the winner.

Detwiler (wearing spikes) boldly ran the waterfall descent off Hosler's Hill, showing little regard for the sharp left to be negotiated at the bottom. Others opted for caution in spots where "the sun that came out at intervals failed to get in its work" and "the runners slipped and there were several narrow escapes from falls." Detwiler's damn-the-ice-full-speed-ahead tactics provided him with a 40-yard lead heading into the hollow, but the chase group reeled him in within 2 miles and it was back to being anybody's race to win.

Indeed, predicting the winner in this particular Berwick would have been a risky proposition. Taking the pre-race favorite—Moore, for example, would have soon proved to be an unlucky wager. The defending champ fell off the pace all through the hollow, as Gregory, McCluskey, and Detwiler began to string out the initial seven. In fact, Henigan—the wily old Irishman with his perpetual grimace so often mistaken for a grin—fixed his brow-knitted gaze on Moore. At one point, Henigan inched ahead of Moore and caught a glimpse of Detwiler up ahead.

And then, for Moore, his race went from bad to worse. As the newspaper noted:

> About 100 yards from the hill just before reaching Martzville, Moore slipped on the ice and fell flat in the roadway. As he struggled to get up the press car came up to offer aid which Moore refused with the word, "I think I can get going again." He continued on, limping slightly in his snow-covered suit and a little later hailed the checkers car and was brought to the finish.

So Moore again arrived first at the finish line, but certainly not in the way that he had envisioned.

As the car brought him back to Berwick, Moore would have seen Gregory out in front, tailed by McCluskey and then—closing rapidly on the significant descent out of Martzville and coming up on the 7-mile mark—the Nittany Lion runner, Detwiler.

> As Martzville turn was reached and the runners faced back toward Berwick Detwiler wobbled around the turn in third place apparently all in and went over to the side of the road

and brushed a parked car as he ran along with every ounce of energy exerted . . . and due to give way to the plodding Henigan 100 yards behind. Gregory and McCluskie [sic] were out front. Moore had just fallen and been compelled to give up . . .

Increasing his stride down Martzville hill the Nittany runner closed up on Gregory and McCluskie [sic] and on the two mile run into Berwick overcame and passed McCluskie, ran down Gregory and continued to increase his lead in the fight in Market and finish strong—the winner of the most spectacular on the hardest fought and most thrilling battles for places ever witnessed by the Briar Creek hills that have been slapped by the moccasined feet of hundreds of America's fleet harriers in many a terrific struggle.

Reading the newspaper account years later, you can't help but feel the writer's excitement (his words stringing out like gasps of breath from the racers themselves . . .) and the magnetic pull toward verbose embellishment. But certainly here was something different from what Berwick Marathon fanatics were used to—a runner, late in the race, charging from third to first. Detwiler rode his wave of adrenaline and passed Gregory just before turning onto Market Street, and then "ran in . . . between the lanes of applauding people and honking horns to a superbly won victory."

Obviously, icy conditions slowed down the times, but Detwiler's triumph in 50:15 was nonetheless honey-soaked. Gregory held together for second and crossed in 50:26, while McCluskey settled for third (50:46). Then came the familiar figure of Jimmy Henigan (4th, 50:57)—once again "in the diamonds" even though it was years after he had hinted at retirement.

Parr, who had led the harriers out Market Street at the start, ran the best race of his Berwick Marathon career. In defiance of his allegedly unlucky race number (13), Parr placed a very commendable sixth (51:47)—just a few ticks behind Shanahan Athletic Club runner John Zack. Behind Parr came some accomplished runners, such as McDade (7th, 52:01) and Bill Agee of Baltimore (9th, 52:58), who would win the US marathon championship in 1931.

11

Jousting with the Jinx

Although Dick Detwiler's stretch drive to win the 1930 race thrilled virtually everyone, Louis Gregory—relegated to second in the final minutes of the Berwick classic—was probably not among that elated majority. Gregory was still in the upswing of his career in the early 1930s, but rapidly becoming a young star on the American and Canadian racing circuit. By 1932 he was recruited to race for the prestigious Millrose AA of New York City. Gregory also made the US Olympic team for the 10,000 meter event in both 1932 and 1936, but failed to place well at either Los Angeles or Berlin.

For most of his life Gregory resided in upstate New York (where he worked on a farm, taught school, and then eventually became a high school principal), but he loved to race and sometimes went to great lengths simply to get to a starting line. Once, in 1940, he won a race in Canton, New York, and then drove 170 miles to a railroad station, whereupon he caught a train to New York City in order to compete in the Metropolitan Cross Country Championships the next day and represent his Millrose club.

Although Gregory could run a quality marathon (he won the 1940 US Marathon title over the challenging Yonkers course and finished second in the 1941 Boston Marathon), his best distances seemed to fall between 6 miles (he won three straight US 6-mile track titles from 1929 through 1931) and 30K (18.6 miles), making Berwick's distance of 9-miles and some yards well within his optimal range.

As for Detwiler, he was looking to repeat and put an end to what seemed to be a budding Berwick Marathon winner's jinx. Perhaps some observers noticed that Phil Silverman had won in 1928—but was forced to drop out, feeling ill, in 1929. Silverman's Brooklyn Harrier teammate Gus Moore charged through the inclement conditions for the win. But Moore came back to defend his title in 1930, only to fall behind halfway through the race, then fall—literally—on the ice. Skinned up and bleeding, Moore attempted to hobble on, but finally he did the smart thing and dropped out.

I
Gregory Moves Up
22nd Berwick Marathon, November 26, 1931

The twenty-second edition of Berwick's holiday racing ritual certainly seemed wide open. The defending champ—Detwiler—and runner-up Gregory were both back, but the list of challengers impressively deep. Dave Komonen, a Finnish carpenter-cobbler (when he could find work at all during the Depression) residing in Ontario, headed the list. A game marathoner (he would win Boston in 1934 when *Time* magazine would describe him as "a pale and unhappy looking Finn") Komonen was considered a pre-event favorite, but he had never felt the race day sting of Foundryville Hill. Komonen's Monarch Athletic Club teammate Wilf McCluskey (3rd in 1930) was back; Philadelphia brothers Paul and Joe Mundy were on hand; and two other former Berwick winners—Phil Silverman and the irrepressible Irishman Jimmy Henigan (who had finally won the elusive Boston Marathon crown back in April)—were also in the field.

The entry list might have been even more stellar, but Gus Moore was a last-minute scratch. As the race write-up of the day noted:

> Of the promised field of 47 runners, Gus Moore was the only outstanding entry missing from the starting field. The negro ace, winner of the event in 1929, was forced to give up the trip at the last minute because of his failure to arrange suitable train accommodations.

Nevertheless, with all the bewildering possibilities, Berwick bettors must have been on the verge of consulting a soothsayer. They would have had a hard time predicting, for example, that the field would be so deep—and the pace so blistering—that experienced former champs like Henigan and Silverman would be reduced to fighting it out for the less than auspicious honor of seventh and eighth place.

In addition to who might emerge the winner with such a talent-laden field prancing on the Market Street starting line—came an obvious second question: Could this be the year that Ville Ritola's course record of 47 minutes, 56 seconds—a mark now nearly a decade old—might be tumbled from its throne?

The weather was proclaimed to be "perfect" and the road conditions pronounced to be fine; it was all systems go.

And the runners barreled off the line, rising to the challenge, as the *Bloomsburg Morning Press* noted:

> The first indication of the speed of the field was brought out at the start, when no less than ten runners, rubbed elbows in the prance out Market . . . with ten more runners sprinkled out over 100 yards to the rear.

About 2 miles into the race, at the Foundryville bridge, Gregory charged to the front, but he was followed closely by McCluskey, Silverman, Joe and Paul Mundy, New York runner Frank Titterton, defending champ Detwiler, pre-race favorite Komonen, and Pittsburgh-area star Frank Cerney. However, the Berwick Marathon jinx was lurking close by, too.

> The bridge and its approach to the long, winding Foundryville Hill sounded the death knell for Detwiler. The 1930 champion stopped and rested until Jimmy Henigan came along, approximately seven places to the rear and offered Detwiler a word of encouragement.

Detwiler resumed running alongside the Boston veteran, but within a quarter mile up the steep ascent, the former Penn State runner (representing Philly's Meadowbrook Club) was once again hunched over with "agonizing pain in the stomach." The race zoomed on without him and the Berwick Marathon winner's jinx was alive and thriving.

Meanwhile, Gregory tucked into Foundryville Hill with all the enthusiasm of a lumberjack ripping into a 20-ounce steak, carving out a 100-yard lead for his effort.

> Gregory maintained his wicked pace into Summer Hill and checked in first at the church, later to re-establish the common belief that the leader at the church is the inevitable winner.

Gregory kept the pressure on, charging up—and down—Hosler's Hill. He looked "full of running" as he zoomed through the halfway mark and banked the hard left at Miller's Hotel. As the former St. Bonaventure star (the papers sometimes referred to him at "the Bonaventure Flyer") took aim at the miles through Kachinka's Hollow, the Canadians—Komonen and McCluskey—moved into second and third and attempted to keep him in sight. No doubt there were bettors back at Berwick (the progress of the race having been telephoned back to Market Street, where it was updated on the finish-line scoreboard) hoping that the favorite Komonen would rally to live up to his pre-race billing. Instead, the unlucky Finn—like Detwiler—ran into unforeseen problems.

Less than 300 yards from the turn, Dave Komonen dropped from the pack and sat down along the dust-laden road. A "stitch" in the side proved the undoing of the Finnish ace, although he turned aside proffers of aid and insisted upon finishing . . . He crossed the finish line in thirteenth place.

That left out one talented pursuer in the now increasingly difficult task of running down front-runner Gregory and—as the local write-up would note—the chase pack was simply "fighting to the last ditch to remain among the first five." Meanwhile, by Martzville turn, the major change in the race order was that Frank Titterton—as far back as eighth in the early miles of the race, whether by choice or relegated there by the sheer speed of the pace—had moved up to third. Titterton, running his best Berwick race in several tries, eventually spurted past Joe Mundy on Market to snag second, but Gregory was a clear winner—nearly 200 yards ahead—and his time of 48:01 a tantalizing 5 seconds off Ritola's still-standing course record.

When Gregory breezed into the tape, he was comparatively as fresh as when he started. But the runner-ups, with few exceptions, were writhing in pain.

Allen Parr, the local leader from Mifflinville, was held to 17th place—the deep field and fast early pace humbling the regional talent. He admitted to the local press that he had never run a race under such pain. Berwick runner Joe Larish (23rd, 63:12) certainly would have concurred.

Joe Larish was another local boy seriously affected by the wicked pace the leaders set. Larish was carried into the dressing room following the finish and required medical aid to combat severe pains in his side and stomach. A physician administered restoratives and ordered his removal to his home for a day of rest, at least.

That Larish rebounded quite successfully was no doubt a tribute to the regenerative powers of youth. At any rate, he was back on the starting line in 1932, a race in which the Berwick lad would respond with a solid effort.

II
McCluskey Finds the Key
23rd Berwick Marathon, November 24, 1932

The 1932 Berwick Marathon had a lot of similarities to the race a year before, starting with an entry list of stars to match the sparkles of the diamond prizes. Lou Gregory, now representing the Millrose Athletic Association, was back to defend his title and perhaps take a crack at Ritola's record that had so narrowly eluded him in 1931.

The Mundy brothers from Philadelphia were back, as was Wilf McCluskey, the 26-year-old Canadian who had placed fourth. They were all now well experienced on the course and quite familiar with its wicked rise up to the Summer Hill churches, where too quick a pace might leave you wondering whether to stop in for a quick prayer or simply retire to the adjacent graveyard.

There also were some new faces on the starting line, such as German American club runners Willy Steiner and Paul DeBruyn—the latter the winner of the Boston Marathon in April, arriving at that finish with his arms stretched out wide and the Fatherland's infamous black eagle prominently displayed upon his racing vest. DeBruyn—who allegedly did some of his training by running up and down stairs at the New York City hotel where he worked as a repairman-waiter—outdueled defending Boston champ Henigan in that race.

Those who liked to place a friendly wager on the outcome of the race might have given strong consideration to a New York-based Finn by the name of Eino Pentti. Pentti was coming off a strong racing season in the metropolitan area, plus he had represented his adopted country—the United States—at the 1932 Olympic Games, although, like Gregory, he had finished well out of the medals in that race.

That interest in the Berwick Marathon was as fervent as ever could be summed up by the numbers of cars and spectators on race day. As noted in the *Berwick Press*:

> The crowd, attracted by the all-star field and the most ideal weather since 1924, lined every inch of the long and tedious route through the colorful and tradition-worn Briar Creek hills. Thousands of automobiles were parked along the road along the nine miles from Sixth street to Miller's turn and back by another route. Trained observers, reinforced by police

figures, estimated the number of on-lookers at 25,000 . . .

As it would turn out, the fans along the finish-line stretch would be treated to one of the most exciting Berwick finishes in the history of the race.

Leaving on the crack of the starting pistol, the field was tightly bunched down Market Street, but by the base of Foundryville Hill—the end of the second mile—several important occurrences began to shake up the field. The first was that the "jinx of the defending Berwick champion" was still very much a diabolical presence, as reported in the *Berwick Press* write-up:

> Lou Gregory, the defending champion and former National six-mile champion, gave up the fight at the foot of Foundryville hill after three futile attempts to run out a painful ankle injury. The 1931 champion withdrew from the field at almost the exact spot that Dick Detwiler, 1930 winner, gave up the ghost in last year's race.

The second big happening was that McCluskey, Paul Mundy, and Steiner hit the Foundryville climb with serious intent, with no man able to open a lead of any significance. Meanwhile, Pentti arrived at the Summer Hill churches in fourth and began a spirited drive on the downhill—and then again after popping over Hosler's Hill. Those downhill surges brought the Finn into contention at the halfway point.

> On the downgrade preceding the turn, Pentti stretched out his arms and let loose on the hill. He closed the gap between himself and Mundy just as they reached Miller's [Hotel] and when Mundy slowed down to take the turn, Pentti passed him and set out to catch Steiner . . .

The Finn caught Steiner 20 seconds or so later, and as the race worked through Kachinka's Hollow only the front-running Canadian remained for him to catch. Running with short but powerful strides, Pentti began to chop away at the 50 yards separating him and McCluskey. When the Finn *did* catch him, McCluskey attempted to go with his challenger, but fell back after about 100 yards of shoulder-to-shoulder running.

> Pentti was running magnificently and no spurt by McCluskey appeared equal to the task which the Canadian faced . . . Into Kshinka's Hollow the two leaders went, race officials, newspapermen and veteran onlookers satisfied that Pentti would finish in first place.

Pentti continued to add to his lead through Martzville and into North

Berwick, perhaps McCluskey's only slim hope of a miraculous comeback resting with the fact that the Finn still felt compelled to give an occasional glance behind. Was it fear? Was Pentti more fatigued than his lead would have led onlookers to believe? McCluskey was still close enough that observers in the pace car and the press vehicle could see the Maple Leaf insignia stitched on his racing vest, bobbing up and down. Still, Pentti seemed a sure winner as he turned onto Market Street with a full 50-yard cushion. He tucked into the final mile and made his way toward the finish line.

As the *Bloomsburg Morning Press* article noted:

> McCluskey was a hopeless second . . . The flashing feet of the flying Finn were fifty yards in front. The race was over, officials, reporters and spectators agreed . . . They cheered the Finn, [who was] apparently still strong. But the cheers reached McCluskey. The Canadian shook the lethargy of tiring legs from him and spurted . . .

McCluskey pulled even at the railroad tracks and into the lead at the Market Street school and—as the Bloomsburg report gushed—"the momentum, the pride of victory, the heart of steel" propelled him to the finish line.

The abrupt change caught everyone by surprise, including the announcer.

> From the end of Market street the word had come that Pentti, the Finn, was in the lead. The announcer was shouting the New Yorker's name to the excited crowd when the heaving green maple leaf was discerned. Then he quickly changed his shout.

Even McCluskey—the victor in 49:09—was surprised, as he was quoted in the Bloomsburg paper: "I didn't think I could do it. I thought he had me beat. But I did it!"

Perhaps from the shock of it all, Pentti trotted in second, 13 seconds behind the Canadian who represented Toronto's Monarch Athletic Club. Pentti promptly exchanged congratulations with McCluskey and vowed to return again next year.

Behind them, the others labored in. Steiner placed third (49:50), followed by Philadelphia resident Frank Nordell (who was coming off a stellar cross-country season for New York University) in 50:27. Ten seconds behind him followed the Mundy brothers—Paul and Joe—who purposely crossed the line together in 50:37. Next came McCluskey's teammate, Lloyd Longman (50:53), while Frank Cerney of Pittsburgh settled for a disgruntled eighth.

"I've had this cold for three weeks," Cerney vented, "and it kept me from winning. I want you to be sure to put that in the paper because no one in the field could beat me when I was right."

Rounding out the top-ten finishers were Paul Kanaly of Boston (the son of the Yale track coach) in 51:31, and the Boston champ DeBruyn (52:01), who had been running fifth past the halfway mark but had faded in the face of the talented field. Joe Larish of Berwick (who raced cross-country for Bloomsburg State Teachers College) finished a commendable 16th (53:51). He was in far better condition at the finish line than he had been the year before when the race doctor ordered him to take some bed rest to recover from the rigors of the Marathon.

As for the crowd, the excitement of such a close race—the rarity of someone coming from behind to snag the first-place diamond in the final quarter mile—no doubt still had them buzzing as they proceeded with the late-afternoon festivities of Thanksgiving celebrated in the curious, traditional style that was uniquely Berwickian.

Photo courtesy of Harry's Sports

Gang of Four: Defending champ Wilf McCluskey of Toronto (5) leads the 1933 race over Lou Gregory (11), Willy Steiner (8), and Berwick "rookie" Scotty Rankine (6)—the latter who charged home for the first of five wins.

III
The Great Zabala Fiasco
24th Berwick Marathon, November 30, 1933

On the national level, the country was hoping that President Franklin D. Roosevelt's "New Deal" enactments would help get some of America's estimated thirteen million unemployed out of the soup kitchen lines and back on the job. The stock market was still up and down like a roller coaster, and most Americans had no way of knowing that economic prosperity was still years (and one big war) away.

In Berwick—a place that seemingly weathered the Depression better than the larger cities—the pre-Marathon buzz suddenly took on an international flavor as the following entry came to light in the local papers. In the *Bloomsburg Morning Press* of November 11, the headline read: "South American Enters Marathon":

> Entry of Juan Zabala, noted South American marathon runner, in the Berwick marathon on Thanksgiving . . . was disclosed yesterday when South American newspapers began making arrangements to have speedy news of his showing flashed to them.
>
> So great is the interest attached to the runner that the South American papers asked for a detailed description of the Berwick course.

Zabala was none other than the 1932 Olympic Marathon champion. In that race Zabala—a 20-year-old orphan—set what was then an Olympic record of 2 hours, 31 minutes, and 36 seconds, nearly collapsing at the Coliseum finish line. By contrast, Sam Ferris of Great Britain galloped in a strong second—just 19 seconds back, but obviously a man who made his move too late. The best US finish in the Olympic Marathon came from Albert Michelsen (whom Berwick crowds were familiar with from his appearances there) in seventh.

Berwick being Berwick, the smart betting money suddenly began to take on a decidedly South American accent, if you will. It seemed unlikely that anyone might be able to mess with the marathon man from Buenos Aires. Merely by entering, the much-vaunted Zabala became a heavy pre-race favorite in the 24th running of the Berwick Marathon, and even defending champ Wilf McCluskey—or 1931 winner Lou Gregory—probably weren't figured to match strides with the swift South American.

There also were new faces on the Market Street starting line, and some of those—such as Canadian Robert "Scotty" Rankine and Boston-based marathon man Johnny Kelley—were destined to make their mark on Berwick racing history. In fact, some were bound to make their presence felt sooner rather than later.

So on race day, Zabala came to the starting line as the strong favorite. No doubt there were some hopeful kibitzers who had wagered on other runners—all now appearing to be long shots of different extremes—and those bettors perhaps surmised that Zabala might blow up on the frequently unpredictable ascent to the Summer Hill churches.

But that never happened.

It never happened because Zabala never even *got* to the infamous Foundryville Hill. Zabala, in fact, ran just a few blocks before retiring from the race. Juan Carlos Zabala was, most likely, suffering from either the flu or a case of food poisoning and had spent the night before the race feeling extremely ill. One report claimed that a physician would not clear him for racing, but Zabala—knowing that the crowds were at least in part gathering on Market Street to see the Olympic champion run—felt some obligation to stride a few blocks before bowing out.

We can imagine that this attempt to placate the fans did little to sooth any men who might have gambled some real money on Zabala winning the race. (There were, however, no post-race reports of bettors tossing themselves off the Berwick-Nescopeck bridge and into the icy waters of the Susquehanna, so perhaps no wagers on the Argentine exceeded more than modest proportions.)

Even in defeat he warranted a few prominent paragraphs in the race story of the *Bloomsburg Morning Post* on Friday:

> Juan Carlos Zabala, of Argentine, the Olympic champion, was stricken ill during Wednesday night, and a physician refused to sanction his start. However, Zabala went out with the field, but after running to Fifth street, dropped out . . .
>
> Zabala, through his manager and interpreter Juan Perez, expressed disappointment after the race that he had not been able to cover the course. "I'm sure I could have broken the record," he said. The Argentine plans to sail December 9 to return to South America.
>
> Early yesterday morning he was stricken with a stomach ailment that left him very weak. Whether he would appear at

all was a question up to the very start of the race. But he appeared rather than disappoint the tremendous crowd and ran to Fifth street.

And so the race roared on, minus the great Zabala, the others locked in battle. The weather was mild, but the runners also bucked a headwind strong enough that they must have suspected it would detract from their final times on the course—not a day for record setting. Rankine and Gregory took a slight lead up "the Hill," with Bill Steiner, young Kelley, and Paul Mundy following. They carried those positions over—and down—Hosler's Hill, and the turn at Miller's Hotel.

By the time the race progressed through Kachinka's Hollow, however, it quite clearly had become a *mano-a-mano* duel between Gregory and Rankine. The intensity of their one-on-one competition pulled them increasingly away from third. In fact, Steiner—running third through 5 miles—was struggling with a side stitch. As the news report noted, he attempted to alleviate it in an inventive (if ultimately ineffective) manner: "Steiner was in apparent pain, and borrowed a belt from one of the occupants of the referee's car in an effort to stop the pain."

Steiner's attempt to rid himself of the side sticker by constricting a belt tightly around his midsection didn't do the trick. Joe Mundy blew by, moving into third, and soon Kelley passed him, too. Meanwhile, the leaders were moving on, virtually joined at the hip.

Up in front Gregory and Rankine were waging a battle of their own. They swept into Martzville side by side, and went down the grade to the Berwick Golf Club with swinging arms almost touching . . . Into North Berwick they swept on even terms, and back through the closely-packed crowd on Market street.

Those spectators jostling for a view on Market Street were soon well rewarded. At 13th Street, Gregory tried to get the jump on his Canadian rival and surged to a yard lead. But Rankine responded with even greater fury.

Then it was Rankine's turn and he stepped on the gas . . . First it was a foot, then a yard, then five yards, then ten. Steadily he pulled away. The speedometer on a press car showed 15 miles per hour as it kept pace with the sprinter.

Rankine powered through the tape in 48 minutes, 35 seconds, and the Maple Leaf contingent had its second straight Berwick champion. About

50 yards behind, Gregory settled for a well-fought second (48:44). More than 30 seconds later, Joe Mundy emerged for third (49:17), and Johnny Kelley—in his first of many Berwick appearances—rounded out the diamond winners in fourth (49:34). Considering the pain in his side, Steiner probably did well to hang on for fifth (49:54), holding off Paul Mundy and defending champ McCluskey, who were both closing fast down the homestretch.

McCluskey understandably could not have been overjoyed with seventh (after winning the year before), but he *did* manage to break the Berwick winner's jinx: He had not dropped out. With Zabala's fiasco, however, you could have argued that the Berwick jinx—like a tricky virus that had re-created itself in order to circumvent antibiotics—had merely struck in a different form, wiping out the pre-race favorite from Argentina.

Back in the pack, there also were some interesting results. Les Pawson, the 1933 Boston Marathon champion from Rhode Island, could only manage a ninth-place finish—one spot ahead of Paul DeBruyn, the 1932 Boston winner.

The local winner was Sterling Yohey of Briar Creek, placing a respectable 14th in 53:40—one spot ahead of Jimmy Henigan, who was back in Berwick, though obviously not in his best racing condition.

Of the 36 starters, there were 29 finishers. Among them was Harold Larish, a fifth-grade student from Bloomsburg. The young lad didn't get his AAU registration card in time to get a number, but he ran and finished anyway. Curiously, although he lacked a number, he was listed in the official results—and he wasn't last—finishing in 25th place in 70 minutes. Depending on how "officially" you view these results, that meant that young Larish had in a sense outperformed Zabala, the Olympic champion.

Zabala, however, vowed to return in 1934, win the race in record time, and prove to the people of Berwick that, had he not been ill, he could have won the 1933. Although he was admittedly surprised by his victory, Robert "Scotty" Rankine also pledged to return to defend his title in 1934. In the midst of the Depression, no doubt the fans of the Berwick Marathon chatted about the expected Zabala-Rankine rematch over their plates of Thanksgiving Day dinner.

12

Rankine's Record Roll

I

Rankine's Return
25th Berwick Marathon, November 29, 1934

Although the return of Juan Zabala, the 1932 Olympic champ from Argentina, never materialized, the Berwick Marathon Association had the makings of a sizzling race for its 1934 edition. The headliners were the Scottish-born Canadian Robert "Scotty" Rankine and Johnny Kelley, the plucky young Irish American from Boston. The Canadian contingent also featured 1932 winner Wilf McCluskey and Walter Hornby.

Although relations between the Americans and their Canadian visitors were almost always friendly, the cross-border factions inevitably drummed up a spirit of high rivalry, too. In addition to Kelley, the Americans countered the lads from the Dominion with the much-experienced Bill Steiner—who had resorted to using a belt in the 1933 race in a vain attempt to subdue a wicked side sticker—and Welsh-born Pat Dengis, an up-and-coming marathon sensation out of Baltimore. (The following spring, Dengis would finish a close second to Johnny Kelley in the Boston Marathon.)

No doubt C. N. MacCrea felt confident that his event—now a quarter of a century old—would produce the kind of competition that the Berwick Marathon deserved for its silver anniversary.

Obviously the race director and his dozens of Berwick Marathon Association colleagues weren't the only ones excited about the 25th edition of the classic footrace. As the field—nearly 40 strong—jostled for position over the first mile, an unlikely point man, perhaps on a rush of adrenaline, surged to the front. Rain and a noticeable breeze greeted the runners and spectators who peeked out from under umbrellas or dripping hat brims to witness the traditional charge. As the *Bloomsburg Morning Post* noted:

> Sweeping out Market street at a fast pace, the field began to
> string out before it reached North Berwick. Louis Bertoldi,
> Bloomsburg State Teachers College harrier, five yards in the

Photo courtesy of Harry's Sports

Racing in the Rain: There was no silver lining in the weather report for the silver anniversary of the Berwick Marathon. Scotty Rankine (12) defended his title. Pittston's Joe Clark (34) was one of the top regional runners of his era, placing sixth.

lead as the field swept out to Summer Hill Avenue. It was a pace, however, that he could not hold and he failed to remain with the leaders for more than another mile or two. Thirteen runners were bunched well through the first mile.

With Bertoldi's gambit proving to be short-lived, the major players emerged just in time to launch a serious assault up Foundryville Hill. It soon became apparent that Rankine and Kelley would match strides and brush elbows for top honors, unless some unlikely event occurred in the late miles.

Kelley had a lead of a couple of yards as the grueling grind up the long hill began. He and Rankine changed places several times, but neither had an advantage of more than a yard or two ... When the Summer Hill churches were reached, Kelley had stretched out a lead of four yards and was running a nice race. Rankine, trailing, appeared content to let the Massachusetts harrier break the rain that was driving from the west ...

When the men began to mount Hosler's Hill, only a yard separated Kelly and Rankine, while Hornby and McCluskey were some distance back. As it turned out that was about the way the field finished.

Hornby and McCluskey hammered the steep descent—"their heels flew down the treacherous macadam toward the turn" said the sports report—in attempt to get back in the race with the leading pair. They made up some distance, but not enough. Rankine and Kelley, spurred by each other, added to their lead all through Kachinka's Hollow, splashing through puddles down the country lane. The entire course was now paved, and therefore the runners were spared the ankle-deep mud that—as sure as it greeted their racing pioneer predecessors—might well have sucked at their racing shoes through that farmland stretch.

Although Johnny Kelley had better credentials over the *full* (26.2-mile) marathon distance, Rankine typically felt confident in distances from 10K to 30K. More of a power runner than the slight and slender Kelley, Rankine—who had outkicked Gregory for his first title—knew he shut down Kelley in any type of sprint finish. Still, Kelley clung to the Canadian—like an ill-cast shadow—as they reached Martzville.

But Rankine opened up some breathing space past the golf course and back to North Berwick. At one point the defending champ may have carved out a 10-second edge. Kelley surged valiantly and gained back half of that as the pair turned onto Market Street and into the puddle-splotched homestretch. The crowds, which had mostly retreated for shelter after the start in deference to the cold rain, rushed back to curbside to catch the final minutes of drama.

Rankine roared home, breaking the tape in 48 minutes and 8 seconds—the third fastest time in the history of the race in its first quarter century and the first successful title defense since his countryman Cliff Bricker did the trick in 1926-27. A tired but still-game Kelley slapped through the wet finish line 3 seconds later. And then it was more than a minute wait until Hornby claimed third, about 90 yards up on McCluskey, who snagged fourth and the last diamond. Only Kelley's gallant runner-up effort had prevented a 1-2-3 Maple Leaf sweep.

Steiner finished fifth (49:44), followed by Pittston's Joe Clark (a LaSalle College grad who represented a team from Germantown, Pennsylvania) in sixth (49:57) and then a slew of Philly runners (John Zack, Harold Auch, Augie Zamperella, Joe Sullivan, and George Rapp) in the 7th through 11 slots. Pat Dengis, who it turned out didn't care much for his baptismal on the long ascent of Foundryville Hill, struggled home 12th and never again returned to race at Berwick.

The locals staged an incredibly close race to the finish, as Sterling Yohey of Briar Creek (15th, 52:46) barely held off Berwick's own Melvin "Fitch" Hons by a mere tick on the clock. Bloomsburg College runner Bertoldi—who had led the field out Market—finished near the dead middle of the field (18th, 53:29) after his brash bolt for glory evaporated in the chilling rain and the flash of faster feet than his own.

Finish Lines: Pat Dengis would win the rugged Yonkers Marathon three times, including a course-record run in 1939. The witty, likable Welshman died in a small-plane crash later in the same year. He was mourned greatly by the running community of his era.

II
Tarzan Brown: Round One
26th Berwick Marathon, November 28, 1935

Robert "Scotty" Rankine was back in Berwick in 1935, and the local papers for much of the week were building up to the fact that a third straight victory would automatically catapult the Maple Leaf star from Galt, Ontario, into the Marathon's elite historical ranks. Only the famed Hopi Indian runner Louis Tewanima and the Flying Finn—Hannes Kolehmainen—had managed to bag three Berwick Marathon crowns. Could Rankine join that prestigious club?

The question became all the more enticing to Berwick Marathon followers when it was learned that Rankine's stiffest competition was likely to come from one of the country's newest—and most colorful—sensations: Ellison "Tarzan" Brown, a Native American runner from Rhode Island. The newspapers—which rarely failed to reflect upon the Carlisle Indian years without lacing their articles with a healthy dose of nostalgia—predictably went headdress-over-moccasins for this latest pre-race angle. Under the title "Noted Indian Enters Race," The *Bloomsburg Morning Press* wrote:

> The most colorful figure in athletics in America and a national title and world's record holder will be in Berwick Thanksgiving Day . . . the appearance of Ellison Tarzan Brown, the Narragansett Indian from Rhode Island, has been assured.
>
> Brown has been the athletic sensation of the past season and

in the brief space of a year has forged to the front by winning the National 20K, 25K and 30K races. In addition, in the 20K event he set a new world's record for the distance of one hour, five minutes and 51 seconds, bettering the record held by Louis Gregory, also entered in this year's events.

Fly Like an Eagle: Ellison "Tarzan" Brown, as the papers put it, was quite "colorful" and sometimes contributed to what might be construed as stereotypical hype—here in a full Native headdress more associated with Indians of the Great Plains.

In addition to Gregory, the paper noted that Tarzan Brown had shown his heels to other great runners quite familiar to Berwick Marathon fans, including Johnny Kelley, Les Parson, Eino Pentti, Paul Mundy, "and every other contender to national honors for the distance events in this country."

> The only runner of note he has not met is the world famous Scotty Rankine and if the doughty Scotchman decides to accept the issue and race here again one of the greatest races, not alone the course has ever witnessed, but the country as well, will result. If these two outstanding men meet here it will practically insure that the course record will be broken.

> Brown is a full-blooded Narragansett Indian, twenty-one years of age, and has only been running for a little over a year. He with his small brother and sister till a small farm near Westerly, R.I. Tall and lanky, he is said to resemble the famous Tom Longboat both in his appearance and stoical manner. Dressed in Indian costumes and accompanied by his manager and trainer he has been the center of interest wherever he has appeared . . .

> His appearance will bring back to the old timers, the great Tewanima who won the race three years in succession in 1909-10-11 . . . It would be peculiarly fitting that, as the Berwick race starts its second quarter century, an Indian should again be the winner. Brown and his trainer will arrive in Berwick next Wednesday in time for a brief workout on the course.

Rankine *was* up for the challenge, of course. He arrived in Berwick on Tuesday before the race—along with Johnny Yeaman, another Scottish-born Canadian residing in Galt—and, on a short training run (according to the Bloomsburg paper), was seen "treating his running partner to his first glimpse of the trying Foundryville hill."

The scribe managed to buttonhole Rankine for a comment after the training run.

> "Yes, I think I have a good chance to break the course record this year," Rankine said firmly but modestly. "Truly I wasn't pressed last year, with all due respects to Johnny Kelley, who placed second. I tried to do my best, but if this Narragansett Indian, Tarzan Brown, is all I am told he is, I'll be pushed more this year than ever before."

And so the 1935 Berwick was not lacking in hype. In addition to the two pre-race favorites, the field was also loaded with quality men who had much experience over the Berwick course—such as 1931 champ Gregory, Eino Pentti (the American Finn and 1931 runner-up), Joe and Paul Mundy, plus Canadian runners Walter Hornby (3rd in 1934), 1932 champ Wilf McCluskey, and Maple Leaf newcomers Yeaman, Bob Morrison, and Milt Wallace.

At first glance, the weather seemed nearly a repeat of the year before—rain. However, the winds were calm and the air mild; all in all an improvement from 1934.

The field was packed tightly out Market Street and even down to the 2-mile point near the Foundryville bridge. Veteran observers of the race, of course, suspected that "the Hill" would soon split up the pack with the precision of a pool shark scattering the multicolored balls on a billiard table. The *Bloomsburg Morning Press* writer couldn't resist some wry comments laced with a dab of the sadistic:

> But the field had not gone a hundred yards up the steep grade when the old ghost of Briar Creek's hills began to get in his work . . . Runners began to hold their stomachs; others began wishing they had oxygen tanks. The field began stringing out . . .

And, perhaps surprisingly, young Tarzan Brown was one of those who had trouble with the Foundryville climb. He was already far off the lead group and not looking like a runner who might regroup for a second-half comeback.

> As the head of the pack approached Summer Hill, the leaders split into three groups. Brown dropped back out of the pace-making group for good . . . The hill took its toll of his stamina.

So those who'd bet on Brown, observing his progress on the course board back at the start-finish on Market Street, would have worn glum faces.

Pentti, the veteran Finn living in New York who had raced for the US in the 1932 Olympic 10,000, was another story. As he had in the 1931 race, Pentti used the downhill off of Hosler's Hill to move way up in the field. Defending champion Rankine led the runners at the sharp turn near Miller's Hotel, but Pentti charged past Yeaman on the descent and moved into second at the hard left turn.

The absence of wind and cold, plus the heat of competition had the top runners zooming along at a fast pace. The weather, however, showed no signs of drying up.

> Through Kschinka's Hollow, where banks of snow lined the
> road, and the rain fell in torrents, Rankine had boosted his lead
> [over Pentti] to a hundred feet. Their legs clicked off the yards
> with surprising speed, and there was not the slightest effort in
> either's running. Every now and then Rankine hitched up his
> trunks. Pentti shot back a glance every couple of hundred
> yards.

Through Martzville and past the golf course, Rankine's edge over the Finnish American wavered between 30 and 40 yards. Given the Scottish Canadian's history of a powerful homestretch kick, however, he must have felt quite confident. And soon he had the vast crowds of North Berwick and Market Street urging him toward the finish line and a third straight victory. In addition, the knowledgeable Marathon fans seemed to sense that this race was destined to be a fast one.

> In through the narrow lane left by the crowd, the leaders
> swept, and the watches were being examined carefully in spec-
> ulation over the possibility of a record smashing performance
> . . . Turning the corner into Market . . . Rankine turned on the
> gas. So did Pentti but the factory worker had a little bit better
> of the argument and increased the lead slightly as the crowd set
> up a cheer.

Rankine's barrel chest snapped the finish-line tape in 47 minutes, 35 seconds—and eight seconds later Pentti raced through the line. In the midst of the post-race glow of victory, Scotty Rankine did not immediately realize that he had—with Pentti's pesky pursuit serving as something of a competitive cattle prod—obliterated Ville Ritola's 1922 record mark of 47:56. Pentti, too, was well under the former record set by the "Pera-seinajoki Wolf" thirteen years before. In all likelihood, the paved roads made a big difference in regard to record-setting on such a rainy day: in Ritola's era such weather would have left Kachinka's Hollow a swampy slog.

Behind Rankine and Pentti, one of the deepest and fastest Berwick fields filed in: Yeaman (3rd, 48:03) and Joe Mundy (4th, 48:16), who snagged the last diamond awards, followed two more Canadians Bob Morrison (5th, 48:26) and Walter Hornby (6th, 48:40). Former Berwick champs Lou Gregory and Wilf McCluskey were forced to settle for respective finishes of 7th (48:58) and 8th (49:08). Despite all the pre-race hype, Tarzan Brown plodded home a lackluster 15th—a mere 3 seconds ahead of local standout Fitch Hons in 16th (52:03).

On his way to the dressing room, Rankine heard the big news from the sporting scribes: In addition to matching the three straight victories of Tewanima and Kolehmainen, he was now the new course-record holder for the Berwick Marathon. As noted in the *Bloomsburg Morning Post,* Rankine's joy was elevated:

> "Whoopee! Hurray!"
>
> That's the way Bob Rankine, the Preston, Ont. Factory worker, felt yesterday when he broke the record for the Berwick Marathon . . . His wine-red jacket around his dripping white shirt and blue trunks, he was on his way to the YMCA after crossing the finish line when a reporter told him he had set the new mark.
>
> "I feel fine. Nice race."
>
> He wasn't even breathing hard, but he confessed he was a trifle tired. A bit later he confided that next week he would enter a hospital for a hernia operation. He is hopeful of a complete recovery before Spring, when he can resume running, and he hopes to make the Canadian middle-distance team for the Olympics.

If Rankine was the happiest guy in Berwick that afternoon, then race promoter Chiv MacCrea was perhaps the next man in line. MacCrea enthused to the press that Rankine was (in the words of the *Bloomsburg Morning Post* writer) "the greatest runner who ever has trampled over the Briar Creek hills on the stiff course that has seen the great middle-distance men of the last quarter century.

"Better than Tewanima, and better than Kolehmainen," MacCrea declared. "Ritola? Yes, Rankine's a shade better than Ritola."

III
Berwick's First Grand Slam
27th Berwick Marathon, November 26, 1936

Robert Rankine's 1936 season had its highs and lows. The hernia operation that he had purposely delayed until after his record-setting 1935 Berwick race dictated a cautious reentry to running in the New Year. Nevertheless, Rankine was fit enough to win Hamilton's famous Around the Bay race (just under 19 miles in length) when that event was resumed after a decade hiatus in March. He clocked a brisk 1:45 and change for the challenging route, the first of a record seven wins in what was—and perhaps still is—Canada's most renowned footrace.

As expected, the powerful-running Rankine made the Canadian Olympic squad that traveled to Berlin in the summer of 1936. Suffering a very rare setback, Rankine pulled a muscle during his 10,000-meter race and was forced to drop out. Despite his luckless experience at the infamous "Nazi Olympics," Rankine was healed up and back in fine form when he arrived in Pennsylvania for his attempt at an unprecedented fourth straight Berwick Marathon title.

In addition to Rankine, the Canadians—at least according to pre-race hype in the local newspapers—were coming south for the American Thanksgiving with designs to grab all the diamonds. As entries began to stream in, the *Bloomsburg Morning Post* issued a sober note:

> Especially strong are the Canadians as they are sending at least eight of the best men in the Dominion here for the great Turkey Day event . . . The Canadians' ambition is not only to win but to sweep all four places . . .

What could foil the lads from the Great White North in such an audacious raid on the Berwick diamond stash? Well, the entry of Johnny Kelley for starters.

> Kelley's entry coming at this juncture, is doubly welcome as it means that Uncle Sam's best will be on hand to dispute the honors with [the Canadians]. Kelly is a great as local favorite as he is in Boston and is rapidly taking the place in the public eye once held by "Smiling Jimmy" Henigan, who retired from distance running last summer.

In addition to Kelley, the Americans also sent experienced men such as Lou Gregory and Bill Steiner to the starting line.

But some observers seemed to think that the US attack would be best served by youth: a surprise attack in the form of Penn State cross-country captain Pete Olexy. Although he had never before run the 9-miles-plus at Berwick, Olexy was coming off a stellar collegiate season that included a recent runner-up finish in the IC4A cross-country championship at Van Cortlandt Park in New York. The young man from Lansford, Pennsylvania—the son of a Polish coal miner—was obviously fighting-fit. The local papers could not resist the urge to draw comparisons to John Romig and Dick Detwiler, Nittany Lions who had pounced for upset wins at previous Berwick races. One quantifying pre-race write-up referred to Olexy as "a dark horse that's not too dark." Norm Gordon, Olexy's Penn State teammate, also entered and was considered a contender for a top-ten placement.

A shot ringing from Jack Harry's starting pistol put lips to rest and bodies in motion. Steiner and Gregory (wisely wearing long underwear under his singlet and shorts, plus a hat) pushed the early pace through 2 miles, perhaps motivated to move fast in an effort to keep warm as the field stepped out in weather cold enough to measure their breathing in little puffs of smoke-like chill. Rankine dogged their progress a few yards back. The men labored against the wind and under occasional flurries of breeze-blown snowflakes.

Veteran Berwick Marathon observers certainly knew one cold truth: "the Hill" would sort out pretenders from contenders—or, as the Bloomsburg paper stated it, "the killing drive up . . . which more famous names have been reduced to second-raters than in any other course in the country."

Photo courtesy of Harry's Sports

Pack of Aces: Among Gregory (hat), Rankine, and Kelley (5) you can account for a total of twelve Berwick Marathon titles. Canada's Morrison (far right) never won, but had the right stuff.

Three-time defending champ Rankine took a stride lead up the mountain, but a trio of Americans followed him—Kelley, Gregory, and Steiner. Near the top, Morrison passed Steiner and moved up to join the leaders. Olexy was not that far back, but apparently at a dear price.

> ... the hill again took its toll, and Olexy was laboring before the top of the hill was reached. The leaders were gradually pulling away ... Gregory, Rankine, and Kelley were running side-by-side, virtually even ... Across Hosler's Hill, where the biting wind was freezing the spectators, the runners went changing positions but little.

By the turn at Miller's, Olexy was out. He later said that the piercing cold and blustery winds had caused him pain virtually from the outset. In addition to Olexy, three other runners would drop from the race. It was so cold that Rankine, a man as tough as the shoe leather he used in his employment, would later admit that the weather conditions had even him on the verge of capitulation.

Presumably, leading the race and shooting for a record fourth straight victory helped keep Rankine's pilot light from going out. The runners gained some relief from the in-your-face wind when they ducked into the lower lane through Kachinka's Hollow, and perhaps even a friendly push at the back as they pounded into Martzville and made the much-welcomed turn for home, hot drink, and food that surely awaited them at the finish line.

Rankine led only by a few feet over Kelley and Gregory as the trio raced past the golf club and tucked into the slight climb toward North Berwick. But the Canadian ace had confidence in his finishing speed.

> But in the final mile, Rankine's sturdy legs flashed a little faster, without losing their rhythm, and at the finish he was some fifty feet ahead of Kelley. Gregory was ten to fifteen feet back in third.

Rankine blitzed across the line, stopping the clock in a near-record time of 47 minutes, 35 seconds. Kelley clambered across just 3 seconds behind, but only 4 ticks ahead of Gregory. It was, at least on paper, one of Berwick's closest races with three finishers within 8 seconds of one another.

But Rankine's toughest opponent might well have been the brutally wind-chilled conditions, as he confessed to the *Bloomsburg Morning Post* reporter:

> "The cold nearly got to me," he said, as he slipped into his

pullover sweater. "I've never run in anything like it. I'm alright now, except for my fingers," and he beat his hands against his legs in an effort to get the blood circulating again.

Kelley and Rankine exchanged exuberant congratulations and some friendly slaps on the back. Despite the tooth-chattering cold, Rankine also was intent on seeing how his fellow Canadians fared and stayed close to the finish line for several minutes.

Toronto's Bob Morrison claimed fourth (48:16) and the last diamond. Steiner (6th) was sandwiched between a pair of Canadians from Ontario—Walter Hornby (5th) and Wilmer "Whitey" Sheridan (7th) in his first of many jaunts through Berwick and its surrounding, unforgiving hills. Three Americans—Rhode Island's Les Pawson (8th), Joe Clark (9th), and Gordon (10th)—charged in next, but they were chased by yet two more Canadians, Alfred Roberts (11th) and Walter Fedorick (12th).

In fact, if you scored the Canadian-American finishers in classic cross-country style (five men count), the "meet" would have been deadlocked at 28-28. One of the few glaring disappointments for the US was the 19th-place finish from Eino Pentti. The American Finn had only recently returned from Europe by ship and was not racing-fit.

As always, the fans also were greatly interested in the local battle. Berwick's own Fitch Hons (15th overall, 52:32) beat Don Karnes of Espy by nearly a minute.

IV
Rankine Speeds the Fifth
28th Berwick Marathon, November 25, 1937

With football season finishing up, basketball poised to tip off, and the splendid leaves long off the trees, Berwick naturally geared up for yet another Marathon. The buildup generally began in early November as official entries began to trickle in, with Chiv MacCrea gradually feeding tidbits to the local sports scribes.

Perhaps MacCrea's most daunting task was to convince spectators and bettors alike that someone other than Robert Bob "Scotty" Rankine could actually win the 9-mile (and a few extra hundred yards . . . 286 yards, it was claimed) race. The sturdy-built Canadian ran uphill decently, downhill like a demon, and had a deadly finishing kick for which none of his Berwick contemporaries seemed to have an antidote.

With four straight victories, nobody could blame Rankine for a display of confidence that stopped just short of brashness. If that confidence needed any kind of an exclamation point, then it arrived in the mail with Scotty's official entry for the 28th running of the Turkey Day tradition. At the bottom of his race application, Rankine had bluntly scribbled to MacCrea: "Mac— I intend to make it five straight and put a new mark on the course."

If that was the equivalent to Babe Ruth pointing his bat at the upper deck of Yankee Stadium, then so be it. If some rival runner was going to prove Rankine wrong, he'd have to be prepared to run faster than any man had before over one of the most demanding courses in the country.

Some of the usual suspects were back to take another shot including Johnny Kelley, Lou Gregory, and Eino Pentti. Anxious to atone for his lackluster showing in 1936, Pentti won the Metropolitan Cross-Country Championship earlier in the month, as if to serve notice that he was on pace for an outstanding Berwick '37.

Once again, however, the press couldn't help but tout yet another Native American runner, this time a man named Russell George who lived on a reservation near Syracuse. It was a familiar theme that the regional papers just loved: Indian runner comes to Berwick and, look out, because this guy could be the "next Tewanima." As noted in the *Bloomsburg Morning Press:*

> The entry yesterday of Russell George, full-blooded Onondaga Indian, threatened to upset "the dope" on the twenty-eighth annual Berwick Marathon. . . . George's appearance will add greatly to the interest in the race, and it will either establish him as one of the most promising distance runners developed in this country or it will relegate him to the ranks of the "also-rans."
>
> The typical Indian runner who still wears his hair long as has been the custom of the Onondaga braves for centuries first broke into prominence when he defeated Lou Gregory at Endicott, New York this spring by a four minute margin in an eleven-mile race . . .
>
> Those who have seen him run are unanimous in predicting a great future for the Indian and many hail him as the next Tewanima. Coming here from Syracuse, he is following in the footsteps of his ancestors who were members of the warlike Six Nations and who, under the British, ravaged this region in

Revolutionary Days.

Upsetting "the dope" was a thinly veiled inference to the wagering that was still going on for the Berwick Marathon. The smart money would obviously be on the four-time champ and heavy favorite—Mr. Robert "Scotty" Rankine, the 27-year-old factory shoe cutter from Preston, Ontario. The introduction of Russell George—along with the fact of his victory over an accomplished runner of Lou Gregory's caliber—suddenly cast some grit into the pre-race stew. An Onondaga brave! With long, wild hair! Could he succeed where Tarzan Brown had fizzled? Could Russell George indeed be—dare they say it (and they did!)—"the next Tewanima"?

As the race turned out, Russell George was never a factor in his Berwick Marathon debut. Tarzan Brown was back again, too, but his run for the diamonds remained lackluster. Joe and Paul Mundy from Philadelphia, and Walter Hornby from Hamilton, Canada, blasted out Market when Tarzan Brown, "the Narragansett Indian who later was to be conquered by Foundryville hill, came up fast to challenge the pace makers." That the pace was *too* frisky might have been evident by the fact that none of the true favorites—particularly Rankine—felt compelled to lead.

By the time the runners reached the Summer Hill churches, the major

Photo courtesy of Harry's Sports

Looking for a Lift: Those cars most have seemed a tempting alternative as the front-runners push up "the Hill" in 1937. Scotty Rankine (8), digging for this fifth straight win, is chased by Millrose stars Lou Gregory (12) and Eino Pentti (9).

players had emerged: Rankine, Gregory, Kelley, Bob Morrison, Milt Wallace, Les Pawson, and the revitalized Eino Pentti, determined to erase the memory of his 1936 Berwick blowup. Rankine and Pentti both employed their downhill running skills to take command by the turn at Miller's Hotel as the race took the slingshot turn into Kachinka's Hollow.

As the front-runners zoomed toward the six-mile mark, Rankine and Pentti had chiseled out a 50-yard lead, but Gregory was still running strong in third. Then—as noted in the *Bloomsburg Morning Press*—the unexpected knocked Gregory off stride.

> It was near this point that one of the official cars, endeavoring to pass another, interfered slightly with Gregory but he saw the car and got off onto the grass nearby. He was watching the car and slipped on the grass, skinning his right arm. He regained his feet without losing his stride, although Kelley was right at his heels . . .

Meanwhile, Rankine and Pentti continued to pound out the miles, neck and neck through Martzville. The sports pages would report that "the two leaders were running strong and appeared exceptionally fresh at the golf course."

But by the turn onto Market Street, the Canadian ace had churned to

Photo courtesy of Harry's Sports

Tight at the Turn: Pentti (9) and Rankine in one of Berwick's most famous duels. The American Finn made the Canadian earn his fifth win. (In the past, Pentti was often misidentified in this photo as Gregory, his Millrose teammate.)

a lead of three or four crucial seconds. And then he got the crowd—estimated to be one of the biggest and enjoying the relatively mild weather—behind him.

> This [the lead] he increased steadily as he raced through the crowd which called "That a boy, Scotty! Go get the fifth straight, boy!" Rankine didn't need much urging.

And—as he had predicted on his race application—Rankine ripped up the record, too. He powered through the finish line in 47 minutes, 16 seconds—slashing more than 18 seconds from his previous mark. Pentti—once again the bridesmaid, but far better than his previous year's performance—clocked 47:36 for second. About 100 yards behind, Lou Gregory sprinted in for third (47:49), while Toronto-based Morrison (48:19) ran a strong fourth—holding off New England stars Kelley (5th, 48:33) and Les Pawson (6th, 49:04) for the last diamond prize.

It was a strong day for the Maple Leaf runners overall, as Canadians claimed four of the next five slots: Milt Wallace (7th, 49:26), Walt Hornby (9th, 50:07), Ab Morton (10th, 50:08) and Whitey Sheridan (11th, 50:29). Andrew Zamparelli from Medford, Massachusetts, managed to sneak in there in 8th, a mere one tick behind Wallace.

The first Pennsylvanian to cross was Joe Clark (12th, 50:30), while Melvin "Fitch" Hons (17th, 52:14) of Berwick won the award for first local. Russell George, the much-hyped Onondaga racer, was forced to settle for 14th (51:12).

Then again, it seemed few runners held much of a chance against Rankine once the dark-haired, barrel-chested Canadian star toed the Berwick Marathon starting line. But—while basking in the glow of his fifth straight victory and a new course record—Rankine alluded to how someone else *might* win the race in 1938. As noted in the *Bloomsburg Morning Press*:

> Yesterday's wasn't the hardest race in the five years he has won the Berwick marathon although he was pressed to a new course record—take it from the champion of champions over the course, Robert "Scotty" Rankine, the 27-year-old shoe cutter who calls Preston, Ontario, his home and the Berwick race his principal Thanksgiving Day recreation.
>
> "I don't mean that Pentti didn't give me a race—far from that. He did. But I had the race in hand all the way. I had it when I needed it and a mile and a half from the finish—when the pain left my side—I knew then I would take it and I did."

Asked whether he would return to Berwick in 1938, "Scotty" smilingly evaded a positive answer: "You know, you can go out once too often," and then hastened to add: "But I'm not afraid of a beating. I have taken them often."

In a rare but fitting moment, the Berwick Marathon race staffers implored the popular champion to address the thousands of spectators swarming around the Market Street finish line area. Robert "Scotty" Rankine graciously complied, but his words once again hinted that he would not be back in '38.

Induced to speak over the amplifier, "Scotty" mounted the judges' stand and told the crowd: "I'm not getting so much of a kick out of winning as I used to. It's getting to be a habit with me. But I do get a kick out of coming to Berwick. I like it here. Maybe now that I have won five times in a row you had better pension me."

No doubt the runners who saw more of Rankine's backside than they ever did his Maple Leaf vest would have been more than happy to chip in a little something to Scotty's pension plan. If Rankine truly meant to take a breather from Berwick, the chances of other runners to win the first-place diamond would automatically improve.

13

Racing on the Brink of War

I
The Great Berwick Blizzard
29th Berwick Marathon, November 24, 1938

True to his word, Robert "Scotty" Rankine did not post for the 29th running in Berwick. If he had, cross-country skis or snowshoes might have been suitable racing equipment, because northeastern Pennsylvania was blindsided by a surprise snowstorm—all the more annoying since only days before the local papers had mentioned an unseasonable stint of "mild weather."

On race day eve, however, the weather switched gears from mild to wild. Blowing snow all but paralyzed automobile travel in the area, with hundreds of cars stranded and drivers resorting to chains on their tires in order to proceed at a slow crawl.

Nevertheless, a brave band of runners arrived at the Market Street starting line for the 29th Berwick Marathon in what still may be the worst weather in the history of the race—certainly worse than even the 1929 and 1930 events.

Some runners were more ready than others. Perhaps guys used to nasty winters—like Lou Gregory from upstate New York, or the New Englanders like Johnny Kelley, Les Pawson, and Tarzan Brown—would be unfazed and figure for the first diamond. The Canadians, too—led by Lloyd Longman and Bob Morrison in the conspicuous absence of five-time champ Rankine—were unlikely to be cowed by a little white stuff and wind.

Among the dark horses was Peter Olexy of Lansford, Pennsylvania, now the freshman running coach at Penn State. A powerful "strength" runner, the 6-foot, broad-shoulder Olexy had dropped out in the bitter cold of the 1936 race. But now he was two years older, stronger, and wiser—the last attribute supported by the fact that he donned a pair of track spikes for traction over what was sure to be a slippery course. Olexy also started the race with what the newspapers described as a "peasant kerchief" on his head, presumably to keep his head dry and to wipe his face off, if needed.

And wiping off your face—in lieu of windshield wipers—*was* indeed needed. As the *Bloomsburg Morning Post* described it:

> Snow was whipped into the eyes of the entire field repeatedly, blinding them momentarily and making the treacherous footing a real peril. Not much of the course had been negotiated until the athletes involuntarily were putting hands to eyes at regular intervals to wipe away the snow that clung tenaciously to eye lashes as though the weatherman were determined to stop this event which annually has focused the attention of marathon fans of the North American continent on Berwick.

The conditions weren't all that pleasant for watching the race, either. The *Post* sports report noted that "only a few hundred of the most hearty watched the start at 2:47." Those who somehow coaxed their cars out to the base of Foundryville Hill—or up the slippery slope to Summer Hill—perhaps were motivated by a slightly sadistic streak, as the *Morning Post* mentioned: "Cars lined the long hill; fans always finding the heart-breaking grind which has taken the toll of so many of the distance greats, of special interest."

It was not the kind of weather in which one expected to come from behind and win. Lou Gregory opened a small lead by the Summer Hill church, but Olexy, Pawson, Brown, Kelley, Pittston's Joe Clark, and the Canadians Longman and Morrison were still very much in contention.

Perhaps feeling semi-confident with his track spikes on, the long-striding, sturdy Olexy ran the steep descent after Hosler's Hill with devil-may-care daring. His willingness to risk took him past Gregory and—briefly—into the lead at halfway, successfully negotiating the slick turn at Miller's Hotel. As the former Nittany Lion plowed into the course through Kachinka's Hollow, he was chased by Gregory (who would soon repass Olexy) and Brown, with Clark—who was running a great race—holding down fourth. Pawson, however, was poised to mount a charge through the hollow that would eventually land him a diamond.

> Keeping time with the rhythm of the whistling wind, the leaders charged into the hollow. Gregory was a step in front much of the way. Big Olexy, as though bringing the challenge to the weather man, ran wide of the leader so he could do his own buffing against the snow . . .

RUN FOR THE DIAMONDS

But positions among that advanced guard changed almost as rapidly as feet hit the hardened, snow covered turf in that endless crunch-crunch through the soft and slippery foundation.

The intrepid trio continued at the front through Martzville, past the golf course, finally arriving back at North Berwick. Behind them, little had changed, except that Pawson had moved into fourth and was gradually pulling away from the plucky Pittston runner Clark. Behind Clark, Kelley—certainly unaccustomed to running so far off the front-runners—and the Maple Leaf pair of Longman and Morrison fought to simultaneously keep their footing and somehow gain on the ghostly outline of Clark, barely visible ahead of them in the blowing snow.

Strangely, the runners arrived in North Berwick to a street that might have been almost peaceful in the swirl of floating flakes except for the huff of their labored breathing and slip-slap of feet seeking traction. But the placid scene changed abruptly, as documented in the *Bloomsburg Morning Press:*

> As they entered the head of that final mile the course seemed almost deserted but once the cry of "here they come" was echoed, the crowd came from nowhere . . . All along the course, deserted seconds before, the course was lined with many deep to watch Olexy put on the drive to win.

Actually, there was a lot of back-and-forth between Olexy and Gregory, the 1931 champion—as Brown fell back enough that the three-man race suddenly became *mano-a-mano,* as written in the *Post.*

> Olexy, his head somewhat sheltered from the cold by a large white cloth knotted peasant-style under his chin and being whipped across his shoulders by the cross winds, entered the straightaway by a stride over Gregory, with Brown at their heels . . . and at Eleventh street Gregory was the pace setter again, Olexy trailing and Brown starting to fall back.

> At Tenth street, Olexy prepared for the finish and threw aside the over-sized kerchief which had served its purpose well in open country . . .

> At Fifth street, three blocks from the finish, Gregory had two strides and he held it until a half block from the finish when Olexy, who hails from Lansford, put on the giant kick which put him over the winner by a couple of healthy strides.

Cold, soaked, but jubilant, the powerful-kicking Olexy clocked 51 minutes, 25 seconds in the horrendous conditions. Gregory was 1 important second behind—2 ticks off of what would have been his second Berwick victory. Tarzan Brown, the Narragansett Indian, redeemed himself for previous dismal performances at Berwick that failed to reflect his true running skill with a diamond-clinching third in 51:33. As noted in the *Morning Press:*

> The Indian runner Brown, who under much better conditions had failed to negotiate the course, was the one runner who found the grind to his liking . . . The little fellow was running in the tenth spot much of the way up the hill but was fresh at the top and at the Miller Hotel he was up with Olexy and Gregory and they failed to shake him.

Les Pawson (52:06), Brown's Rhode Island rival, was almost 2 yards back in fourth, snagging the last diamond, while Clark placed a gutsy—and career Berwick-best—fifth place (52:51).

The sixth through tenth slots comprised Longman (53:01), Kelley (53:13), Morrison (53:17), Whitey Sheridan (53:35), and Philly's Shanahan Catholic Club runner Joe Sullivan (53:46).

Bloomsburg State Teachers College had enjoyed a competitive cross-country season, and one of its top harriers won the local laurels. Don Karnes, of nearby Espy, Pennsylvania, finished 15th overall in 57:02.

For Pete Olexy, the victory was one of the most cherished of his running career and more than made up for the DNF he suffered in the extreme cold of two years before. The triumph also placed him in good company when it came to Penn State men, joining previous Nittany Lion luminaries such as John "Blondy" Romig and Dick Detwiler in the Berwick winners' circle.

In addition, Olexy led a first-through-fifth "sweep" by the Americans. It was the first time in six years that a Canadian had not won the Berwick Marathon. As events would turn out, Dwight D. Eisenhower would be in the White House before the Canadians would crown another Berwick champion.

Photo courtesy of Fran Oxley

Fleet Pete: Like a lot of World War II-era runners, Pete Olexy probably lost his best running years while he was in the service. Winning Berwick in 1938 was one of his biggest victories, but he was back in shape to win the New England 25K championship in Gloucester, Massachusetts, by 1946.

II
Lou Gregory's Berwick Bounce-Back
30th Berwick Marathon, November 23, 1939

Lou Gregory, the enthusiastic racer from upstate New York known as the "Bonaventure Flyer" in his collegiate days, most likely didn't relish racing Penn State runners—or former Penn State runners—when it came to the homestretch down Berwick's Market Street.

In 1930, PSU runner Dick Detwiler charged from behind to steal what appeared to be Gregory's first-place diamond. Then, in the blinding blizzard of '38, it was another Nittany Lion—powerful-churning Pete Olexy—who clawed past Gregory in the final 100 yards to snag first.

But perhaps these near-misses also served to fire up Gregory for the next year, because in 1931 he came back to win, and in 1939 he again responded with a fantastic race. Gregory came into the 30th edition of the Berwick classic with all the building blocks of an already successful season: he won the 1939 US 10,000-meter track title in the summer, then performed typically well in various road races and cross-country competitions in the late summer and autumn.

Despite his experience—or perhaps because of it—the 34-year-old Gregory could not have expected an easy win at Berwick. Defending champ Olexy—strong as a country plow horse—was back, as was the erratic but talented Tarzan Brown, who had chased Gregory and Olexy to the tape in the '38 snow-fest. Brown's racing stock may have been at an all-time high: The Narragansett Indian won his second Boston Marathon title the previous spring and had raced well since then.

Veteran New England marathoners such as Les Pawson (4th in '38) and Johnny Kelley also could not be discounted. Gregory also brought along Mel Porter—his former Ithaca High School teammate and Millrose AA clubmate—who had twice finished in the top five of the Boston Marathon.

In addition to the Americans, the Canadian Lloyd Longman—who had represented his country in the British Empire Games in Australia in 1938—was back and in prime racing shape. As the *Morning Press* noted several days prior to the race:

> Longman comes to Berwick in the pink of condition, having especially prepared for the event and will arrive here the day before in order to insure a good night's rest before the race. Last year, he did not reach Berwick but an hour or two before the event was run and he does not wish to make that mistake this year when he will be called upon to meet a field made up of the best the country affords.

The field—a whopping 48 entries—broke from the starting line and, in great contrast with the previous year, enjoyed mild fall weather and the support of a large crowd of spectators. Gregory was never far off the front as various runners took turns there, including Longman. At Foundryville bridge, Tarzan Brown charged to the front, but his attempt to wrestle the pace-setting chores from the others soon evaporated on the infamous hill, as documented in the *Morning Post*:

> Ellison (Tarzan) Brown, the Narragansett Indian from Westerly, R.I., who on the basis of past performances this season was the pre-race favorite, went out at the top of the more than a mile-long Foundryville Hill, a hill that has sounded the death knell to the Berwick Marathon hopes of many of the distance running games' greatest stars.

Les Pawson, the 1938 Boston Marathon champ and diamond winner in Berwick the previous year, soon joined Tarzan in what was for Pawson a rare DNF. Another familiar standout of races past—Eino Pentti—also called it a day without finishing.

Meanwhile, Gregory used the steep descent off Holser's Hill to take a 40-yard lead into the abrupt turn at Miller's Hotel. He was exactly 24 minutes flat at the 4-mile mark, with the hardest part of the course behind him. Longman—described in the *Post* write-up as a "bespectacled studious appearing wearer of the Maple Leaf"—ran second, but not far ahead of the likes of his fellow Canadian Duncan McCallum, Kelley, and a pair of Philadelphia's finest harriers, Joe Sullivan and Dick Blackwell.

As if a testament to the talent-laden field, some top runners in the second group were going to the well simply to stay in the top ten—a pack that included defending champ Pete Olexy, Bill Steiner, Porter, Penn State's Norm Gordon, and Canadian mainstays Ab Morton and Whitey Sheridan.

Gregory sped far ahead, oblivious to the jousting of the also-rans behind him. His arms swinging front to back in the fashion of a runner who has found his rhythm, Gregory gradually—like an accomplished poker player bolstering his chip stack—added to his lead through Kachinka's Hollow. Judging from the Post account, Gregory was—as we might put it in modern terms—"in the zone."

> He kept his eye straight ahead although the many turns on the course allowed him enough glances at the trailing Longman to keep him pretty well posted . . .
>
> In Kschinka's Hollow, a peaceful host today but a reigning terror a year ago when its treacherous ice was covered with falling snow, Gregory remained 40 yards in front of Longman, with Kelley then running in the third position he retained.

Gregory was not about to take any chances on a coin-flip sprint down Market Street. He arrived in Martzville with at least a 15-second cushion and promptly hammered the next 2 miles in 10 minutes and change. He raced home to snap the tape in 47:50—at the time that was fourth fastest in the era, behind a trio of Scotty Rankine's clockings. No doubt the great racing conditions, along with the incentive not to be second yet again, kept the educator concentrating on his task. As the *Morning Post* put it:

> The ideal weather, the cheering crowd be-decked in holiday finery and the largest field ever to respond to the starter's gun for the event all served as a background for little Lou and his steel-spring legs.

Longman ran a commendable second (his all-time-best Berwick) in 48:08, while Kelley—still in search of his first Berwick victory—found himself back in the diamonds with a solid third (48:40). Newcomer Joe Sullivan (4th, 48:45) bagged two diamonds—one for this top-four placing and the second gem for the honor of being the first Pennsylvanian. In addition, Sullivan paced the Shanahan Catholic Club to the first ever official team trophy, as Gordon (10th) and Philly's John Zack (15th) provided the necessary backup support.

McCallum (5th, 48:51) outlegged Blackwell (6th, 48:58), and they were followed more distantly by Steiner (7th, 49:38), Olexy (8th, 50:08), Porter (9th, 50:10), and Gordon (10th, 50:25.) Bloomsburg State's Don Karnes repeated as top local runner: The Epsy man finished 32nd (56:55), nearly a minute ahead of veteran Allen Parr of Mifflinville.

III
Tarzan Brown's Biggest Rebound
31st Berwick Marathon, November 28, 1940

In an era before Sports Channel, e-mail, or cell phone plans, word often traveled the old-fashioned way: letter.

In mid-November 1940 (with most of the world at war and America on the brink of joining in), race director Chiv MacCrea received a correspondence from none other than Ellison "Tarzan" Brown—the Narragansett Indian whose performances seemed to match the Berwick terrain: up and down with a lot of rough spots.

Perhaps Brown was writing to assure MacCrea that he was ready to rock and anxious to atone for his DNF blemish of 1939. In fact, Brown's 1938 race—in the blizzard, banging cold elbows with the likes of Pete Olexy and Lou Gregory en route to a diamond-winning third—was Tarzan's lone

Berwick performance that was worth letting out a jungle yell.

The rest of his races in Berwick? Lackluster, at best. Despite much pre-race hoopla insisting that he would give Rankine a tough race, Tarzan trudged along in 14th in his 1935 debut. Brown was back in 1937, but once again melted down on Foundryville Hill, as Rankine cruised on for his fifth straight win and a course record to boot.

Nevertheless, Tarzan Brown went on the record in 1940, stating he was in outstanding shape and ready for Berwick. Perhaps he needed to justify his expense money to a wary MacCrea. Regardless, the race director passed on the word to the local scribes, and the *Bloomsburg Morning Post* wrote:

> In a letter received from Brown yesterday he writes that he is in excellent form and is very confident of winning. His task will certainly be no easier . . . Not only must he defeat those who took his measure a year ago . . . but a number of new men . . .

The pre-race blurb then continued with:

> In the past season Brown has also broken 11 records. He is a temperamental runner and if he has one of his good days he is unbeatable, hitherto the "hill" has bothered him in the Berwick run but it would not be surprising to see him first across the finish line on the 28th, despite the fact that to do so he must defeat every outstanding distance man in this country and the race surely will be a struggle of giants.

If a "struggle of giants" smacks of a bit of hyperbole, the field (although again without Scotty Rankine) was quite competitive. Defending champ Gregory was back, as were Johnny Kelley and Les Pawson. Philadelphia sent a slew of good runners, led by Dick Blackwell who had placed fourth in 1939.

Already fully involved in World War II, the Canadian invasion was down to an Army of One: a dark-haired dapper little man with a Quebec-ois accent named Gerard Cote. Cote's first big victory was the 1940 Boston Marathon, and because he ran down Johnny Kelley *and* Robert "Scotty" Rankine en route to that win, Berwick fans gave him a lot of pre-race re-spect. Cote also beat defending Boston Marathon champ Brown in that race after—according to some accounts—a hungry Tarzan wolfed down two ice cream bars in the Newton Hills stretch and predictably got sick and was forced to drop out. (Brown, however, returned the favor and thumped Cote in the Salisbury Beach Marathon about six weeks later.)

Like all races, this one had to be settled on the running course and not in the newspapers. Most of the course was snow-covered, with patches of ice here and there, and a persistent nose-nipping wind out of the west. It wasn't nearly as bad as 1938, but it wasn't close to being pleasant.

Eleven men clustered about at the mile mark, almost as if it were a pre-agreed attempt to stay warm. The road was still bare until they reached the outskirts of town, the details noted in the *Morning Post:*

> Pawson took over the pace setting job . . . As they moved out of Berwick on the blacktop the highway was covered with snow, with a shallow film of ice in the car tracks. Up to that time the paving had been bare where the boys were running and those with spikes were having trouble. At the end of the paving Pawson, Blackwell, Brown and Kelley were in that order and a little later smiling Johnny Kelley had moved to second and "Tarzan" Brown was back to fourth and many believed he was already starting to fade out of the picture.

Dashing Through the Snow: Three-time Boston Marathon champ Les Pawson (Pawtucket vest) took over the pace-setting chores in 1940. But Tarzan Brown (10, running fourth) ran down Pawson on Market Street for a huge victory.

Photo courtesy of Harry's Sports

But rather than fade, Brown in fact kicked it up a notch and ran "the Hill"—his archnemesis (as the paper described it, "that killer of wind and hopes, the two-mile long grind . . .") in past Berwick races, smartly and smoothly. He moved up gradually, and by the Summer Hill churches, the two Rhode Island men were giving the rest of the field something to chase. Brown apparently felt strong enough that he bucked what the newspaper described as "a wind that spectators can testify was plenty cutting."

It was not a day to come back on the leaders. As the *Post* writer quipped: "It was slippery in the hollow and the runners resembled automobiles without chains as foot traction every once in a while skidded and made the runners appear as if they were on a tred [sic] mill."

Brown and Pawson essentially held their lead through Kachinka's Hollow and into Martzville, while Blackwell battled Kelley for third and fourth. Behind that quintet—which was looking more and more to be the diamond winners—New Yorker Joe Kleinerman and Joe Clark from Pittston went by the much-heralded Cote (ranked by many as a pre-race favorite) who eventually faded to tenth.

As they had in 1938's horrendous conditions, the down-in-numbers crowd deserted Market Street after the runners took off, but returned abruptly to catch the finish. Only two strides separated Les Pawson and Ellison "Tarzan" Brown as they swung onto Market Street, but—as the *Post* stated:

> . . . it was the moment the Indian had been waiting for ever since he started coming to Berwick and he not only kept his lead but lengthened it slightly to break the tape as the crowd did two things with the same motion, applauded the victor and got some circulation back into their hands.

And so, true to his pre-race letter, Tarzan Brown was both in great racing shape and confident of his success. He breasted the tape in 50:35, with the always game Pawson—racing his seventh Berwick—plowing in behind him 5 seconds later. Blackwell (3rd, 51:05) and Kelley (4th, 51:27) secured the two remaining diamonds. It was nearly a minute before Kleinerman trudged in 5th, about 30 seconds in front of Clark.

Don Karnes (19th, 62:32) repeated as the top local, as the Espy resident won for his third straight year. He was one spot behind Eugene James of Plymouth, who just happened to be the nephew of Pennsylvania's governor.

Among those who didn't finish were defending champ Lou Gregory and Daniel Kemple, the latter having been a top-notch college harrier at Bloomsburg.

From the give-this-guy-a-diamond-for-effort department comes this nugget via the *Morning Post:*

> Most hearty of the runners was Michael J. O'Hara of the Glencoe Athletic Club, New York, who came in thirteenth after he shed both shoes and socks somewhere along the course.

Well, it was the Berwick Marathon and nobody ever said it was going to be easy.

Downtown Tarzan Brown: Ellison "Tarzan" Brown did some of his best running in foul weather. Here he wins a wet Boston Marathon in 1939.

IV
Encore: Gregory vs. Kelley
32nd Berwick Marathon, November 27, 1941

There's no doubt that Lou Gregory of New York and Johnny Kelley of Arlington, Massachusetts, raced each other dozens and dozens of times, if not hundreds. In the full marathon, Johnny Kelley had better lifetime performances, but Gregory was no slowpoke at 26.2 miles, either, having second-place finishes in both the Yonkers and Boston marathons during his long career. That said, Gregory probably preferred distances between 10K and 30K—and the Berwick Marathon was somewhere in between. On November 17—just ten days prior to Berwick—Gregory handily won a 15-mile race in Queens, New York City, so he was ready to roll for the 32nd Berwick Marathon. Kelley had raced the arduous Yonkers Marathon on November 9, so the obvious question might have been less about readiness and more about recovery.

It was almost a foregone conclusion that Kelley and Gregory would battle at Berwick every Turkey Day, since both men were popular, long-standing entrants in the race. Gregory, however, had two first-place victories, and Kelley had a frustrating string of near-misses—something the 1935 Boston Marathon champ and 1936 Olympian was quite eager to correct.

Never one to hide his true feelings, Kelley had even been quoted (prior to the 1939 race when he tabbed Gregory and Tarzan Brown as the guys to beat) in the *Berwick Enterprise* emphatically stating: "I certainly have a warm spot in my heart for Berwick and outside of the Olympic and Boston marathons, there is no race in the world that I would rather win than Berwick."

Normally, Les Pawson would have been mentioned as a contender—especially on his strong runner-up effort to Tarzan Brown at Berwick the year before and his 1941 Boston Marathon victory. But Pawson—in a variation on the same curse that had and would plague some top Berwick runners for decades—got the worst of a vehicle mishap the previous month. Because of his bad luck, Pawson probably did quite well just to finish 7th at Berwick in 1941. As Johnny Kelley remembered it (in *Young at Heart*):

> In October of '41 we went to run an 18-mile race from Salem to Lawrence. I was in the lead at about 7 or 8 miles and I heard a noise behind me—poor Les was struck by an automobile. The car went by me and he was stretched out all cut up—the bumper of the car and went in so deep that it caused a serious injury—it used to ache like a toothache. From that day on he was never really the same.

With the war looming on the horizon (though nobody would have predicted the surprise attack on Pearl Harbor was a mere ten days away), the field for the 1941 race was conspicuously small. Only 22 men went to the line, with only two former winners—Gregory and Pete Olexy—among them. As the *Bloomsburg Morning Post* noted:

> Many distance runners, who always return for the Thanksgiving Day attraction, were not on hand, either because of

being in the service or because of employment in the defense industry.

By the Summer Hill churches, the race had already come down to Gregory vs. Kelley, with the rest of the field already strung out far behind the official cars that toured along with the front-runners.

The Berwick Marathon still drew an incredible crowd, especially on a relatively nice-weather day like this one. As usual the start and finish—plus "the Hill"—were the most popular places to watch. But even the most rural stretches drew dozens of spectators. Some of the fans were—as we would put it today—multitasking, as reflected in this nugget from the *Berwick Enterprise*:

> Several sportsmen who wanted to hunt yesterday selected locations near the course of the marathon and when the race approached they stopped hunting and joined the throngs of spectators who lined the course.

An accomplished downhill runner, Gregory broke to a 40-yard lead at the halfway mark, as he zoomed down the steep side of Hosler's Hill and rounded the curve at Miller's Hotel. Gregory maintained his lead through Kachinka's Hollow, but when he broke out onto Martzville Road the front-runner suddenly had company—but it wasn't from a fast-closing Kelley. As noted in the *Berwick Enterprise*:

> Officials who recalled how a dog paced Ritola on his record-breaking run in 1922 thought that the unusual incident might be repeated yesterday, for a white dog started chasing Gregory on Martzville Road. For a while, it looked like the dog might continue the run, but there was a moment's hesitation and the owner intervened.

Even without his canine escort, Gregory kept up the pace. In fact, the Millrose AA runner added slightly to his cushion over the final 2 miles to win in a nonplussed 48 minutes, 25 seconds. Kelley trotted in second, 25 ticks later, and probably well aware that he had once again—in this his eighth try—failed to snare the top diamond. After Kelley, John Coleman of Worcester, Massachusetts, held off Joe Kleinerman of the Millrose AA for third in 49:35.

Not only did Kelley once again have to settle for something less than first, but—as if to add a punctuation mark to his dismay—some hulking, overly exuberant fan on Market Street smacked him—hard—on the shoulder. The zealot allegedly was aiming for his back, but Kelley tried to be his usual cheerful self about it. As the *Berwick Enterprise* quoted Kelley after the race:

> "He meant well . . . Those things happen every once in a while. I wouldn't have minded so much, but the fellow came into the 'Y' to apologize and nearly crushed my hand with his grip! I then realized what a slap on the back he would have given me if I hadn't ducked out of the way."

Kelley wasn't so good, however, at hiding his disappointment at finishing second in one of his favorite races.

> "I really wanted to win this Berwick race . . . I ran in the Yonkers Marathon on November 9th, and it takes about a month to train for a shorter race after you've been training for longer ones. I really didn't feel right in training until last week, but then I thought that I had succeeded in getting down to this distance."

But that was racing. Lou Gregory was now a three-time Berwick champion—tying him with the likes of Tewanima and Kolehmainen—and, at least in theory, giving him a shot to move on Rankine's record five victories. As for Johnny Kelley, there were eight attempts—most of them valiant ones—but still no victory.

14

Kelley's Grand Shamrock Slam

Even taking into account that Johnny Kelley was well schooled in the Irish art of blarney, the Berwick Marathon was clearly one of his favorite races.

Kelley first ran Berwick in 1933 and placed a promising fourth. He was still ascending to the zenith of his running career. More than two decades later, the two-time Boston Marathon champ, and three-time US Olympian was still placing in the top ten in the Thanksgiving Day classic.

Because past Boston Marathon winners like Smilin' Jimmy Henigan and Clarence DeMar were some of Kelley's most important role models, he surely had heard of the Berwick Marathon years before he even toed the line on Market Street. Kelley (in his biography—*Young at Heart: The Story of Johnny Kelley—Boston's Marathon Man*) said: "Jimmy Henigan was a little gentleman. He was one of my idols when I was coming up . . . He was a big help to me and an inspiration."

Kelley was eager to follow the leads of the old-time Boston runners, and—like Henigan—he would become a fan favorite at Berwick. Back in Kelley's era, that would have meant giving races like Berwick—and Hamilton's Around the Bay—a "good go": Berwick and The Bay would have served as important measuring sticks for those with lofty Boston Marathon aspirations.

In addition to the race itself, Kelley soon made numerous friends and acquaintances in Berwick. For the vast majority of his Berwick visits, Kelley stayed as a guest with Robert Eshleman—a prominent member of the Berwick Marathon Association, a local nurseryman, and the runner who (as a high school lad) had finished second in the inaugural race in 1908. Over the years, Kelley mentioned to various people how much he always enjoyed the post-race dancing at Berwick's West End Park on Thanksgiving evening.

But look no farther than *Young at Heart* for more proof of his affinity with the Berwick event. Wrote authors Fred Lewis and Dick Johnson (in co-operation with Kelley) in their book, published in 1992:

Photo courtesy of Harry's Sports

On the Lookout: Kelley raced hard at Berwick, but after eight prewar attempts, the Irishman was still looking for a first-place diamond.

Johnny wasn't in the Army two weeks when he ran his first race as Private Kelley. He got a three-day furlough for Thanksgiving, which he used to compete in a nine-mile race in Berwick, Pennsylvania. He won the race for the first time in nine tries and was awarded a diamond ring, which he still wears on his pinkie . . .

The year that Private Kelley first won the Thanksgiving Day race was 1942, and it served as the start of his Berwick Marathon "grand slam"—a shamrock slam of four straight victories. Kelley also had a slew of near-misses over the Berwick grind—placing second five times. (Similarly, he placed second seven times at Boston, in addition to his wins in 1935 and 1945.) Like a lot of runners of his day, Kelley was attracted to the Berwick races because of the top-shelf prizes—diamond rings and watches. Over the course of his career, it seemed like Kelley could have opened his own shop with his race booty alone—as attested to in *Young at Heart*. Said Kelley of prizewinning in a pre-Nike, pre-running boom era:

"They did have good prizes at some of the races: diamond rings, record players, radios, silverware, suitcases . . . I won 22 diamond rings and 118 watches. I gave every member of my family a watch. I remember one time Les [Pawson, one of Kelley's friendly racing rivals] and I tied at the finish of a race in Worcester. I couldn't hear him coming up behind me because of all the cheering of the crowd. He caught me and we finished in a dead heat. We flipped a coin between two 21-jewel watches: a wrist watch and a pocket watch. I won, and took the wrist watch. We won everything but money."

Of course, aficionados of the Berwick Marathon race history know *exactly* where all those diamond rings came from.

I
Nine's the Charm
33rd Berwick Marathon, November 26, 1942

In a travel essay, the writer Jan Morris once quipped: "The luck of the Irish is a wish more than a characteristic."

No doubt Johnny Kelley—like Jimmy Henigan before him—would have nodded knowingly and relinquished a wry smile at that line. Eight times Kelley had raced at Berwick, but first place had eluded him each outing, including (at that point in time) *three* runner-up efforts (two to Rankine in the mid-'30s and one to Gregory in 1941) in previous Berwick Marathons.

How to move up a notch? That was the question. Defending champion Lou Gregory was back for the 1942 race and always a game opponent, although one whom Kelley typically beat over the 26.2-mile distance. But Gregory was always tough to top between 10K and 20 miles, and Kelley would have entertained no false hopes about that.

One of the first major hurdles Kelley had to face in the 1942 race was simply this: getting there. Just weeks into his military service, it took some string-pulling among army brass to arrange a three-day pass. The always affable Kelley—fairly well known because of his 1935 Boston Marathon victory and 1936 Olympic appearance—had his fans even among army officers. It didn't hurt his cause that he won the New England 10-mile championship race just the Sunday before Berwick and then presented his first-place medal to his company. (It does, however, make one wonder how it might feel to run a 10-mile race just days before taking on Berwick, but those working-class runners of Kelley's day apparently had no qualms about such challenges.)

Race day unfolded with fairly nice racing conditions—cloudy, mild, and breezy, according to Berwick Marathon records. Kelley's competition included a hard-charging, well-muscled young runner named Eddie Cook. Cook, who attended an agricultural college in Massachusetts, set a fast early pace down to Foundryville, with Penn State cross-country captain Norm Gordon and a new Nittany Lion standout named Curtis Stone running hard to keep contact.

Three-time winner and defending champ Lou Gregory also was close to the leaders, but went down with an injury at the bottom of Foundryville Hill—and suddenly the race took on a different spin. Gregory, certainly the favorite, was out. But the runners steamed on—knees lifting, arms pumping, and lungs ever-thirsty for oxygen—with Cook, Kelley, and Gordon virtually together, and Stone a few yards back.

Cook still clung to a slim lead at the top, down the slight grade, and up again to the top of Hosler's Hill. But Kelley made his big bid for the lead through Kachinka's Hollow, and Cook finally had to yield to his more experienced rival. In fact, Kelley had not been at all rattled by Cook's pushing of the early pace; it was something he had seen quite recently.

"Cook and those Penn State runners set a terrific pace," stated Kelley in the post-race *Berwick Enterprise* write-up. "I was pretty sure I could beat Cook because I had defeated him last Sunday at Boston in the 10-mile race. He started out in that race just like he did here, but I got him in the end."

Kelley led the rest of the way, cheered down Market Street en route to a victory that had taken the better part of a decade to nail down. He scooted home in 48 minutes, 55 seconds. About 90 yards back, the lanky Gordon (49:11) charged in just ahead of his teammate Stone (49:15). Millrose Athletic Association runner Bill Steiner moved up well to claim fourth (49:21), followed by Coleman and first Canadian runner Whitey Sheridan (in what was his highest Berwick place ever). Cook—suffering the effects of his brash, crash-and-burn strategy over a grueling course he had never raced on before (and never did again)—struggled home in seventh.

Tarzan Brown—never really digging out from a somewhat nonchalant start—settled for eighth, just ahead of Baltimore's Don Heiniche and the recent Yonkers Marathon champ Fred McGlone. Despite Gregory's DNF, Kelley's first win came against a deep and potentially talented field of footracers. His post-race interviews were brimming with gratitude and graciousness toward his opponents.

"This is one race where age really helped," exclaimed the 35-year-old Kelley in the *Enterprise*. "I had the advantage of experience, especially experience on this course. Those fellows could really run!"

There was no mistaking how much Kelley wanted his first Berwick victory, however.

"I did want to win this one before quitting and I hope to get back next year," said Private Kelley. And then he admitted: "You remember how disappointed I was last year, but this sort of makes up for it."

Young Lions: Curt Stone (2) was a promising young runner in 1942. He's pictured here with PSU teammate Norm Gordon (3), '42 winner Johnny Kelley, and the fourth diamond winner Bill Steiner. Stone would win in 1949.

Lou Gregory, who had a lot to do with Kelley's disappointment the previous year, was somewhat philosophical about his fortunes this time. "It's all in the game," Gregory told reporters. "Some days everything is just right, and you can't help winning. When things aren't right, there's not much you can do about it."

Keeping in mind the "hope to get back next year" part, one of Kelley's first actions after winning Berwick was to dash off telegrams with the news to his father back in Boston, but also his post commander Colonel Winfield H. Shrum. Shrum, along with a Captain Haagar, had showed sharp interest in Kelley's running career, and news of his Berwick victory would have been almost as eagerly received as it was dispatched.

With the war ever-present, the runners who weren't already in uniform were just waiting for the call-up and were cramming in races. So just two days after the quad-pulverizing Berwick race, the young Penn State guys Norm Gordon and Curt Stone found themselves racing on a mud-sloppy cross-country course in Newark, New Jersey's, Weequahic Park in the National AAU meet, representing Philly's Shanahan Catholic Club.

"I have a hard time believing how I could have done all that racing in November of '42," recalls Curt Stone, who (now a young 85 years old) resides in his boyhood village of Brooklyn, Pennsylvania. "We raced at the IC4A cross-country championships. Then we won the NCAA cross-country title at Michigan State in '42 and I believe that was Penn State's first national title in any sport. Then I must have run Berwick and then the national AAU race where we won the team title for Shanahan."

Stone remembers the roads at Berwick as "really rough, the stones were large and stuck up sharply." Whatever the rigors of the Berwick course, a young Stone—posing with Gordon, race winner Kelley, and the fourth diamond winner Bill Steiner—looks none the worse for the winner in a post-race picture that was most likely snapped in the lobby of the official race headquarters, the Berwick Hotel.

As if a testament to youthful regeneration, Gordon (7th) and Stone (8th)—just 48 hours after racing Berwick—supported Shanahan's Dave Williams (3rd) and Jerry Carver (5th) en route to the National AAU cross-country team title.

The fifth man for the winning Shanahan squad was a skinny, precocious high school kid from New Jersey who placed 9th. His name was Harris Browning Ross.

In the near future, Ross was bound for the US Navy, then—after the war— Villanova on the GI bill. In the long term, he was destined to make two US Olympic teams and win a record number of Berwick Marathons.

II
King Kelley Retains Crown
34th Berwick Marathon, November 23, 1943

If it can be said that Berwick can be won "with ease" (and that's exactly how the Associated Press blurb *did* describe it), then Johnny Kelley's 1943 Berwick Marathon victory probably fit the bill. In the middle of World War II, the field was one of its smallest—a mere dozen starters, and one of those was the "vertically challenged" local lad "Shorty" Balazs, who was in it exclusively to finish the course.

The veteran Kelley—the monkey of *not* winning now off his back since snapping the jinx the previous year—ran near the front pack down Market. Around the mile mark, Kelley grabbed control of the pace, and he led the way down to the base of the mountain. Then he promptly added to his cushion all the way up Foundryville Hill. Behind him, Ab Morton—now a member of the Royal Canadian Air Force—carved out an equally solid position in second. Morton—who typically represented the Galt Track Club out of Galt, Ontario—was arguably enjoying his greatest year of running, having won Hamilton's important Around the Bay (around 19 miles) in October.

Kelley churned on, enjoying some rare miles at the front without pressure, and acknowledging fans along the course, since—like Jimmy Henigan and Tom Barden before him—he was a popular Irish runner whose gregarious personality attracted much backing from local observers.

Kelley's special shoes—of which the local papers made note of during the war years—would have had him feeling "light" as he clipped around the familiar course in cool, clear weather. As Kelley once told the *Berwick Enterprise:*

> "They weigh only 5½ ounces a piece and I wear them only
> in the big races, and I wear them only in the big races because
> it's hard to get another pair like them. They're light as a feather,
> and when I'm running I hardly know I have them on."

Kelley—special shoes, special Irish grin—snapped the tape on Market Street in 48 minutes, 47 seconds. You could have enjoyed a small glass of beer before the next man arrived. Ab Morton checked in about 2 minutes later, a distant runner-up, but well ahead of Ed Shephard, who was representing the Todd Shipbuilding Corporation from Gorham, Maine. In his highest career finish at Berwick, Baltimore's Don Heiniche (who represented the White Horse Club) placed fourth, just ahead of New York's Bill Steiner.

Back in ninth place was Boston Athletic Association runner John "Jock" Semple. The Scottish-born Semple—famous for his sometimes irascible temper—would one day ascend to high official rank in conducting the Boston Marathon. In 1967, Jock became infamous—worldwide—when he attempted to tear off Kathrine Switzer's number during her famous run from Hopkinton to Back Bay. In typical Jock logic he reportedly said (delivered in his trademark Scottish burr): "I am not prejudiced against women; they just can't run in my race!"

Although the field was a small one, it proved unusually worthy: Everyone who started the race finished the course. That included Berwick's own stubby-legged Shorty Balazs, his motivation no doubt increased by a small wager that claimed he could not go the distance. Shorty—an orphan who was something of the town mascot—*did* complete the course; it just took him a very long time.

Photo courtesy of Berwick Marathon Association

Kelley Wins! The Berwick crowds loved Johnny Kelley—and by all accounts he loved the race through the Briar Creek Hills.

III
Rankine vs. Kelley
35th Berwick Marathon, November 23, 1944

It might well have been Kelley's back-to-back victories that brought Robert "Scotty" Rankine back to Berwick after a seven-year sabbatical. Although the two men were quite friendly, there was always a keen rivalry between the Canadians and Americans—with Boston, Berwick, and Yonkers (and less frequently, races in Canada, such as Hamilton's Around the Bay) serving as venues to prove whether the Maple Leaf or Stars & Stripes ran supreme.

Rankine, who held both the Berwick course mark and the race record for career victories (five), was a force from the Great White North that Kelley was quite familiar with and never would have underestimated. Although Rankine had not run Berwick since 1937 and was certainly past his best running years, he was far from retired. For example, Scotty had won the Around the Bay event in Hamilton six of the last eight years, including the 1944 event that had been held just a month before Berwick.

The conditions on race day were windy, cloudy, and cold. Rankine, on leave from the Royal Canadian Air Force, tucked in with Kelley—his familiar rival—as the field headed down to Foundryville. Although these two experienced Berwick veterans certainly would have ranked as strong co-favorites, Forrest Efaw—former Oklahoma A&M runner and several times the national AAU steeplechase champion—would have warranted some concern. Efaw (who was on leave from the Naval Training Center in Sampson, New York), however, was getting his first taste of "the Hill."

In addition to Rankine, the Canadians also had strong entries with the likes of Ab Morton (also in the RCAF) and Walt Fedorick of the Hamilton Olympic Club.

But by halfway, the race was down to Rankine and Kelley, neither of whom was pushing the pace too hard—perhaps because of the wind, or simply because they were saving something for the finish. As it turned out, Rankine couldn't quite deliver the thunder down Market Street as he had so often in the previous decade; Kelley pulled away to his third straight Berwick win in a rather modest 49:20. Rankine scooted home 15 seconds later, far ahead of Fedorick (3rd, 50:05) and Efaw (4th, 51:00). Morton placed fifth (51:25), holding off Baltimore's Don Heinicke by 10 ticks.

Perhaps the surprise of the race was 7th-place finisher Jack St. Clair, running for the Nativity Club out of Philadelphia. St. Clair—just 17—collected the Pennsylvania prize diamond as top finisher from the Keystone State.

Led by Efaw—and supported by marathoner Fred McGlone (9th), Robert Donnally (11th) and Jock Semple (12th), the Naval Track Club from Sampson won the team title.

Charles Bedio of Berwick was the first local to finish, placing 16th in a field of 18 finishers in 1 hour, 5 minutes, 37 seconds. Matthew "Shorty" Balazs was the only other Berwickian in the race. Shorty finished last, but—as reported in the *Bloomsburg Morning Press*—"got the biggest hand of the day."

IV
Kelley Goes for Four
36th Berwick Marathon, November 23, 1945

For Johnny Kelley, 1945 was the best of times and the worst of times—to paraphrase the start of a famous novel.

Ten years after capturing his first Boston Marathon, the 37-year-old Kelley revisited the winners' circle in Back Bay in April 1945. Kelley charged all the way from fifth place in the second half of the race, but was far enough ahead at the end that the Irishman blew kisses to the crowd.

A few weeks later he won the Medford, Massachusetts, race for the seventh time, but those who knew Kelley well could tell he was somewhat troubled and distracted. His somber mood was not without explanation: His brother Edward—an airman in the Pacific theater of the war—had been reported missing. Finally, in June, word came from the US War Department confirming the death of Staff Sergeant Edward Emmett Kelley. Johnny had written his younger brother a letter describing his Boston Marathon victory, but the letter was returned to him unopened.

Despite his grief—or perhaps because of it—Kelley plowed on with his running season. In late October, he scored a rare American victory in Canada's most competitive race—winning the Around the Bay event in Hamilton, Ontario. (Kelley won the 19-miler a mere 27 seconds ahead of Rankine, while Whitey Sheridan snagged third.) A win at Berwick, then, would give Kelley an unprecedented triple in one calendar year—the "three B's" of Boston, Bay, and Berwick.

The field, however, would be highly competitive. Oklahoma native Forrest Efaw (still stationed with the US Navy in Maryland) was back and now well aware what "the Hill" meant. Rankine, pumped for a rematch with Kelley, also was entered. Perhaps with a wee bit of exaggeration, race director Chiv MacCrea was quoted in the *Morning Post* to the tune of: "It's a wise man indeed who would attempt to pick the winner or even name one of the first three men."

In addition to Rankine, many of the other consistently tough Canadian runners—such as Ab Morton, Milt Wallace, and Whitey Sheridan—were set to return. According to the *Morning Post,* they were also bringing along some special support from up north.

> Many of the Canadian harriers will be accompanied by their wives. Some of them will be making their first trip to the United States. Some of the ladies are as enthusiastic as the runners themselves, fans have noted.

If the Americans needed another top gun to support Kelley against the herd of galloping Canadians, than that man appeared to be Lou Gregory.

Gregory had not raced at Berwick since 1942, but—according a story documented in the *Morning Post*—the event was never far from his mind. While stationed in Hawaii in 1945, Gregory—a US Navy lieutenant—competed in a rather large all-military track meet. Bob Kisbaugh, a marine from Berwick, thought he recognized the perpetually fit-looking distance runner and pushed through the crowd to get a better look. Sure enough, Kisbaugh realized this was Lou Gregory, the man he had watched win the Thanksgiving Day race in his own hometown.

"You don't know me, but I know you!" Kisbaugh shouted to Gregory.

Naturally curious, Gregory responded: "Who are you?"

Kisbaugh said: "Well, I'm from a small town in Pennsylvania and I saw you run there!"

Gregory immediately enthused: "Berwick! You tell the fans I'll be there to race on Thanksgiving Day!"

As Kisbaugh related to the papers, Gregory easily won his military race that day in Hawaii. And now, true to his word, he was lined up once again at Berwick. As a three-time race champion, Lou Gregory—although he now limped when he walked from a bad car accident—could not be discounted as a contender.

In addition to past champions Kelley, Rankine, and Gregory, there was yet another former star on the entry list. The prospects of picking—and for more than a few Berwick race fans this still meant betting on—the top finishers in 1945 event didn't get any easier when Ellison "Tarzan" Brown opted in. The newspapers loved it, of course, as the *Morning Post* noted:

> Shouts of "Tarzan's back!" began echoing among Berwick Marathon fans as the entry of the outstanding Indian runner— Ellison "Tarzan" Brown—was announced by Director C. N. MacCrea . . .

> The presence of Brown indicates that the racing dope sheet may be upset and the Berwick fans who knew of Tarzan's ability are counting on him to lead the pack home.

And then, as if to quantify such grandiose predictions, the article laced in a cautionary thread at its close:

> A victory in the Turkey Day classic would do much to restore Brown's standing which has suffered during the past several seasons through his laxity in keeping in physical condition for marathons.

A stiff wind slapped around the runners as they headed out Market on race day. The front-runners were still close together on the run down to Foundryville. But then Kelley put all speculation to rest with a major move that started at the bottom of the infamous climb. As the *Morning Post* described: "It was a timely strategy and staged at such an unexpected moment that he widen the gap rapidly . . ."

None of the other runners was able to match Kelley's attack, and by the Summer Hill churches he had forged to a sizable lead that only got bigger through Kachinka's Hollow. Efaw and Rankine hunkered down to fight for second . . . Tarzan Brown was way back, already relegated to also-ran status . . . and Lou Gregory dropped out.

Kelley was never really pushed—unless one counted the pushing from the wind, which served only to slow his overall time. Kelley had time to wave his clenched fists above his head—like a victorious boxer—as he covered the final yards to the tape, crossing in 49 minutes, 16 seconds. He had his fourth straight Berwick win—a grand slam—if not in a lightning-quick time.

There weren't any great battles for the next few places, either, as the runners came in almost evenly spaced: Forrest Efaw—although slowed by a side stitch for much of the race—charged home in second (50:02), while Rankine settled for third (50:24), and Morton placed fourth (51:06). Baltimore's Don Heinicke finished fifth (51:36) and Whitey Sheridan—in one of his highest finishes—placed sixth (52:47).

As if to add emphasis to the postwar boom, the Berwick field of 28 featured a runner from Alaska, Mainhardt Brendt (7th, 53:50), and another from the West Indies, Oswald Kissoon of Trinidad (12th, 55:23).

The Berwick crowd reserved its most thundering applause for the first local finisher—Berwick High School runner Morris Doty (23rd, 1:04:32). Shorty Balazs finished 28th and last, but his 1:09:04 was his fastest time in three Berwick runs.

Finish Lines: Johnny Kelley and Don Heinicke had both qualified for the 1940 US Olympic Marathon team, but as World War II ignited, the Games were canceled.

15

The New Fast Gun

I
Brownie's First Berwick
37th Berwick Marathon, November 28, 1946

The Berwick Marathon was such a Thanksgiving Day tradition that apparently some people decided skybox seats—literally—might be the way to go as the 37th running of the classic footrace awaited the starting pistol. As the *Berwick Enterprise* reported:

> Yesterday's Marathon had more aerial viewers than any previous race. A number of planes from Center Airport and from Berwick Airport were aloft throughout the race, keeping a tab on runners along the course and at the field.

While the airborne spectators might have enjoyed an artful overview as the field of 30-plus runners snaked their way around the hilly course, they would have missed the close-up jousting of the lead runners and—as it turned out—one of the most surprising upsets in the history of the race. Regardless, it was a good day for flying—be it in the air or on the course—the late fall weather clear and brisk and invigorating.

Enter the ambush express: one Harris Browning Ross, a 22-year-old Villanova freshman (after a stint in the military like many young men of his era), unarguably to become one of the most important forces on the American running scene and absolutely the most dominating runner in the history of the Berwick Marathon.

Super Nova: As a young Villanova runner, former navy man Ross Browning burst on the Berwick scene with immediate impact.

When the 1946 race went to the Market Street starting line, nobody—especially Ross himself—would have predicted his victory. But once he won, Ross would rate favorite or at least co-favorite status for more than a decade—essentially the boss man of Berwick.

Ross rightly considered Johnny Kelley—coming in with four consecutive Berwick victories—and Canadian standout Walt Fedorick (having notched 10 wins in his last dozen races in the Great White North) as the co-favorites. Kelley, however, reportedly warned that Ross—a resident of Woodbury, New Jersey—would be a factor in the race before it was over. It proved to be an on-target prediction.

Nevertheless, as the runners labored up Summer Hill toward the lofty churches, it was Fedorick who led the charge, followed not far back by Kelley, Canadian star Scotty Rankine (who, although past his prime, took the lead briefly at the top), and New Yorker Bill Steiner. Ross was a few steps back, running with another Canadian, Ab Morton. Although it *had* been done before (first by Dick Detwiler in the 1930 race), knowledgeable Berwick fans still knew it to be a rare deed for someone *not* leading at the Summer Hill churches to find a way to win.

Ross waited longer than that. It wasn't until after the runners jostled through Kachinka's Hollow that the wiry young man from South Jersey suddenly surged to the forefront. Probably it was little consolation for Kelley to see his pre-race foreshadowing of Ross's running prowess proving to be true . . . unfolding before the veteran marathoner's eyes. Ross had relatively long legs and a stride to match, versus Kelley's classic marathon shuffle—and the young man began to slowly heat up the pace.

Finally Ross burst into the lead about 300 yards from the Martzville turn. At first it was only about three yards but Ross kept up the killing pace as if he was just starting out in the hill and dale chase.

Past the golf club and en route to North Berwick, Ross gradually added to his lead. Fedorick, meanwhile, attached himself to Kelley, as if both men were forced to acknowledge that the race was looking increasingly to be one for second and not first. Ross held a 40-yard edge turning onto Market Street, and soon he banked a right onto 11th Street, since this edition of the Marathon—for the first time—was going to finish in the packed football stadium at Crispin Memorial Field. The runners scampered along the sidelines just as the second half was about to get under way.

Inside the gate . . . where about 4,200 fans watched the football game and the marathon finish in one of the greatest sports innovations Berwick has ever seen, Ross was leading Kelley by about 60 yards . . .

Ross raced on unbothered to about a 75 yard lead and crossed the finish line nearly as "fresh as a daisy," for one of the biggest upsets in marathon racing history. He had beaten the best in the business . . .

Ross's time of 48 minutes, 35 seconds was a "new record," but one with something of an asterisk, since—with the Crispin Memorial Field finish—it was a slightly different course over the last half mile. He finished a solid 100 yards ahead of Fedorick (2nd, 48:50)—who ran down Kelley (3rd, 48:56)—for runner-up honors.

The popular Scotty Rankine powered home fourth (good for a diamond ring award), followed by Morton, Steiner, and Hamilton Olympic Club warhorse Whitey Sheridan in 7th.

Philadelphian Jack St. Clair, representing the US Army, placed 8th, was followed by Don Heinicke of Baltimore. (St. Clair also snagged the Pennsylvania diamond award when it was discovered that although Ross attended Villanova, he actually lived in the Garden State). Herman Goffberg (Penn State runner and 1952 Olympian) placed 11th, and was sandwiched between two game coal region runners—Joe Clark of Pittston (10th) and Robert McCormick of Mahoney City. The first Berwick runner to cross the line was high school boy Ben West (24th, 1:01.9). West snapped up *two* gold watches for his efforts—one for first local, one for first high school finisher.

II
Ross Repeats
38th Berwick Marathon, November 27, 1947

Ross was back to defend his title in 1947, but needless to say this time he entered the race as the favorite. Jack St. Clair, who several years later would star at Penn State on the 1950 NCAA championship team, had other ideas and took the pace out hard. He led at the bottom of Foundryville Hill and then promptly attacked the ascent with enthusiasm. St. Clair's brave charge was not missed by the local sports scribes:

> St. Clair, a Philadelphia boy who was counted upon strongly
> for a good fight for the state title, fooled the race fans along the
> way with his brilliant showing . . . Three-quarters of the way up
> the hill St. Clair widened his lead to ten yards over Ross.

St. Clair led at the top of Summer Hill, with Scotty Rankine trailing him in second; a few steps behind him labored the ever-enduring Johnny Kelley, with Ross an inch off his shoulder. But this time Ross did not wait as long to apply the pressure: He surged into the lead on the slight downhill after the churches, kept the pace hot up Hosler's Hill, and then added to it on the steep descent to the halfway mark. By the time the men were racing through Kachinka's Hollow, the Villanova standout—now more experienced—had carved out a 40-yard advantage.

In Ross's wake, Kelley chipped away at the fast-starting St. Clair, moving into second, and the Yanks in turn were chased by a trio of Maple Leaf men—veteran Rankine, the 1946 runner-up Walt Fedorick, and Ab Morton.

But in the end, Ross won easily—even if his final cushion over Kelley was about 100 yards—as he sailed into the football stadium just as the first half was ending.

> Running a strong race all the way, Ross never looked tired
> and he finished with a lot of pep before nearly 5,000 fans as-
> sembled at Crispin Memorial Field to watch a combination grid
> game and the running of the 38th annual Marathon.

Ross's time was 48 minutes, 37 seconds—just 2 ticks shy of his debut victory. Kelley churned in at 48:52, with St. Clair gamely clinging to third in 49:02. The Canucks held the next three slots in the field of 36 finishers, with Rankine (4th, 49:12), who snared the last diamond award, then Fedorick (5th, 49:27), and Morton (6th, 50:09). John Leiss of Washington DC (7th), Don Heinicke of Baltimore, Joe Clark of Pittston, and Walter J. Berger of Binghamton, New York, followed, rounding out the top ten.

Photo courtesy of Michael Sheridan

Elmer and the Saint: Elmer Guy, an old-time runner from the Jeanette (Pennsylvania) Harriers, finished 9th in 1945. Behind Guy is Jack St. Clair—Penn State runner—who bravely led Browning Ross up to Summer Hill in 1947.

III
Triple Threat—Ross Rolls On
39th Berwick Marathon, November 25, 1948

If Browning Ross was something of a surprise in his initial running, and a strong contender/slight favorite in his second outing, then by 1948, it would have been virtually impossible to find someone to bet against him finishing first in the 39th running of the Berwick Marathon.

Why? Because in the previous year, Ross had only added to his list of accomplishments and built upon his racing experience. Ross's résumé now included an NCAA steeplechase championship which he won in the spring for Villanova, and then followed up with an appearance in the 1948 London Olympic Games in the summer. In London, Ross made the 3000-meter steeplechase final and placed seventh (in 9:23.2) overall. Not necessarily expected to make the finals (he had been third in the US trials), he was at the front with two laps to go when the Scandinavian runners swept by him.

In addition, the ever-popular Johnny Kelley—Ross's chief challenger—wasn't getting any younger. Kelley was still considered a strong, consistent runner, but the Boston Irishman certainly could not be expected to match Ross in terms of finishing speed, in the unlikely event that they even found themselves running head-to-head in the final mile.

In terms of mystery, then, the 1948 Berwick Marathon had little to offer. Ross took control early in the race and breezed on to his "triple" victory—the usual cast of contenders jousting for the also-ran spots behind him. Ross's time—without being pushed in the late miles—was his best so far, clocking 48:24. About 200 yards back ran Kelley, the never-say-die Irishman in 49:04. The next three finishers were similarly spaced: Louis White of Philadelphia (3rd, 49:21), Scotty Rankine (4th, 49:51), and Jack St. Clair (5th, 50:12). The Canadians secured the team title, as Rankine (who once again snatched the last diamond), Ab Morton (8th) and Arthur Wilson (17th) combined for the winning total of 32 points.

Of course, as events would unfold, 1949 would be a different story for Berwick's newest three-time champion.

Finish Lines: Jack "The Saint" St. Clair went on to coach at Temple University for many years. His burley, bear-like physique in those years veiled his past as a svelte runner on Penn State's NCAA Championship winning cross-country team and a diamond winner at the Berwick Marathon.

16

The Lion's Share

I

A Fast Rolling Stone
40th Berwick Marathon, November 24, 1949

Just went it must have looked like nobody could stop H. Browning Ross's annual "run" on Berwick Marathon diamonds, along came a couple of Lions—former Nittany Lions, that is, as in Penn State running stars Horace Ashenfelter and Curtis Stone. Ross knew these rivals well, and had matched strides with them many times over in cross-country and track races. He also was an Olympic teammate of Stone's in 1948 and would be again (along with Ashenfelter) in 1952. Ross was well aware both Stone and Ashenfelter were fierce competitors and tough, dedicated runners.

Due largely to his 1952 Olympic steeplechase gold medal performance (in a World Record at the time of 8:45.4), Ashenfelter is relatively well-known to followers of American distance running. Stone, perhaps, is a man less in the historical limelight. However, Curt Stone made three US Olympic teams (1948, 1952, 1956), won numerous AAU titles on the track, plus raced to a US cross-country title in 1947. And, in a rarely accomplished feat, Stone would (in 1952) win both the 5000 and 10,000-meter races at the US Olympic Trials (the so-called "Woolworth's Double").

Indeed, according to Herman Goffberg, his late Penn State and Olympic teammate, Stone might have snagged an Olympic medal at the 1948 London Games, but a cloud burst prior to the 5000-meter final worked against him. "The runner in front of him kicked mud up on his glasses and he couldn't see," Goffberg recalled in an interview (with Penn State's *Daily Collegian*) in the fall of 2000. Nevertheless, Stone managed a sixth place in the 5000 final (narrowly won by Belgium's Gaston Reiff over a fast-closing Czech star Emil Zatopek in what was then an Olympic record 14:17.6) in a quality time of 14:39.4.

Regardless, with Stone and Ashenfelter, Ross knew he was going to have a run for his money—or, more accurately, his first-place diamond and a chance at a fourth straight Berwick title.

Ed Hoffman Jr. of Berwick had a lot to do with the appearances of Stone and Ashenfelter. Hoffman knew both men well; not only because Hoffman was once the Nittany Lion track team manager, but also because all three men were fraternity brothers at the Sigma Alpha Epsilon house. "When I was in school," Hoffman recalls, "Curt Stone was known as the runner who looked like a college professor."

Understandably, Hoffman couldn't resist urging the former Penn State runners to "run for the diamonds." He even helped secure "expense money" for Stone and Ashenfelter from Chiv MacCrea to cover their travel and lodging costs. (In a recent interview Hoffman recalled: "The word was that if you wanted expense money from Chiv MacCrea then you were wise to get it *before* the race rather than after.")

The weather broke clear, cold and breezy on race day 1949, so Stone—especially racing in a decade when Berwick's roads were paved—wasn't going to have mud kicked up on his glasses. A field of 45 men—considered rather large in its era—toed the Market Street start line.

Perhaps partly for his role in securing the fleet-footed Lions, Hoffman copped one of the best seats "in the house"—a place in starter J. Howard Remley's car.

"J. Howard Remley had a yellow Chevy convertible," remembers Hoffman. "Once he started the race, he, his wife, Chiv MacCrea and Chiv's wife would hop in the car and ride around the course to see the runners. They let me go with them. I think I remember seeing Bill Ashenfelter—Horace's brother (and a national-class runner himself)—cheering for Horace, Curt Stone and Browning Ross near the halfway mark, at the turn."

As if they were some sort of fleet-footed scouting party, a small group of five—among them the now-42-year-old marathon warhorse Johnny Kelley—broke away from the main pack. In addition to Ross, the pair of former Penn State men, and Kelley, Luther Burdelle of Philadelphia kept contact through the early miles—but he was destined to a distant fifth place finish by the end of the race.

In a recent interview, Horace Ashenfelter—now a "young" 85-years-old—said, "I don't remember a lot about Berwick because I only ran there one time. I do remember Curt saying, 'Wherever Brownie goes, *you* go . . . .' And that's exactly what we did. Oh, yes . . . And I do remember the Hill. It reminded me of some of the cross-country races we used to run in

Schenley Park in Pittsburgh."

Only longer, of course . . . As the leaders smacked into the heart-thumping ascent toward the Summer Hill churches, *The Berwick Enterprise* noted:

> Ashenfelter, appearing in his first race here, turned in a magnificent performance. The rawboned athlete was captain of the Nittany Lion cross-country team last year and he poured on the rugged element going up the Foundryville Hill and kept it that way until the end of the race.

Stone, of course, had plenty of the so-called "rugged element" himself, but he was bidding his time. Stone passed Kelley, the tough little old Irishman, going up the hill, and kept contact with Ashenfelter and Ross. Then Stone—as if taking a page from Ross's book of tactics when the Villanova man prevailed in his first two Berwick races—roared to the front through the small, wave-like hills of Kachinka's Hollow. But Ross grudgingly grabbed a step in front near Martzville. The trio arrived in North Berwick appearing strong, and then Ashenfelter—a man destined to be an Olympic champion and world-record holder in the steeplechase—surged into the lead.

Meanwhile, more than 6,500 "race-football fans" awaited the arrival of the marathon leaders at Crispin Field. They were not disappointed, as the top three men bolted onto the track within seconds of each other, but Stone gave no ground in the final loop around the cinders—bulling past Ashenfelter and bursting across the line in 47 minutes, 19 seconds. Ashenfelter sprinted in next, just three ticks back, but well he had to, since defending champ Ross raced across the line four seconds later. Three men in the space of a mere eight seconds!

"I was surprised that Brownie didn't go with us," remembers Stone (who, like his friend "Nip" Ashenfelter, is 85-years "young") who resides in his boyhood town of Brooklyn, Pennsylvania, Wyoming County. "Brownie had 48-second quarter-mile speed. He was fast enough to run a leg on the mile relay in some big meets if he was needed."

A minute later, the popular veteran Kelley labored in—and then it was 90 seconds more until Burdelle could claim fifth.

As if to testify just how tough this starting field was, Robert "Scotty" Rankine was kept out of the diamonds for the first time, placing a commendable sixth. Third in 1948, Louis White, now representing the Boston Athletic Association, placed ninth.

Stone's speedy clocking evoked discussion of whether or not he would have broken the traditional Market Street finish record of 47:16 set by

Rankine back in 1937. Some of the race "wags" speculated that the stadium track finish, with its slightly slower turns (as opposed to a straight-arrow finish on Market) might have cost Stone the trio of precious ticks. Nevertheless, Stone—who represented the Shanahan Catholic Club out of Philadelphia—doubtlessly was pleased with his twin-win diamond performance. He snared one diamond for the overall victory, of course, and the second for being the first Pennsylvania resident across the line.

One of the few honors that escaped Stone that day was first-place team laurels. That title went to the Penn Athletic Club (19 points), with Ashenfelter, Ross, and 14th place finisher Tom Sander—who was sandwiched between Canadian Ab Morton and Ted Dobroski, a soldier out of Fort Bragg, North Carolina, in the highly competitive field. The Hamilton Olympic Club—with Selwyn Jones (7th), Whitey Sheridan (10th), and Walt Fedorick (11th), captured team runner-up honors with 28 points, one better than the Shanahan C.C.

With a name that could serve as a description of the 9-mile course, Rollin Hill—a Berwick High School runner—was the first town resident to finish. Hill clocked a respectable 59:30 and finished 50 seconds ahead of Hershel Hileman, who in turned was chased by another Berwick resident runner, Sheldon Grassley. Like Stone, Hill "double-dipped" at the awards presentation; he collected a gold watch for first Berwickian, and a second one as the first high school finisher.

Finish Lines: Horace Ashenfelter still does some light jogging and walking these days, in addition to (on his good days) shooting a round of golf in the low 80s. His gold medal from the 1952 Helsinki Olympic Games is on display at the Penn State All-Sports Museum located near Beaver Stadium in State College. Ashenfelter gave his medal to the museum with the stipulation that his grandchildren can take it for show-and-tell if they wish.

In addition to his Olympic gold (when he defeated Russian Vladimir Kazantsev, the previous world record holder, charging ahead over the final barrier), Ashenfelter won numerous US titles in indoor and outdoor track, and two US cross-country titles (1955-56). His brother Bill Ashenfelter—also an Olympic qualifier in the steeplechase—won the US cross-country crown in 1951. Ashenfelter resides in Glen Ridge, New Jersey, a town that hosts the Ashenfelter 8K Classic every Thanksgiving Day!

Horace "Nip" Ashenfelter: He won the 1952 Olympic steeplechase gold in World Record time. In the 1949 Berwick Marathon, he had the lead until teammate Curt Stone passed him on the Crispin Field track.

17

The Second Streak

I
Browning Ross's Record Run
41st Berwick Marathon, November 23, 1950

Browning Ross was back at Berwick for the 41st running, but the former Nittany Lions—Stone and Ashenfelter—were not. There was, however, no lack of competition, as the Boston Athletic Association sent down Jesse Van Zant. Along with Van Zant, the young Canadian runner—Selwyn Jones—was back and as would soon become evident, fast-improving.

Like many marathoners that put the Pennsylvania event on their race schedule, Berwick almost served as fall speed training; 9-miles up and down was certainly solid prep work for the Boston Marathon, even if that famous event was still months—and a long winter—away.

Van Zant—like Clarence DeMar before him—was definitely more of a pure marathon runner. In 1948, Van Zant had placed third in the Boston Marathon in 2:36 (one place and a full minute ahead of Johnny Kelley). His best all-time performance arguably came in 1951: Van Zant won the US Marathon title with a 2:37:12 clocking over the notoriously rough Yonkers Marathon course.

Marathon specialist or not, Van Zant opted for a headstrong strategy at Berwick. When the 1950 race blasted off the Market Street starting line, he looked more like an aggressive miler. He pushed right to the front, with only the teenager Jones game enough to tag along (almost) with him. Meanwhile, Ross—now a sage traveler over the bumps and thumps of the Berwick grind—cautiously glided along in third. As the local *Berwick Enterprise* described:

> Van Zandt (sic), wearing a woolen cap which he tossed away at the mile and a half mark, led the field with a strong and determined start, just as the experts predicted he would. His first mile was designed to put the field to the hardest test possible . . . At first he was challenged by Jones who was only about ten yards behind and keeping a fast pace. Ross trailed by about 30 yards in third place.

Three-time Berwick champion Ross managed to pull even with Van Zant by the Summer Hill churches, but not without much expended effort.

Glancing frequently at his watch, Van Zant lost his stride a bit as the racers headed up the last few hundred yards toward the top of the incline . . . Van Zant and Ross were running even at the Summerhill Church and Browning was having trouble with his side. He had developed a stitch. Van Zant continued to pour out a stiff race which had a lot to do with setting a record in the event.

Ross, as he had in several of his earlier Berwick appearances, found the quick up and down dips of Kachinka's Hollow to his liking. The newspaper account reported that Ross and Van Zant were "as close as hand and glove" at the top of the first Hollow hill following the abrupt left turn just after the halfway mark. But Van Zant was fated to pay for those aggressive early miles, as the newspaper account noted: Van Zant was "beginning to show the strain of the race in his grimaces."

Whether Ross deduced this with a sideways glance or by listening to his opponent's labored breathing, he picked the next slight descent to attack.

Ross captured a lead of ten yards and never gave up the advantage for the remainder of the race . . . Constantly the distance was being lengthened as Ross sought to build up insurance against a sudden burst by Van Zant.

But by the Martzville church, Ross risked a quick glance back and noticed he had legged out a 100 yard cushion on the Boston-based runner. As had hampered Ross earlier in the race, Van Zant suddenly was struck by a knife-like side "stitch." Behind Van Zant—and not in Ross's field of vision—the old war horse Kelley and the Canadian youngster Jones were trading surges and counter-surges.

Like a horse galloping back to a barn he knew well, Ross was "running with all his speed" as he hit Market Street, banked a left onto Eleventh Street, and bee-lined to Crispin Field where the Turkey Day footballers were finishing up the first half. Van Zant, having shaken off the stitch, ran strong in second—but now more than 150 yards back.

The stadium crowd roared a familiar greeting to Ross's ears and this time he wasn't chasing Stone and Ashenfelter, but the "ghost of Scotty Rankine's past." Ross knew he was running fast and the Berwick Marathon record—barring an untimely stumble—was about to be shattered.

The Villanova star stopped the clock at 46:50—nearly 27 seconds faster than the time that Rankine ran in his great 1937 race that ended at the Market Street finish. The clocking left little to debate: H. Browning Ross was now the fastest man to have ever toured the challenging Berwick Marathon course on Thanksgiving Day—even if the finish line was in a slightly different locale. Van Zant—who no doubt deserved an assist on Ross's record run for attacking the early miles with devil-may-care audacity—placed a solid second (47:20) a time that would have won all but two of the previous races.

Behind the two men who made the race upfront, Jones—who in the middle of the decade would help Michigan State win two NCAA cross-country titles—out-legged the 43-year-old Kelley for third (48:39) by a mere six seconds. Kelley grabbed the fourth diamond award, more than a minute ahead of Walt Fedorick. Jones, Fedorick and the ever-steady Wilmer "Whitey" Sheridan (9th, one spot ahead of teammate Barry Lush) clinched the team title for the Hamilton Olympic Club.

Although the field was drastically smaller than the 45 runners of the previous year, all 19 of the starters finished the race. The first Berwick man was, once again, Hershel Hileman (14th, 59:49). Berwick's Don Bedio was the first high schooler (16th, 60:37).

II
Record Repeat
42nd Berwick Marathon, November 22, 1951

In the days prior to the 42nd running of the Berwick Marathon, there were rumors that Curtis Stone and Horace Ashenfelter—the former Nittany Lion duo who relegated Browning Ross to an unaccustomed third place in the 1949 race—were "on board" for the 1951 edition. The rumor proved half true—Curt Stone showed (although not in tip-top racing shape), but Ashenfelter (who was working for the FBI in New York and running for the New York Athletic Club) bowed out at the last minute due to the recent birth of a child in his young family.

Nevertheless, Ross had plenty of competition and they weren't reluctant to unveil their speed. In the early going, Valdu Lillakas—the Flying Estonian, technically a "misplaced person" representing the Montreal Track and Field Club—hit "the hill" with all his might. As the leaders lifted knees and puffed out lungs up to the Summer Hill churches, Lillakas chiseled out a very slight edge over Ross and accomplished marathon runner Vic Dyrgall. Perhaps Lillakas was still pumped up from a harried journey to Pennsylvania that brought him to the Hotel Berwick a mere 40 minutes before race time; his rambunctious start may also have resulted from not seeing the arduous ascent before he was actually running it.

Ross may have sensed the pace was "hot" and purposely kept something in reserve. The leaders were still tightly bunched through Kachinka's Hollow—a stretch where Ross had charged into first in the past. In fact, Dyrgall—who had placed second in the 1949 Boston Marathon—still led by a stride or two at the Martzville Church.

H. Browning Ross ran up hills quite comfortably, a smooth rhythmic form that wasted little energy. But his relatively long legs really opened up on the descents and it was his ability to run those so aggressively that made him so speedy on a rollercoaster course like Berwick. He demonstrated his downhill attack mode after the left turn at Martzville as the race headed back to Berwick. With that big move, Ross immediately opened up a gap on Dyrgall, Lillakas, and Philadelphia-based runner Luther Burdelle. Despite suddenly being alone at the front, Ross continued with all available speed over the final two miles and hit the stadium track with all cylinders pumping adrenalin.

> **The ex-Villanova great finished the race in fine shape and built up a 150-yard lead . . . With fans imploring Ross to "pour it on," Browning ended in a sprint for the tape before 4,000 applauding fans . . . Undoubtedly, it was his greatest race to date.**

In addition to a new record of 46 minutes, 41 seconds, Ross's number of career victories at Berwick was now bumped up to five—tying him with Canadian great Scotty Rankine. Rankine, however, still stood as the lone runner to ever win five *consecutive* Berwick Marathon titles. In effect, it still gave Ross something to chase—other than diamond rings or gold watches—when he towed the line each Thanksgiving. In addition, there was still this lingering, nagging debate that the stadium finish was slightly faster than the Market Street finish. (It was a question that Ross would eventually make a mute point.)

Dyrgall, the marathon man representing the Millrose Athletic Association, trudged in second, posting a fine time of 47:19—16 seconds ahead of Lillakas, the Estonian runner with "displaced person" status who trained and resided in Montreal. Luther Burdelle of Philly (representing the Mutual of Omaha insurance company) placed fourth in 47:56. Stone—the 1949 Berwick champion—had to settle for fifth in 48:59.

Behind the pre-race favorite and the various contenders, Thomas Jones of Lincoln University (6th, 50:08), held off Johnny Kelley (7th, 50:15) and Tom Sander of the Penn AC (8th, 50:19)—though with Ross and Sander leading the charge, the Penn AC won the team title. Behind Sander, Alton General—the Canadian Indian—crossed the line in 9th, just one spot ahead of Whitey Sheridan.

In the race within the race—to see who would be the first Berwick-ian—Don Bedio of Berwick High School placed 13th overall in 56:11. Second local was Herschel Hileman (17th) of Nescopeck, who apparently ditched his shoes at the Martzville Church (blisters?) and finished the last few miles in his stocking feet.

Some pre-race kibitzers might have thought Curt Stone would once again get the best of Ross, but he simply wasn't "race sharp" as he had been in 1949. In Stone's defense, he hadn't raced seriously in the months prior to Berwick because he had "peaked" way back in February for the first Pan American Games that were staged in Buenos Aires, Argentina. After the Pan Am Games, Stone went to England and raced quite well in their spring season.

All Stone had accomplished in Argentina was a gold medal in the 10,000-meters and another (but more controversial gold) in the 3000-meter steeplechase. The reason that Stone's steeplechase race resulted in an uproar was that he purposely waited for his American teammate and crossed the line in an unintentional (at least on Stone's part) tie! Stone's US teammate was not Horace Ashenfelter, but one H. Browning Ross.

"I had already won the 10,000," remembers Stone, "and I wanted Brownie to pass me. But he wouldn't! And that's how we ended up in a tie."

The officials from Argentina at first pushed for disqualification of the American pair, claiming that their tie—which they believed to have been deliberate—was a violation of the rules (not surprisingly, it was a runner from Argentina who had placed third), but they eventually withdrew the protest. Ross went on to win the Pan Am 1500-meter gold, though—in-credibly—his chief rival from Argentina (who was over 6-foot) purposely held onto the back of Ross's shorts to slow him down! Ross—at 5-8, 130—was fuming at the finish line. "I never saw Brownie so mad!" recalls Stone, with a light chuckle.

In a feature story that ran in *The Runner* (December, 1983), Ross con-firmed that he had boiled over: "The most amazing thing," he admitted, "is that after the race I took a swing at him!"

Finish Lines: Fourth place finisher Luther Burdelle continued to race long after his swiftest years had passed. In 1998, Burdelle placed well in the top half of Philly's "Run For The Hill Of It" 5-miler and averaged well under 8-minutes per mile. He was 73-years-old at the time.

Appealing to their usual thirst for stories concerning the Native American runners, Berwick Marathon fans learned from the local newspapers that the 19-year-old Alton General—an Iroquois—had once felled a 198-pound buck with his bow and arrows to celebrate the Canadian Thanksgiving.

III
The Three-Peat Feat
43rd Berwick Marathon, November 27, 1952

Browning Ross came into the 1952 Berwick Marathon in what had now become his usual set of pre-race circumstances: he was the favorite and he was in superb running shape to back it up.

That said, there *was*—at least on paper—competition that could not be totally dismissed. The Estonian refugee, Valdu Lillakas was back and once again representing the Montreal Track and Field Club. One major difference for Lillakas this time was that he arrived long before the race went off and he also knew what the course entailed, particularly its rigorous grind up to Summer Hill.

The Canadians also once again sent forth Selwyn Jones, racing for the Hamilton Olympic Club. He was still relatively young to be knocking heads with a proven war horse like Browning Ross, but he had raced on the course three times before and was looking to improve on his third place showing from 1950.

But, in truth, both Lillakas and Jones probably went to the line more worried about Ross than vice-versa. When would be make his move? Probably at the top of the hill, if past history was any indication. Browning Ross ran the ascent aggressively enough, but he knew just how to pace it—typically saving his knockout punch for the brief level stretch at the summit, or the quad-thumping descent off of Hosler's Hill.

In the event someone was still close, the former Villanova star and two-time Olympic steeplechaser also was prepared to fire in a flurry of "mini-surges" through Kachinka's Hollow. That race strategy, in fact, was simply a mirror reflection on a common training run he conducted; during workouts Ross would often surge for the length of two or three telephone poles along the road.

Just *knowing* when or what Ross might do, however, didn't necessarily mean a rival runner could *do* anything about it. It was a bit like the tale of the mice all agreeing a bell should be placed on the tomcat's neck so the rodents could benefit from an early-warning system—a capital idea, but *who* could pull it off?

True to form, the pace unfolded with Ross content to run with others down to Foundryville. All but a few good men fell back as the hill was attacked; then at the top Ross blasted off with one of his patented long, punishing pace accelerations. Nobody could hang with him, and by halfway his lead was 150 yards. Lillakas established himself in second through Kachinka's Hollow and out to Martzville, but he never was able to make any serious inroads on the defending champion's lead.

What was left? Well, the record! Ross, riding the wave of cheering fans down Market Street and en route to the Crispin Field finish line where a packed stadium was killing time between halves of the Berwick-Newport football game. Ross came through—if only by a tick of the clock—with a new course mark of 46:40. Twenty seconds later Lillakas strode across to claim second (47-flat), while Jones (48:58) out-sprinted Ed Aylmer of Michigan State Normal School (49-flat) for third. The ever-popular Johnny Kelley placed fifth (49:34).

In the next wave of runners came Maple Leaf entry Keith Dunnett (6th, 49:54), John DiCommandrea of Michigan State Normal School (7th, 49:57), Don Mitchell of the Penn AC (8th, 50:33), Harry Groves (who later coached at William & Mary and then had a Joe Paterno-like stint at Penn State) of the Penn AC (9th, 50:49), and Lou White of the New York Pioneer Club (10th, 51:27).

The depth of field was fairly outstanding, as Dick Hart, Whitey Sheridan, and Les Pawson chased in White, all within 20 seconds. A last minute entry, Edo Romangnoli, represented the New York Police Association and finished 15th overall in a well-balanced time of 52:52. The first Berwick finisher was high school entry Don Bedio (55:39) in 25th—a few places better than his father Chuck Bedio (1:08.22).

Finish Lines: The Michigan State Normal School that John DiCommandrea and Ed Aylmer raced for was located in Ypsilanti, Michigan, and eventually became known as Eastern Michigan University . . . Selwyn

Jones, however, raced for the Michigan State Spartans, based in Lansing. DiCommandrea was still racing well in New England events well into his mid-70s. He also was voted Coach of the Year in Massachusetts while directing track and cross-country at Wakefield High School in the 1970s.

IV
Four Straight & Seven of Eight
44th Berwick Marathon, November26, 1953

In his prime, Browning Ross brought so much momentum, so much knowledge to the starting line (not to mention running skill and conditioning), that he must have demolished any true semblance of a typical wagering system among the "sporting" set in Berwick. Clearly, until proved otherwise for several years in a row, this man was your favorite. Any other runner in the "Browning Ross Era" at Berwick came to the line a long shot—and it would take Olympic caliber runners along the lines of Stone and Ashenfelter to mess with the King of the Briar Creek Hills.

Dick Hart, a University of Pennsylvania runner, would one day have the credentials—at least on paper—to be considered a long shot against Browning Ross. But Hart was still several years away from his peak running; in 1955 he would win the AAU 6-mile championship on the track and the following year he won the US 5000-meter title. He also qualified for the US Olympic team bound for Melbourne, Australia in the 10,000-meter run in 1956.

Hart led the 1953 race down to Foundryville, but it was almost as if Ross *allowed* this early development. Once the front-runners slammed into the twisting climb to Summer Hill, Ross took over with authority.

For the other runners in the rather smallish field of 25 runners, it must have been a bit like watching the Master Magician run through his usual—but still brilliant—repertoire and, try as they might, still finding themselves dumbfounded, the phrase: "Now *how* does he *do* that?" poised on their gasping lips.

Ross held a lead of several seconds at the top of the hill, but lengthened that considerably up and down Hosler's Hill and was in firm command of the race as he whirled around the sharp left onto Kachinka's Hollow Road. He was more than 100 yards ahead of Hart, who in turn was chased by the veteran Johnny Kelley, John DiCommandrea, and the top Canadian entry, Barry Lush of the Hamilton Olympic Club.

By the Martzville church, Ross's comfortable cushion was more than 200 yards, and Hart was an equally solid second. Ross was well on his way to his fourth straight Berwick Marathon win and perhaps the only question that remained was if he would arrive on the Crispin Field track with a shot at breaking his own course record? The cool, calm conditions were on his side, and soon the Berwick spectators would urge him on—anticipating something extraordinary.

And like Houdini, Ross still found a way to amaze the crowd—even if there was no serious competition on hand; he zipped into the stadium and raced in for a new course mark of 46:38—two seconds faster than the year before. Hart charged home for runner-up laurels in 47:28, but he hadn't truly worried the winner.

For Ross, the victory simple added to his growing stack of Berwick achievements, the most glowing being: his seventh win in eight races, his fourth straight victory, and his fourth straight course record!

The crowd, however, still had something to get excited about, other than a second half of Bulldog football. "Here comes Kelley!" swept through the crowd, as the old time favorite scooted around to take third (49:48)—more than two minutes behind Hart, but clinching his 20th diamond ring in 21 appearances.

DiCommandrea grabbed fourth (49:58), while Lush (5th, 50:18) held off Iona's Jim Mahoney (6th, 50:23) and Millrose A.A. mainstay Joe Kleinerman (7th, 50:57) to snag the fifth and last diamond award.

The mid-pack attack came through with some excitement, as runners battling for the 8th through 13th slots were all on the track at the same time, sprinting for places and awards. They were: Canada's Keith Dunnett (8th, 51:17), Walt Berger of Binghamton, New York (9th, 51:20), Jack Barry of the Shanahan Catholic Club (10th, 51:23), Joe Martin of Penn AC (11th, 51:26), Ed Aylmer of Michigan State (12th, 51:31), and Hamilton Olympic Club chief "Whitey" Sheridan (13th, 51:43.)

V
Browning Ross Takes The Fifth
45th Berwick Marathon, November 25, 1954

The 45th edition of the Berwick Marathon might as well have been started with a loud yawn as opposed to a pistol shot. If ever there was a "ho hum" race in the history of the Run for the Diamonds, then let us designate that dubious distinction to the 1954 "race." If auto racing uses the checkered flag, then the 1954 Berwick event should have unfurled the white flag of surrender—virtually from the gun, the field (except for one runner) let the champ cruise along uncontested.

But who could blame them? Ross stepped on the line with *four* straight course records on his resume and more knowledge concerning the course than Newton had about the laws of gravity. What could mere mortals offer against that? As the local papers summed up:

> H. Browning Ross . . . repeated yesterday as champion of the Berwick Marathon when he won the local race with ease over 35 U.S. and Canadian distance stars. He held a lead of 500 yards from Summer Hill until he crossed the finish line at Crispin Field just 47 minutes, 15 seconds after he left the "Y" starting line . . . The Woodbury, New Jersey, school teacher thus won his fifth race in a row and got his eighth first [place] prize in nine years of competition here.

The man who *did* challenge Ross was a top Canadian runner (and former Drake University star) named Gordon Dickson, although he was taking graduate courses at NYU at the time and representing the New York Athletic Club. Dickson dueled with Ross through two miles, but he cramped up badly on the arduous ascent to Summer Hill and was forced to drop out. (A fine runner, Dickson returned for a future crack at Berwick and his result was considerably better.)

The best race of the day actually came between two Mt. Lebanon Track Club teammates, as Bernie Luterancik and Don Summick—a pair of former Pitt Panthers-battled down Market Street for the runner-up slot. Luterancik got the nod at the line, although both runners were timed in 49:15—about 600 yards behind Ross who never really put the gas pedal down as he arrived in the stadium; there was no need.

Bill Welsh of the Millrose A.A. clocked 49:35 for fourth and held off George King of New York University (5th, 49:43.)

Rounding out the top ten were Tom Duffy (6th, 50:13) of Philly's Penn AC, the ever-ready Irishman Johnny Kelley (7th, 50:19), Ron Kiehl (8th, 50:22) of Penn AC, Joe Kleinerman (9th, 50:35) and Ted Corbitt (10th, 50:42) of the New York Pioneers.

The first Berwickian to cross the line was high school runner Steve Fraind (28th, 1:04.03), who beat defending local Don Bedio by one place.

Miles of Style: High-tech running gear was still a few years away. Canada's five-time champ Scotty Rankine (front, 2nd from left), Oswald Kissoon of Trinidad, and young Whitey Sheridan (2nd from right) display fast fashion. Ab Morton is hidden

VI
Nine Out Of Ten: Ross Rides Again
46th Berwick Marathon, November 24, 1955

Not every football team wanted to come play Berwick at Berwick on Thanksgiving Day and when that tradition ended in 1955, the Marathon rolled on—albeit back at the original YMCA finish. The Crispin Field finish—admittedly the site of more than a few electrifying races including Ross's solitary loss in 1949—would be silent for the first time in nearly a decade.

The change back, of course, brought on some speculation. Would Ross be able to equal his course record times that he clocked en route to the Crispin Field finish?

Chiv MacCrea—a.k.a. "Mr. Marathon"—felt compelled to weigh in on the matter in a pre-race *Enterprise* write-up:

"The return to the original marathon course after eight years, during which period it finished at Crispin Field, poses the question of the time made during that period. The course used with the finish at Crispin Field is certainly fifty feet less than the original course and in addition considerable grade was with the runner down Eleventh Street to Vine," proclaimed C.N. MacCrea.

Perhaps some of MacCrea's motivation is raising the question came from finding *something* H. Browning Ross could race against—and the clock seemed like a better bet than did a human rival.

Although Ross's 1953 mark of 46:38 was the official race record, the course mark with the YMCA finish still technically belonged to Robert "Scotty" Rankine and dated back to 1937.

Race day weather wasn't on Ross's side—for the second straight year it was cloudy, cold and, worst of all, windy.

Pittsburgh's Bob Carman—who would make his mark in the Berwick race before the decade expired—led for most of the first mile. But by the time the field turned onto Summerhill Avenue, Ross already had moved up front. He had a small lead at two miles, but he quickly extended that on the now-well-familiar (to him) climb up to the Summer Hill churches.

And then Ross did what he often tried to do; while his would-be pursuers tried to recover as "the Hill" finally-but-briefly flattened out, Ross put the hammer down. The result was a 200 yard lead as he zoomed down Hosler's Hill and through the halfway mark. The race was essentially over. As recorded by the *Enterprise*:

> The Woodbury, New Jersey, racing champ widened his lead considerably at the top of the hill . . . He led Dickson by 200 yards at that point, with John Holt of the Millrose A.A. another 50 yards back. Then came Joe Barry who ran one of his finest races here. Those four positions held all the rest of the way around the course with neither man picking up much on the other.

Accompanied by the cheers of spectators braving the chilly afternoon, Ross smoothly finished up his solo run. Although the newspaper headline read: "Ross Wins 9th Marathon Title in 10 Years, But Misses Record by Five Seconds"—one certainly could have argued that it *still* was a new record. His time of 46 minutes, 43 seconds—yes, five ticks off his course mark with the Crispin Field finish—nevertheless demolished Rankine's 1937 mark set on the original course with the standard YMCA finish line on Market Street.

Nearly two minutes back, Gord Dickson—the talented Canadian wearing the New York AC garb with its trademark "winged foot" insignia—placed a distant second (48:38), but a vast improvement from his first Berwick race. Holt was exactly two minutes behind Dickson (50:38), while Barry snagged a solid fourth (51:08).

The next three slots actually provided the Market Street fans with the best races of the day, as three prominent runners all finished within 18 seconds of each other. Carman grabbed fifth (51:32), and Ted Corbitt—the US Olympic Marathon team member in 1952 and a prominent New York Pioneer—ran his best Berwick ever, placing sixth in 51:42. That was six seconds up on the ever-feisty Johnny Kelley (7th, 51:48).

Other notables in the top 20 included Millrose's Joe Kleinerman (12th, 52:44) and Wilmer "Whitey" Sheridan (19th, 54:08).

The top Berwick finisher was once again Steven Fraind (39th, 1:03:40), who also improved his time slightly from his rookie race.

Finish Lines: Although Berwick's mere 9-mile course was too short for Ted Corbitt, he obviously had a special fondness for the Diamond event. As his son Gary says with a smile: "At our house, Thanksgiving dinner was always on Friday!"

Photo courtesy of Michael Sheridan

Ross Rocks Market: H. Browning Ross set a record for the Market Street finish in 1955 and 1956, to go along with his Crispin Field finish mark.

RUN FOR THE DIAMONDS

Shooting For Double Figures
47th Berwick Marathon, November 22, 1956

Ten times! Ten victories—in eleven attempts; for some reason, it all sounded *so* much better than nine wins.

But H. Browning Ross—the Boss Man of Berwick—wasn't counting his diamonds before they were mined and cut. In the days leading up to the 47th Thanksgiving Day classic, Ross made it clear that—despite his easy win the year before—he wasn't about to get complacent. When contacted by the local press to confirm title defense, Ross couldn't resist asking: "Are any of the Canadian runners coming?"

When he was told that runner-up Gord Dickson was coming back, Ross told the *Enterprise*:

> "Well, Dickson is a very serious threat to me. He is really terrific and will probably give me trouble this year. Only recently he won the 15-mile road race at Dundas, Ontario . . . I held the record there, but Dickson lowered that mark by three minutes."
>
> Ross was also told that Don Fay of the Boston A.A. had also entered.
>
> Ross answered: "That boy is also very good."
>
> And so it went. The top runners will all be here but Ross has a fierce competitive spirit and he would be the last one to run out on a meeting with them.

But when the printing presses stopped and the gun finally sounded in the 47th sendoff around the Briar Creek Hills, Ross found himself in a full-fledged, run-on-the-edge-of-death duel with a runner who originally hailed from far warmer climes.

That man was Rodolfo Mendez, a top-notch Puerto Rican runner representing the New York Pioneer Club. Mendez had hoped to represent Puerto Rico at the 1956 Melbourne Olympic Games in the 10,000-meter event, but those plans fell through at the last minute. He entered Berwick late Tuesday might and when Ross heard, the defending champ knew that Mendez would probably be his main threat.

Mendez did not disappoint. He scooted into a lead of a few steps down at Foundryville. Then Ross took over the pace-setting chores as both men tore into the teeth of the grueling grade up to the Summer Hill churches. As if hitched to the nine-time champion's hip, Mendez shadowed the favorite to the top. Whatever pressure Ross applied at the summit—his patented move—it was matched by Mendez. They were shoulder to shoulder down to the turn at Miller's corners.

Or would elbow to elbow be a more accurate description? Gary Corbitt—the late Ted Corbitt's son—recalls his father mentioning some glancing of elbows between Ross and Mendez as neither man would willingly give an inch to the other. In the process, it became a two-man race—more than a minute behind them Penn AC runner Luther Burdelle matched strides with Canadian star Gord Dickson.

The front-runners blew through Martzville and swept down the hill past the golf course. Finally, Ross gained a few yards. He added to it ever so slowly, but by the time he reached North Berwick and the right hand turn for home, the former Villanova star had carved out a 30 yard lead. Ross more than doubled that lead down the homestretch, but he had to dig deep for every half-second he gained—Mendez had made sure of that. As the *Enterprise* dutifully summed up:

> The Berwick champion said after the race that Mendez is a strong runner and that he gave him plenty of trouble and concern. It showed at the finish line as Ross didn't break with his usual burst of speed at the end. In fact he slowed up at the line and might have broken the record with a little burst of speed.

Ross's time of 46 minutes, 39 seconds left him just one tick shy of his own race mark (set at the Crispin Field finish, allegedly slightly shorter/faster) but he decisively erased Rankine's route record over the finish-at-the-Y course. (The BMA, in fact, awarded Ross with a special wrist watch for running a new best for the YMCA finish layout.)

Ten seconds later the tough-running Mendez checked in (46:49). Burdelle (3rd, 48:19) delivered his best effort ever at Berwick, outlasting Dickson (4th, 48:27), while Burdelle's club teammate John Cunningham nailed down fifth (49:53.)

From the whatever-it-takes-to-run-Berwick department, the 1956 race featured Bob Goldie of Toronto. Goldie ran a steady race to finish in 6th place (50:28)—but perhaps it seemed comparatively easy considering what he went through just to get there. Goldie and several other Canadian runners were halted by a swirling snow storm near Buffalo en route to Berwick. The others opted to go home, but Goldie—with his wife—

pressed on through the storm, only to arrive in Berwick 10 minutes before the smoke would curl from the starter's pistol.

Other notable finishers in the field included Johnny Kelley (8th, 51:10), 44-year-old Joe Kleinerman (12th, 52:30), and Ted Corbitt (14th, 52:59). One of the pre-race contenders, Don Fay of the Boston A.A., showed that the Berwick course could still put a rookie through the wringer; Fay salvaged 17th. The first local to cross the line was Lynn Karshner of the Berwick Marathon Club in 1:01.19—26th out of 37 finishers.

Harris Browning Ross and Running

Berwick Marathon fans tend to remember Harris Browning Ross as the man who dominated the race: 10 victories, 7 in a row—a course record-setter (including the route that ended at Crispin Field, a record that still, in the technical sense, belongs to Ross).

But Browning Ross *beyond* Berwick—in the wider American running community—is regarded as a much larger, much more important figure, beyond his own running. His sudden death from a heart attack in April of 1998 left the running community and a vast array of friends and family understandably stunned, but not at a loss of words about his many influences.

"Turtle" Tom Osler—a Ross protégé and friend—has been quoted as saying: "He is to running what George Washington is to this country." (This has been paraphrased or repeated in various ways.) Kathrine Switzer compared his founding of the Road Runner's Club of America (RRCA) in 1958 to Martin Luther's Reformation in the foreword to *Boom! Forty Years of Running and Writing with the RRCA*.

Browning Ross, of course, in his typical manner—humorous, understated, self-depreciating—talked about that founding in less grandiose terms. About that seminal meeting at the Paramount Hotel in New York City, Ross told Hal Higdon (writing for *The Runner* in December 1983), "We were supposed to be a national convention and it was six guys meeting in a dingy hotel room." (Among that half-dozen RRCA originals were Ted Corbitt and Joe Kleinerman, both who were hugely instrumental in launching the New York Road Runners, today one of the most important running clubs in America.)

That formation was, more or less, in response to the dismissive (and sometimes heavy-handed) treatment from the Amateur Athletic Union.

"Browning was banned by the AAU for selling running shoes from the trunk of his car," said Freddi Carlip of the *Runner's Gazette* (and a former RRCA president) upon presenting Ross to the National Distance Running Hall of Fame in Utica, New York in 2002. "He put the needs of runners first. Runners needed shoes; Browning provided them. He was banned a second time when he took a young woman to a marathon in Philadelphia and told her to run, over the objections of the race officials."

H. Browning Ross also was one of the first to spread the word through publication—his *Long Distance Running Log,* a 30-page monthly newsletter, now rightfully enjoys cult status in the realm of publications in our sport. The *Log* (1957-1975) went out to about 1,000 runners at its zenith. As Higdon wrote: "For those of us before the boom, before even the hint of such a boom, the *Log* was the most important communication to arrive during the month, a publication of epic importance, destined to be examined on the walk back from the mailbox . . . destined to be read and re-read." It is not a stretch to trace the roots of *Runner's World* or *Runner's Gazette* (which exudes the home-spun qualities of the *Log*) to Ross's publication.

He was also a character. Jack Heath—long-time friend and co-coach at Gloucester Catholic in South Jersey—has hundreds of Browning Ross stories, such as Ross's remedy for slight injuries. For example, a high school runner with a sore calf might be told to "rub peanut butter on it." Heath, of course, had a close friendship with Ross. "If someone broke the world record in the mile I had to call him right away . . . Unless he called me first," he once wrote.

Ross hosted many "competitive fun runs" in South Jersey. Berwick Marathon Association member Fred Takacs recalls traveling to some of these races—and the motley array of race prizes spread out haphazardly on the trunk of Ross's car.

As Takacs wrote (*Runner's Gazette,* January, 1999) in a remembrance to Ross, "It was classic old-fashioned road racings all right. There was no digital clock at the finish, no pin-on numbers, no sponsors, and no waiver to sign . . . Entrance fees ranged from $3 to $5, depending on how many runners showed up or what he had to offer in prizes."

Ross's love of road races as a competitor was legendary. His wife Sis used to beg him "not to bring home any more trophies." Legend has it that the famous Villanova coach Jumbo Elliott—fed-up with Ross sneaking off to run road races during the college season—once threatened to boot him from the squad. "Go up to the dorm and pack your bags!" Jumbo allegedly thundered. "You're back on the tomato farm!" (The last most likely a barb directed at Ross's South Jersey roots.)

According to Higdon, Ross loved no race more than Berwick.

> Ross's favorite race was the Berwick Marathon, actually nine miles, held each Thanksgiving Day in the town of Berwick, Pennsylvania. "They'd pay my expenses. Everybody in town turned out. I won it ten or eleven times. First prize was a diamond ring, worth $130 so they claimed."

On top of that, the applause and cheers at Crispin Field and—at the end of his career Market Street—were, of course, worth a lot more than that. Berwick loved Browning Ross just as much as he loved Berwick.

Olympic Memories: H. Browning Ross holding a photo of himself in his Olympic blazer. He made two U.S. Olympic teams in the steeplechase.

Photo courtesy of *The Runner's Gazette*

18

Changing of the Guard

Just as Robert "Scotty" Rankine and Johnny Kelley before him, even H. Browning Ross had to finally slow down and give way to younger runners. But to steal a line from the Welsh poet Dylan Thomas, he did "not go gentle into that good night." His final races at Berwick—a highly-competitive event that he had dominated for a full decade (with one little "blip" in 1949 when the twin Lions—Stone and Ashenfelter—roared up in his otherwise unblemished path)—were nip and tuck affairs in which he made his competition win the old-fashioned way; they had to *earn* it.

I
Kyle Ends Maple Leaf Drought
48th Berwick Marathon, November 28, 1957

Coming into the 48th Berwick Marathon, there were two streaks on a collision course. Browning Ross had won seven straight Berwick Marathons and—conversely and somewhat astoundingly—the Canadians had not put a man first across the finish line in 20 years. Twenty years! Two decades! Somewhere Bob "Scotty" Rankine must have been shaking his head in disbelief.

In the end, this collision of two streaks going in opposite directions came down to *one second* and one man's fast-twitch muscle fiber twitching ever so slightly faster than his rival's.

Canadian Doug Kyle had certainly been on a roll in 1957, including several key victories over Ross at 15-miles and the nearly 19-mile Around the Bay event, both in Hamilton. Perhaps even more worrisome to his competitors was the fact that Kyle (who had competed for Canada at the Rome Olympic Games and then enrolled as a graduate student at Michigan) had absolutely demolished all the Yanks in the US AAU National 6-mile race on the track over the summer. Kyle had clocked 29 minutes, 22 seconds for the race—more than 150-yards ahead of second place.

Not surprisingly, it was Whitey Sheridan who brought Kyle down to

Berwick—although Whitey himself was injured and unable to hobble more than a few blocks before reluctantly stepping onto the sidewalk. It was a decent day to run, but not perfect—cloudy (which was good), but also breezy and a bit muggy. Had he been physically able, Whitey certainly would have opted to slug it out over the Briar Creek Hills.

Prior to the start, Ross admitted that Kyle—a 1956 Olympian for Canada—would be a hard man to beat and allowed that his best shot would be in gaining some ground up "the Hill."

For his part, Kyle knew Ross would take him to the limit. More than 50 years since the event (speaking by phone from his home in Calgary, Alberta), Kyle recalled:

"Well, Browning knew that course like the back of his hand . . . Every hill, every twist and turn. I knew that I couldn't let him get far ahead of me, or I might never catch him again. All I knew was that if I wanted a chance to win, then I had to stick with him."

So that's how the race unfolded. Browning Ross hit the hill hard—and gained a few yards on Kyle. But not long after both men flew down the backside of Hosler's Hill, Kyle pulled even with Ross and the pair of Olympians dueled through Kachinka's Hollow, through Martzville, and back to North Berwick. Their head-to-head battle was furious enough to have forced Gordon McKenzie—a two-time US Olympian and a great runner in his own right—to third place.

When they arrived back on Market Street, the men were still right together. Finally, with less than a minute of racing left, Kyle went to his kick. But it wasn't until the last 50 yards that he clearly gained daylight—and victory by one tick of the watch in 46:40 to Ross's 46:41. As the *Enterprise* wrapped it up:

> The likeable and friendly Kyle was very modest over his victory. He called Ross a top performer and said that he was worried all the way. He wants to come back next year he indicated.

McKenzie, representing the New York Pioneer club, ran to a solid third in 48:04 (cheered on around the course by his wife Chris who hitched a ride with a local doctor), while John Church of Toronto's Gladstone AC nailed down fourth in 48:41. Jack Barry of the Shanahan Catholic Club took fifth place in 50:06. Back in 11th (50:47), was one of Berwick's grand old stars—Johnny Kelley—still competitive in a field of more than 50 runners.

David Hetler of Berwick, the first local, posted a modest time of 1:02.08

Doug Digs Deep: Kyle (22) gets ready to kick, as Ross cannot shake his Canadian shadow.

and placed 41st. But Hetler received a rousing hand as he arrived by the YMCA finish line on Market. As the *Enterprise* couldn't resist noting:

> Hetler's fine finish was watched with interest at the Crispin Memorial Football Field. Hetler has been working in the press box, helping keep statistics on the Berwick Bulldogs. Those who worked there weren't aware that he was running until he made the disclosure about a week ago.

As far as race statistics went, however, the major change was that for the first time since 1949, H. Browning Ross would not be listed in first place. In 1958, Ross would aim to be back in a more familiar place—the winner's circle.

Finish Lines: A graduate of the University of British Columbia where he competed in cross-country and track, Doug Kyle competed at the 1956 Melbourne and 1960 Rome Olympic Games. He also won a silver and bronze medal at the 1959 Pan American Games, in the 10,000 and 5000 meters respectively. In 1961, Kyle won the Canadian Cross-Country title. He never did get back to Berwick to run, but in 1963 he helped start a full marathon in Calgary, Alberta, the city in which he now lives.

In addition to his Olympic appearances at Melbourne and Rome, Gordon McKenzie won the national US Cross-Country title in 1954, placed second in the 1960 Boston Marathon, and won a silver medal in the 1963 Pan American Games Marathon.

His wife Chris McKenzie was a former world-class 800-meter runner in England. As early as the 1950s, she became active in the early pioneering efforts to gain participation rights for women in US road races.

II
Carman's Finish Line Crash
49th Berwick Marathon, November 27, 1958

In 1958 a college runner for West Virginia University named H. John Rogers had just finished a cross-country meet at Schenley Park in Pittsburgh when something somewhat unusual happened. Recalled Rogers in an essay for the 1997 Berwick race program:

> Bob Carman, the Carnegie Tech coach, came over to our locker room afterwards for a visit. He was a friendly, gregarious fellow, and I learned later, a graduate student working on his Ph.D. He was just filling in as track and cross-country coach.
>
> Carman was also one of the leading distance runners in the East . . . At some point in his visit, Carman started talking about the Berwick race. He was going up and taking several of his runners. "It's nine miles," he said, "a good way to end the season."
>
> Here was a great adventure staring this 18-year-old in the face and all I had to do was say "yes." It was, I suppose, a little like the call to arms in 1917. Not only was it an adventure, but

of equal importance to my youthful incarnation. It was a test of my manhood . . . I told Carman I'd let him know, but my mind was already made up.

My coach didn't like the idea, but since cross-country season would be over, he really couldn't tell me not to go. A trip to Berwick meant giving up my first trip home in nearly three months. It would be hard to tell Mother that I would be passing on the turkey that year. But that's what I did. "If that's what you want to do," she said over the telephone.

But the decision was probably made when I heard Carman say "nine miles", and after school on the Tuesday before Thanksgiving I hitchhiked up to Pittsburgh and stayed overnight with Carman and his wife. On that Wednesday, seven or eight of us traveled in two cars to Berwick . . . .

Although young Rogers was aware Carman was a talented runner, he certainly wasn't a "shoo-in" to win Berwick. After his loss to Doug Kyle in 1957, H. Browning Ross was ready to roll out all his strategic wisdom over the course to recapture his crown in 1958. Carman, however, arrived in Berwick with a big plus on his side; he had defeated Ross in the AAU National 30K Championship race in York on November 2. Despite that win, Carman readily acknowledged that "we all had a lot of admiration for Browning Ross. He was a great runner."

Although Kyle had moved out West in 1958 and was unable to return to Berwick, there were—in addition to Carman—at least one other man had to be reckoned with and he had a very fast mile time on his resume. His name was Bob Seaman, the former UCLA mile standout (he had clocked 4:01), who was stationed in the service at Fort Lee, Virginia.

Both Ross and Carman were aware of Seaman's speed and had no intention of allowing such an accomplished miler to get a free ride until the Market Street finish line came into view. They heated up the pace quickly enough that J. Howard Remley's starting pistol shot was all but still hanging in the cold air. The runners bucked a stiff breeze as they headed out Market, and Seaman tucked in behind the two long distance men, determined to stick as long as possible.

As long as possible proved to be the top of Summer Hill. And, then— like a boxer who had fended off too many punches for too many rounds— Seaman, the pure track man, finally had to let go.

"As soon as we hit the top of the hill, Browning accelerated," recalled Bob Carman during a phone interview from his Santa Barbara, California home where he resides in retirement. "And I went with him . . . Then we were shoulder-to-shoulder the rest of the way."

As for Seaman, he was now cut adrift—in "no man's land"—with the two front-runners pulling relentlessly away, and the tired runner's knowledge that the others, playing vulture, would be doing their best to come collect his spent, wobbling carcass. As the *Berwick Enterprise* recorded:

> Seaman stuck on the heels of Ross and Carman until the trio hit the top of the hill at Summer Hill. The hill tired Seaman as he dropped behind and by the time Ross and Carman had made the turn at Miller's Hotel, Seaman had dropped 25 yards behind and it widened the rest of the way.
>
> Seaman indicated that the hill had been a tough one and that he suffered greatly during the latter stages of the race. Several times, he indicated, he felt like dropping out.

Meanwhile, Ross and Carman blazed toward the finish, and—for his part—Carman knew that he'd have to summon all of his reserves for any hope of a victory. The long-striding Carman *did* have good finishing speed, however, noting he had once been clocked in 10.3 for 100 yards—an unusual weapon for a distance runner to have in his quiver of arrows.

"Browning Ross wasn't going to just let you have it," recalls Carman. "He was going to make you *work* for it! He'd throw in these little surges, get a few yards on me, and then I would have to reel him back in."

With about a half-mile left in the race—hammering down Market Street, the crowd roaring—Carman counter-surged "just to test him" and, although Ross responded, Carman began to feel like he might be able to win on a sprint.

"With about 150 yards to go, I made another move—a lot harder—and then with about 50 yards to go I heard Browning let out a loud sigh . . . And I thought: 'I have it!'" Carman remembers.

Carman still had one major obstacle in his way—a rather large photographer had parked himself right in the middle of the finish line, no doubt in an effort to snap the best possible finish line shot.

"He was kind of a doughboy type of guy," Carman lightly chuckled. "I was simply too tired to go around him, so I just closed my eyes, crossed the finish line, and banged right into him."

The big photographer somehow grabbed hold of Carman and held him up, so he didn't plunge to the pavement. Four seconds after Carman's finish line crash, Browning Ross finished—second for the second straight year.

Meantime, Seaman was trying to claw his way in. Jack Barry was hunting him down, but Seaman rallied enough to hold on to a hard-won third (49:43). Barry—recording his highest Berwick finish in his career—charged in for fourth (49:48) just five seconds later.

After Barry, came another man with an Irish name—and a name Berwick Marathon fans knew well—John A. Kelley. At age 51, Kelley put together an outstanding race, copping fifth in 50:21

It was almost as if Kelley was thanking the Berwick race fans. On Thanksgiving Eve, the Moose Club had hosted a special "Johnny Kelley Night" to honor his 25th appearance in Berwick. As the *Enterprise* noted several days before the 49th running:

> Kelley is to the Berwick Marathon what cinders are to a track. His green and white knit cap always announces to his many Berwick fans, "Here comes Kelley!"
>
> As a reward to Johnny, Berwick sports fans are going to be able to show their appreciation by presenting him with a "night" and with an engraved wall plaque with the inscription: Presented to Johnny Kelley in honor of his 25th running of the Berwick Marathon from his legion of Berwick followers.
>
> Local fans who wish to be a part of Johnny Kelley's reward may donate any sum, not matter how large or small, at Harry's Sporting Goods Store, West Front Street.

As if a testimony to both age and youth, the runner who chased in the much-celebrated Kelley was a talented high school runner: Ralph Houdeshell of York, Pennsylvania, placed sixth (50:57). Rounding out the top ten were Dick Donahue of the Boston A.A. (7th, 51:34), Olympic marathoner Ted Corbitt of the New York Pioneers (8th, 51:42) in one of his best Berwick races, George Tracy, a high school runner from Warren, Ohio (9th, 51:48) and Richard Hamilton, who was—like the race winner Carman—representing the Ammon Recreation Center of Pittsburgh (10th, 51:54).

Finish Lines: Jack Barry twice won the Philadelphia Marathon (1956 and 1957) and he often gave Browning Ross a run for his money in Philly area races, once beating Ross in a Mid-Atlantic 30K event.

III
The Golden Year: Berwick Turns Fifty
50th Berwick Marathon, November 26th, 1959

As one might imagine, Berwick did not let the 50th running of its race approach without a little bit of pre-event fanfare. When the *Enterprise* listed the official entries in the Wednesday paper, the headline referred to the Marathon as the "Golden Anniversary Race." The papers were packed to capacity with various stories on the history of the race, including some reminiscence from C.N. "Chiv" MacCrea—"Mr. Marathon" himself. Obviously, the town was well aware that their enduring event was something special.

In addition, with Bill Heller as the driving force, the BMA added a 5-mile high school run. Clearly, the officials—while enjoying the Golden Anniversary of the 9-mile event—had an eye on the future, too.

As for the "Marathon" itself, Bob Carman was on board to defend his title. In fact, the papers made note that Mrs. Lyn Carman wrote to the *Enterprise* after her husband's 1958 victory "expressing appreciation for the kind treatment received by her husband on his visit here. She indicated that he would make every effort to be back and defend his title."

The obvious choice for chief rival would have been Browning Ross, but the 10-time champion—nagged by some occasional injuries—was not back in his best racing condition and made it known weeks before that he would not be among the starters.

The Berwick Marathon Association, however, had real hopes that Gordon Dickson—who had landed a bronze medal in the Pan American Games Marathon back in August in Chicago—would be with the Canadian contingent. In addition, Rudy Mendez of the New York Pioneers—the runner who had pushed Ross so doggedly back in 1956—had registered.

Unfortunately, neither Dickson nor Mendez showed up on race day. But Jim Green of the Boston Athletic Association did, and despite the fact that Green had never raced on the Berwick route, he became an instant co-favorite (along with Carman) by virtue of the fantastic races he'd run earlier in the year. Those races included a third place in the Boston Marathon and a silver medal in the Pan American Games Marathon (won by John J. "the younger" Kelley), about four minutes ahead of Dickson.

Green's affable manner perhaps belied the fact that he was once boxed prior to becoming a runner. But he was able to transfer the mental toughness required in the ring to the rigors of serious road racing. So when the starting gun banged, Green went right to work, as if it were Round One and he needed to establish just who was boss.

By the time the runners approached Foundryville and the two-mile mark, the New Englander had strung out the field and dispatched virtually all potential threats except for one—the long-striding, bespectacled Carman. As the front-runners warmed to the task, their breath produced tiny smoke-like wisps in the chilly, 35 degree air.

Carman stuck with Green to the Summer Hill churches, but he was clearly working to keep contact. Green—as if stealing a page from the H. Browning Ross playbook—then took off at that summit and quickly established a 100 yard lead. By the time Green negotiated the sharp left at Miller's turn, he'd doubled his cushion. Green doubled it again from Martzville in and—when all was said and done—he won by nearly a quarter-mile.

However—in these days before light-weight plastic running watches—Browning Ross's course record escaped Green by 15 seconds. Green stopped the watches at 46:54. After the race, the Groton, Connecticut, English teacher admitted to the *Enterprise* writer that he "still had plenty left, but I had no way of knowing how close I was to the mark."

Carman buckled down and ran well enough to hold second (48:05), more than 50 seconds up on Toronto's John Church of the Gladstone AC (48:57). Another Canadian, Bill Smith—the transplanted Scotsman racing for the Hamilton Olympic Club—captured fourth (49:30). Just 20 seconds later, Baltimore's Frank Pflaging—destined for bigger Berwick deeds in the next decade—snagged fifth.

The Shanahan Catholic Club packed three men in the next five to fuel their successful bid for the team title, as Jack Barry (8th, 50:00), Berry Crawford (9th, 50:10), and Bill Prater (10th, 50:12) ran in a pack. Wayne Gallatin (6th, 49:52) of the BOC and Sy Villa, a US Army entry from Fort Bragg, North Carolina, (7th, 49:56) scurried in just ahead of the Shanahan band.

Running a good race in 11th was Terry Engleman of Bloomsburg State Teachers College. Engleman clocked 50:28 and held off the likes of Dick Donohue (12th, 50:33) of the Boston A.A. and 1952 Olympian Ted Corbitt (13th, 50:44).

Special mention in the *Enterprise* deservedly fell upon the shoulders of "Whitey" Sheridan, as the paper noted:

> When the veteran Wilmer "Whitey" Sheridan crossed the
> finish line in 31st place he received a very warm round of ap-
> plause. In his many appearances here the very friendly Cana-
> dian has gained many friends and they were on hand to extend
> their greetings.

Just a few seconds behind Whitey, the first local sprinted in. As the *Enterprise* recorded it:

> Nescopeck's Donnie Young followed Sheridan to the tape
> and the first local runner had finished the event. He looked in
> good shape after the long run and was quite happy.

Young wasn't the only finisher in a celebratory mood. In a rare occurrence, all 56 starters finished the race. Perhaps they knew that special gold medals would be awarded to all finishers at the post-race buffet at the Berwick Fraternal Order of Eagles.

Regardless of motivating factors, each and every one of those runners deserved their gold medallions. On a day partly meant to honor one of America's finest footraces, they had fought the good fight, run the honest race, over the rough, hilly course on the traditional Thanksgiving Day. After all, it was the Golden Anniversary Race—a half century of racing in Berwick, Pennsylvania!

Those 13 original runners that had paused on that start line in 1908, waiting for Domville's pistol shot to send them forth down the muddy street—off toward the long twisting hill and those lonely, rutty back-country lanes—would have nodded knowingly with pride. Their successors—the 56 finishers of 1959—had kept faith with the original 13.

And then the Angel of History flew on.

The Canadians

Sometime in the 1990s, I got a chance to hear "Whitey" Sheridan hold court with one of his many Berwick stories—a story that was both simple and illuminating.

"During World War II, rubber was rationed," Whitey explained, "so good tires were hard to come by. But we still wanted to make the trip down to Berwick for the race . . . So a bunch of us got together with our cars and we picked out the tires with the most tread. We took one off one car . . . one off of another . . . until we had the four best tires. We put them all on one car and then we headed to Berwick for the race."

To me, the story spoke to the very core of commitment the Canadians had to the Berwick race, and they were not going to permit a little bit of wartime rationing to ruin their fun. (The Canadians had plenty of meat, though, and they sometimes would bring it down to their American running friends, like Johnny Kelley, during the war years.) If they had to go to great lengths to travel hours upon hours, for the sheer joy of running a 9-mile race with a nearly two-mile uphill, well, then they would simply do what was necessary.

The Canadian commitment to Berwick, of course, came from inception. It would be safe to say that the race would be vastly different without Canadian input and participation, but the truth is we cannot say for sure that there would even *be* a race in Berwick without Canadian influence.

It is, in fact, recorded in Berwick town history that A.E. Domville—the Hamilton, Ontario transplant who came to Berwick to work in American Car & Foundry management ranks—was "the spirit behind the race." It was Domville who knew of the Around the Bay race (dating back to 1894) and passed on the enthusiasm for such a footrace to C.N. "Chiv" MacCrea and Professor James Sigman. It was a short step from that to: "Why not in Berwick?"

The deeds of the great Canadian runners at Berwick are well recorded in these pages in the individual race write-ups: Cliff Bricker (1926 and 1927), Wilf McCluskey (1932), Robert "Scotty" Rankine (1933 through and including 1937), Doug Kyle (his "photo finish" win over Browning Ross snapped the latter's seven-year win streak in 1957), Dave Northey (two record runs, 1971 and 1978), Rob Legge (1975) and Rob Earl (1983 . . . third man to run sub-44 minutes) head the Maple Leaf winners list.

In more recent times, the Canadians have checked into the winner's circle with the likes of Ken Martin (1990) and Matt Kerr (2005).

The lone Canadian woman to win Berwick was Muffi McLeod in 1984. More recently, Whitey Sheridan's daughter—Lynda Deboer—won the women's Masters in 2005. Lynda no doubt felt she had to keep pace with her brothers—Michael and David—who frequently placed (and still place) in their age brackets at Berwick.

Of course, if we listed all the diamond awards that Canadians have won in Berwick and carted back north of the border, it would run for several pages and look like an advertisement for a jewelry store.

The first Canadian to race at Berwick won no diamonds, ran against the Carlisle Indian School runners, and raced in absolutely horrendous weather and over snow-covered roads. His name was Don McQuaig and he came from Hamilton, so it is likely that Domville had something to do with his presence. He finished fifth—right in the thick of the Carlisle Indian School onslaught led by Louis Tewanima. McQuaig—a green shamrock embroidered on his racing vest—slugged his way around the slippery route in a more than respectable 58:21. He was the first non-Carlisle runner to cross the line in a field of 30-plus registered runners.

Some of the pre-World War I stars from Canada included Jimmy Duffy—who finished only 8th at Berwick, but (finding longer distances better suited to his talents) won the 1914 Boston Marathon the following April. Arthur Jamieson—a Native Canadian runner—was a close third at Berwick in 1914. Sadly, both Duffy and Jamieson would die in Europe during The Great War. The Irish-born Duffy died almost exactly a year after winning Boston. During a nighttime mission, he was fatally wounded while storming a German machine gun nest hunkered down in thick woods.

Running writer David Blaikie (who has published some of the best research on the early Canadian runners) noted in his book *Boston: The Canadian Story* that Duffy's death stunned many of his friends and fans at home. Perhaps George Richards, one of Jimmy Duffy's friends and fellow runners (they had both won Round the Bay titles; Richards in 1911, then Duffy in 1912 and 1913), said it best: "I hoped that the report of Duff's death was not true. He and I were the best of pals and I can't convince myself that he is dead. He was a great runner and a fine fellow."

In the 1920s, Charlie Snell—who finished third behind countryman

Kid Shamrock: McQuaig was the first Canadian to race at Berwick.

Bricker in 1926—got lots of ink in the regional papers. Snell earned his living as a fur trapper in the Canadian wilderness and the local press obviously saw this as a unique tidbit that was worth a mention.

But the man who served as "the connection" between the 1930s and the present day Maple Leaf contingent was the same man who told me the story about the car tires—Wilmer "Whitey" Sheridan. As early as 1936, young Whitey proved his competitive merit with a seventh place finish. His top Berwick efforts yielded a pair of sixth place finishes (1942 and 1945), but Whitey's true legacy—one that true long distance runners can relate to—was his love of the sport. Fast forward to 1996; Whitey trudged his way around the rugged route—by most counts, his 50th Berwick race.

Whitey Sheridan was—first and foremost—a hard-nosed "runner's runner"—a guy for whom the capital "T" stood more for "try" than it did for "talent." That nearly was enough to land him a spot on the Canadian Olympic Marathon team in 1948; the trial finished on a track in Montreal and Whitey came into the stadium first. As a recent news article summed up, "He might have been confused about the number of laps he was sup-

227

posed to run or just too tired to put on a finishing kick. But two other runners suddenly appeared in the stadium and sprinted past him to the finish. Only the top two got Olympic berths."

Whitey Sheridan passed away on February 2, 2008. As age-defying ace Ed Whitlock (he ran the first sub-3 hour marathon for a man over 70 in the history of the planet) described Whitey's "Runner's Roost" bungalow in Waterdown, Ontario, it was "an Aladdin's cave of running memorabilia."

A frequent Berwick racer himself, Whitlock—in a beautiful balance of homage and humor—went on to say: "[Whitey] was a fierce competitor who was hard on himself and others when they showed any shortcomings. He could generally come up with something to needle someone about even if you ran well . . .

"If one was associated with Whitey, one was expected to run. Even though the daughters got out of it, somehow their husbands were not exempt. . . . Whitey worked for Stelco as an open hearth furnace operator. The heat probably kept his weight down in the days before ubiquitous bottled water. Of course there was none in the races in those days either, but that would have been an excuse that would give one no escape from his needling. . . . All the best Whitey, you won't be soon forgotten!"

Fit for his 50th: Whitey Sheridan finishes at his 50th Berwick. Susan Mitchem-Conner of Berwick performed the honorary pace-setting task.

Speaking of Ed Whitlock, he's my new hero. When I used to be a young runner, trying like hell to break 2:20 in the marathon (I never did it; 2:22:30 was the best I could muster), the typical studs—Bill Rodgers, Frank Shorter, etc.—were the guys I wanted to be like. But now that I am in my 40th year of racing, I want to be more like that Whitlock guy.

Whitlock allegedly does the bulk of his running around a cemetery near his home, because he doesn't trust cars out on the road. (Did I mention he's smart too?) Prior to his sub-3 hour marathon—at age 72—he ran three hours a day, at a relatively slow pace, for 20 days straight. He then ran 2:59:09.3 in the Scotiabank Toronto Waterfront Marathon in September, 2003, placing 26th overall in a field of more than 700 starters.

A native of Great Britain, Whitlock once ran a 4:31 mile at age 17. Rumor has it that he also once beat Gordon Pirie (British Olympian and a former World Record holder for 5000-meters in the 1950s) in a junior competition—but then he immigrated to Canada and got locked into employment demands for a few decades. Relatively late in life, Ed Whitlock made his running career comeback—in a big way. Whitlock's performances, frankly, can border on the unbelievable. For example, in the 2004 "Run for the Diamonds" Whitlock—age 73—clocked 57:45, a time that would have placed even in the 35 to 39 bracket. That may have been the race after which I overheard somebody say: "Until I found out who that old guy was, I just figured he must have cheated . . ."

Clay Shaw Photo

Mister Ed: Whitlock is the real deal—the fastest man on record for age 70-plus with his sub-3 hour marathon.

Lest you get the impression that the Canadians were always all business when they came south to Berwick, I might mention that they also—on occasion—would have a good time. Sometimes *too* good, like the year Ted McKeigan decided he would dazzle the onlookers in a Bloomsburg tavern (in defense of Mr. McKeigan, this was a *post*-race performance) with the classic yank-out-the-tablecloth trick.

It seemed like a great idea at the time.

When the stunt went awry, McKeigan (not to be confused with Harry Houdini or David Copperfield) allegedly shrugged and mumbled: "Didn't work." The tavern owner (staring at much shattered glassware) managed to contain his enthusiasm for McKeigan's deft sleight of hand, and requested that the overly festive runners—perhaps half a dozen Canadians among them—vacate his premises at their earliest convenience. The Canadians, affable fellows one and all, complied.

The Tumultuous 1960s

With the dawn of a new decade, the town of Berwick was about to encounter changing times. For the town, 1962 brought an announcement that American Car & Foundry—long the economic pillar of the riverside community—planned to close its doors in a year's time. At its zenith, the sprawling industry had employed close to 4,000 workers—some of them men whom had weathered even the Great Depression by making subway cars for New York City and who had absolutely helped win World War II by cranking out tanks to subdue the Axis powers.

In addition to its own specific trials and tribulations, Berwick, of course, felt the shock waves of national events. On November 22, just days before the 1963 race, readers of the *Berwick Enterprise* were hit with the stunningly sad news—delivered in huge, black-lettered headlines—of President John F. Kennedy's assassination. Near the end of the decade the tumultuous and divisive years of the Vietnam War swept the country—and small, semi-rural communities like Berwick were not immune to its effects.

Against the backdrop of these very real and troubling events, the Marathon remained a constant part of the town's Thanksgiving holiday. The true operation of the race began to fall increasingly on the able shoulders of Bill Heller—although the aging Chiv MacCrea was still lauded as "Mr. Marathon" in the papers and listed as "in charge of race" in the race program.

I
V as in Victory, *Z* as in Zoom
51st Berwick Marathon, November 24, 1960

If you ever want to win a bet with someone in your local running group, here's a probable winner: "What Villanova runner was the only Wildcat to win an NCAA men's cross-country title?" After reading about the exploits of H. Browning Ross in this book, that would be an educated guess. Then there were the great milers—Marty Liquori, Eamonn Coghlan, Marcus

O'Sullivan, Dave Patrick, Olympic champ Ron Delany, or Sydney Maree (who also ran the 5000 meters close to 13 minutes!). Maybe a pure cross-country guy—like Irish import Donal Walsh would be the right answer? All good guesses—all wrong.

In 1963, Victor Zwolak won Villanova's only individual men's NCAA cross-country title for Coach Jim "Jumbo" Elliott's famed distance legions. (There have been plenty of Villanova women to win the distaff NCAA harrier crown, by the way.) Zwolak, a powerfully built runner from Delaware, was also an accomplished steeplechaser and twice won the NCAA title in that event, too. In 1964, Zwolak won the NCAA steeple-chase title and followed that up just weeks later with a runner-up per-formance in the US Olympic trials. At Tokyo in the '64 Olympic Games, he narrowly missed making the finals in the steeple.

Given those credentials, perhaps—in retrospect—it isn't a huge surprise that Zwolak won the Berwick Marathon in 1960. But when you consider that he was still in his freshman year at Villanova and that he also set a course record (breaking the mark of another Nova steeplechaser, H. Brown-ing Ross), then his accomplishment becomes all the more eye opening.

Zwolak's Attack: Used to the rigors of cross-country and the grueling steeple-chase on the track, Vic Zwolak was all-systems-go on the Berwick course.

In addition, the start of the race was delayed for more than an hour while officials fretted and waited for the arrival of one of their headline stars—marine captain Alex Breckenridge, a Villanova grad and a US Olympic marathoner in 1960. After flying in from Camp Lejeune, North Carolina, Breckenridge finally arrived by limousine from Avoca Airport near Wilkes Barre, hurriedly warmed up, and then toed the line with the other runners—some of whom were openly miffed about the long delay. The pistol shot that sent the field of 57 runners down Market Street—under perfect racing conditions of cloud cover, mild temperatures and no wind—finally resounded at 3:08 PM.

According to the *Berwick Enterprise,* "Veteran Jim Montague merely started and then moved to the sidewalks. He was upset by the late start, as were many other runners and fans."

But while the disgruntled Montague was stepping off the course in a huff, Vic Zwolak and former Oberlin College (after transferring from Yale) standout George Foulds were blasting down Market Street. Their shoulder-to-shoulder duel right from the start relegated a talented field—among them Breckinridge, Canadian Olympian Bob Buchanan, accomplished steeplechaser Berry Crawford, Puerto Rican star Rudy Mendez, and Frank Pflaging (a man who would figure greatly in future Berwick races) of Baltimore—to a second pack. As the *Berwick Enterprise* noted:

> Zwolak, a freshman student at Villanova, staged a duel right with Foulds right from the start. The two moved right ahead of the pack and were never bothered by the other runners as they headed back into the hills. First one and then the other would lead, but never by more than a few yards. At Summerhill they were even and they continued to Miller's turn about the same way.

Strong and confident, Zwolak applied the pressure through Kachinka's Hollow and carved out an ever-increasing lead. By the Martzville Church, he was about 150 yards ahead of Foulds. But suddenly Zwolak—wearing the dubious number 13 on his racing vest—was struck by a side stitch and forced to slow down as he reached the Berwick country club. At slightly over 6 feet tall, Foulds stretched out his long stride and quickly gained back ground—closing the gap to 50 yards as the pair worked their way to North Berwick.

But Zwolak somehow got rid of his stitch and again began to pour on the speed. Then the fans at the top of Market Street got into it, urging the

Villanova freshman sensation toward the tape. Foulds's counterattack had faded in the wake of Zwolak's kick, but his pressure during the race certainly had provided the necessary incentive, as documented in the *Enterprise*.

> . . . it was a Pittsburgh harrier, George Foulds who did the pushing and Zwolak responded with a fine record of 46:25. Foulds finished just 12 seconds off Ross's [old] record [of 46:38 in 1953] with a 46:50.

It was an extraordinary show of running power for Zwolak and Foulds, since both of them were racing Berwick for the first time. Behind them came Breckenridge (3rd, 48:05), Buchanan (4th, 48:18), Crawford (5th, 48:29), and Pflaging (6th, 48:43). Behind Pflaging, a spirited scramble for top-ten spots came from the likes of Angie Gioiosa (7th), Dick Haines (8th) and Browning Ross's old rival, Rudy Mendez (9th).

Although Pflaging had fallen off a place when compared with his 1959 showing, the clock indicated better days might yet be coming; the Baltimore Olympic Club runner had sliced more than a minute off his previous best over the diabolical course.

II
Shirey Rolls for "the Rock"
52nd Berwick Marathon, November 23, 1961

As often happened with collegiate runners, there was no guarantee they could return to defend a Berwick Marathon title—*if* they were fortunate enough to win one to being with. Sometimes college coaches weren't all that keen on their thoroughbreds—especially ones on a full-ride scholarship—racing such a rugged event as the Berwick Marathon. And sometimes it was simply a case of recovering from the college cross-country season and resting up before launching into a vigorous indoor season.

With the NCAA cross-country championship meet staged earlier in the week down in Louisville, Kentucky, Vic Zwolak did not return to defend his Berwick title in 1961. He did, however, leave a more-than-challenging course record to chase for those in the 52nd running who might have "the right stuff."

With the powerful-running Zwolak out, George Foulds, Alex Breckenridge, and Canada's Bob Buchanan must have thought their odds greatly improved. Foulds, however, was nursing a slight injury and nursing a serious cold—and that did not bode well for confronting all that the Berwick course could dish out. The weather, too, was less than perfect—a cold drizzle greeted the runners.

Breckenridge—a man who made the 1960 US Olympic Marathon team and competed on the cobblestones of Rome—attacked the hills in the first half of the course and held a slim lead at the sharp left turn onto Kachinka's Hollow Road. But the US Marine officer perhaps felt the presence of an unknown—but obviously gung-ho—college kid dogging his heels.

The runner was Dick Shirey, wearing his Slippery Rock running shirt, the lucky number 7 (in contrast with Zwolak's Number 13 in 1960), and a knit cap to keep his head warm in the damp conditions. He won the Pennsylvania cross-country title among all the state teachers colleges—the PSACs—early in the month. Then, in what probably served as the perfect Berwick tune-up, Shirey placed fifth overall in the small-college national cross-country meet on November 18. He arrived in Berwick in peak condition and without any pressure to live up to pre-race expectations—not even the most savvy of Berwick race handicappers would have known much about him.

In the second half of the race, Shirey pulled slowly away, then galloped down Market Street to break the tape in 47:38—far off Zwolak's record run from the previous year, but 13 seconds up on Breckenridge. Buchanan charged in third, while Foulds—laboring on his bad leg and attempting to breathe with a heavy cold—managed fourth in 49:01. Foulds, in fact, had rallied gallantly down the steep slope of Hosler's Hill, and briefly moved into second place at Miller's corner before giving way again to Breckenridge and Buchanan through Kachinka's Hollow.

It definitely qualified as a small upset, as the college kid held off the much-experienced Breckenridge. In addition to his Olympic Marathon experience (he had finished 30th in Rome—essentially in the middle of the race that was won by the barefooted Ethiopian great Abebe Bikela), Breckenridge had also placed sixth in the Pan American Games 10,000 meters. In Breckenridge's defense, his duties in the US Marine Corps did not always make for regular training routines and—perhaps even more of a factor—allowed him to race less often than was ideal.

Officially representing the Penn Hills Striders, Shirey received solid support from Angie Gigiosa (5th overall) and Matt Gregory (8th overall) to take the team title over the Delaware Valley AA.

Other notable top-ten finishes came from former University of Kansas steeplechase standout Berry Crawford (6th) and Philadelphia high school runner Moses Mayfield (7th).

While the Canadians were pleased to place Bob Buchanan among the top four, Wilmer "Whitey" Sheridan drew well-deserved applause from the Berwick fans, too. The Hamilton Olympic Club veteran placed 26th—exactly halfway in a field of 52 runners in the 52nd annual event—with a respectable time of 55:45. The local papers could not resist comparing Whitey to "Ole Man River"—"the likeable towhead just keeps rolling along and apparently is determined to break Johnny Kelley's record of 25 Berwick races, the present record number of appearances." In fact, the ever-ready Whitey was destined to *double* Johnny Kelley's Berwick appearance mark.

III
Picking Quinn to Win
53rd Berwick Marathon, November 22, 1962

The pre-race rumor mill was working at high speed as the 53rd Berwick Marathon approached. Not only had defending champ Dick Shirey signed up, but highly touted Fred Norris, a force from New England (by way of Old England) was entered as well.

If there ever was a runner who rated "favorite" status without having actually run the Berwick course before, then that man was Norris—a tough, wiry, working-class bloke who had once mined coal for a living. He had raced for Great Britain in the 1952 Helsinki Olympic Games, placing a respectable eighth in the 10,000 meters. Although he was 40 years old, nobody was expecting Berwick's climb to Summer Hill to be much of a bother for Norris; just that June he had zoomed to the summit of Mount Washington in New Hampshire (essentially 8 miles of uphill on the mountain's auto road) in a stunning time of 1:04 and change. (Norris's time that day was a Masters record that stood for forty years.)

Unfortunately, Norris did not show. A late letter arrived, expressing regrets and mentioning a strained muscle. The defending champ Shirey, too, was a late scratch. Suddenly the Thanksgiving Day classic was up for grabs. Die-hard handicappers of the race—and there were still some who reportedly liked to lay a five or a ten on the outcome—must have been in a quandary.

Once again, it seemed that Breckenridge and Buchanan might move up a spot or two and fight it out for a Berwick crown. There were some other runners who rated a brief mention—whispers of dark-horse roles and such—and among that wild herd was Kevin Quinn, recently graduated from Saint Joseph's College and teaching history at Roman Catholic High School. Representing the Delaware Valley AA at Berwick, Quinn's teammate Pat Walsh was also considered a runner who could place in the top half a dozen.

Berwick Marathon Association official Bill Heller knew Quinn was sharp because he had seen him win a cross-country race in Harrisburg, a mere four days before. Quinn had twice won the Middle Atlantic AAU cross-country title, and his mile record at St. Joe's indicated that he could call on better-than-average finishing speed—if needed—down Market Street.

A miserable, goose-bump-inducing rain greeted the runners on race day. Perhaps trying to keep out of the dismal elements for as long as possible, several runners arrived a few crucial seconds late to the starting line. That included the main Maple Leaf hope, Bob Buchanan, and his tardiness cost him a few precious seconds, as the field was off and running down Market before he belatedly left the line—approximately 20 yards behind. Bob Zollenhoffer of the Boston Athletic Association also got caught by the gun; he was removing his warm-up pants and shirt when the starter's pistol barked. He eventually worked up to 12th place, after initially giving away 15 yards.

Quinn, however, was ready to roll—even though he had only *heard* about the Berwick hill and had not scouted it out first hand prior to the race. Armed with the power of blissful ignorance, Quinn whipped through the easy opening 2 miles before tucking right into the climb toward the Summer Hill churches.

After the race, Quinn admitted to Bill Heller (his insights appearing in Heller's "Sportracings" wrap-up column a few days later) that he really hadn't planned for the climb to be quite so tiring and tedious.

"Every time I went around a curve, I though sure that the top was near but the road seemed always to stretch upward and endlessly ahead," mused young Quinn. "I think I might have held back had I been aware of that long hill ahead of time."

But once committed, Quinn—like the famed St. Joe's mascot, the Hawk—clutched the lead and refused to relinquish it. He recovered somewhat on the long descent from Hosler's Hill, and took about a 35-yard lead into the Kachinka's Hollow stretch. In fact, Quinn's clubmate—Pat Walsh—briefly swept into second at Miller's turn, but Breckenridge soon counterattacked and again took up the pursuit of the front-runner. Meantime, Buchanan had dug out from his miscue at the start and moved into a solid fourth position, his eyes fixed on the hardworking men ahead of him.

The rain increased in the final miles, but Quinn more than matched it with pressure of his own through Martzville and past the Berwick country club. Once he was back on Market Street, the crowd—despite the dreary day—got behind him. Drenched but jubilant, he raced to the tape and clocked 47:35—far off Zwolak's record time, but a few ticks faster than Shirey had won with the year before. Kevin Quinn's performance won him the first place watch (presented by Berwick-born Pennsylvania state senator Zehnder Confair) and a paragraph of well-deserved praise in Heller's post-race column. Wrote Heller:

> His time of 47:35 was remarkable in light of the fact that it
> was his first time over the course and that he also battled a cold
> wind and some heavy rain over the last half of the course.

Breckenridge again was forced to settle for runner-up honors (2nd, 48:26), with Buchanan again third (3rd, 49:24). Walsh hung on for fourth (49:41). Along with Dick Donahue (8th, 51:18), Quinn and Walsh combined to give Delaware Valley AA the team title, with Altoona AC (led by Angie Gioiosa, 5th in 49:53) placed second.

Other notable performances in the field of 40 finishers came from Bloomsburg State College sophomore Jan Prosseda, who placed 10th in 51:47. Berwick High School's Dave Stoker led the local lads (19th, 54:49).

As for the tuckered but happy Quinn, his last comments to Heller before he climbed into his car to head home to Philadelphia and a scrumptious Thanksgiving feast were: "I'll return next year."

The Road of Life being a series of potholes, Quinn never did get back to Berwick for another race. And one day, while Quinn was out for a training run, someone with sticky fingers stole the first-place Berwick watch from his gym locker. As the melancholy writer Kurt Vonnegut might have mused: "So it goes."

20

Pflaging's Tour de Force

I
Pflaging's Second Half Charge
54th Berwick Marathon, November 28, 1963

Although Kevin Quinn's parting words were a well-intentioned promise to defend his title in Berwick, the following year came and he did not
arrive. Instead, a letter did, noting that a tear in his Achilles tendon would
have him on the mend and not on the starting line. Quinn dashed off a
letter to Bill Heller, the assistant race secretary, lamenting his reluctant
withdrawal from the event. The *Enterprise* reprinted a portion of Quinn's
note:

> I am very sorry that I can't defend my title this year—but I
> am sure that you understand. Winning your race was one of the
> great thrills of my career and I will always remember the
> Berwick Marathon.

There was, however, a competitive race shaping up, although it would
be without the likable former St. Joe's star.

Bill Heller's years in the Baltimore area (coaching at St. Paul's) helped
keep the 1950s and 1960s at Berwick stoked with some of the top running
talent that Maryland had to offer. Arguably the best at Berwick was a quiet-
spoken, bespectacled former Georgetown University standout named
Frank Pflaging. He first raced at Berwick in 1959, placing a more-than-
respectable fifth. And although he dropped to sixth the following year, he
sliced more than a minute off his time—and all that hinted of fast races yet
to come.

Heading into the 1963 race, Pflaging had something else going in his
favor: George Foulds—the runner-up to Zwolak's record run in 1960—
was back again, and the area papers promptly pronounced Foulds as the
pre-race favorite. The day before the race the *Enterprise* wrote:

> The appearance of Foulds here is met with high interest for
> he is the one that pushed Vic Zwolak of Villanova to the pres-
> ent course record of 46:25, set in 1960. Running here in 1961,

with a bad leg and heavy cold, the ex-Yale distance star placed fourth in the field with a good time of 49:01. This will be the third appearance here for Foulds.

With most people in a somber mood—if not still in actual shock—from the fatal sniper ambush of President Kennedy's motorcade just days before in Dallas, the race nevertheless went to the line on Thanksgiving Day at 2 PM.

The Marathon most likely did add a small feeling of normalcy. Plans unfolded for the race as if it were just another year. As per usual back in these days before runners gorged on the obligatory heaping plates of pasta, the Berwick Moose Club and the town's Fraternal Order of Eagles treated the entries and their guests to a pig roast *and*—for good measure—sauerkraut on the side, on Marathon eve. (One can only venture a guess what sort of intestinal trickery this meal may have caused for the distance runner of that day.)

Nothing, however, slowed down George Foulds, who bolted off at the crack of J. Howard Remley's pistol. He zeroed in on another fast starter—Doug Thomas of the Harrisburg A.A.—but unleashed his long stride and broke to the front around the 1-mile mark.

Thomas eventually faded back to 22nd place, but Foulds—as if to live up to the Number 1 pinned to his shirt—hammered down to Foundryville and then parlayed his front-running momentum right into the face of "the Hill." It was some gutsy running on a typical late-fall day, a hint of winter hanging in the cold breeze.

In Foulds's wake trailed the largest field in Berwick Marathon history—74 starters, of whom only two would fail to finish. The previous record number of runners had been 56 in 1960. Near the front of the pursuit pack were two Baltimore Olympic Club runners—Pflaging and Rich Frampton.

Foulds attacked the hill with reckless abandon and was rewarded with a 150-yard lead at the top. But Pflaging gained some of that back on the flat at the top and the second climb and descent of Hosler's Hill. At Miller's Corners, Foulds's cushion was down to 30 yards. Pflaging patiently chipped away through Kachinka's Hollow's small, rolling rises and descents and was a mere 5 yards back at the Martzville Church.

By the Berwick golf club, the two hardworking runners were essentially even. Some distance behind them Frampton held down third, just ahead of William and Mary harrier Bob Lawson. Rich Lampman, a Nittany Lion runner, was dueling with a precocious schoolboy star—Steve Gentry of State College.

As the front-runners approached North Berwick, Pflaging unfurled his best running. As the *Berwick Enterprise* later put it:

> From then on Pflaging moved into the front and he set the pace all the way to the finish line. The winner appeared in fine condition when he crossed the line.

Pflaging stopped the clock in 46:50, just 25 seconds off Zwolak's fine mark. Hanging on for a solid second was Foulds in 47 minutes flat. With diamond rings back as race awards, both Pflaging and Foulds had turned in racing performances worthy of the hard gem.

It was almost 2 minutes more before Frampton checked in for third, a full 100 yards ahead of Lawson in fourth. Gentry, who had earlier in the month won the Pennsylvania state 3-A cross-country title, ran a solid fifth—exactly 3 minutes behind the winner. The boys from Baltimore—led by Pflaging and Frampton—easily won the team title, with the Nittany Lions Track and Field Club settling for second.

Did anyone on the Berwick Marathon Association roster envision a field that might soon top 100? Most likely. Did anyone think in terms of 1000-plus or a race with hundreds of women in the mix? Most likely—nobody!

II
Pflaging's Encore Tour
55th Berwick Marathon, November 26, 1964

As the 55th annual Thanksgiving Day race approached, the local papers were abuzz with two recent letters that had winged their way to Bob Eshleman—the nurseryman from just west of Berwick and one of the original 13 men who had toed the Market Street line in 1908.

One was from Johnny Kelley, Eshelman's friend for several decades. The four-time race champ often stayed with Eshelman when he came to Berwick and no doubt Kelley, the former florist, and Eshelman discussed growing flowers when they weren't talking about the Marathon.

In a response to Eshelman's letter inviting Kelley to come tour around the course in a lead car during the race, the flinty, battle-tested veteran quipped:

"If I came to Berwick, it would be to run, not ride around the course as an 'Honored Guest' . . . I am in good shape and still running. Competed in eight races thus far this year and came home in the first 10 on 5 different occasions."

Around the same time, Eshelman also received also received a letter from the 10-time winner Browning Ross. Ross had not raced at Berwick for five years, but the 40-year-old road warrior strongly implied he was anxious to return, writing:

"Surprisingly enough I am in real good running condition at the moment (no usual nagging leg injuries) and if everything holds up I will run in the Berwick Marathon. Probably have a job winning but feel sure I can place in the first three. It would definitely be my last Berwick Race as a runner, for at 40 I am just too old to keep up with these kids."

And then Ross added: "I still consider the Berwick Marathon the finest race in the country and would rather win there than at any National Championship."

Unfortunately, when race day actually rolled around, Ross was ambushed by the flu—he called race officials on Thanksgiving morning and bowed out. He had a sore throat, a 101-degree temperature, and, if that weren't enough, doctor's orders not to run. Vic Zwolak, his 1960 course record still the mark to beat, had also planned to race at Berwick, but he, too, had the flu. Scratch another top runner from the field.

Frank Pflaging, the Baltimore Olympic Club point man, was back to defend his title. He even turned down a chance to compete in the conflicting US cross-country championships in order to race at Berwick.

It turned out to be a good choice, as Pflaging turned in a near-flawless race and cranked out a new personal best on the course, despite some occasional spurts of cold rain. Pflaging also landed his second straight C. G. Crispin Memorial diamond ring.

If they gave out "assists" in road racing, then Pflaging's BOC teammate Larrie Sweet would have gained that accolade in the 1964 Berwick Marathon. Although Lou Coppens of the Ridley Township Striders ran point down to Foundryville, it was Sweet who led Pflaging over the tough miles—the infamous ups and downs that still make Berwick's course what it is today. Even by the time the BOC men crested the top of "the Hill," it was clear no other runner was close enough to help them out with the pace or threaten them, either.

After Coppens fell off the leaders, Steve Gentry—the 17-year-old high school star from State College—took over third. He wasn't, however, quite strong enough or experienced enough to pressure a veteran road racer like Pflaging.

But Sweet fulfilled the "pushing" role quite well. Pflaging took the lead through Kachinka's Hollow, but didn't really pull away until the downhill stretch out of Martzville. He arrived in North Berwick looking strong and dashed through the finish line in 46:46.2—trimming 3 seconds off his winning time from the previous year. Sweet stuck in there and cracked 47 minutes—if just barely—with 46:59.

Gentry, with a rare diamond-winning performance from a high school runner, held on to third in 48:35. He also won a wristwatch for being the first scholastic finisher, and an engraved trophy for being the first finisher from Pennsylvania. Louis Castagnola of the American U Track Club of Washington, DC, moved up nicely to secure fourth (48:58), outkicking the Altoona veteran Angie Gioiosa (5th, 49:02) who snagged his third fifth

Photo courtesy of Berwick Marathon Association

Baltimore's Best: Frank Pflaging led the charge for the Baltimore Olympic Club in the mid-1960s, posting three straight Berwick victories.

place in four years—this one good for a diamond. Coppens, a former Delaware Valley College standout, managed to place sixth (49:15) despite his headstrong start. Former Bloomsburg State star Jan Prosseda, representing the Harrisburg AA, held off Bill Greenplate for 7th (49:31).

Back in 20th place—in a modest time of 51:30—was one Charlie Messenger, a Kenwood High School star who also ran on the BOC team. Two years down the road he would post more than a few places higher on the Berwick Marathon finishers list.

III
Pflaging's Hat Trick
56th Berwick Marathon, November 25, 1965

Even the pre-race hype in the *Berwick Enterprise* didn't attempt to pretend that Frank Pflaging was anything other than the favorite as the 56th event finalized entries. Pflaging had once again bypassed a chance to compete in the US cross-country championships, opting for a Thanksgiving Day jaunt through the Briar Creek Hills instead. He also was in fantastic shape, having run some excellent track times over 3000 and 5000 meters in Europe during an AAU summer tour. As the paper reported:

> It's hard to go against a winner and Frank Pflaging with two consecutive victories over the Berwick course has been cast in the favorite's role. Pflaging pretty much had his own way in 1964 as he finished well ahead of Larrie Sweet with a fine time of 46:46.

If there was one man out there who just *might* have messed with Pflaging's shot at a third straight first-place diamond, then that runner probably was Chuck Leuthold. Representing the Nittany Lion Track and Field Club, Leuthold came into the event off a good cross-country season for Penn State. The *Enterprise* referred to him as "one of the real good young distance men in the east . . ."

On race day, the runners were greeted with excellent weather—a slight cloud cover, mild temperatures, and (best of all) no wind. As the runners arrived at the 2-mile mark near the Foundryville bridge, Pflaging took control of the pace. But Leuthold tucked right in behind—essentially taking on the role of "pressure man" that Larrie Sweet had occupied the year before. Their climb up the mountain to the Summer Hill churches essentially turned the race into a two-man battle, as the *Enterprise* recorded:

> Pflaging gained the lead at Foundryville with Leuthold right behind him and their positions never changed as the champ withstood the strong challenge . . . In fact Leuthold's challenge is the reason a new record exists today.

Once he opened up some breathing room—perhaps 50 yards or so at halfway—Pflaging kept the pressure on. He knew any slacking of the pace would allow Leuthold to reestablish contact. The two-time defending champ worked all the way through Kachinka's Hollow, Martzville, past the golf course, and—once back on Market Street—he pressed all the way to the tape.

The result was a new course record. The Baltimore Olympic Club star snapped the tape in 45 minutes, 57 seconds—not only shattering Vic Zwolak's five-year mark (46:25) but also establishing the first sub-46 on the course. Although he looked smooth racing into the finish, Pflaging admitted to being "tired and sore, but happy" after his record run.

Leuthold kept digging deep, too, and was rewarded with the second-fastest time ever run on the Berwick layout; his 46:11 was also well under Zwolak's old record. And although third place—which went to "Turtle" Tom Osler in a brisk 47:10 that seemed to fly in the face of his nickname—was far off the two leaders, a domino effect seemed to sweep the field: 14 men dipped under 49 minutes, a new Berwick first.

Rounding out the top ten after Osler were Tom McCarthy of New York's Gaelic American Club (4th, 47:27), James Smyth of Drexel Hill (5th), Ray Smith of the Nittany Lion Track and Field Club (6th), John Acri of John Harris High School (7th), Lamont Smith, Empire Harriers (8th), the Altoona AC veteran, Angelo Gioiosa (9th), and Lou Castagnola of the American U Track Club (10th). Larrie Sweet, who had pushed Pflaging to such a great race just the year before, fell back to 14th.

Acri, who had won the accompanying Berwick 5-mile high school race in 1963, arguably turned in one of the most impressive performances of the day. He clocked 48:16, a faster time than Steve Gentry had run to clinch third in 1964.

Pflaging's win, of course, immediately placed him in rare company. He joined the ranks of Louis Tewanima, Hannes Kolehmainen, Lou Gregory, Scotty Rankine, Johnny Kelley, and H. Browning Ross in the "three victories" circle—making him a runner who even in the ever-accumulating history of the Berwick Marathon would deserve special mention.

Finish Lines: "Turtle" Tom Osler did some of his best running in the mid-1960s. In addition to his Berwick third, he won the Philadelphia Marathon in 1965, plus—in 1967—he won the AAU National 30K title and broke 2:30 (19th place) at Boston a month later. A math teacher at Rowan University, Osler once claimed he started racing to escape "nerd status."

21

Record-Smashing 1960s

I
Messenger Delivers
57th Berwick Marathon, November 24, 1966

The 1960s at Berwick were marked by some hit-and-run raids, so to speak, by college hotshots—including the record-setting Villanova's Vic Zwolak, Slippery Rock standout Dick Shirey, and St. Joe's Kevin Quinn (a graduate, but only recently so) at the start of the decade. Amazingly, none of those young men had even run the course before. All that flew in the face of the old Berwick lore that had suggested the experienced runner (a man who had confronted "the Hill" once before)—if not an actual battle-tested veteran—stood the best chance to snap the finish-line string on Market Street.

Frank Pflaging's trio of victories, then, was something of a return to normalcy. Pflaging had placed well (5th and 6th) in his two earliest forays and then ascended to the winners' circle, presumably well schooled on how to run the course—as his reeling in of the front-running Foulds in 1963 seemed to reflect.

But in the middle of all that so-called normalcy came another Villanova Wildcat—another brash rookie (at least in terms of the Berwick beast)—who would, as the old-time bettors on the race so quaintly stated it, "upset the dope."

Charlie Messenger was a college kid who fit the upset mold. Defending champ Pflaging, for one, would have been well aware of Messenger's abilities because he enlisted him to run for the Baltimore Olympic Club. Also, Messenger had starred at Kenwood High School in Maryland (along with Dick Patrick, another thoroughbred miler in Villanova's stable). And if you were looking for more recent proof, Messenger was coming off a fantastic cross-country season in which he (and Nova teammate Tom Donnelly) had led the Wildcat charge to the NCAA title just days before.

Messenger, in fact, swept out Market Street like a kid still riding that adrenaline high from helping his team clinch the collegiate crown. At the top of Summer Hill, fans needed a long look back to even catch a glimpse of the pursuit pack—the young Wildcat had clawed his way up the mountain and opened up a significant lead of more than 100 yards. Although sometimes front-runners at the top gave some back on the crash-and-burn tumble down Hosler's Hill, Messenger, in fact, *doubled* his lead. Bill Falla of the BOC ran second at Miller's turn, but he had worked very hard just to be there and was still 200 yards behind Messenger.

Meanwhile, cagy veterans Pflaging and Herb Lorenz of New Jersey picked up the pace through Kachinka's Hollow, passing runners who had perhaps put too much energy into the first half of the race. They were racing each other and also hoping to catch a glimpse of Messenger in the process. But even their spirited duel never really put them in contact with the Villanova thin-clad. And even if they had caught him, Messenger—an accomplished track runner who had performed superbly in such pressure-cooker situations as the Penn Relays—surely could have summoned a finishing spurt.

But it never got down to a kick. Not even close. Messenger blitzed down Market Street, his face seemingly without a sign of strain. While there was some doubt the previous year if Pflaging could sneak under the 46-minute barrier, Messenger dropped the record—like a wayward elevator missing an entire floor—by a huge amount. The new mark to shoot for was 45:36—and it now that mark belonged to Charlie Messenger.

Nearly a minute later, Lorenz claimed runner-up honors (2nd, 46:32), just ahead of Pflaging (3rd, 46:36), who desperately held off hard-charging Dan Payne (4th, 46:37). Payne did his collegiate running at West Virginia University, but he had his local followers since he hailed from nearby Wilkes-Barre. Payne's superb effort gave him the state and tricountry awards.

II
Scharf Storms To Victory
58th Berwick Marathon, November 23, 1967

The 58th running of the traditional race was greeted with dismal conditions in the morning—rain and cold. The rain subsided by the time the field assembled on Market Street, but the chilling wind and damp cold engulfed the runners, many prancing around in an attempt to keep warm.

Only 49 of the registered 60 runners answered the call, the weather no doubt part of the reason. It was already known that Villanova's Messenger would not defend his title, as the Wildcats had been concentrating on their collegiate season. (Led by Messenger's 10th place finish, Villanova successfully defended its NCAA harrier title out in Laramie, Wyoming on the Monday after Berwick.)

In the minutes leading up to the gun, Bob Scharf of the Washington Sports Club—one of the co-favorites—opted to pull a yellow jersey over his racing vest (and race number); not a bad idea in such conditions.

When the gun sounded, Ray Somers of the Baltimore Olympic Club surged to the front, apparently helping pace BOC ace and three-time Berwick winner Frank Pflaging down to Foundryville.

Having never run the course before, Scharf was content to allow Pflaging to take him around the course. However, just before the leaders reached Martzville Church—on the hill—Scharf grabbed the lead. He soon lengthened it to 25 yards as he hung a left and headed back toward Berwick. By the time Scharf hit the top of Market, he had hammered out a healthy edge of more than 20 seconds.

Berwick fans were not sure who this front-runner was for the first 7 miles, as noted in the *Enterprise* article:

> Scharf was a mystery man for most of the race, for he wore a yellow shirt over this uniform hiding his number (55). He wore the jersey to keep himself warm and about two miles from home he shed the garment to reveal his identity.

Striding down Market, Scharf hit the tape in 46 minutes, 11.2 seconds. BOC veteran Pflaging placed second, half a minute behind. Lou Castagnola—Scharf's Washington Sports Club teammate and the winner of the Washington's Birthday Marathon (2:22:46) back in February—took third (46:40).

Rounding out the top seven finishers were Somers (4th, 47:29), Frank Glanz (5th, 48:03), and Charlie Koester (6th, 48:09), all of the Baltimore Olympic Club; and seventh was Dave Leuthold of State College in 48:31. Along with Pflaging's runner-up effort, the BOC's four men easily carried the team title, despite WSC's 1-3 start from Scharf and Castagnola.

Back in 22nd place was a young runner from St. Francis College by the name of Steve Molnar. He clocked a modest 51:19, but was destined to run much faster and place much higher in some future diamond runs.

III
The Flying Irish: Patrick's Prediction
59th Berwick Marathon, November 28, 1968

Patrick McMahon, an Irishman residing in the US as an undergraduate student at Oklahoma Baptist College, came to Berwick with Olympic Marathon credentials (12th at Mexico City, in a highly competitive field and despite the high altitude) and a whole lot of confidence. Clearly, this wild Irish rose—who sported a kelly-green warm-up suit— was not to be mistaken for a shrinking violet . . . Upon his arrival in town, the 24-year-old McMahon immediately made an astounding pronouncement: He claimed that the Berwick course was "a fast track" and furthermore he predicted he could run the route in 44 minutes and 30 seconds!

If that dropped some jaws among the local Berwick Marathon aficionados, then McMahon quickly did the same to the field in the 59th edition of Pennsylvania's longest-running hit. Only three-time Berwick champ Frank Pflaging of Baltimore could stay close enough to even witness McMahon's unbridled attack of the course. Two miles into the race, the lanky (5-foot-11-plus) but well-muscled Irishman held a 30-yard lead over Pflaging; by the Summer Hill churches he had tripled his cushion.

And Pflaging was running fairly fast, too, far ahead of third. The pack had busted up faster than a pack of billiard balls subjected to the precision break of a pool shark. This particular race was destined to be one of those rare Berwicks when the front-runner's pace was so hot that it promptly strung out the field in its exhaust fumes. In other words, it wasn't all that different from Messenger's one-man assault in 1966.

McMahon's run through Kachinka's Hollow and Martzville was a lonely one in terms of competition; only the spectators were there to cheer him on, then craning necks and casting eyes back down the road in search of the next running rival. The wait was significant. The weather was less than perfect—cold and breezy.

When it was over, McMahon's time prediction was a minute off. He settled for a mere course record of 45 minutes, 19.6 seconds. Pflaging, the runner-up, crossed more than 2 minutes after in 47:34—and he was more than a minute in front of Glenn Brewer, the Pottstown Pacer entry who placed third (48:37). Pflaging—who rarely had much to say about himself after winning a big race—was quick to laud Patrick McMahon's running prowess.

"He's a great runner," Pflaging emphatically informed reporters. "He stepped right out and no matter how hard I tried I couldn't catch him."

Behind the front-runners, Bill Showers from nearby Milton (where he had just won the PIAA Class B cross-country title) came in 5th in an attempted tie with Wayne McBride, another scholastic star out of Harrisburg. Both boys clocked 49 flat, just 3 seconds behind fourth place finisher Eric Walther of Jamaica, New York, but Showers got the nod.

Rounding out the top ten were: Mark Moreau from Brown (7th, 50:01), Dick Geiger, Spring Grove, Pennsylvania. (8th, 50:05), Robert Brown of the Harrisburg AA (9th, 50:11), and Gordon Michener of the Hamilton Olympic Club (10th, 50:14).

In the next group of ten, two names jump out to lifelong fans of the race: Lanny Connor (16th, 50:57), who posted for the Berwick Ramblers, and the young Canadian he was chasing—David Sheridan (15th, 50:49), one of Whitey's running sons.

IV
The Silver Fox Slips In
60th Berwick Marathon, November 27, 1969

The Berwick Marathon Association usually made a concerted effort to bring back the reigning champion to defend his crown over a course that the real old-timers still sometimes referred to as "the Briar Creek Hills."

There is no doubt the BMA would have wanted to see the fleet-footed Irish Olympian and new Berwick record holder—one Patrick McMahon—back on the starting line in 1969. It's quite probable that talks of "expense money"—and how much was enough—came into the equation of bringing back McMahon, who was now based in Boston and running for the Boston Athletic Association.

McMahon, for his part, certainly seemed interested in coming back. He sent a letter to Berwick officials and—in his typically blunt fashion, skipped right over any pretense of false modesty—wrote: "I am running great at the moment, and this year, I am sure I could get very close to 44:30 for 9.3-miles . . ."

In McMahon's defense, this was no mere bit of blarney. Back in April he had placed eighth overall in the Boston Marathon (in 2:23), won the rugged Cape Ann's 25K in August, and on October 25 won the 30K (18.6 miles) Around the Bay Race in Hamilton, Ontario with a solid time of

1:38:20. Given Berwick's direct hotline to Hamilton (i.e., Whitey Sheridan and the boys), the BMA would have been well informed on McMahon's victory there.

But something must have gone awry—possibly a gap too wide to bridge involving expense money—because McMahon was not back in Berwick. Instead, he opted for a much shorter race (and the Irishman was obviously more lethal at the longer stuff): the Manchester, Connecticut, Thanksgiving Day run of approximately 4.8 miles.

In a way, McMahon suffered a double loss that day. He managed a close second to Amby Burfoot (1968 Boston Marathon winner and long-time *Runner's World* editor-writer) up in Manchester, and, later the same day, his sterling Berwick Marathon record was broken—by less than a second and a half.

Newcomer Jim Howell of the North Carolina Track Club set a brisk early pace, no doubt energized in the cool, calm conditions—perfect for long-distance running. Meanwhile, veteran Berwick runners Frank Pflaging and Herb Lorenz kept contact a few yards back.

Eventually Howell slipped back to third by midway, while three-time winner Pflaging and Lorenz (1966 runner-up to Messenger's record run) went *mano-a-mano* in a spirited battle. Lorenz, who would gain the nickname of "The Silver Fox" in his Masters Division years because he raced so smart, opened up a very slight lead over Pflaging near the Martzville Church and then added to it gradually over the final 3 miles.

Lorenz, of Mount Laurel, New Jersey, had something other than just his talent going for him when it came to that final push. Sure, the tall and powerful Lorenz had long strides. But that something extra was fear.

"I could hear Pflaging's footsteps over my shoulder and was fearful that he might come on strong at any moment," Lorenz said in a finish line confession to the local press.

That fear proved to be a great motivator and most probably cost McMahon his Berwick record. Lorenz thrust his torso through the tape and stopped the clock at 45 minutes, 18.2 seconds.

Pflaging's great effort—albeit second best—nevertheless paid off with a bonus: a time faster than any of his three victories. The Baltimore Olympic Club ace was timed in 45:42. He didn't have much time to spare, as John Loeschorn (3rd, 45:46) and his North Carolina Track Club teammate Howell (4th, 45:47) barreled in next. British-born Brian Drewitt, representing the Hamilton Olympic Club, placed fifth (46:20).

With Loeschorn (who later in his career became an accomplished marathoner and ultramarathoner) and Howell, and third man John Jayro (6th, 46:37), the boys from the Tar Heel State carried the team title quite convincingly.

Regional standouts Wilkes-Barre's Dan Payne (48:00) and Milton's Bill Showers (48:04) placed ninth and tenth, while Upper Merion's Bill Louv—having won the PIAA cross-country title earlier in the month, placed 16th (49:13) over the rugged route.

22

The Sizzling 1970s

Running in America was on the verge of a new era when the 1970s began. The decade would see the emergence of two major American marathon stars—first Frank Shorter (his Olympic Marathon win in Munich a pivotal moment for American distance running) and then Bill Rodgers. Canadian standout Jerome Drayton emerged with similar brilliance north of the border. Although none of these great runners ever competed at Berwick (Shorter came oh-so close!), the inspirational effect of their world-class performances arguably raised the competitiveness of young runners who hovered at the levels just slightly below them.

Glance at the sheer depth of the Berwick results from the mid-1970s and spilling into the 1980s and you cannot but help utter "Wow!" Times that might win a diamond in today's era would have had you fighting for a spot in the 20s or even the 30s in Berwick's most competitive heyday.

In addition, a second important aspect of the Berwick Marathon began to emerge: the fields began to get bigger—and bigger! The first stage of the so-called running boom was exploding by the mid-1970s and Berwick, in terms of size and quality of front-runners, began to gradually reap the benefits of that trend. The crowds certainly were not as big as in the pre-TV era, but the number of actual runners began to increase—cracking the 100 mark for the first time in 1973.

You could argue that the Running Boom continues to reshape itself and evolve (the most obvious being the continued rise of women participants). It is not out of the question that Berwick will top 2,000 runners for its 2008 and 2009 events. Some of that obviously will because of the celebration of the 100th anniversary since Domville's starting pistol snapped and sent 13 intrepid locals down a muddy Market Street and also the actual 100th race in 2009. But part of this rising trend in participants—despite Berwick's tough, no-nonsense course and its not always convenient Thanksgiving Day date—is that running continues to evolve into an all-embracing sport of the masses.

I
Jerry! Jerry! Richey Rolls at Berwick
61st Berwick Marathon, November 26, 1970

In 1970, the pre-race hype centered on Jerry Richey—an accomplished miler at Pitt and former North Allegheny High School star—as one of the favorites. He had won two PIAA State 3-A titles in cross-country (and four more on the track) and now was the leader of his Pitt Panther squads.

Richey's entry set up one of those interesting pre-race dilemmas for Berwick Marathon handicappers. Could a young college runner—with proven speed credentials (Richey had already run the mile in 3:58.6 at Pitt in 1968)—handle "the Hill" and beat the veteran long-distance types? Although he had run only so-so in the recent NCAA cross-country championships staged in Williamsburg, Virginia, earlier in the month, he'd placed second at the IC4A harrier meet, indicating he would be sharp for racing.

Herb Lorenz did not return to defend his title (he opted for a race in Puerto Rico instead), but Baltimore Olympic Club standout Frank Pflaging—a three-time Berwick champ—certainly fit the bill as wily veteran.

Richey, however, was not the only hotshot collegiate runner in the field. The Canadians had an entire team—Waterloo University of Ontario—headed by Maple Leaf ace David Northey.

As Northey recently recalled, "I think there was just a few of us that came down that first time. There was a guy at school who was from Hamilton, and that's how we first heard about it. He said, 'Hey, there's this race down in the hills of Pennsylvania and they give away diamond rings as prizes . . . ' So we decided to go down and give it a go."

The race weather (mild, clear, a tad breezy) was more cooperative than J. Howard Remley's starting pistol, which initially failed to fire. On Remley's second and successful attempt, the field bolted out Market Street. Puerto Rico's Carlos Ortiz soon zoomed to the front and set the pace down to Foundryville.

As the course entered its torturous phase, it was Northey who took over the pace-setting chores and Pflaging who attached himself to the young Canadian's hip. Richey ran a few yards back and steadily climbed 'the Hill"—not gaining ground, but not losing much, either. Also moving well was Lock Haven State College coach and former University of Michigan runner Jim Dolan.

Richey ran well down Hosler's Hill and moved right up to the leaders.

He whipped around the hard left where Miller's Hotel had once stood and—shortly after—the Panther star pounced. As he told reporters after the race: "I laid back waiting for a chance . . . When we came around this little turn I went for the lead and once I got it I knew I could keep it."

Said Pflaging about Richey's big move: "I heard him coming and I tried to stay in front of him, but there was nothing I could do . . . He just breezed right by me."

Northey established himself in second and took up the task of pursuing Richey. Pflaging kept contact with the Canadian, a few yards back.

In fact, Northey vs. Pflaging soon became the most interesting tussle of the day, as Richey continued to pull away through Kachinka's Hollow, Martzville, and North Berwick. He never really had to reach for his miler's kick as he cruised home for the win in 45 minutes, 29.6 seconds. Richey clinched the C. W. Crispin first-place diamond for his effort and also the Con Dellegrotto Memorial Trophy for being the first Pennsylvanian to finish.

Northey also dipped under 46, clocked 45:51 as he gradually relegated Pflaging to third (46:09) over the final miles. Dolan, gaining on Pflaging in the final drive to the tape, finished fourth (46:15). Northey's strong debut performance (which certainly hinted of bigger things to come) and teammate Paul Pearson's 10th place spearheaded Waterloo U's team title win of 27 points, just 3 better than the Dolan's Lock Haven Track Club.

Rounding out the top ten finishers were Richey's Panther teammate Mike Schurko (5th), Cornell frosh Phil Collins (6th), Chambersburg High School runner Tim Cook (7th), Dan Payne of Wilkes-Barre and West Virginia University (8th), North Carolina runner George Phillips (9th), and Pearson. The first regional finisher was West Chester runner Bill Showers from Milton (12th).

In addition to Richey's first place, Pittsburgh-area runners also had the last finisher. Mark Danton of Jeannette finished 65th (out of 68 starters—three men dropped out), but was honored nonetheless with the Carl "Red" Canouse Trophy given to the oldest finisher. Danton was mere 57 years old—a youngster compared with some of today's graying gazelles.

Politicians have often been on the peripheral fringes of the race, frequently donating prizes (including diamond rings) to Berwick runners. At the 1970 event, Congressman Daniel J. Flood presided at the post-race celebration, handing out awards—even though it was his birthday.

Flood—with his waxed mustache and eloquent Shakespearean speech tones that earned him the nickname of "Dapper Dan" in Washington circles—was known for his visibility in his district. On Thanksgiving Day, you couldn't get better visibility in the region than attending the Berwick Marathon.

Finish Lines: The early 1970s were productive running times for Jerry Richey. He won the NCAA indoor 2-mile title in 1970 (8:39.2!) and in 1971 anchored the Panthers' distance medley relay quartet—with Mike Schurko running the 1200-meter leg—to an NCAA indoor title as well. Richey recently handed out awards at the Pittsylvania Mile track mile races; the 16-19 bracket runners compete in the "Jerry Richey Mile" race in that event.

As for Congressman Flood—beloved by many in his district—he was forced from office in 1980 after he was stuck in the muck of a massive bribery scandal. One reason Flood enjoyed the Berwick race was that he supposedly ran cross-country in college.

II
Blasting Through Barriers
62nd Berwick Marathon, November 27, 1971

If you want to win a bet for, say, a beer at the Elks Club, try this one: True or false: The Berwick Marathon (aka Run for the Diamonds) has *always* been run on Thanksgiving Day.

Answer: False. Reason? In 1971, a humongous snowstorm that blew in on Wednesday night and left the roads all but paralyzed—plus numerous runners stranded en route to Berwick—forced the race to be postponed for the first (and only) time in its history.

"It was a difficult decision," admitted Berwick Marathon Association president David Dickson, "but the general consensus was that the weather conditions were too severe and we felt the general welfare of the athletes should come first."

The Baltimore Olympic Club members, led by three-time race champ Frank Pflaging, were less than pleased by the postponement. They *had* (somehow) made it to Berwick and—with holiday plans still scheduled back in Baltimore—slogged through the snow-covered roads on their own and then headed back home. BMA officials held out the slim hope that the miffed BOC runners would return for the 1 PM start on Saturday—but they didn't.

The difficult decision to postpone, however, had an opposite effect on an intrepid band of Canadian runners who—during their journey to Berwick—were stuck on Route 81, north of Scranton, for ten hours. When the roads were finally clear enough to travel, the Canadians—being relatively close to Berwick—decided to visit town and friends they had made in their first year anyway. They were pleasantly stunned to find out that the race had been postponed to Saturday and that they would, after all, get a chance to run.

Like a prisoner who suddenly receives a last-minute reprieve from the governor, David Northey—the 1970 runner-up to Richey (who didn't make it in to defend his title)—must have wanted to make the most of it. The two-day delay, in fact, turned out to be *doubly* good for Northey because he had run hard the previous weekend, finishing third in the Canadian cross-country championships held in Halifax, Nova Scotia. The extra recovery time certainly helped his race-weary legs.

Maple Leaf Express: Like the avalanche of snow that forced a race delay of two days, Northey took Berwick by storm, posting the first sub-45-minute effort in the history of the event.

Any tiny traces of fatigue from the race in Halifax were outweighed by the boost in Northey's confidence. The Canadian runner knew he was in great shape, and he flew off the line expecting to win. The weather was rainy, but fairly warm. The pace was sizzling, and by the time the front-runners hit "the Hill," Northey found he had dropped everyone in the field (down to 37 runners due to the postponement) except one. That one happened to be Paul Pearson, his own Waterloo University teammate—and even his presence seemed normal, as if they were pushing through a hard workout. As the *Enterprise* described it:

> Pushed by Pearson, Northey never let up. Finally with less than four miles to go, Pearson developed a "stitch" and he had to drop back. Northey, however, never broke his record-breaking stride and he breezed home to the applause of the fans lining the course. "The applause really helped," Northey stated later. "I had no idea I was breaking the record, but the applause just made me want to run that much harder."

The clapping hands and encouraging words spurred Northey to not only a new course record, but also the first sub-45-minute clocking in the history of the Berwick Marathon—an astounding 44 minutes, 55.2 seconds—obliterating Herb Lorenz's mark (45:18) established just two years before.

"It was just one of those days, you know, when you just feel like you're going to have another gear, if you need it," Northey said recently.

But the extra gear never really needed to be engaged, as Northey—looking somewhat like the missing member from Sergeant Pepper's Lonely Hearts Club Band, with his John Lennon glasses, long hair, and flowing mustache—glided home, looking nonplussed.

Pearson charged in next (2nd, 45:43) with Millersville State College ace Jeff Bradley, representing the Lancaster Boys' Club, nailing down third (46:40). Rounding out the diamond winners were Baaz (4th, 47:03); Bloomsburg State's top man Tim Waechter (5th, 47:10) and William and Mary's Tim Cook (6th, 47:44), both running for the Harrisburg AA, and Waterloo's Dave Anderson, who captured the final diamond (7th, 47:55), nipping fellow Canadian Kip Sumner at the line.

Farther back were West Chester State's Dave Patterson (13th, 49:07) and young Tom Carter, who received his Berwick baptismal, trudging home in 27th (54:50). Both runners would enjoy loftier places before the decade was out.

III
Bradley's Berwick Breakthrough
63rd Berwick Marathon, November 23, 1972

Ten years after his first Berwick Marathon victory, Frank Pflaging of the Baltimore Olympic Club was back again. He must have felt something of an elder statesman as the field headed out Market Street—the front-runners surrounding him were virtually all college runners or recent grads. One was a smooth-striding junior from Millersville State College named Jeff Bradley—the talented point man on some of Coach Eugene "Cy" Fritz's most powerful Marauder teams of that decade. Bradley and William and Mary runner Tim Cook (former Chambersburg High School star) set the early pace down to Foundryville, with Mike Sabino—Pflaging's younger teammate on BOC—among those in contact.

Back in the pack of 71 starters, surprisingly with minimal fanfare, two young women were running down Market Street, too. One was Laurie Ruggieri, who was cruising along with her father Nick—a long-time participant at Berwick. Both father and daughter were representing the Triple Cities Running Club from New York's Binghamton area. The second woman was Claudette Lehman, who—like Ruggieri—had arrived at the race with family. But in Claudette's case, her brothers—Garry and Randy—were already far ahead of her, mixing it up in the competitive surges of the mid-pack. She was running steady, but almost immediately at the back.

When the front-runners hit "the notorious hill" (as the *Enterprise* referred to it), Bradley grabbed a solo lead. He never relinquished it the rest of the way, but neither did he get far enough ahead to relax. Behind the leader, Sabino, Cook, the veteran Pflaging, and Penn State-Berks runner Bruce Skiles took turns heading up the pursuit pack.

At Martzville, Sabino emerged as the man most likely to bridge the gap. But Bradley kept the pressure on, past the golf course, up the gradual rise toward North Berwick. Then—like many a Berwick leader before and after him—he rode the crowd support down Market Street and the finish. He stopped the clock at 46:03.

Quoted in the *Enterprise,* a jubilant Bradley admitted: "I was aware of footsteps behind me all the way around the course, but I just concentrated on keeping my stride and kept hoping that no one would pass me."

And nobody could. Sabino raced home second in 46:15, with Skiles

10 seconds back in third. Early co-leader Cook placed fourth (46:51), while West Chester College standout Bill Showers (from nearby Milton) ran a strong second half of the race to capture fifth (47:15).

Rounding out the top ten were Pflaging (6th, 47:30), Heinz Wiegand of Maryland (7th, 47:51), Millersville frosh Gary Baynon (8th, 48:02), Steve Molnar of the Richland Striders (9th, 48:16), and PSU-Berks runner Doug Mack. (In fact, PSU-Berks—which also placed Joe McCool, Jack McDaniels, and Brian Skiles in the top 20—would have won the team title, except there was some question regarding whether or not they were registered with the AAU)

The *Berwick Enterprise* did recognize the pioneering pair of women runners, but arguably in a strangely dismissive manner, stating:

> **The two female entries, the first in the history of the marathon, Laurie Ruggieri and Claudette Lehman, both finished, although way back. Ruggieri was 63rd and Lehman last.**

Well, nobody ever expected a race at Berwick to be sugarcoated. Nevertheless, Ruggieri and Lehman had established a bridgehead of sorts, a stage on which future (and faster) female stars would reveal their brilliance.

Finish Lines: Millersville's multi-All-American Jeff Bradley still holds some records there, including the indoor 2-mile (8:57) and outdoor mile (4:11.0). In 1976—while competing in the Boston Marathon's infamous "Run for the Hoses" race—he was among the leaders at halfway before fading slightly in the 90-degree-plus heat and finishing 39th. In 1976, Bradley placed third in the AAU cross-country championships and in 1977 he was an alternate on the US International cross-country team.

In addition, Bradley helped mold two future diamond winners—Mark Amway and Greg Cauller— during his coaching career at Hempfield High in Landisville, Pennsylvania.

IV
Top Chef: Tim Cook's Berwick Sizzle
64th Berwick Marathon, November 22, 1973

There were 115 runners on the Berwick Marathon starting line in 1973—the first time in the history of the Thanksgiving Day traditional footrace that the field had cracked the century mark. And while "quantity" may have caused some pre-race buzz, the "quality" of the field was something to marvel at as well.

Jeff Bradley, coming off another highly successful cross-country season at Millersville, was back to defend his title. Mike Sabino, the 1972 runner-up from Maryland, was on hand, too.

But it was the entry of Dave Northey—the first man to snap 45 minutes on the arduous layout—that had footracing fans savoring a Northey-Bradley duel, with Sabino perhaps having a say in the order of finish.

In addition, two former University of Pennsylvania stars—Karl Thornton and Julio Piazza—were in town and whispered to be contenders. Both had been All-Ivy League performers in 1971 for Coach Jim Tuppeny's team—Penn's best cross-country team in the history of the program. The Quakers (led by Dave Merrick, Thornton and Piazza) scored a landslide victory at Heps and then placed a solid third at the NCAA cross-country championships over a hilly course in Knoxville, Tennessee. In addition, Thornton and Piazza had run the Penn Relays Marathon in April 1973, with Thornton winning the event.

Perhaps the prestige of being the defending champion weighed on Bradley's mind. The Marauder ace led the race down to Foundryville, but as the front-runners headed up to the Summer Hill churches, Tim Cook—the William and Mary standout who was fourth at Berwick the year before—moved right up to him.

Cook worked the severe upgrade hard and steady. In the early stages of the ascent, he pulled up to Bradley's shoulder; then his natural pace and rhythm simply swept him to the front. At the top, he suddenly had that feeling—extremely rare for most of us—of being *alone*. He bucked a slight breeze at the top, but his breathing seemed remarkably well controlled after the steep climb. No doubt about it: He was leading the Berwick Marathon and nobody else was, at that precise moment, close enough to claim contact.

Where was Bradley? Where was Northey, the course record holder? Why weren't they with him?

Unexpected front-runners can sometimes fuel a race off these vague feelings of apprehension. And Cook did exactly that. He didn't dare look back—but if he had, Cook would have noted a lead of nearly half a football field. He later spoke to the *Berwick Enterprise*.

"I couldn't believe I was in the lead," said Cook, who was racing for the Harrisburg AA that day. "I kept waiting for someone to catch up to me."

But as Cook stuck to the task through Kachinka's Hollow, he had in fact increased his lead. By the Martzville Church, he was a full 20 seconds ahead. Behind him, Thornton—in his first and only time on the Berwick course—had charged into second place and was attempting to reestablish contact with the leader. If he had been able to get closer, Thornton might have posed a serious threat down the homestretch—he had 4:06 mile speed to draw upon if it came down to a kick.

But Cook pulled away even more as he hammered past the golf course, heading for North Berwick, his confidence soaring as he remained unchallenged and the miles melted away. Sabino, meantime, began to fight Thornton for second, with Piazza and Marty Sudzina of the Jeannette Harriers also in the mix.

But as Cook turned right onto Market Street, the others were clearly racing for second and other descending places. Cook galloped through the tape in a fine time of 45 minutes, 33.9 seconds. Some 50 seconds later—almost 300 yards back—Sabino charged in. Second for the second straight year, Sabino (46:23) also led the Baltimore Olympic Club (with teammates Steve Mathieu 6th and Jim Wich 7th) to the team title.

Thornton (3rd, 46:29) and Piazza (4th, 46:38) held off Sudzina (5th, 46:43), while Bradley (8th, 47:52), Canada's Dan Anderson of the Sudbury Track Club (9th, 47:58), and Bruce Skiles (10th, 48:06) rounded out the top finishers. Obviously off his best form, Northey finished 31st overall—but the course-record holder would be back in better shape in some Berwick races yet to come.

Berwick's own Bill Bull finished 26th overall (50:36) and that was more than strong enough to make him the first local. Tim Cook's twin brother Tom placed 40th, while Whitey Sheridan—at age 57—came in 90th.

Only one woman ran the race—Berwick's own Debbie Focht, a student at Lock Haven State College. Focht, who had competed in the scholastic races at Berwick during high school, finished the course in 1 hour, 24 minutes. She placed 106th, beating three men and a few others who failed to finish.

Finish Lines: Tim Cook continued to race well in college and post-collegiate competition. He also became a highly successful coach at Chambersburg High School, mentoring the girls' cross-country team to a Pennsylvania state title in 1977. His Trojan teams won nine District 3 titles and added a second PIAA crown in 1989. He was selected to the

William and Mary Hall of Fame.

In December 2002, Tim Cook and his wife, Susan, died in a multi-vehicle crash on Route 81 after a truck crossed the median strip and collided with their car. The school honors Cook's memory with the Tim Cook Track & Field Invitational and the Tim Cook Memorial Cross-Country course.

Julio Piazza went on to set a record for the short-lived Provident Marathon in Philadelphia in 1977, clocking 2:20:18. He also won the inaugural Philadelphia Distance Run in 1978. Piazza has long served as the Lafayette College cross-country/track coach.

Marty Sudzina ran 2:19:55 and placed 13th at the 1976 men's US Olympic Marathon trials. He also won the Penn Relays Marathon twice (1977-78).

V

Bison Blitz at Berwick
65th Berwick Marathon, November 28, 1974

Penn State had long played an important and visible roll in the history of the Berwick Marathon. Nittany Lion winners at Berwick such as Romig, Detweiler, Olexy, and Stone were all woven into the very fabric of the event's history. The Lions continued to be a presence at Berwick and, in fact, even their coach Harry Groves sometimes took on the Briar Creek Hills.

But by the mid-1970s, another college distance running program in central Pennsylvania began to emerge—the Bucknell University Bison, under the gruff, no-nonsense guidance of Coach Art Gulden. Between 1975 and 1992, Gulden mentored the Bison to 18 straight conference championships and captured a trio of IC4A cross-country titles. The Bison men also qualified for the NCAA championships nine times in 20 years. Under Gulden's tutelage, the Bucknell women qualified for the national meet in 1999.

One of the runners riding Gulden's first competitive wave was Lou Calvano, a student athlete from Carle Place, Long Island, New York. It was only a matter of time until some of Bucknell's better runners learned of the Thanksgiving Day race that happened to be just down the road from Lewisburg. In 1974, Calvano—at the urging of teammate (and future ultramarathon runner) Dan Brannen, who recommended the Run for the

Diamonds—arrived on the Market Street start line.

Calvano was in great shape, having just completed his junior cross-country season under Gulden, by all accounts a stern taskmaster. He had the added advantage of showing up somewhat under the radar. Dr. Clyde Noble, the cross-country coach at Bloomsburg State College and a Berwick Marathon Association member, had seen Calvano in action during the season and did label him a dark horse worth watching.

The favorite's role, of course, fell on Tim Cook. And like Jeff Bradley the year before him, Cook may have felt some obligation to defend his title at the front. The William and Mary standout seized the lead at the base of the ascent to the Summer Hill churches, and—to his credit—hit the mountain with a mighty move.

Perhaps a little *too* mighty. Cook led by 100 yards at the summit. But behind him, a pack was working together, including Calvano, Baltimore Olympic Club runner Steve Mahieu (6th in 1973), and Canadian standout Rob "Legger" Legge. The veterans Wayne Vaughn (Cumberland AC) and Mike Sabino (twice Berwick runner-up) were also still running within themselves, despite the wicked climb.

"No, I didn't think I had it won at that point," Calvano later was quoted in the *Berwick Enterprise*. "I glanced over my shoulder and saw a couple of guys behind me. I knew I had to run."

Calvano emerged as the man who perhaps measured out his reserves in the best possible way. He caught Cook around the halfway mark, and they ran more or less even through the dips of Kachinka's Hollow. In Martzville, however, it was Calvano who had pulled out to at least a 10 second lead by the golf course. Cook fought gamely but failed to make any serious inroads over the final 2-plus miles.

Calvano zipped through the finish line in 45 minutes, 39 seconds. Cook (2nd, 45:50) dug deep and held off a late charge from Mahieu (3rd, 45:52). There was more than half a minute's gap back to Legge in 4th (46:29), as the young Canadian had some breathing space before Vaughn (5th, 46:37), Sabino (6th, 46:41), BOC's Vic Nelson (7th, 46:42), and Puerto Rico's teenage sensation Jose de Jesus (8th, 46:52) crossed the line. Bruce Skiles (9th, 47:05) and West Chester State's Dave Patterson (10th, 47:10) rounded out the top bunch, while course-record holder Dave Northey (11th, 47:17) turned in a better race—but still was far off his 45-minute busting form of 1971.

If Clyde Noble was somewhat pleased to see his Calvano prediction rise to the fore, he also was happy to see his star Husky harrier—Lou Gunderman—post a 14th-place (48:52) showing in the field of more than 100 starters. Ed Pascoe, his Bloom teammate, finished 23rd (50:53).

Lanny Conner was back to his winning local ways, as the Berwick Rambler rambled home in 31st (52:23).

Waterloo University from Ontario was so bullish on Berwick that they brought *two* teams down to compete. Waterloo A took the team title (over the Baltimore Olympic Club) with Legge, Northey, Murray Hale (15th), and Nigel Strothard (20th) leading the charge.

Finish Lines: Lou Calvano went on to become a successful marathon runner, representing the Millrose AA He finished 14th in the 1976 New York City Marathon—the first to travel through the five boroughs—in a time of 2:22:46. In 1978, Calvano won the inaugural Long Island Marathon. He also competed in the 1980 US Olympic Marathon trials. In 1983, Calvano ran 2:20:29 at New York City.

23

The Record Tumbles Twice

With the second half of the 1970s beginning, Berwick's footrace was now officially known as the Run for the Diamonds—although most locals and newspaper write-ups continued to refer to it as "the Marathon."

Regardless of label, the race was in a fine state. Most noticeably, the numbers were slowly increasingly. The so-called running boom had a lot to do with that, of course, and the jump up in numbers was being fed by several little streams. Older runners were tending to stay in the sport longer, and gradually—ever-so-gradually—more and more women were taking part. The accompanying Berwick youth races also began to introduce more boys and girls to road racing, and some of them inevitably filtered into the longer event when they turned 17.

In terms of competition, the post-collegiate runners were flocking to clubs (the best to shoe-company-sponsored teams), and that guaranteed that the racing at the front, and—in the bigger races—even in the mid-pack would be fierce.

Berwick benefited greatly from these changes. Gone forever were the fields of just a few dozen runners. At the front, the course record—already a blistering mark under 45 minutes (i.e. a sub-5-minute-per-mile pace on a tough course)—would tumble twice more before the decade ended.

As for the town and its people, it could be argued that they were increasingly aware that the race—regardless if you called it the Run for the Diamonds or the Berwick Marathon—was part of its historical makeup; a colorful, unique mosaic that consistently added a new piece each year.

The town had certainly sensed the importance of the race back in the late 1950s when it approached its 50th running and the event's golden anniversary. But now Berwick was hurtling onward, accumulating more years, more decades. The race was a piece of history, and townspeople continued to nurture it.

As if to illustrate this understanding of history, on the day prior to the 1975 Run for the Diamonds, the *Berwick Enterprise* ran a short item on a local woman who found an original program from the 1908 inaugural race. The paper showed a picture of Mrs. Drew Eyer of Nescopeck hold-ing the item—and the *Enterprise* also ran a copy of the 1908 program with its race preview, depicting both the course map and the listing of that first wave of intrepid "marathon" runners.

Mrs. Eyer had found the program in the belongings of her late father, Samuel Creveling. The race program had been preserved in the center of the family Bible. Creveling also took the competitive plunge in 1923 and ran the Berwick Marathon—finishing 18th and last, but finishing nonetheless. He also was the first local finisher in 1924. Creveling had taken part in a ritual that was part of the regional history. Sam Creveling must have felt some humble pride in that fact, and securing an original 1908 program of the Marathon obviously was a cherished memento to him.

I
Get A Legge Up: The Hill, Round Two
66th Run for the Diamonds, November 27, 1975

Rob Legge left Berwick in 1974 with a diamond ring and something else: a healthy respect for "the Hill."

A scholarship runner for Indiana University in his college days (he fin-ished 18th in the NCAA cross-country championships in 1968—good for All-American honors and one spot ahead of some guy named Frank Shorter from Yale), Legge was used to the demands of competitive running. Before his first Berwick, Legge's fellow Canadians had warned him about "the Hill." But that wasn't the same as actually *running* it. Despite his suc-cessful Run for the Diamonds debut, Legge couldn't suppress a lingering regret that "the Hill" had won Round One.

As the *Berwick Enterprise* noted:

> Through the years, 66 of them, "the hill" is what has sepa-rated the best from the very best. It took its toll on Legge in 1974. Running in his first marathon, Legge had to settle for a 4th place.

Conditions—cloudy, cool, but perhaps a tad breezy—were reasonable when the field of 117 starts bolted down Market Street. Knowing what to expect, and having prepared for it in practice, Legge took control on the ascent to Summer Hill, hammering up at a strong, steady pace. He arrived at the top with a 100-yard lead that he never gave up en route to a winning time of 45 minutes, 8.5 seconds.

"I was ready for the hill this time!" exalted Legge in the *Berwick Enterprise* report. "I heard a lot about the hill last year, but once I got out on the course I wasn't ready for it," he admitted. "It really knocked me out."

With a year's experience behind him, Legge used the hill to knock out the rest of the field in Round Two. "This year I came here with the idea of hitting my stride early, getting up the hill in good shape, and then just striding in," he said.

If Legge was striding, then they were *fast* strides he was putting down around the Berwick layout. His time essentially put him right at a 5-minute per mile pace. At the time, only Dave Northey, the course-record holder at 44:55, had gone faster. Although he was close to the record, Legge told reporters he really wasn't the kind of runner to lay down a blistering kick at the end. Nevertheless, his hard, steady pace carried the day with ease.

Behind Legge, regional running fans were excited to see young Jimmy Lyons, former Bishop Hoban (Wilkes-Barre, Pennsylvania) star, busting out a grand Berwick debut. Lyons, who had just finished a solid freshman cross-country season at Pennsylvania Conference powerhouse Edinboro State (under Coach Doug Watts's watchful eye), snatched the second-place diamond in 45:50. Ten seconds later, Tim Cook—the champ in 1973 and second in 1974—raced in for third (46:00).

Wayne Yetman (4th, 46:09)—who along with Legge helped lead the Toronto Olympic Club to first-place team honors (Paul Pearson and Larry Reynolds completed TOC's scorers)—held off the veteran Mike Sabino (5th, 46:15) of the Baltimore Olympic Club in the homestretch. Steve Molnar (6th, 46:30) of the Human Energy Running Club and former Millersville mainstay Charlie Trayer (7th, 47:03), representing the Appalachian Athletic Club, rounded out the diamond winners.

The Canadians' presence might have been even more noticeable, but they split some of their best men into two teams, as Waterloo University— led by Mike Lanagan (10th, 47:56) and Ted McKeigan (12th, 48:25)— also entered a team. Shore AC (paced by Gary Pierce—who just missed a diamond ring in 8th—and Dave Patterson in 9th), however, placed second to TOC.

Ten years after his last Berwick victory, BOC stalwart Frank Pflaging finished a respectable 23rd (50:06).

After Lyons, the regional watch focused on Lou Gunderman of Bloomsburg State College in 14th. Former University of Scranton runner Jack Brennan, representing the New York's Central Park Track Club, placed 16th overall.

The Berwick Ramblers made a strong showing, with a handful of runners in the top 50. Leading the way for the locals was Steve Johnson (30th, 50:44), with Ken Sweeney (34th, 51:11) not far behind.

Finish Lines: Rob Legge made the Canadian international team that competed in the 1971 Pan American Games held in Cali, Colombia. Legge competed in the 5000 meters (won by Steve Prefontaine) and the 10,000 meters (won by Frank Shorter).

Wayne Yetman's lone Berwick appearance was in 1975, but the following year he landed a spot on the Canadian Olympic Marathon team. Competing in Montreal (and fighting the aftermath of a bad cold), Yetman finished a respectable 33rd overall in 2:23 and change. (He also met the queen and Prime Minister Trudeau.)

One of the top racers in the region, Lou Gunderman went on to compete well over the full marathon distance. Gunderman also was an accomplished coach at both West Hazleton and Hazleton Area high schools.

II
Tom Carter's Berwick Blast
67th Run for the Diamonds, November 25, 1976

In the weeks leading up to the 67th race, Berwick Marathon Association members were beside themselves with joy! They had landed Frank Shorter—the 1972 Olympic Marathon gold-medal winner and, most recently, the 1976 Olympic Marathon silver medalist—to come run for the diamonds.

But as it had in the past, the flu bug raised its ugly mug, and—just like that—Berwick's dream of Frank Shorter, arguably the biggest name in long-distance running, was out. Old-timers perhaps thought back to 1933 when the flu bug ambushed poor Juan Carlos Zabala and hammered the Olympic Marathon champ to such a weak state that he was able to jog just a few token blocks before dropping out.

Not only did Shorter's late cancellation rob Berwick of the most visible name runner it would have had in decades, but it also decreased the likelihood for a new course record—or so race followers might have logically surmised. You could almost feel the lament seeping through the *Berwick Enterprise* write-up:

> The Berwick Marathon, 67th edition, will have a record field of over 200 runners on Thanksgiving Day, but it won't have Frank Shorter, the nation's biggest name in marathon competition. Shorter, who won gold and silver medals in the last two Olympic Games, had to withdraw from the 9.3-mile event because of illness. He telephoned Rick Heller, race secretary for the Marathon Association, late Tuesday night to express his regrets and his apologies.

And so, as the paper, went on to state, the race "has been thrown wide open." Doubly so, because 1975 champ Rob Legge opted to compete for the Canadian national cross-country team in the US AAU harrier championships in Philadelphia.

Even without Shorter and Legge (and, overall, a reduced Canadian presence than in recent years), the '76 race drew some great runners. Among the contenders had to be diminutive dynamo Jose de Jesus. De Jesus was a known talent to Berwick race aficionados, by virtue of his 8th-place finish in 1974 and his 1973 Bill Heller Memorial Schoolboy Race victory.

But those who *really* followed running closely would have known even more—maybe more than they wanted—about de Jesus's fantastic season. Back in April, despite 90-degree-plus temperatures at the Boston Marathon (aka the Run for the Hoses, because some spectators cooled off the runners with garden hoses along the 26-mile route), de Jesus placed a gutsy third. In addition, he competed at the Montreal Olympic Marathon in late July and finished a very respectable 23rd. in 2:19:34.

In fact, de Jesus spearheaded a powerful Puerto Rican team that also included Eduardo Vera, Pedro Santiago (who broke de Jesus's record in the Bill Heller Memorial Schoolboy Race in 1974 with a blazing 22:47 for the 4.8-mile route), and Carlos Quinones. In a Shorter-less, Legge-less Berwick, suddenly it was the guys from the Caribbean island—not the Great White North—who looked like the favorites.

Nevertheless, Lou Calvano (1974 winner) and Tim Cook (1973 champ) were both in the field and ready to run, so fans were expecting a good race—even sans Shorter.

Calvano and Cook were both in the mix with the Puerto Rican runners as the field bolted down to Foundryville. De Jesus and Vera tore right into the climb up to Summer Hill—they were used to racing a similar hill in

Coamo, in Puerto Rico's famous San Blas Half Marathon, and harbored no fear of the terrain. Meanwhile, Calvano, feeling sick, was forced to pull over temporarily, losing precious time and momentum.

By the time they reached the top, a third runner pulled up not too far behind them. His name began with a C—but it wasn't Calvano and it wasn't Cook. Running for the Rochester Track Club (but wearing a racing singlet that read VESTAL from his Triple Cities, New York, stomping grounds) was young, bullish Tom Carter, his rather well-muscled, 6-foot frame in sharp contrast with his tiny foes. Carter had done some good collegiate running, first for Niagara University and then the University of Tennessee, but his top performances arguably came later in his road racing career.

Carter's decision to come to Berwick was fairly last minute. He, too, had planned to concentrate on the AAU cross-country race. But then something changed his mind.

"The weekend before Berwick I had a hard workout scheduled," recalls Carter. "I was going to run a track workout, and then jump in a local 3.5-mile club run right after it. When I got to the track, there was like a small blizzard, but I got out there and ran a 4:13 mile in the snow. Then I ran a half in 2:10 and finished the track part with a 56-second quarter. Then I jumped in the 3.5-mile race and ran 16:57. And I was like, 'Geez! I'm pretty fit . . . Maybe I could place in the top 15 at Berwick . . . ' I was still a little intimidated by Berwick, because the first time I had run there it was really tough."

Coming off that fantastic session, Carter talked his training partner Gary Wallace into making the trek. Both men post-entered, warmed up, and took off with the Puerto Rican contingent.

Soon Carter, de Jesus, and Vera were locked in a back-and-forth three-way racing donnybrook—trading surge for surge. The lead changed hands nearly half a dozen times by the time they bopped over Hosler's Hill, ripped through Kachinka's Hollow, and got up to the Martzville Church. The pace was historically quick. The perfect weather conditions—clear, calm, and crisp—dovetailed nicely with their hot pace. Not far behind the trio of front-runners, waging an equally spirited battle for the four through seven slots, were Santiago, Shore AC's Bill Scholl, and Wallace.

As the trio turned onto Martzville Road and headed back toward Berwick, Carter hammered the long downhill. He grabbed the lead—10 yards, and then 20—as he fired past the golf course, churning toward

North Berwick and the welcoming fans awaiting the leader back on Market Street.

"I just hit my stride and I felt good," Carter told the *Enterprise* reporter later. "I knew those guys were behind so I wasn't about to let up."

That inspiration nipping at his racing flat heels added fuel to Carter's powerful, long-sustained drive down Market. His feet were blistered and bleeding, but his adrenaline rush kept the pain to bearable levels. With both fists raised and noticeable grin splashed across his face, Carter broke the tape in 44:16—nearly 40 seconds sliced off Dave Northey's 1971 mark! De Jesus (2nd, 44:46) and Vera (3rd, 44:52) also dipped under the former record. Those quick times certainly soothed some of the "no Shorter" sting.

Photo courtesy of Berwick Marathon Association

TC—Totally Competitive! Tom Carter ran sub-9:20 for the last 2 miles of his record-setting Berwick run in 1976—and still had energy to celebrate.

Carter immediately removed his shoes, explaining that he had actually borrowed them from his brother and found them to be about half a size too small. "They hurt," he admitted, "but with the position I was in, I wasn't about to quit."

But looking back on that race with three decades of hindsight, it isn't proper-fitting shoes that Carter wonders about.

"You know," Carter said recently, "I sometimes wonder what I might have been able to run that day if I had not waited so long—because at the top of the hill, it honestly felt *incredibly* easy! Like I was just floating along . . . But I was too scared to go that early, so I waited."

Of course, waiting put also put a lot of punch in Carter's final 2 miles: "The split I remember most is that I ran my final 2 miles in 9:20," he says.

Rounding out the diamond winners were Santiago (4th, 45:12), Scholl (5th, 45:14), Wallace (6th, 45:18), and the '75 runner-up Jim Lyons (7th, 45:37).

Some good runners populated the next wave of finishers as well, with Dave Patterson (8th, 46:13), first Canadian finisher Ted McKeigan (9th, 46:18), 1973 champ Tim Cook (10th, 46:22), Quinones (11th, 46:30), Steve Molnar (12th, 46:34), East Stroudsburg State runner Joe Worden (13th, 46:41), Bucknell's Bob Braile (14th, 46:52), Baltimore Olympic Club standout Mike Sabino (15th, 46:54), and Millersville's Charlie Trayer 16th, 46:54.5) all—incredibly—under the 47-minute barrier.

The Puerto Rican AA, in addition to pushing Carter to an outstanding time, cleaned up in the team competition—scoring a stingy 14 points for four men. There were a dozen other squads in the team battle, with Shore AC a distant second with 44 points, just nipping Waterloo Track Club.

In a new addition to the Run for the Diamonds, the officials recognized a Masters Division (40 years and older) for the first time. West Chester College cross-country coach Bill Butler took first in that category with 51:09 and 50th place overall. Butler was followed by Penn State coach Harry Groves (2nd) and Robert Wood (3rd) of Harrisburg.

But the new masters were comparative youngsters next to Whitey Sheridan, who at age 60, nearly broke 60 minutes (well, okay, 1:02.02), and Ben Roseto, who at 63 was the elder statesman of the entire herd.

Carter's time wasn't the only record set. Very quietly, the women were getting faster. Sharon Jarrey clocked the first sub-hour performance, leading a few ladies in a time of 59:58.

The Berwick field also had a record number of finishers negotiate the 9-mile course—183. Could the 200 mark be far away?

Finish Lines: In addition to Berwick, Tom Carter won the 1979 Utica Boilermaker—a brutally hot day befitting the race name. In typical Carter fashion, he had slept in his Chevy Nova the night before, then ran down the pre-race favorite in the final mile. Carter also won Schenectady's feature event—the Stockadeathon—in 1983, topping Barry Brown of the famed Florida Track Club.

The ever-colorful Carter has also performed halftime shows at various basketball arenas around the country. Carter entertained crowds by twirling the basketball on the end of some very long sticks. TC is still very active in running circles, coaching at Broome Community College in New York and also serving as president of the Triple Cities Runners Club. At age 55, he ran a sub-5-minute mile.

III
One Shot Wonder: Bo Brennan's Berwick
68th Run for the Diamonds, November 24, 1977

In 1977, Tim Cook was back for another round. Lou Calvano was also in the house, and so was Canadian Bob Legge. For those counting, that was three former Berwick champions on the prowl for more first place diamonds.

But Tom Carter—the sensational new course-record setter—was not, electing instead to run the AAU national cross-country meet down in Texas.

Still, Berwick being Berwick, there was always a chance a new gun would wander into town on Thanksgiving Day and give it a shot. This time that new fast gun was Edward "Bo" Brennan, a former Phillipsburg, New Jersey, high school standout fresh off a successful cross-country season for Farleigh Dickinson University in which he had cracked the 25-minute barrier on several 5-mile layouts.

Brennan's successful season in the college hill-and-dale competitions only added to his already solid belief in his own abilities. Those who had raced against Brennan before were not totally surprised to learn that Bo was heard to say prior to the race, "I think I can win this thing."

A runner with that state of mind might be tempted to take off at the start—guns blazing. But Brennan wisely kept some ammunition in reserve, having never raced on the course before. He got up "the Hill" just fine, keeping contact with the early front-runners without expending too much energy. Dave Felice of State College (who would eventually fade to 12th) was running point for much of the early miles—but Brennan flashed into the lead through Kachinka's Hollow, with Cook moving into second.

As Brennan bolted out onto Martzville Road and stretched out his stride down to the golf course, he had carved out a 100-yard cushion. Cook attempted to mount a counterattack, but the FDU runner had more than enough to win, clocking 45 minutes, 12 seconds for the first-place diamond.

"The Berwick course is suited for me," Brennan told the *Enterprise* after his win. "Nine miles is my range. I felt good all the way."

Tim Cook readily agreed that Brennan must have felt good—maybe better than that. Brennan was just too fast for the 1973 winner on this particular day. Although Cook had yet to duplicate his victory of several years back, he had nonetheless run some other solid Berwick races, accumulating a pair of seconds and a third.

Ted McKeigan, representing the Ontario Track and Field Club, charged in third (45:44) in a new personal Berwick best. The lanky, good-natured Canadian was just 4 seconds behind Cook. (Not in top racing condition, Legge—a winner two years before—had to settle for 28th place.)

Lawrence Schemelia of New Jersey placed fourth, just ahead of Calvano (5th, 45:51)—a diamond-winning performance that no doubt did much to erase the memories of his illness-plagued race in1976.

Perhaps barely noticed in all the hoopla was 19-year-old Karin Von Berg from Ithaca, New York, who quietly sliced nearly 2 minutes off the best women's mark at Berwick. Von Berg clocked 57 minutes, 58 seconds, beating more than a few men. Behind her came her sister Karen Von Berg and Wilkes-Barre teenager Mary Wazeter.

There was one other record that also was easily broken: The Berwick starting field swelled to 265. All but 15 of those runners finished the rough, rolling route.

Finish Lines: Although she did not get a mention in the *Berwick Enterprise* race write-up, two years later Karin Von Berg would go on to win the US women's 10K road title at Freihofer's in Albany with a speedy 34:26.

IV
Northey's Return and Bulldogs Romp
69th Run for the Diamonds, November 23, 1978

For the Canadians, the annual pilgrimage to Berwick served a dual purpose—competition and fun. They took both seriously, and weren't above a post-race party or two to make sure they accomplished the second goal.

Sometimes the Canadians would arrive on Wednesday and stay until Sunday. But they were usually fairly well behaved prior to the big race; they took their performances in Berwick seriously.

As it turned out, the lads from the Great White North blew into Berwick for the 69th annual event with all the speed and bravado of an Alberta clipper. On the way down to Pennsylvania, they decided to name their team "the Canadian Bulldogs"—a tip of the hat to the Berwick High School nickname.

They arrived well after midnight. Dave Northey pulled up some floor space at Bill Bull's apartment after dining on a peanut butter sandwich and listening to some Neil Young on Bill's stereo.

But the next morning the Canadians—despite their self-assigned Bulldog moniker—proceeded to go out and run like greyhounds. It was an astounding show of Dominion dynamite that not been approached by any other team in the decades since.

Leading the attack was a refocused Northey. He came to Berwick in great shape, judging from some of his recent races in Canada, including a third-place finish at the highly competitive 12K Springbank race in London, Ontario.

However, Carl Hatfield—who won the AAU Marathon title in October in 2:17 and change—was signed up. The first All-American in the history of West Virginia University back in the late 1960s, Hatfield (who was a descendant of the Hatfield clan involved in the infamous feud with the McCoy clan of West Virginia) arrived in Berwick on Wednesday and took on the role of a slight favorite. Coming from the mountainous state, it was generally assumed the course would be a plus for him.

And Hatfield *did* come through with a very good race; it just didn't match up well against Northey's *great* race.

Hatfield set the pace out Market Street and down to Foundryville, with Northey right behind. The other top Canadian runners were gathered near the front, too, so Northey must have felt at home. The conditions were clear, cool, and close to ideal, except for the occasion intrusion of a brisk breeze.

But when it came time to climb, it was the Canadian—not the former Mountaineer—who pushed to the front and threw down the gauntlet. Hatfield tried to stay close, but by the top of "the Hill" it was Northey riding a 10-second lead. And then it became more—200 yards. Pounding down the steep side of Hosler's Hill, coming to the halfway point,

Northey's quads did feel tight from the descent. A moment of doubt crossed his mind that Hatfield might come back to challenge him.

But then both doubts and tightness were gone. Northey snapped back into his long-striding rhythm through Kachinka's Hollow and his lead increased. By the time he breezed through Martzville and past the golf club, the question became one of speed—how fast?—not place.

Northey answered the "how fast" question with a new course record. He blew through the finish line in 44 minutes and 3 seconds. "I knew I was close to breaking 44 minutes, so I was running hard at the end," said Northey in a recent interview. "It would have been cool to be the first guy to break 45 minutes *and* 44 minutes."

It was more than minute before Hatfield crossed in second (45:05), and then there was a pack of Canadian Bulldogs hammering home—Joe Sax (3rd, 45:21), Ted McKeignan (4th, 45:25), and 1975 champ Bob Legge (5th, 45:30)—sorting out the diamonds among themselves. Not that the Americans weren't battling—they were: Bucknell's Lee Edmonds (6th, 45:33) and Boyertown's Tim Groff (7th, 45:39) and Steve Molnar (8th, 45:41) were very much in the hunt for supporting places.

Despite all the firepower at the front (never had eight men busted 46 minutes so convincingly in the history of the great race), regional runners performed well. Ed Pascoe of the Wyoming Valley Striders (15th, 47:39), University of Scranton standout Joe Haggerty (18th, 47:50), and Jeff Brandt (19th, 47:54), former Bloomsburg State harrier and Danville High School cross-country coach, all turned in solid efforts.

Steve "the Hare" Johnson led all Berwick Ramblers, placing 28th in 48:45—another testament to the depth of the overall field. Lanny Conner gave a serious scare to the 50-minute barrier, placing 33rd (50:09).

Meanwhile, Beth Guerin of Wyomissing smashed the women's record, clocking very close to 6-minute-per-mile pace (55:03) for the roller-coaster route. She finished 84th overall in another record field that saw 387 people go the distance—placing her in the top one-fourth of the fastest, deepest field in Berwick history. Behind Guerin, there were two other female finishers who had competed the year before—Pennsylvania high school runners Mary Wazeter of Wilkes-Barre and Eileen Hornberger of Reading.

Somewhere in that mass of finishers, Whitey Sheridan was completing his 42nd run. The veteran runner was also basking in the incredible success of the Canadians—something he had predicted would happen before the starting gun.

Northey, perhaps understandably, was enjoying the afterglow of his redemption run. He readily admitted that his comeback (he had been, for him, a lackluster 30th as Carter obliterated the course mark in 1976) had germinated somewhat in disgust with his own complacency.

"I got tired of being out of shape," he told the *Berwick Enterprise*. "I got tired of watching other guys run well. So I got to work."

Hatfield was gracious in a defeat that may have come as something of a surprise to him. He was, after all, in the midst of one of his greatest seasons of running.

"I knew it would take a strong runner to beat me," Hatfield said. "Northey proved to be that individual. He ran a great race."

As did Hatfield; only the West Virginian's strong effort had prevented a Maple Leaf sweep of the first four diamonds.

Finish Lines: Joe Sax only ran Berwick one time, but he was one of Canada's best in his era. He competed for Canada at the World University Games, the Pan American Games, the World cross-country championships, and he was also a finalist in the 1978 Commonwealth Games. Sax won the 1981 Around the Bay 30K in a smoking time of 1:34:14. In November 2004, the running community was stunned to hear Sax had died of a sudden heart attack. He was only 52 years old.

V
A Tie Offered—A Tie Refused
70th Run for the Diamonds, November 22, 1979

In 1979, the Run for the Diamonds was beginning its seventh decade. But far from needing Medicare, the race had never been more robust— 423 runners started the race and only one dropped out.

Despite being in his prime racing years, former West Chester State standout Dave Patterson felt something like a Berwick veteran. Patterson had first made the Berwick pilgrimage as a high school runner out of Altoona, Pennsylvania, placing among the top kids in the C. W. Heller Memorial Schoolboy Run (a race that day won by a young Greg Fredericks out of Wilson High School in the Reading, Pennsylvania, area).

As Patterson stepped on the line for Berwick '79, it was his eleventh appearance in town. He had yet to finish better than eighth—tantalizingly close to winning one of Berwick's precious diamond ring awards. But Dave Patterson was a hard-core runner, always up for the challenge of long-distance running. For example, in 1976, Patterson placed 8th at Berwick and just three days later *won* the Philadelphia Marathon in 2 hours, 24 minutes, 59.6 seconds.

Patterson also was in the midst of a big breakthrough. He had bolstered his miles per week in training, become more selective in what races he would run, and watched his times grow dramatically faster. As he arrived in Berwick, he was ready for a great race.

Unlike Patterson, Steve Eachus—who went to high school in the West Chester area where Patterson attended college—had never run Berwick before. Eachus, however, was known to students of the regional running scene because he had been an NCAA Division 2 All-American cross-country and track athlete at Bloomsburg State. In fact, the lanky, long-striding Eachus had finished as the national runner-up in the NCAA D-2 cross-country championships in 1978.

Patterson and Eachus got out well as the 70th Run for the Diamonds race blasted down Market Street in record numbers. But it was Jim Cooper of the Nittany Valley Track Club who took on the pace-setting burden down to Foundryville Hill. As the climb began in earnest in the cold, clear, and breezy conditions, Patterson and Eachus took over, with Cooper barely hanging on until the top. Soon after, however, it became a two-man race between Patterson and Eachus.

Patterson had run Berwick so many times (first introduced to the race by his Altoona High School coach, Angie Gioiosa) that he had developed a simple theory. Basically Patterson believed that wherever a runner happened to be at halfway—with the major hills behind and the field typically spread out—his finishing position would most likely change only a place or two in the second half.

As the pair of front-runners zoomed through Kachinka's Hollow and Martzville, neither man could gain any real separation. When they arrived back in North Berwick, Patterson did something rare in the annals of Berwick race history: He offered his friendly rival a tie.

"Third place isn't going to catch us, so what do you say we ease up and finish together?" Patterson said, according to post-race reports in the *Berwick Enterprise*.

Eachus politely declined. "We're really moving now," he said, "so let's run it out."

In a recent interview, Patterson confirmed exactly that story. "That's right . . . I offered him a tie. I guess I didn't see any reason in us killing each other at that point . . . But he turned it down, and then he sort of blew up in the last half mile."

Patterson, too, mustered a decent kick en route to a speedy victory in 44 minutes, 29.2 seconds. Eachus finished 5 seconds after him. And 45 seconds later the fans were treated to a near photo finish between Mike Ludivici, a top runner out of Bucks County, and Craig Woolheeter of Carnegie Mellon. Ludivici got the nod on a lean, although both runners were clocked in 45:14.4.

Then Ted McKeigan turned in a gutsy performance to overhaul Cooper for fifth. McKeigan had a throbbing stress fracture in his foot—but Berwick being Berwick, and McKeigan being McKeigan, he simply laced his racing flats slightly tighter and saddled up. The Canadian snagged another diamond (5th, 45:39), with Cooper sixth (45:42.)

Berwick race connoisseurs still had some quality running to observe, as Bill Reifsnyder of Williamsport High School barreled home to grab the 7th—and final—diamond ring, just ahead of Canada's Tommie Pearson (8th, 45:54), Carnegie Mellon's Dario Donatelli (9th, 46:03), and Canada's Joe Sax (10th, 46:19.1).

Reifsnyder, who had won the PIAA 3-A cross-country championships just several weeks before, clocked the fastest all-time Berwick time by a high school runner with his blistering 45:48.1—still the event record some three decades later. But Reifsnyder had even more to add to his Berwick résumé before his racing career would come to an end.

Regional performances of note came from Francis Awanya, a native Nigerian who ran for Kings College (Wilkes-Barre), as he placed 15th overall in 47:00.6. Not far behind him were Danville's Jeff Brandt (16th, 47:20) and Scranton's Joe Haggerty (47:29.3).

The women's field expanded, with ten women breaking 66 minutes. The first-place runner was Karen Warlow in 58 minutes, 55 seconds—almost a minute in front of the runner-up, Carol May (2nd, 59:47). June Mankoski finished third in an hour and change.

Patterson was quick to credit Berwick's race day magic for the great results on the day, and not just his own. (His own time was quite impressive, trailing only Northey's and Carter's winning efforts in the years just before.)

"I love to run here," Patterson told the *Enterprise*. "It is a highly competitive field and there is a lot of tradition in this race. The crowd is great, too. I'll be back next year."

And "next year" turned out to be one that runners, years later, would be proud to say: "I was there in 1980, when . . ."

Finish Lines: Dave Patterson went on to compete in the 1980 Olympic Marathon trials and finished 13th in 2:15.09. He also won the Philadelphia Marathon in 1981 in 2:17.25. Patterson had several outstanding runs in the Boston Marathon, including a 2:14:18 (19th place finish) in 1981. Steve Eachus won back-to-back Brian's Run 10K titles (a major race in the Philly area) in 1978 and 1979. He was inducted into the Bloomsburg University Hall of Fame in 1995. Ninth-place finisher Dario Donatelli went on to a highly successful coaching career at Carnegie Mellon University in Pittsburgh.

THE WOMEN OF BERWICK

Fast Women: Misti Demko (2), Lisa Haas (5), Wendy Nelson-Barret (4) put the hammer down in their quick 1998 race.

Clay Shaw Photo

As previously noted in the 1972 race write-up in this book, Laurie Ruggieri of the Triple Cities Running Club (near Binghamton, New York) and Claudette Lehman, who represented the Appalachian Athletic Club of Pennsylvania, were the first women to officially complete the Berwick Marathon. No doubt they were encouraged by family members, as Laurie ran with her father Nick (a longtime Berwick participant) and Claudette came with her brothers Randy and Garry. The brothers zoomed off at their own pace and left Claudette to fend for herself. However, as noted by Daniel Spadoni in a short overview history of the race he did as a graduate school thesis project back in the early 1980s, the women's story at Berwick was always shrouded by a persistent rumor that refused to fade away. As Spadoni wrote in the 1983 race program:

> Although females did not officially compete at Berwick until 1972, there was a young woman from England named Chris McKenzie who reportedly ran unofficially way back in 1955. Even though no mention was made of her feat in the papers, McKenzie, who now resides in Long Island, New York, was most

probably Berwick's female pioneer. The chances are good that McKenzie would not have been allowed to run if she had filed an official entry, as women of that time were considered to be far too weak for such a far and demanding distance.

So . . . yet another Berwick mystery! Like the Berwick ring in Germany . . . the bloody moccasin prints . . . Ritola the Pup. Here was yet another nugget that needed to be examined more thoroughly if one was to get close to the truth.

Chris McKenzie turned out to be the wife of Gordon McKenzie—a two-time US Olympic runner from New York. Gordon first met Chris at a meet in England where she was running the half mile in a track meet (An accomplished track runner at that distance, Chris ran close to 2 minutes and a couple of ticks at her peak.)

Chris McKenzie *would* have been the perfect pioneer for women's running at Berwick because she was very passionate about women being allowed to compete over the same distances and courses that male runners did. No shrinking violet, she once wore a T-shirt to a 10-mile race in Washington, DC (in the era long before the AAU allowed women to compete in long distances), that proclaimed in bold letters: IF WOMEN CAN HAVE BABIES THEY CAN RUN 10 MILES!

McKenzie also once jumped in the Thanksgiving Day Road Race in Manchester, Connecticut—despite an AAU ban on female participants—and was beating several dozen men (and two other women runners) when—her statement clearly made—she veered off just a few yards before the finish line. (An 18-year-old Smith College student named Julia Chase—whom McKenzie was there in support of—*did* continue on to cross the finish line, although she was not counted in the official results.)

But the picture is clear: Chris McKenzie was *exactly* the kind of woman who might have jumped in the Berwick race and run it—just to prove that she could.

Well, McKenzie was in Berwick during the 1950s, but it turned out to be 1957 and she was there to watch Gordon (who placed third behind Doug Kyle and Browning Ross) compete—not to run the race herself.

"I do have a story about Berwick, though," she said in a recent interview. "I was so excited to see how Gordon was doing out on the course, that I flagged down a car I saw downtown and asked a man to drive us [her mother was with her, too] around the course . . . The man didn't say much, but he did it. It was only afterward that we found out he was a doctor who had just finished a house call when we ran up to him."

The famous Kathrine Switzer—the first woman to officially run the Boston Marathon (stealthily registering as "K. V. Switzer"), in 1967—never ran Berwick. But interestingly, some of the major players in her infamous '67 Boston run *did* compete in Berwick Marathon races. One was Arnie Briggs—a Syracuse-area runner who helped Ms. Switzer train for the marathon; the other was the irascible Jock Semple himself—the B.A.A. Scottish-born curmudgeon who attempted to rip K. V. Switzer's number off her sweat top when he discovered there was a woman running in the race.

Switzer also turned out to be a powerful influence on the woman who still holds the Berwick course record—none other than Katy Schilly Laetsch.

"When I was about 14, I was at a 10-mile race (in central New York State) . . . just to watch," recalls Laetsch. "I was running track at the time, but I never dreamed I could run races that far. Well, Kathrine was there running and she saw me and came over and said, 'You should be running this!' . . . I think I said: 'I could never run 10 miles!' . . . And she said, 'Sure you could!' . . ."

Not long after that chance meeting, young Katy Schilly became a top cross-country runner on her Central Square, New York, high school team (she was co-captain her senior year and ran as high as third on a squad that was—except for her—all boys). Kathrine Switzer even took her to an occasional road race.

Although Katy Schilly Laetsch still has the course record at a sizzling 50 minutes, 54 seconds (set in 1981 in her lone appearance), there have been some other eye-opening performances on the women's side at Berwick. High on the list are two-time winner Misti Demko—her 51-flat clocking in 1992 just half a dozen ticks off the CR—and the only three-time women's race winner, Wendy Nelson-Barrett (1993, 1995-96). Tammy Donnelly Slusser also makes the multiple-winner list, notching victories in 1985 and 1989.

The women's race history at Berwick is already a storied one. Several women who have competed in the Run for the Diamonds have also competed in the US Olympic Marathon trials. Even by the late 1970s, Berwick was already attracting some serious women racers. (In addition, it should be noted that Berwick was actually *ahead* of the curve when it came to the scholastic 4.8-mile races; it had girls—such as Wilkes-Barre Meyers's Debbie Trubela—racing in the shorter event as early as the mid-1960s.)

But the biggest change has been in the numbers! By the mid-1990s, the BMA bumped up the number of diamond prizes (the women are awarded diamond pendants) for the "open" women to equal the "open" men's—seven because the number of female competitors continued to increase. In fact, Berwick is on pace to attract well over 300 women runners for the 2008 and 2009 events.

New Wave: Tracy Wartman, 1996 women's champ, had both high school and college running experience prior to Berwick—something the "pioneers" lacked.

Clay Shaw Photo

Maple Leaf McLeod: Muffi McLeod is the lone Canadian woman to place first at Berwick. She won in 1984 with a zippy 51:50.

24

The Pfitzinger Phenomenon

I
Pfitzie vs. Fredericks: Smashing 44 Minutes
71st Run for the Diamonds, November 27, 1980

There had always been some validity to the theory that a runner who had already experienced the arduous Berwick course in combat would logically have some advantage over a runner totally new to the rugged route. That theory generally yielded correspondingly intelligent results over the decades of Berwick competition.

But there were occasional rare exceptions, and those rare exceptions came to fruition when enormous talent, or sheer will—or both!—came to Berwick the first time and simply snatched the snarling beast of a course by the scruff of its bristle-haired neck and *shook it.* Those rare happenings, of course, tended to blow the experience theory all to smithereens.

Photo courtesy of Berwick Marathon Association

Pfitz at the Front: Future two-time Olympian Pete Pfitzinger (4) spearheads a large pack early in his 1980 record run. Former Penn State star Greg Fredericks (2), plus 1976 champ Tom Carter (12) and defending champ Dave Patterson (partially visible behind Pfitzinger) go with the flow.

In the case of the 71st running of Berwick's traditional trot beyond the confines of town and back again, there were two tremendous talents who arrived for the event. Neither man had raced on the course before, but those truly fine-tuned to the distance running scene knew immediately that both men were capable of winning.

One was Greg Fredericks, former US record holder for 10,000 meters on the track and also a proven cross-country runner. The former Penn State great (multi-All-American, 1975 AAU national cross-country champ) was arguably a bit disillusioned since the 1980 Olympic Games had come and gone—without American participation because President Jimmy Carter opted to boycott the Moscow Games due to world tensions over the Soviet invasion of Afghanistan. Fredericks had qualified in the 10,000-meter run, but it had been something of an exercise in futility. Fredericks—and many other great American athletes—were denied a chance to test themselves against the world's best in Moscow.

The other was 22-year-old Peter Pfitzinger, who—younger than Fredericks—still had his best chances for Olympic participation ahead of him. A graduate of Cornell, "Pfitz" had won the AAU 15K (the same advertised distance as Run for the Diamonds) title earlier in the year. He had also been tearing up the roads all summer, close but not in the winners' circle at the Cascade Run-Off and Peachtree Road Race during the summer with two solid third-place efforts.

Pfitzinger also was a skilled hill runner, so—like a blind date that comes highly recommended by reliable sources—the Cornell graduate student was anxious to engage the Berwick beauty for a prance around the legendary layout. A beast to most, Berwick for Pfitz turned out better than a Match.com commercial—it was true love at first flight.

In a recent interview, Pfizinger recalled: "I was living in Ithaca at the time and regularly running up 2-mile-long hills in practice, so the [Berwick] course suited me perfectly."

The pre-race picture became even more interesting, however, when you included the slew of former Berwick champions poised to toe the line and take on the two highly hyped co-favorites. Those former victors included the super-competitive Tom Carter (1976), two-time winner and course record holder Dave Northey (1971 and 1978), Tim Cook (1973), and the defending champion Dave Patterson. In addition, Carl Hatfield—who had pushed Northey to his record run in 1978—was back, too.

All in all, you didn't have to be a mathematical wizard to figure out that the chances of a hard working runner of good (but not great) talent moving up to steal a diamond ring in such fast company were dietary: slim and fat.

The weather was clear, breezy, and cold enough that most of the runners opted for long-sleeved running shirts under their races vests, running gloves, or both.

If the weather was cold, the pace was predictably hot—on fire, in fact. Pictures of the race—even in the early miles prior to hitting "the Hill"—readily reflect the effort etched on most of the faces of the front-runners.

Pfitzinger was running according to his pre-race plan: specifically, let someone else lead for the early miles, then work hard up the hill and grab the lead there, if possible. However, that plan was soon slightly altered, simply because Pfitzinger found himself running point on the lead pack as they approached Foundryville. Incredibly, Pfitzinger—with Fredericks providing much of the reason for it—would hammer out the uphill mile in 5:36.

"After many back-and-forth surges between Greg and me, a few hundred meters from the top, I made a move just when a helicopter was close overhead and I could not hear Greg," remembers Pfitzinger. "But I just kept pushing as hard as I could, figuring that—as a faster 10,000-meter runner—Greg was probably a better downhill runner and might pass me back . . ."

But as Fredericks later told the *Berwick Enterprise:* "I figured if I got over the two hills in good shape, I'd be all right, but I didn't make it over the second hill [Hosler's Hill] very well. The hills make this race. They tell who is going to win it."

For Pfitzinger's part, he was leaving nothing to chance. He didn't want to risk a glance back—in his mind, the equivalent of placing a COME GET ME sign on his back.

"I never looked back because I didn't want him to know how much I was hurting," says Pfitzinger, some 28 years later, "so I didn't really know how close behind he was."

The answer, until about the 8-mile mark, was close. Pfitzinger was able to pad his lead in the dash down Market Street, crossing the finish line in 43 minutes, 20.9 seconds. Pfitzinger's phenomenal run over the roller-coaster hills of Berwick had shattered Dave Northey's previous mark of 44:03. Fredericks, too, dipped under 44 and the old record with 43:41.5.

Looking back on the race more than 27 years later, Fredericks mused in a recent interview: "I don't remember a lot about the race, but I remember getting to the top of the hills and realizing that Pete had a pretty big lead. I thought, 'I better close the gap now . . . I can't wait . . .' And I *did* initially gain some back, but then it seemed like I spent the second half of the race working hard to catch up and I just never got that much closer. Pete just ran really well . . ."

Behind them came numerous quality performances, as Tom Carter—sporting a Woodstock-era look complete with headband—charged home third (44:37).

"Those guys weren't that far ahead of me at the top of the hill," recalls Carter. "But then they started to pull away even more, and I thought: 'Geez . . . I must be having a *really* bad day!' And then on the home-stretch—I would have needed binoculars to see them—so I was still thinking, '*Bad day*' . . . So when I finished, I was surprised to see I ran pretty fast and they were just that far ahead. It was kind of . . . well . . . *humbling*!"

Dave Patterson (4th, 45:14), Carl Hatfield (5th, 45:20), Henry O'Connell (6th, 45:23), and Shore AC standout Bill Scholl (7th) rounded out the diamond award winners. Penn State's Larry Mangan (who would crack 4 minutes for the mile several times in the next decade) missed a diamond by mere seconds—clocking 45:28 just in front of two-time champion Dave Northey (9th, 45:34) and Steve Molnar (10th, 45:35).

The next wave of ten finishers—nine of whom broke 47 minutes—had some proven runners in it, too, including: Nittany Valley Track Club's Jim Cooper (11th), Francis Awanya (12th), Peter Bortolotti (13th), 1973 champion Tim Cook (14th), former West Chester standout Pat Quirk (15th), former University of Tennessee track star, Dave Lapp (16th) , Danville's Jeff Brandt (17th), Penn State's Gary Black (18th), Scranton's Brian Bosley (19th), and Bill Kvashay of Dallas, Pennsylvania (20th). To put the depth of the race in context, Kavashay's time of 47:12 would have landed him a diamond ring in most races just a decade before.

With all the fire at the front, the women were waging a great race, too. Kathy Warlow of Palmyra, would break the record of her twin sister, Karen, set in 1979. Warlow—who in 1982 would qualify for the NCAA women's 10,000 meters for the University of West Virginia—clocked 55:04.2 for the win and 104th place overall in a field of 500-plus. Warlow needed her record run to stay ahead of Laura deWald, who would go on to notch 8th the next year in the US women's marathon rankings. DeWald ran 55:29 for runner-up honors.

With Fredericks and Cooper leading the way, the Nittany Valley Track Club won the team title, holding off Penn State and the Appalachian AC.

In the blast-from-the-past division, nobody could mess with Milt Wallace! At age 69, the former Canadian star—a diamond winner back in the 1930s and a 1936 Olympic participant in the 10,000-meters—toured the course one more time. Wallace negotiated the old Beast of Berwick in 1 hour, 35 minutes, and 12 seconds. He placed 495th and finished before a handful of other participants.

Finish Lines: Making the 1980 Olympic team was understandably somewhat bittersweet for Fredericks. ("There was an Olympics that year," he says wryly, "we just didn't go.") But in addition to setting a US record for 10,000 meters (28:08, breaking Billy Mills' previous mark) in 1972 and winning the 1975 US cross-country title in Annapolis, Maryland, Greg Fredericks says one of his career highlights was finishing a close second to the late great Steve Prefontaine (13:31) in the 1972 NCAA 5000-meter final at hallowed Hayward Field in Eugene, Oregon. "I gave him a good race—at the time we had raced to the fourth and seventh fastest 5000 times ever run by Americans—and he asked me to take a victory lap with him before his home crowd. That was a side of Pre that I think most people don't know about."

II
Pfitz Defends, Schilly Destroys
72nd Run for the Diamonds, November 26, 1981

A common request to Berwick winners—from both BMA officials and the local press (and sometimes those hats were worn by one and the same)—was: "Will you come back to defend your title?"

Sometimes still in the process of getting a minute trickle of oxygen back to the brain and still semi-euphoric on the drug of victory, nine times out of ten the runner would gush: "Yeah . . . I plan to be back!"

Pete Pfitzinger had nothing but great acclaim for the race following his Berwick debut.

"This is a good, challenging course and it's ideally suited to me," he said. "The field of runners was excellent. I definitely want to return to defend my title."

Pfitzinger had already dabbled in full marathons even prior to his first

Berwick race, but in 1981 he continued to improve at the 26.2-mile distance—a distance that would turn out to be the Olympic answer for his running. However, he came into the 1981 Run for the Diamonds after having run a new personal best of 2 hours, 12 minutes, 41 seconds at the Nike Oregon Track Club Marathon in September, placing third in the bargain. After a gradual recovery from that solid performance, Pfizinger admitted he wasn't *quite* as fresh as when he appeared in 1980. In fact, a sore heel had forced the former Cornell University star to miss a month of training.

The 1981 Berwick field, although just as deep, did not include Greg Fredericks. After the 1980 Olympic boycott fiasco, Fredericks understandably began to drift slowly away from the sport that he had excelled at for the last decade. That the field was sans Fredericks may have lessened Pfitzinger's "AA" factor—both his anxiety and adrenaline would pump at lower levels.

Knowing that his leg turnover might be somewhat lacking since he had been unable to weave in a lot of quality sessions prior to Berwick, Pfitzinger nonetheless had a plan—a plan that, if properly executed, had proved quite successful in the history of the race.

"My strategy," said Pfitzinger, "was just to blast everyone on the Hill."

And that's exactly what he did, although "everyone" turned out to be primarily Don Norman, who was representing the West Virginia Track Club, because Norman really was the only once close enough to *get* blasted.

Although Pfitzinger did gain a lead up the hill that he never surrendered, Norman did well hanging tough in second. He was rewarded with a fast time of 44:34—29 seconds behind the defending champion.

Rounding out the men's diamond winners were Steve Molnar (3rd, 44:45), Penn State's Gary Black (4th, 44:56), former Bucknell cross-country and steeplechase standout Jim Knight (a.k.a. "The Night Man" in 5th, 44:59), Shore AC ace Bill Scholl (6th, 45:07) and Mark Neal (7th, 45:15).

Meanwhile, the women's race proved to be nothing short of historic. Katy Schilly—already an accomplished runner and a former All-American at Iowa State— churned out a dazzling time of 50 minutes, 54 seconds. Schilly, who was running for Iowa United and Nike at the time, found out about the Run for the Diamonds race from her sister—Chris Daymont—whose husband, Dick Daymont, coached at Bloomsburg State at the time.

Clay Shaw Photo

Shattered By Schilly: Katy Schilly (now Katy Schilly Laetsch of California) made her one run at Berwick count. With power and grace, she hammered out a course record (50:54) that still stands.

"What I remember about the race is that I felt phenomenal when I was running the race," said Katy Schilly-Laetsch, in a recent interview that came more than twenty-five years after her record-setting race. "I remember the hill, of course! But I was thrilled by my time and thrilled by the race. I still have my diamond in its little box."

But the course-record setter for women also remembers that her timing was almost off for her Berwick blast, because Schilly must have been just on the verge of the flu, as she found out later in the day, but—lucky for her—*after* the race.

"What I remember is that later in the day I developed a fever," Katy recalled. "Everyone was eating Thanksgiving dinner and I just wanted to go curl up in a corner somewhere."

Schilly's time placed her 52nd overall in a field of 580 finishers—and that in an era in which the men's competition up-front was extremely fast. (In fact, the men's race was so deep and quick that Tom Carter clocked 45:23, which gained him the "honor" of the man with the fastest "non-diamond-winning" performance in the hundred-year history of the race.)

In fact, the female competition behind Schilly was speedy, too. Sue Crowe, racing for Allegheny-Nike, clocked 52:30 for second, and Kris Bankes of the Reading Athletic Attic Track Club took third in 53:46. Defending champ Kathy Warlow finished fourth (58:05), with Schilly's sister Janine (59:06) and Lori Adam (59:12) all cracking the 1-hour mark behind her.

Top 20 regional performances came from steady performers like Scranton's Joe Haggerty (16th) and Billy King (19th), plus Danville's Jeff Brandt (17th.) The top Berwick finisher was Bill Bull (31st) in 48:46—racing to a new record for a local.

PFITZ FOR THE FIGHT

Although Peter Pfitzinger didn't return to Berwick until 1995 as a guest speaker, his "diamond days" are still much talked about. His 1980 mark has stood an amazing test of time, and survived despite some other great runners who have won.

"The [Berwick] race was a big confidence booster for me," Pfitzinger reflects, "because Greg had made the Olympic team in the 10,000 meters a few months earlier."

Pfitzinger, of course, went on to make two Olympic teams of his own—both in the marathon. In 1984, Pfitz shocked most "track heads" (but perhaps not himself) when he not only made the team (he was seeded in the teens going into the event), but came back to *win* the men's US Olympic Marathon trials up in Buffalo. The course was not far from Pittsford, New York, where Pfitzinger grew up prior to attending Cornell University.

Not unlike the same courage he had at Berwick in 1980 when he sailed right into the teeth of the major climb up to Summer Hill, Pfitzinger made a bold move in the 1984 trials. As Pfitzinger reflected upon his most memorable race in an interview with MensRacing.com:

"In the Trials, there were 12 of us together at halfway and I decided my chances to make the team would be better if the pace was faster. I picked it up and because everyone was keying off of Alberto [Salazar] and Greg [Meyer], no one went with me. By 21 miles, I had a 30 second lead, but then John Tuttle and Alberto started reeling me in, and caught me at 25."

And just as he had when racing Greg Fredericks at Berwick, Pfitzinger strongly resisted a glance backward!

"I never looked back and hung onto Alberto and John for dear life so as not to become a footnote that said, 'Pfitzinger led from 13 to 25 miles only to get passed by the pack and finish ninth . . . '

Instead, with 600 to go, it was Tuttle who looked back. Pfitzinger saw that glance as a green light to pass. He surged ahead of Tuttle, and—once he'd pulled the trigger on his kick—saw the much-favored Salazar come into his "kill zone." The race was part instinct, part ingrained practice—Pfitzinger had actually practiced sprinting at the end of his long runs with his training partner Tom Radcliffe, thinking at the time that rehearsing that final do-or-die spurt to the line just *might* make the difference for third or fourth place, and a trip to the Olympic Games.

Pfitzinger's kick won the day—first place in 2:11:43, just one tick ahead of Salazar, the US record holder and the man who had won both the New York City Marathon and the Boston Marathon.

With only eleven weeks until the Olympic Games, Pfitzinger took a brief few days of recovery before going back into training. In Los Angeles, Pfitzinger proved his trials win was no fluke: He was the first American finisher, with an 11th place effort in 2:13:53.

In 1988, Pfitzinger once again called upon a late surge to blow by Paul Gompers and place third (2:13 and change, plus the $20,000 he won) behind surprise winner Mark Conover and one of the top contenders Ed Eyestone. Once again, Pfitzinger performed well in the Olympic Games. On a warm, humid day in Seoul, South Korea, Pfitzinger placed 14th. Unfortunately, injuries were already nipping at his fleet heels, and Seoul turned out to be the final marathon of his outstanding racing career.

As for Berwick's Run for the Diamonds, it's obvious that the race has a special spot in Pfitz's memory bank.

"The atmosphere and town spirit are unsurpassed and I wish I could return to run that hill again and catch up with old friends," he wrote in a recent e-mail from New Zealand.

Of course, back in the day, when Pete Pfitzinger ran that hill, nobody—friend or foe—could catch up with *him*!

25

Berwick's Big Boom: The 1980s

The Pfitzinger-Fredericks battle in 1980 led some to believe that Berwick would attract more big-name runners. However, it might be more accurate to say that the race sometimes landed very promising runners as they were in the process of *becoming* big names. Although BMA officials are not hesitant to waive an entry fee for a top runner, or to chip in for gas money, they do not—at least in recent decades—pay so-called appearance fees.

What *did* continue to build at Berwick, however, was the sheer numbers of participants. That phase began slowly at the tail end of the 1970s and the trend was consistently higher through the next decade. In fact, one could argue that Run for the Diamonds is once again in a growth spurt as the race zooms toward its special anniversaries in 2008 and 2009.

I
John Doub's Shake 'n Bake
73rd Run for the Diamonds, November 25, 1982

John Doub came into the 1982 Run for the Diamonds with a plan and then he had the guts to run with it.

"I first heard about Berwick from Tim Cook," recalled Doub of Waynesboro, Pennsylvania, in a recent interview. "He said it was a great race, so that's how I first came up to run it."

Doub's debut at the Diamonds came in 1977, just after his cross-country season for the Shippensburg Red Raiders had finished. He placed a commendable 13th in a solid field, chasing in early race leader Dave Felice of Penn State and holding off Charlie Trayer. It was a promising first jaunt over the challenging course, and Doub obviously took some mental notes in the process.

By 1982, Doub was physically stronger, vastly improved, and far more experienced. His pre-race strategy centered on staying competitive up the hill, but to fire in his major burst at the *top* of the mountain where the course briefly flattens out before dipping—and then cruelly rising again at Hosler's Hill. (Doub was essentially rehashing one of Browning Ross's favorite riffs on how to win Berwick; one that had worked successfully a number of times for the old master from South Jersey.)

"The crucial part of this race isn't really the hill," Doub would remark after the race. "It's once you crest the hill. You can't relax thinking the hard part's over."

As the race unfolded, Doub, in fact, *never* had the luxury of relaxing. And some of that started soon after he hammered out the first stage of his plan.

"The only problem was," recalled Doub, "I might have surged just a little bit *too* hard at the top of the hill."

Doub's competitive nature may have been elevated a notch or two by the presence of Terry Baker. Since Baker was located in Hagerstown, Maryland, and Waynesboro, Pennsylvania, was just across the border, the two talented runners often went head-to-head on the roads. The early 1980s were particularly productive racing years for Baker, too. He set a record for the Annapolis 10-Miler in 1980 (48:09), twice won that mountain goat grind known as the Charleston Distance Run 15-Miler in West Virginia (1981-1982), and also notched 7th at the Boston Marathon (2:16:32) in 1982.

So as Doub attempted to avoid self-combustion from his own sizzling surge, Baker began to chip away at the lead, working hard to reestablish contact. In fact, Baker—hammering down Hosler's Hill to the halfway mark—drew virtually even with Doub as the rivals entered Kachinka's Hollow. In addition, Mark Neal of the West Virginia Track Club—seventh in 1981—was chasing both, perhaps 20 or 30 yards behind.

But Doub, who had recovered somewhat from his big move earlier, reached deep down and . . . responded with a serious countersurge!

"Baker had to surge to catch me," Doub told Rick Heller (who in addition to his role as BMA race secretary penned the event write-up for the *Enterprise*) after the race, "so I put on another surge and opened up a 50-yard lead."

Doub's gutsy response cut him loose from Baker and Neal. In fact, Tom Carter—who uncharacteristically had paced himself a bit more conservatively in the early miles—and Steve Molnar of Johnstown, Pennsylvania, eventually overtook Baker and Neal.

Meanwhile, Doub, having fired in two serious surges during his race, arrived back on Market Street with those conflicting sensations that affect many front-runners—he was understandably fatigued from his efforts, but also sniffing the sweet proximity of the finish line. "I didn't run eight miles that hard to give it away in the last mile," Doub says.

And so he dug deep again and tried to ride the cheers of the crowd to the finish. For all he knew, his rival Terry Baker was gathering his last reserves for one last-ditch rally. For Doub, there was no time to savor the anticipation of a first-place diamond that was not yet his.

But it wasn't Baker who almost stole Doub's glory at the finish line. That role went to Tom Carter—his big, powerful running form closing so rapidly on Doub that it was as if he had popped out of a side street, fresh and full of running.

Oh, what Carter would not have given for 30 more yards of race to be run! One minute he was racing Molnar stride for stride for seemingly what would have to be second place, and then—suddenly—he realized, in the middle of an arm-pumping, knee-lifting, lung-stretching kick, that Doub's 50-yard lead was evaporating right before his eyes.

"I usually could run my last quarter of a road race in 60 seconds," Carter said. "It was just a little too late. But, then again, he might have had something more, too."

Doub drove to the tape in 44 minutes and 19 seconds. And a mere 2 ticks after him Carter plowed through. Molnar grabbed a close third (44:27).

"I didn't know where he was," Doub said, later admitting that Carter nearly stole the race from him.. "I felt pretty comfortable and then he came out of nowhere . . . He must have run a super half-mile."

Molnar certainly could attest to those facts, and did, in the *Enterprise* race story. "I was just trying to beat Carter, but he was really moving at the end," he said.

After the top three came Baker (4th, 44:59), Neal (5th, 45:07), former Millersville standout Al Treffinger (6th, 45:15), and Canadian racer Roger Cawkwell (7th, 45:18), rounding out the diamond winners. Don Norman, runner-up to Pete Pfitzinger in 1981, placed 8th (45:27).

Laura deWald of Arlington, Va., won the women's crown, though admittedly her race was less dramatic than was Doub's. She finished 67th overall, but wasn't overjoyed with her time of 53:23—which she attributed partly to not being pushed. Although deWald won by several minutes, the depth in the women's race was obviously getting better. Lori Adams (2nd, 56:07), Anne Marie Sick (3rd, 56:32), Eileen Shovelin, (4th, 56:40), Freeland's Michele Pingar (5th, 57:50), Jennifer Helton (6th, 58:22), Janine Schilly (7th, 58:32) and Barb Swann (8th, 58:41) all were well under an hour, on a windy day.

On the regional and local level, Greg Pealer—who was in the midst of an outstanding All-American running career at Susquehanna University—placed 16th overall in 47:02. He was just ahead of Scranton's Joe Haggerty (17th, 47:12), Danville's Jeff Brandt (18th, 47:21), and Berwick's own Bill Bull (21st, 47:59).

The West Virginia Track Club quartet—led by Neal (5th), Ed Burda (13th), Joseph Wangugi (14th), who hailed from Kenya, and veteran Carl Hatfield (15th)—easily defended their team title over the Nittany Valley Track Club and the Canadian Bulldogs, among other squads.

Finish Lines: In 1983 Neal, Burda, and Wangugi all competed for the West Virginia Mountaineers that qualified for the NCAA cross-country championships staged at Lehigh University in Bethlehem, Pennsylvania.

Laura DeWald was already quite accomplished over the full 26.2-mile distance, winning the Osaka Marathon in Japan in 1982 with 2:34.59. She competed in the first-ever US Women's Olympic Marathon trials in 1984, placing 62nd (out of more than 200 starters) and clocking 2:44:36.

II
The Earl Of Berwick
74th Run for the Diamonds, November 21, 1983

It was rainy, cool, and windy. But Canadian standout Rob Earl was apparently ready to scorch the famed Berwick course, come hell or high water—or, for that matter, a side sticker.

Earl took a quick tour—by car—of the course one hour before the race. Legendary Coach Paul Poce (founder of the Toronto Olympic Club) hinted in the pre-race *Press-Enterprise* article that Earl would "do well." Those words were brimming with understatement.

Nevertheless, Earl—a Berwick rookie—decided his best strategy was to run "the Hill" conservatively and just keep contact with the leaders.

But the 24-year-old Canadian—a man who had run 14:23 for 5000 meters when he was still a junior (20-and-under) in an indoor track meet—found himself leading anyway. By 3 miles, Earl, who was a bit surprised that nobody went with him up the steep and winding road, held a five or six second lead. It was a lead he soon extended. After zooming through Summer Hill village and then up and down Hosler's Hill, Earl suddenly saw that cushion grow to nearly a minute at the halfway mark.

There was just one problem. Earl had a fairly persistent side sticker. And as he told the *Press-Enterprise* afterward, he didn't even dare clutch at the cramp with his hand—reason being that would have alerted the chase group that he was possibly catchable.

But nobody was catching Rob Earl on this day. Despite the stabbing pain in his side—which fortunately soon subsided—Earl was about to pop the third fastest time in Berwick race history. Although he slowed slightly in the stretch run ("I was pretty tired. I just tried to make it to the finish line," he admitted to sports reporter John Michaels), Earl still crossed the line in 43 minutes, 47 seconds—with only Pete Pfitzinger and Greg Fredericks (who was chasing Pfitz that day!) having posted faster marks.

Defending champion John Doub—perhaps not at his peak after running two marathons in recent months—checked in for second place in a time (44:37) that would have been good enough to contend for the win in most years. Back in fourth at one point in the race, Doub steamed back over the final miles to take the runner-up position.

Former Pennsylvania state mile champ Robert Snyder chased Doub in for third (44:41), while West Virginia runners Ed Burda (4th, 44:57) and Joseph Wangugi (6th, 45:12) collared diamonds, too. Marathon runner Don "Spiny" Norman was sandwiched between the two Mountaineers.

Kevin Ryan, an accomplished long-distance runner who had made two New Zealand Olympic teams and once placed sixth (2:11:44) at the Boston Marathon, was considered one of the pre-race favorites. However—citing too much hard training in the days leading up to the race—Ryan was somewhat flat and struggled to eke out the last diamond award (7th, 45:17).

The rainy weather might have been cool, but the times were hot—especially when you consider the depth of field. Two more men—Erik Steudel (8th, 45:44) and Joel Carpenter ((9th, 45:56) broke the 46-minute barrier but couldn't snag a gem. Susquehanna University's Greg Pealer (10th, 46:21), former race winner Tim Cook (11th, 46:22), Bruce Kemmerer (12th, 46:27), John Ausherman (13th, 46:29), and Jeff Brandt (14th, 46:42) all produced great efforts as they battled in the second-ten bunch of finishers.

In the ever-important local scramble, Steve Johnson (48:08, 17th overall) relegated Bill Bull (48:26, 18th overall) to a rare second in the battle of Berwickians.

In the women's race, Barbara Swan beat her cold and the rest of the female field en route to first place in 55 minutes, 23 seconds. It was a huge leap forward for the 23-year-old former Nittany Lion runner, as she had placed a modest eighth in 1982.

Swan overcame a slow start, as she got boxed in for a few blocks—trapped in the Market Street madness of 691 starters. But the diminutive runner weaved her way to the front of the women's race in short order and won by almost 4 minutes. Second place, however, was noteworthy in that 15-year-old Eileen Gallagher (59:15) had won the C. W. Heller Memorial schoolgirl race on Saturday and took on the "big" race just five days later. Gloria Quinn (3rd, 59:22) was right on Gallagher's fleet young heels, with Julie Haggerty (4th, 59:38) and Bloomsburg's Kathy Staib (5th, 1:00:41).

Finish Lines: Rob Earl still holds the junior record in the indoor 5000 for Ontario. Rob—and his twin James Earl—are familiar faces on the Ontario Masters cross-country scene.

Three Kings of Diamonds: Budd Coates (5) leads John Doub (2) and defending champ Rob Earl of Canada up the infamous ascent, en route to his debut Berwick victory. Coates won again in 1991.

Clay Shaw Photo

III
This Budd's for Berwick
75th Run for the Diamonds, November 22, 1984

Coming into the 75th Run for the Diamonds, Budd Coates—fitness director at Rodale Press in Emmaus—had never run at Berwick and, of course, had therefore never raced on "the Hill."

But à la Pete Pfitzinger, Coates had never actually met a hill he didn't like—at least not when he was fit.

And coming into the 1984 race, Coates was *very* fit—despite the fact that he had dropped out of the New York City Marathon some four weeks before, on the brink of collapse from the intense, unseasonable heat during that run.

If heat could sometimes stop Coates, hills never seemed to. Some of Coates's 20-mile-plus training runs purposely incorporated the nastiest, quad-simmering climbs he could find (including the Lehigh Valley's South Mountain); the kind of hills you might describe as scenic if you were in a convertible sports car with a picnic basket in the backseat, but—as a runner—had you looking down at your shoelaces for long, agonizing minutes at a stretch.

On race day, the weather was slightly overcast, breezy, and cold enough that a number of runners (including Coates and women's winner Muffi McLeod of Canada) opted to race in tights.

The field was deep, with 1982 champ John Doub, defending champ Rob Earl, and 1976 winner Tom Carter all ready to roll for more diamonds.

Coates tucked in behind others as the field bolted out Market Street. But by the time the front-runners hit "the Hill" a trio—Doub, Earl, and Coates—had gained a few yards on a second group headed up by Mark Amway, Billy King, and Carter.

Coates's pre-race plan had been to fire in a surge just near the top of the hill, gain a few precious yards of breakaway, then see what happened. But he felt too good to hold back and moved into the lead halfway up the climb to Summer Hill.

"I was running comfortably and walking away," Coates later told the *Press-Enterprise.* "I never really looked back because I didn't hear any footsteps."

And the good old knowledgeable Berwick crowd helped him, too. They kept telling him how big of a lead he had. So Coates just kept sailing along, nice and rhythmic, adding to his cushion of safety.

Budd Coates had always run well uphill, but he was probably even faster on the descents. If anything, he added to his lead down Hosler's Hill and zipped through the halfway mark. He enjoyed about a 150-yard lead through Kachinka's Hollow.

John Doub was admittedly less comfortable. "That year I had been fighting off the flu and wasn't fully recovered," he said in a recent interview. "But I decided to try it anyway. I don't remember a lot about that race except when I finished I ended up in the back of an ambulance."

Coates hit the finish line quite comfortably in 44 minutes and 6 seconds, his white gloves held high in the air in the runner's patented salute to victory. A slight smile stretched about his face, parallel to the snap of the finish line across his Rodale Press racing vest.

Doub, meantime, having fallen back to fourth place, reached way down and sprinted past both Earl and Amway—grabbing second in 44:42. On the verge of a feverish collapse, Doub was immediately steered toward the ambulance and medical assistance. Amway raced home for third, just ahead of Earl (44:47)—the latter happy with a diamond since he was coming off surgery back in August and wasn't in top racing condition.

Rounding out the diamond award winners were King (5th, 45:09, in his lifetime Berwick best), Carter (6th, 45:12) and a man who would be heard from again, Shippensburg State senior Steve Spence (7th, 45:30).

These being Berwick's boom years in terms of depth of talent, the places just missing a diamond were still quite fast: Spence's Red Raider teammate Rob Berkebile (8th, 45:44), Bucknell grad Tom Richardson (9th, 45:48), and former East Stroudsburg runner Joe Worden (10th, 45:54) all cracked the 46-minute mark.

On the regional level, Steve Gasper of Hazleton ran one of his best races at Berwick, clocking 47:43 for 18th—just one spot and 11 seconds faster than Berwick's Bill Bull.

Like Coates, women's winner McLeod—who resided in Hamilton, Ontario—was racing the Berwick course for the first time. And like the men's winner, the race yielded a fast outcome—her 51:50 clocking the second fastest ever by a woman (trailing Katy Schilly's record by just short of a full minute) over the challenging route. She placed 55th overall in the field of 700-plus starters. Runner-up Carol Myers—a York resident representing the Adidas Western Pennsylvania squad—checked in with 53:05. Sue

Crowe of State College ran a strong third, crossing the line in 53:46, while former Kutztown runner Lori Lawson took fourth in 54:09. Fifth place went to Sue Carden, former East Stroudsburg State standout, in 55:24, with Ann Sick not far behind in sixth.

In the team tally, the Adidas Western Pa. squad easily won the title on the men's side. For the women, the Wyoming Valley Striders defended their team crown.

Finish Lines: In 1984, Budd Coates had already competed in the first of his four US Olympic Marathon trials races. He placed 24th in 2:18:54 on the Buffalo course—the race won by Berwick course-record holder Pete Pfitzinger in his upset victory over Alberto Salazar.

Sue Carden also had competed in the 1984 US Olympic Marathon trials. She placed 50th in 2:43 in the race won by Joan Benoit in Olympia, Washington.

Susan Crowe, top runner out of State College, was tragically lost to her family and the running community on February 18, 2006, when she was killed in a car crash in North Carolina. Runners in State College hold the Sue Crowe Memorial Arts Fest 5K and 10K races in July in honor of her.

Just Chill: Mark Amway (2) and Billy King (5) set the pace: Bill Reifsnyder (4) bides his time off Amway's shoulder.

Clay Shaw Photo

IV
Rainy-Day Reifsnyder
76th Run for the Diamonds, November 28, 1985

A cold, slanting rain slapped at the faces of the runners as they headed out Market in the 76th edition of the Thanksgiving Classic. Virtually all of them would be most thankful to reach the finish line and seek dry clothes and warmth in the YMCA or the now-gone Moose Club. The weather was dismal enough that there were few post-race entries and the field ended up more than 100 runners below the previous year's tally, but 572 intrepid finishers nonetheless trudged through a goose-bump-inducing rain.

Of course, some people got back to the finish line faster than others. Former Bucknell All-American Bill Reifsnyder hung out for the first two miles—following a race strategy designed by his coach Charlie Maguire (former 1973 NCAA 10,000-meter champ for Penn State), who was perched on the back of the press truck.

Reifsnyder and the other front-runners may have dodged a potential disaster when, according to the *Press-Enterprise* report:

> Less than a mile into the race, while Reifsnyder and [Mark] Amway ran side by side just ahead of the field, a potential calamity occurred when a car traveling into town on Summerhill road ignored police warnings to pull over and headed into a blind curve with the runners on the other side. The car skidded to a stop just a few feet in front of the leaders.

The skidding car might have been the last thing with the potential to stop the 23-year-old Reifsnyder, a runner in the process of becoming a world-class road racer.

In the early stages of the climb to Summer Hill, Reifsnyder began to pull away. He knew the course from his astounding 1979 run—7th in 45:48, a still-standing record for a high school runner at Berwick—as a Williamsport schoolboy star. When he reached the top—lacking in its usual throng of spectators due to the weather—trudging past a few brave souls huddled below umbrellas or peeking out of raindrop-streaked car windows—he had a comfortable lead. Amway—a Berwick veteran at this point—was the last man to let go during the ascent and established himself in second.

Reifsnyder cruised on to victory in 44 minutes, 19 seconds. The muscle-tightening conditions—combined with a slightly sore hamstring—did, according to Reifsnyder, deter him from making a run at a faster time. The Berwick race was also a preparation race for the former Bucknell star, as he was already inked to race the Honolulu Marathon early in December.

Amway posted what was to be his highest Berwick finish, taking runner-up honors in 45:20. He told reporters afterward that Reifsnyder was "in a different class from the rest of the field . . . This was more of a workout for him."

Rounding out the wet road warriors who won diamonds were Waterloo Ontario's Mark Inman (3rd, 45:29), Millersville grads Erik Steudel (4th, 45:33) and Billy King (5th, 45:41), Penn State standout Paul Mackley (6th, 45:54), and another former Marauder, Greg Cauller (7th, 46:14).

One runner who seemed to fluff off the rain, wind, and 35-degree temperatures was Bill Bull. All Bull did was stampede to his fastest Berwick finish ever—clocking 46 minutes, 55 seconds, good for a very solid 11th place. Bull's performance placed him just ahead of some proven runners, like Robert Snyder and Greg Pealer.

Looking back on that landmark race (still the fastest ever by a local), Bull says: "I was in pretty good shape that year and I remember that I kind of laid low in terms of doing stuff *before* the race . . ." (By which he means his duties as a BMA member, helping with race preparation.)

Like Reifsnyder, women's champion Tammy Donnelly came into the race in fantastic shape. An accomplished runner at the Indiana of Pennsylvania University (IUP), Donnelly had placed 4th in the NCAA D-2 Cross-Country Championships earlier in the month. Her biggest challenge came from the weather conditions, which she admitted afterward were a bit much: "I usually like running in the rain, but it was colder than I like."

Donnelly's pace, however, was sizzling. Her first 3 miles passed at under 6-minute-per-mile pace (17:55 at 3 miles) and—with the big climb behind her—she had blown open a big lead. She scooted around the course for a soggy but fast victory of 52 minutes, 33 seconds. (She finished 24 seconds ahead of the shirtless Ben Hyser of Reading, who won the men's 50-54 age group.)

Behind Donnelly, the other top female finishers were Barb Swan (2nd, 56:40), Barbara Griggs (3rd, 58:09), Carol Davis (4th, 59:48) and Sandra Jenkins (5th, 60:23).

Finish Lines: Ten days after his wet win at Berwick, Reifsnyder hammered out a 2:14 runner-up effort at a hot and humid Honolulu Marathon (bowing to a record-setting Ibrahim Hussein of Kenya). Reifsnyder (along with Keith Brantley) would lead the 1992 US Olympic Marathon trials for more than 20 miles before falling back to fifth.

Runner-up Mark Amway, a familiar face in Pennsylvania running, clocked a 2:18:26 at the 1991 Boston Marathon—a time that qualified him for the 1992 US Olympic Trials. Amway has owned and managed the popular Inside Track running store in Lancaster, Pennsylvania, since 1989.

V
Fast-Driving Ferrari
77th Run for the Diamonds, November 27, 1986

Like most runners who envisioned a chance of winning the Berwick race, Brian Ferrari had been forewarned about "the Hill." With that advice tucked away in his pre-race brain, Ferrari opted for some early deference in regard to the upgrade. So he bided his time, content to just hang close to a pair of former (and, to him, familiar) Pennsylvania Conference "name runners"—former Clarion runner Bruce Kemmerer and former Lock Haven star Mark Amway. All three men knew one another well, having competed often in the collegiate ranks.

Kemmerer, who had good half-mile speed, found the somewhat conservative early miles to his liking. Could he perhaps entice the other two to keep the pace semi-friendly until they got back on Market Street? If so, then Kemmerer's chances to win would get dramatically better.

But it was Ferrari who arguably had the most impressive credentials of the three. In 1983 he won the NCAA D-2 cross-country title; he also notched back-to-back NCAA D-2 10,000-meter crowns on the track.

For a first-timer on the Berwick course, he had a good plan. After his just-stick-with-them strategy up the hill, Ferrari—with echoes of Browning Ross—switched gears at the top. Neither Kemmerer nor Amway answered, and he soon found himself alone at the front. He parlayed his lead into an even greater one up Hosler's Hill.

Ferrari did, however, deal with some nagging doubt, as he later told the *Press Enterprise:* "I was surprised at the top of the hill when they didn't respond to my move. I was pretty scared because I figured they had run the course before and knew something I didn't . . ."

But as most runners know, sometimes a little fear is a high-octane fuel. Ferrari roared down the steep descent, through the halfway mark, and took about a 100-yard lead onto Kachinka's Hollow Road. Amway and Kemmerer jousted for second and third; still somewhat in striking distance but not gaining ground on the front-runner.

As Ferrari turned out onto Martzville Road and headed back to Berwick, his confidence soared and he ate up the downhill past the golf course with long, hungry strides. He increased his lead over the last two miles, snapping the finish-line tape in 44 minutes, 43 seconds. Kemmerer's kick did secure second place (45:26), while Amway took third (45:38).

Like many Berwick winners before him, Ferrari praised both the competitiveness of the field *and* the infamous course.

"The course was very hard, especially the hill," he admitted, "but it's a popular race and the competition is really tough. It was a perfect day for the race."

After the top three, Canadian stalwart Ted McKeigan hammered home (4th, 46:25)—with former Millersville standouts Steve Koons (5th, 46:33) and Erik Steudel (6th, 46:36), plus former Berwick champion Tim Cook (7th, 46:37), applying some stretch-drive incentive.

Following the top seven diamond winners, were Canadian Paul Barron (8th, 47:11), Steve Molnar (9th, 47:15), Scranton's (and Millersville's) Bill King (10th, 47:23), and Bob Snyder (11th, 47:32). Bill Bull—running one of his best Berwick races in terms of place—finished 13th (47:56.6), just two-tenths of a tick behind Reading's Dean Feinauer.

The women's race was more hotly contested, particularly when defending champion Tammy Donnelly was a late scratch due to a slow-healing muscle pull. Donnelly, however, told one of her faster teammates—Christina Skarvelis—about the Run for the Diamonds.

The result was a tight pack through 3 miles, but by 5 miles it was down to Skarvelis, the Pittsburgh-area runner, and Lori Adams of Bethlehem. They were still together when they got back to Market Street, but Skarvelis knew—without looking back—that her lead was very slight because people in the vast crowd kept encouraging in the plural—"come on girls!" Besides, the 25-year-old Skarvelis later admitted she was too *scared* to look back.

Adams raced in with a fine performance—55:27. But it was 2 seconds shy of Skarvelis's winning time, as the Allegheny Nike club runner held on for the victory. Skarvelis and Adams finished 87th and 88th respectively in

Clay Shaw Photo

Close Call: Christina Skarvelis scoots home just before Lori Adams.

the overall results, in a starting field that topped 650. As Adams recently recalled, "Late in the race, I think I noticed her shoelace was untied. And I kept thinking, 'Why can't I catch this woman with a loose shoelace?'"

Rounding out the top seven women finishers were Barb Swan (3rd, 55:56), Bloomsburg's Brenda Bisset (4th, 56:08), former East Stroudsburg State standout Sue Carden (5th, 56:15), Eileen Shovelin (6th, 56:42), and Gloria Rawls (7th, 58:23) of the Wyoming Valley Striders.

Western Pennsylvania Adidas won the team title with a mere 15 points, with the Toronto Olympic Club second and the Berwick Ramblers third.

Finish Lines: Brian Ferrari competed at the US Olympic Marathon Trials held in Columbus, Ohio, in 1992, placing 48th in 2:32.03. He coaches cross-country and track at Hagerstown Community College in Maryland.

Christina Skarvelis finished 14th in the 1987 women's field at the Boston Marathon in 2:46:52. In 1988, she competed in the US Olympic Marathon trials held in Pittsburgh, placing 87th out of 159 finishers in 2:50.30.

VI
Speedy Spence and Persistent Adams
78th Run for the Diamonds, November 27, 1987

Racing would be more predictable if fate wasn't always getting in on the act. Consider the wrong turn, the loose shoelace, or the dropped cup of water at the aid station . . . or, one of my all-time favorites, the freight train that cut off everyone but a handful of front-runners in the 1907 Boston Marathon.

For 25-year-old Steve Spence—the former Shippensburg All-American and National D-2 5000-meter champion on the track—fate, in the negative sense, intervened in a simple form of the common pothole while he was racing a 10K in Baltimore the Sunday just prior to Berwick. Spence wisely called it a day and retired from the battlefield that day instead of hobbling on and doing more damage. (Spence had recently become an assistant coach at his alma mater, and we can assume he was heeding the kind of advice he might dispense to his college runners.)

So the pothole was the bad news. But the good news was, Spence was not seriously hurt, and in a roundabout way not finishing that race left

Clay Shaw Photo

Unfinished Business: Steve Spence (seen here in 1984) finished 7th in an earlier Berwick, but three years later he came back for a big win.

him well rested for the 78th annual Run for the Diamonds. The weather was cooperative, too—overcast, slight breeze, and cool, but not cold enough to warrant gloves for most runners.

As the race unfolded, Spence found himself battling former Edinboro University ace Greg Beardsley, who had won the NCAA D-2 cross-country title in 1982, on the grind up to Summer Hill. Nearing the top, they were joined by hard-nosed former Bucknell runner Carl Kemmerer—but Kemmerer had expended a lot of energy to close that uphill gap. When the Bison runner fell back, it soon became a two-man race between Spence and Beardsley.

As coincidence had it, Beardsley had run in, and finished, the 10K in Baltimore just five days before—the same race Spence had been forced to bow out of at the 2-mile mark. As Spence raced down Hosler's Hill and toward the halfway mark, he kept that fact in his mind. Certainly he had to be a bit fresher than his former Edinboro rival.

On the first short hill on Kachinka's Hollow Road, right after making the sharp left turn, Spence blasted off on an ambush surge. He gain 10 to 15 yards in short order, and Beardsley never did reestablish contact after that. As Beardsley noted to the *Press-Enterprise:*

> "I tried to get ahead of him on the uphill but it was fruitless
> . . . I know Steve has good leg speed and once [someone gets]
> that far ahead, it's tough to make up . . . And even if I would
> have caught him, he's tough enough that he'd have had some-
> thing else up his sleeve."

Spence, spurred on both by his growing lead and the ever-enthusiastic Berwick crowd, kept churning out fast miles. He zoomed down Market Street and hit the tape in 44 minutes, 19.8 seconds. Beardsley was able to hold on to second place in 44:52.2, while Craig Thompson (3rd, 45:12) held Canadian entry Jeff Martin (4th, 45:34) at bay. After his early bid to go with the leaders, Kemmerer still managed to grab fifth (45:45.9), as Greg Cauller (6th, 46:03) and Kevin McGarry (7th, 46:24.3) nailed down the last diamond-winning spots.

In the women's race, Lori Adams of Bethlehem and defending champion Christina Skarvelis of Pittsburgh flip-flopped on their places of the previous year. Adams—a Run for the Diamonds veteran who was representing the Emmaus Road Runners—prepared specifically for Berwick in her training. Translation: She went on a mountain goat diet of hills, hills, and *more* hills—including some runs up the Lehigh Valley's South Mountain. It all paid off for the soft-spoken and humble athlete as she seized the lead halfway up "the Hill" en route to a new personal best of 54 minutes, 12.8 seconds.

Skarvelis actually ran a few ticks faster than she had in her 1986 victory, clocking 55:22 for runner-up honors. Despite a pesky cold, Barb Swan of the Adidas Western Pennsylvania team secured third in 56:05. Rounding out the rest of the top seven for the women were Tammy Slusser (4th, 56:43), Kim Sweda (5th, 57:31) and Carol Davis (6th, 58:50) both of the Berwick Ramblers, and Carol Livermore (7th, 59:17).

Finish Lines: Steve Spence's best races were still ahead in his career and they came at the full marathon distance. Spence landed a bronze medal with an extremely patiently paced race in the World Championship in Tokyo in 1991. The next year he won the US Olympic Marathon Trials in Columbus, then—despite a touch of the flu—placed a very respectable 12th in the 1992 Barcelona Olympic Marathon.

Lori Adams clocked a 2 hour, 50 minute, and 12 second marathon in 1987—with the handful of seconds the only thing between her and a US women's Olympic Marathon trials qualifying time. Although the race director offered to shave the seconds off her time (because she had not started at the front of the race), Adams politely declined.

VII
Ruch Captures Berwick Crown
79th Run for the Diamonds, November 24, 1988

The Runner's Gazette (aka "America's First Running Newspaper) once quoted former LaSalle University running star Kevin Ruch on his racing philosophy. Ruch had it well thought out.

"In every important race," Ruch said, "I try to find the fine line which exists between running in control and running with your eyeballs popping out."

But about 3 miles into the 79th annual Run for the Diamonds, Ruch certainly was close—if not a fraction over—that fine line, and if his eyeballs weren't exactly popping out of his head, they didn't particularly care for what they were observing, either. The race prognosis was mixed: Ruch certainly was on pace to land a gem, but it did not seem very likely that it would be a first-place diamond.

That's because two of Coach Arthur Gulden's former Bison runners—Carl Kemmerer out of Palisades (Bucks County) and Rich Stark from Tunkhannock—had just knocked the stuffing out of "the Hill" (of course, the Hill had exacted its own punishment in the process) and were at least 100 yards ahead as the race headed to the halfway mark. Also running back near Ruch was the 1987 third place finisher Craig Thompson.

But Ruch was also benefiting from the hard-boiled, no excuses allowed wisdom of Art Gulden, a former military officer who had served in Vietnam. Although Ruch had graduated from LaSalle, he was all too familiar with the unbridled success of Gulden's Bucknell Bison. So Ruch, who resided in Camp Hill, Pennsylvania, sometimes journeyed up the Susquehanna River to Lewisburg to work out with Gulden's legions, or conferred with the Bucknell mentor by phone concerning his workouts.

Clay Shaw Photo

Bold on the Shoulder: Ruch (right) paces off Rick McGarry (Philly singlet) early in his 1988 Diamond victory.

313

So Ruch wasn't ready to quit. In fact, both Ruch and Thompson were able to regroup through the roller-coaster ride of Kachinka's Hollow—those rapid waves of short ups and downs—and Stark and Kemmerer finally began to come back. Thompson, the former Tennessee Volunteer runner, caught them first.

But no sooner had Thompson taken the lead when he heard footsteps behind him; a much-rallied Ruch came steaming up and attached himself to Thompson's shoulder. For the next 3 miles, they virtually matched strides back to North Berwick, but when they turned onto Market Street, Ruch began to heat up the pace. He pulled gradually away to a 7-second win, clocking 44 minutes, 41 seconds. Thompson took the runner-up position in 44:48.

After the dueling duo, Kemmerer charged home (3rd, 45:15) just ahead of his Bison teammate Stark (4th, 45:34). Brian Ferrari, the 1986 Diamond king, placed fifth in 46:01. Rounding out the diamond winners were Canadian runner Paul Barron and Greg Cauller, who won the college division of the IC4A Cross-Country Championship when he raced for Millersville. The next few places were laced with some frequently seen names in Berwick history: former Council Rock High School runner Terry Permar (8th), Rick McGarry (9th), Scranton's Billy King (10th), 1976 champ Tom Carter (11th), Hazleton's Steve Gasper (12th), and Berwick's Bill Bull (13th).

Although Craig Thompson was a near-miss for top honors, he no doubt drew more than a little consolation from the results of the women's race: His wife Eileen won! Eileen Hornberger Thompson, a former Reading-area runner who raced for some championship Lady Vol cross-country squads in the early 1980s, charged right to the front early on and then concentrated on keeping pace with the men around her. When she crossed the line in 53 minutes, 45 seconds, it was her first win in four shots and placed her 63rd overall in a starting field of 700-plus. Defending champ Lori Adams of Bethlehem ran a solid second in 55:20, but she confirmed that Thompson's fast start forced her into a catch-up role early on.

Filling out the top finishers for the women were Barb Swan (3rd), Karen Flanagan (4th), Sue Carden (5th), Brenda Bisset (6th), and Sandra Stefanski (7th).

Runner-up Adams echoed a familiar refrain for most Run for the Diamonds participants, remarking to *Enterprise* reporter Gary Smith: "I've run this race five or six times and it is terrific. The crowds are just great."

Finish Lines: Kevin Ruch competed in the 1992 US Olympic Marathon trials held in Columbus, Ohio, and placed 28th in 2:24:46. In 2005 Ruch helped organize the inaugural Run Sober Drive Sober 5K, a race to bring attention to the dangers of alcohol-related crashes.

Team Thompson: Eileen won the women's title in 1988, while Craig matched her with a first in 1989.

VIII
Craig Thompson on Top
80th Run for the Diamonds, November 23, 1989

The snow brought a white Thanksgiving to Berwick and might have reminded some of the 1971 blizzard—except this time it was the light, fluffy stuff. There were no runners stranded out on the highways and no postponements. It was just cold enough to put the racing gloves on, though some runners added hats to their racing attire.

With defending champion Kevin Ruch a last-minute scratch due to an injury, Craig Thompson—third in 1987, second to Ruch in 1988—was looking for a simple one-place improvement. Was that too much to ask?

The overnight snowstorm proved to be mostly a nonfactor, as most of it melted under some mild sun. There were some sloppy spots that the runners had to work through or around.

But there was no avoiding a stiff headwind (unless you tucked in behind others) as the runners headed down to Foundryville and prepared to gather their physical and mental resources for the climb to Summer Hill. The temperatures didn't even reach 30 degrees, but the race, of course, generated its own heat.

The wind was strong enough that it made the ascent doubly difficult and the pace—at least to Thompson—seemed quite slow. The runners bunched up in a pack, with nobody eager to break out on their own.

What may have seemed like a nonaggression pact continued up and down the major hills, and then on through Kachinka's Hollow.

Then Jack Ditt—a former Annville-Cleona high school standout who went on to set some records (including a 14:20 5000 meters on the track) at the Virginia Military Institute—ambushed the front-runners at around the 6-mile mark and shook up the order. As the pack strung out behind them, Thompson and Ditt turned it into a two-man race as they turned onto the Martzville Road—Berwick-bound and with the wind finally at their backs.

Thompson, decked out in Reebok racing regalia, then took a page from the Kevin Ruch race strategy book: He waited until Market Street to pass Ditt and build to a speedy finish.

"Kevin Ruch took off on me at the eight-mile mark last year," he told Chuck Souders of the *Press-Enterprise,* "so I kind of imitated him this year. . . . I ran behind Jack . . . and then took off on him."

It was a nice step up for the 28-year-old Knoxville, Tennessee, runner, as he snapped the string in 45 minutes, 52 seconds. Ditt—representing the US Air Force—charged in for second about 12 ticks later.

Third went to Budd Coates (46:30). The Lehigh Valley standout might have been in the mix with Thompson and Ditt, but a late arrival (partly due to the weather, partly due to a training partner—who shall remain unnamed) left him no time to change into his racing flats. He ran the race in his training shoes.

Rounding out the diamond winners were Tom Carter (4th, 46:43), Rich Stark (5th, 46:58), Edinboro State runner Mike Renninger (6th,

47:02), and Jim Simpson (7th, 47:24).

Eight and ninth went to Lehigh Valley runners Mark Will-Weber (47:33) and Mark Gerber (47:48), but it was Berwick's Bill Bull posting his highest finish (10th, 47:57) in his long race history that drew the focus of local fans. Bull, who fought off a mid-race side stitch en route to his fine performance, sent a new local record for consecutive victories—six of them! (Bull surpassed the previous local mark of five straight wins achieved by Allen Parr of nearby Mifflinville. Parr won local honors from 1927 through and 1931.)

Bull led a fine showing from the Berwick Ramblers, as the local club also put Steve Gasper (13th) and Jim Lyons (15th) in the top 20. The West Hazleton High School alumni team was also well represented in the top 20, as the brothers Joe and Gary Sluck (12th and 20th respectively), along with Bob Radzwech (14th) did the old Wildcats proud.

Tammy Donnelly Slusser won her second Run for the Diamonds title in 53 minutes, 10 seconds. The former Indiana University of Pennsylvania All-American thought she was cruising along, just racing the men around her, when she slightly bumped a runner next to her. That runner, upon Slusser's closer examination, happened to be Reading Athletic Attic ace Beth Guerin, wearing a knit-wool cap to ward off the cold. That surprise gave Slusser can extra jolt of adrenaline and she picked up the pace en route to the first-place diamond. The veteran Guerin ran strong to snag runner-up laurels, just two places and 12 seconds behind.

Slusser's performance—coming just three weeks after she raced in even more windy conditions at the Chicago Marathon—placed her 51st overall in a field of more than 600 finishers.

Other top finishers in the talented women's field were Diane East (3rd, 54:07), Lori Adams (4th, 56:28), Craig Thompson's wife Eileen Thompson (5th, 56:40), Kim Gasper of the Berwick Ramblers (6th, 58:37) and Barb Swan (7th, 59:13). The top three women won diamond awards.

Finish Lines: Tammy Donnelly Slusser, an IUP Hall of Fame athlete (as is her husband, Don Slusser), is fast approaching 100 lifetime marathons—including several in the women's US Olympic Marathon trials. She has run a marathon on every continent except Antarctica.

26

Berwick Gets Bigger

I
Martin's Market Street Move
81st Run for the Diamonds, November 22, 1990

No less than a running philosopher than Coach Harry Groves of Penn State once said: "The problem with big kickers is they often lose to *other* big kickers." It is, essentially, a reworking of the ancient adage about living by the sword and dying by the sword.

Craig Thompson's Berwick experiences seemed to have a lot of Market Street dramatics woven into them. In 1988, Thompson lost in the final stretch to Kevin Ruch—a guy with a 1:53 personal best over 800 meters. But Thompson turned around in 1989 and zapped Jack Ditt in the final mile to clinch the first-place diamond.

And, as if to make matters even more complicated, Thompson had held off Canadian Jeff Martin—for third place—in the 1987 Berwick won by Steve Spence. In between Diamond races, however, Thompson and Martin had raced each other a few times—and it wasn't close in most of them; one guy would beat the other convincingly. Martin also had the endurance end covered—he had won some full marathon races in his career.

As fate would have it, Thompson led much of the 1990 Run for the Diamonds, but as the front-runners arrived back in North Berwick, who but Jeff Martin was perched just off his shoulder. Like one of those High Noon western shoot-outs, this one apparently would be settled on the main street, before lots of curious onlookers.

Martin, from St. Catherine's, Ontario, delivered the big burst and bolted through the finish line in 46 minutes, 1 second. Thompson, the former Tennessee runner, had to be content with second—five ticks behind. Third went to Penn State standout Aidan O'Reilly (46:16), a man who would captain the Nittany Lion cross-country team the following fall.

The four through seven diamond spots fell to Eric Shafer (4th, 46:32), who ran for IUP in college, former Millersville runner Kevin Stover (5th, 46:41), Dave Berardi (6th, 46:52) of Maryland, and Canadian war horse Ted McKeigan (7th, 46:54) whose homestretch gallop took him past the writer of this book for the last diamond.

Canada's Paul Barron placed ninth, just ahead of Berwick's Bill Bull (10th), Hazleton's Steve Gasper (11th), and former champ Tom Carter (12th). Joining Bull and Gasper, the Berwick Ramblers' Jim Simpson had a strong race, placing 13th.

In the women's race, Kirsten Harteis of Chambersburg, Pennsylvania (now married to Steve Spence), took the lead by herself over the last half of the race, but she didn't really like the feeling. As she told the *Press-Enterprise:* "From like five miles on I was by myself and it was really stressful."

As it turned out, Harteis won in 54 minutes, 19 seconds (good for 62nd overall out of 744 finishers), but Molly Mitke of Allentown charged in just 6 seconds later for runner-up laurels. Barb Swan (3rd, 54:38), former Cornell runner Pam Hunt (4th, 55:12), Deb Grossman (5th, 55:15), Ellen Thompson (6th, 56:25), and Amanda Dudley (7th, 56:50) rounded out the top finishers in a competitive women's field.

One of the most eye-opening performances of the morning had to go to ultrarunner John Clark of Sunbury. Clark *ran* to Berwick from Sunbury (32 miles!) prior to the event, then raced the course and placed 231st in 1 hour, 2 minutes. That's either a long warm-up, or a long cool-down, depending on how you look at it.

II
Budd Coates's Double Diamond
82nd Run for the Diamonds, November 28, 1991

With a mile to go, Budd Coates of Rodale (a company that stakes its reputation on healthy lifestyle choices) was looking for "the arches"—but not the golden ones that are home to Ronald McDonald.

It was just one of those races in which Coates felt *good*—but not *great*. However, now a wily road racing veteran and much experienced over the Berwick layout, Coates hung in there long enough to script a very successful ending.

"I just kept concentrating on the arches," said Coates in a recent interview.

He was, of course, speaking of the white arches that once spanned Market Street about 100 yards before the race finish. Coates zipped under the arches and on to a string-snapping victory—his second first-place diamond—in 45 minutes, 11.5 seconds.

The top three finishers were all within eight seconds of each other. Dave Berardi of Catonsville, Maryland—who had run his personal best of 2:21 in a full marathon about a month before Berwick—placed a close second (45:13), while ever-steady Mark Amway captured third (45:19). Berardi made a nice jump up from his sixth place the year before.

Amway had a step or two lead on Coates and Berardi at the 5-mile mark. In a recent interview, Amway lauded Coates's competitive nature: "Anytime you had to run against Budd Coates, you knew it was going to be a really tough race."

But unlike his 1984 Diamond victory, Coates did not jump to a comfortable lead on "the Hill." That meant he had to rely on his kick.

In his post-race interview for the *Press-Enterprise,* Coates claimed that—being a "marathoner"—he didn't *have* "much of a kick." Nevertheless, Coates—who once ran a 4:10 mile in a summer twilight track meet—could still conjure up a solid finish when needed, though perhaps it was a kick generated more from tenacity than pure fast-twitch muscle fiber.

After the top three men, the diamonds went to Mike Renninger (4th, 45:59), Terry Permar (5th, 46:03), Greg Cauller (6th, 46:23), and—for the second straight year—Ted McKeigan scooped up another seventh-place (46:31) gem. Former East Stroudsburg runner Drew Davis outleaned Kutztown (and PSAC steeplechase champ) standout Bart Wasiolek at the line for eighth place.

A notable name in 13th place (47:27) was Malcolm East—the British-born runner living in the Pittsburgh area who once clocked a 2:11 marathon (good for 5th at Boston in 1981) and a sub-28-minute 10K. Steve Molnar won the Masters diamond (16th, 47:40), and Bill Bull (18th, 47:48) repeated as top local finisher.

Like a lot of Berwick participants, women's winner Molly Mitke of Allentown needed a break-in race to get used to "the Hill." In fact, Mitke admitted to the *Press-Enterprise:* "Last year I was intimidated by the mountain . . . This year, once I got on top, I knew it was pretty much all downhill the rest of the way and I just took off."

Mitke also took off a big chunk of time from her Berwick debut, touring the course in 53 minutes, 33 seconds. That put her more than a minute ahead of veteran Diamond runners Barb Swan (2nd, 54:46) of Lewisburg, Pennsylvania, and Debbie Grossman (3rd, 54:55) of Shavertown.

Rounding out the women's top seven were Karen Koehler (4th, 55:11) and a trio of Penn State runners, Kris and Kim Kelly of Pittston (5th and

6th in 57:29 and 57:30), and Kelli Hunt (7th, 57:30) from nearby Hazleton. The Nittany Lion teammates essentially ran together for the race. The Masters winner was former Hazleton resident Deborah Gebhardt of Maryland in 1:02, the first of her three wins in the 40-plus bracket.

Those who left quickly after the race to get ready for Thanksgiving dinner would have missed one of the most courageous endurance efforts of the day. Wearing a Bloomsburg sweatshirt, Tony Cerminaro Jr. became the first person with an artificial leg to complete the rough 9-mile course. It took him 3 hours, 44 minutes and change. When he arrived at the Market Street finish, he got a big hug from his mother Kathleen.

Finish Lines: In 1990, Budd Coates competed in the USA vest at the Goodwill Games in Seattle, finishing fourth. His stellar running career—one that must be said to be ongoing judging by his 2007 New York City Marathon time of 2:35 at age 50—includes qualifying four times for the men's US Olympic Marathon Trials. Coates had competed in various countries around the world—including Japan, Bermuda, Morocco, and Malaysia.

The early 1990s were good racing years for Molly Mitke. In 1992 she ran 17:56 at the Alburtis (Pennsylvania) 5K—a time that remains the women's course record there.

III
Haas, the Hill & O'Reilly
83rd Run for the Diamonds, November 26, 1992

Randy Haas of Orwigsburg, Pennsylvania, had heard about Berwick's Run for the Diamonds for more than a decade—and most of those "conversations" almost came as challenges from his training partner (and former mayor of Pottsville) Joe Muldowney. "Randy! You gotta run Berwick . . . You gotta run Berwick!"

But Haas, who had speed to burn as a young runner when he won both the 800 and 1600 state titles in the state Double-A (small schools) division, always manage to dismiss Muldowney's remarks as a wee bit of malarkey. But having won most of the races in northeastern and central Pennsylvania, this Berwick thing *did* start to get to him.

"One Thanksgiving I sitting down to eat turkey and I saw Mark

Amway coming across the line at Berwick—because they would show it on our local news station," Haas laughed. "And I thought, 'Maybe I should run it . . . ' "

Not long after—with Muldowney once again imploring him to "Run for the Diamonds"—Haas finally acquiesced.

"I had heard about the Hill, but when I got up there, I didn't want to see it," said Haas. "But I was in good shape that year—I think I had placed like fifth at the Philadelphia Distance Run (half marathon) and back in April I had run 2:17 at Boston [Marathon]. So I just went out and ran hard . . ."

Not only did Randy Haas not know that much about the course, but he knew nothing about the guy in the Asics racing vest striding powerfully along next to him as they zipped through the 2-mile mark and began to ascend to the Summer Hill churches. Not knowing might have been just as well; that guy happened to be Gerry O'Reilly—a 1500-meter Irish Olympian at Seoul in 1988 and a stud at Villanova in his collegiate days.

Of all the runners who have ever competed at Berwick, none of them had a mile PR to match O'Reilly's—a world-class, positively smoking personal best of 3 minutes, 54 seconds. At the 1986 Penn Relays, O'Reilly had also anchored the Villanova distance medley relay team to a performance that broke the existing world record in that event—the only problem being that he was photo'ed at the tape by Georgetown's Mike Starr in a heart-breaking outcome that was decided by mere *one-hundredths* of a second. Although Haas also was without question one of the fastest finishers on the Middle Atlantic road racing scene at his peak, O'Reilly might have had an edge in a sprint finish in which both men were relatively fresh.

But Berwick being Berwick—and the early pace having been aggressive—it was clear that nobody was going to arrive back on Market Street completely fresh. O'Reilly drafted directly behind Haas up Hosler's Hill and was still right behind Haas at halfway. But the eventual winner whipped around the corner onto Kachinka's Hollow Road and blasted up the first gradual hill there; a move that broke him loose from the former Wildcat.

Clay Shaw Photo

Rocket Rookies: Neither O'Reilly (633) nor Haas (22) had run Berwick before their classic 1992 duel. Haas broke away from the Irish Olympian and world-class miler around the 5-mile mark.

Just past 5 miles, Haas didn't hear footsteps anymore and he sensed that if he just kept working hard the Run for the Diamonds title would be his.

And so it was. A jubilant Haas—resplendent in the green, black and white silks of his Adidas sponsor—raced down Market Street and breasted the tape in a fine time of 44 minutes, 39 seconds. O'Reilly—in his only Berwick appearance—placed a solid second (45:31), but nearly a minute back at the end. Former Bucknell runner Rich Stark captured third in 46:17.

After the top three came Greg Cauller (4th, 46:44) with his best-ever Berwick finish, a strong performance from Terry Permar (5th, 46:48), Mark Gerber (6th, 46:55), former East Stroudsburg standout and a participant in the 1992 men's US Olympic Marathon trials, and—snaring the final open diamond—the powerful-running Bob Schwelm. Canadian Frank Lewis blitzed the Masters field with a terrific race, clocking 47:11 and placing eighth overall.

While Haas and O'Reilly were "enjoying" their classic duel at the front, former Shippensburg star Misti Demko was blasting away on her own in the women's field. All Demko did was turn in the *second* greatest single female performance in the history of the race—and even Katy Schilly's record run of 1981 just barely escaped her.

Looks Are Deceiving: Misti Demko looks fresh at the finish, but she said she was sore days later. Starter Dinny "Two Gun" Noonan points her home.

Demko, of Hershey, Pennsylvania, clocked 51 minutes flat, a scant 6 seconds off Schilly's mark. A trio of Penn State runners—Kim Kelly (2nd, 53:31), Kelli Hunt (3rd, also in 53:31) and Kris Kelly (4th, 53:33)—all scooted in together, but two or so minutes behind the winner. Rounding out the top seven women finishers were Molly Mitke (5th, 53:53), Barb Addis (6th, 54:35), and Lisa Reilly (7th, 55:46). Deborah Gebhardt won the women's Masters diamond in 1:01:25.

"I think it was Mark Amway who got me to run it," said Demko recently. "I typically trained about 50 miles per week, so a 9-mile race was a *long* way for me! The race was as hard as I expected . . . maybe more . . . I was sore for several days."

Finish Lines: Haas qualified for the 1992 men's US Olympic Marathon trials but elected not to compete because he would have had very little recovery time after his Boston Marathon run. However, by virtue of being the second American finisher at Boston, Haas was invited to Japan for a 15K road race in 1993—an experience that he still considers one of the highlights of his racing career.

Demko had other great races in her career, including a 1:14 half-marathon (the longest race she ever ran) at Philly that placed on the US World Half-Marathon team that competed in Brussels, Belgium, in 2002. She also ran under 32:44 for 10K. A mother of four, Misty might return for some Masters competition in the near future.

IV
Bodnar's Berwick Break-In
84th Run for the Diamonds, November 25, 1993

Just as Randy Haas needed a nudge (or two) to initially race at Berwick, another great champion of the 1990s needed some spirited encouragement from his running peers to make the effort. That guy was Jason Bodnar, a runner with 4:02 mile and 13:37 5000-meter credentials.

A star runner at Laurel Highlands High School (Uniontown, Pennsylvania) and also on some of Coach Jim Lear's best Pitt Panther squads in college, Bodnar had—and still has—strong ties to the western Pennsylvania running community.

"I first heard about the Berwick race from some of the older western Pennsylvania runners like [Don] 'Spiney' Norman [Berwick runner-up to Pfitzinger in 1981] and Brent Hawkins . . . They said: 'You should run that race!' . . . But to tell you the truth, before that I only knew about Berwick because Ron Powlus played quarterback there before he went to Notre Dame."

However, when Bodnar actually traveled to Berwick and prepared to race the Run for the Diamonds he also had heard about "the Hill." Although like Randy Haas the year before, he never actually experienced the arduous ascent until he was in the race.

Bodnar seemed to think a smart strategy was to stay with the front-runners until the hardest part was behind them.

"Maybe people really built it up to me, but I actually expected it to be worse than it was," Bodnar recalled in a recent interview. "In fact, after we got up there, I think I even asked some of the other guys 'Hey . . . Is this the top?' because I thought there might be more to it . . ."

There was still a fairly large pack of contenders as they pounded down the steep descent of Hosler's Hill toward the halfway mark and the abrupt left-hand turn. Then the pace got hot in a hurry, as the runners began to string out on that first gradual hill at the start of the Kachinka's Hollow Road stretch.

As the runners neared Martzville, Randy Haas had fallen off slightly, while Bodnar, Budd Coates, and Mark Amway were still close together at the front. "I remember thinking we needed to keep the pace honest," says Coates, "because with Randy's finishing speed, you really didn't want him close to you at the end."

Of course, Bodnar (with his 4:02 mile PR) could jet at the finish, too. He put together a fast second half of the race, complete with a solid kick down Market Street, to win in 44 minutes, 27 seconds. Coates (2nd, 44:51) barely held off Amway (3rd, 44:54), while a fast-closing Haas (4th, 45:01) kept Dave Berardi (5th, 45:14) and Mark Wimmer (6th, 45:18) at bay.

The seventh-place diamond went to Polish-born marathoner Antoni Niemczak (45:29), a controversial figure in racing circles due to his 1986 disqualification (and subsequent two-year suspension) for testing positive for steroids after a runner-up finish at the New York City Marathon.

The field was a particularly fast, as reflected in the fact that former Berwick champ Kevin Ruch (1988 winner) blasted a time of 45:41—and still missed a diamond by one spot.

Frank Lewis of Canada defended his Masters title, winning the 40-plus diamond with a time of 47:35.

Wendy Nelson-Barrett—a former PIAA state champion in cross-country and top Nittany Lion runner in college—easily won the women's race in 51 minutes, 38 seconds (at the time, Berwick's third fastest clocking ever for females) in her Berwick debut. Lisa Reilly ran a solid 53:31 for second place. Rounding out the women's top seven were Mary Ellen Kelly

(3rd, 54:27), Laurel Park (4th, 54:58), Connie Buckwalter (5th, 56:17), Barb Swan (6th, 57:29), and former Bloomsburg University star Tina Wikoski (7th, 57:44). For the third straight year, Deborah Gebhardt won the women's Masters.

The top Berwick finishers were Bill Bull, who clocked 48:10 (just 18 seconds up on Jamie DeFinnis), and former Bulldog runner Justine Johnson, who was timed in 1:02:11 as she paced along with friend and Moravian College teammate Carla Thomas.

The Sheridan family from Ontario made their trip down a worthwhile one: Whitey Sheridan was recognized as the race's oldest finisher, while his sons Dave and Mike both placed in the 45 to 49 age bracket.

V
Bodnar's Fleet Repeat
85th Run for the Diamonds, November 24, 1994

Sometimes just getting to Berwick turns into a competition—man vs. Mother Nature—and such was the case for the 85th annual Thanksgiving Day classic. With major snowstorms blowing across Pennsylvania, defending champion Jason Bodnar saw what typically was a three-hour trip to Berwick degenerate into twelve hours of drudgery and uncertainty.

Nevertheless, he was on the line for the crack of Dinny "Two-Gun" Noonan's famed starting pistols (and Dinny's well-rehearsed starting-line speech that admonished in advance any would-be gun jumpers) and a shot at becoming Berwick's first successful title defender since Pete Pfitzinger started off the 1980s with back-to-back wins.

The weather had come around—spots of bright sun had broken out to melt the snow—but the runners still bucked a noticeable wind as they headed out Market Street. Perhaps in deference to that breeze, Bodnar tucked behind Toronto's Henry Bickford and Randy Haas, as a big pack headed toward the first mile marker. Also in that bunch was 1986 Berwick champion Brian Ferrari.

The big bump—yes, "the Hill"—strung out the runners, as did the subsequent downside off Hosler's Hill. By the time the leaders zoomed through the halfway mark and began to hammer through Kachinka's Hollow, it was Ferrari and Bodnar in control, with Haas about 50 yards back in third. Sweeping down the Martzville Road, past the Berwick Country Club and heading for town, it was still Bodnar and Ferrari shoulder-to-shoulder, with Haas hoping to reestablish contact.

But as they reached Market Street and the final mile, Bodnar was pulling slightly ahead and added to his lead in the final minutes with a fluid and powerful finish. He clocked 45 minutes, 17 seconds to defend his title.

Haas closed the gap on Ferrari down Market, but Ferrari held on to finish second (45:42). Haas was 5 ticks back in third, while Bucknell University ace Chris Preistaf captured fourth (46:10).

The rest of the diamond-winning positions went to former Bloomsburg University standout (under Coach Lanny Conner) Dan Pszeniczny

Clay Shaw Photo

Tough Enough: Bodnar (1) and Ferrari (2) went shoulder-to-shoulder while Haas tried to chip away at their lead. All three men had one Diamond win at this point—and were looking for their second!

(5th, 46:29), former Bucknell runner Joe Cresko (6th, 47:01), and Canadian Gary Westgate (7th, 47:10), who held off Masters Division winner Terry Permar by just 1 second. Regional standouts Jim Simpson (47:16) and Drew Davis (47:21) ran strong to finish ninth and tenth.

In the women's race, Lisa Reilly ran *exactly* the same time (53:31) as she did in 1993—but with one important difference: She finished one place higher, and that put the Minersville resident in the winner's circle.

"It was an exciting win for me," recalls the winner, now Lisa Haas. "Randy [Haas] had won it, so it was nice that I could, too." About 200 yards behind the winner, Laurel Park of Michigan checked in for second-place laurels in 54:08, a place better than in 1993. Katie Dosser of Ontario mustered a quick kick near the finish to hold off Penn State runner Kim Kelly by 1 second in 54:30. Former Millersville State runner Connie Buckwalter (55:02) held off New Jersey's Barbara Addis (55:06) for fifth, while seventh place went to Mary Ellen Kelly of Columbia, South Carolina in 55:40—edging Penn State runner Kris Kelly (Kim's twin) by 1 second.

Margaret Betz, 58 years old, captured the Masters diamond in a brisk time of 1 hour and 1 minute flat—a time that beat all the 40-year-old women in the deep field. Betz of Conklin, New York (near Binghamton) was destined to be one of the top age-group runners in the US, although she never even took up the sport until she was over 40.

Not long after his second Berwick triumph, Bodnar says he felt he hit the best training stretch of his career. "I was just running some *crazy* workouts and feeling great!" he said in a recent interview. "I was doing stuff like repeat miles in 4:10 and three times 800 in 1:55 . . ."

But instead of reaping new personal bests on track and road, Bodnar—as fate would have it—came down with pneumonia. Then, to make matters worse, he had a reaction to some of the medication he was given. He missed months and months of training. "I did get back in shape eventually," he says, "but I felt that I never got back to where I was just before I got sick."

Finish Lines: Margaret Betz once won her age group in the Los Angeles Marathon (1984) and the Boston Marathon (1993), but perhaps more noteworthy were the US women's age-group (65 to 69) records she set in 2003—21:16 for 5K, 35:38 for 8K, and 1:36:28 for 20K.

VI
Randy Rides Again
86th Run for the Diamonds, November 23, 1995

That old Credence Clearwater Revival song called "Up Around The Bend" could have been Randy Haas's theme song in the 1995 Run for the Diamonds. Like an accomplished performer, Haas held steady as Colombian native Miguel Upegui steamed through the opening mile in 4:45—jumping to an early lead of more than 50 yards.

"I didn't know who he was," Haas, the 1992 champion, later admitted, "but I knew what was coming up around the bend."

Of course "what was coming" happened to be "the Hill"—and Haas, now a veteran of several Thanksgiving Day races, knew that the climb would exact its punishment on anyone who recklessly attacked the opening miles. Since Colombia is a high-altitude country that includes the northern part of the Andes, most endurance athletes from that nation—be they runners or cyclists—can climb quite well. But Upegui (who had been living in the US for a length of time) nevertheless had to pay for his frisky first mile.

Haas caught the South American just before the churches in Summer Hill, and then blew open a big lead on the subsequent descents. In fact, as Upegui fell off, one of the region's better-known runners—former Northwest High School star and Bloomsburg University All-American Dan Pszeniczny—moved into second.

Virtually unchallenged in the second half, Haas cruised on en route to his second career Berwick victory, thrusting his right arm in the air and crossing the line in 45 minutes, 29.5 seconds. Pszeniczcny charged home second—more than 200 yards back—in 46:17. Upegui settled for a distant third in 47:01.8.

After the top three, the remaining diamonds went to Canada's Paul Barron—who snatched two gems because he also was first Master—in 47:30 (4th), Chambersburg's Tim Schuler (5th, 47:34), Rich Stark (6th, 47:46), and James Garrett (7th, 48:45) of Bennington, Vermont, who outleaned Canadian Henry Bickford by 1 crucial second.

The women's race may have been even less of a mystery, as heavily favored Wendy Nelson-Barrett bolted out to a strong opening, blasted up the hill, and never saw another female rival. She won comfortably in 52 minutes, 50.5 seconds—her second Run for the Diamonds victory. The former Penn State runner also finished 29th overall in a field of more than 700 finishers.

Although Alice Thurau of Fisher, Pennsylvania, was a distant second to Nelson-Barrett, her time of 53 minutes, 42 seconds was still an outstanding performance—doubly so because she also won the Masters diamond. Former Berwick winner Molly Mitke (3rd, 55:41) held off Barb Addis (4th, 55:45), while the battle for fifth was even closer, as Ann Sick (5th, 58:18) of nearby Millville nipped Wilkes-Barre high school runner Michele Wolyniec (6th, 58:19). Patty Turney of Silver Springs, Maryland, nailed down seventh (58:52).

For the local bragging rights, once again Bill Bull galloped in first in 52 minutes flat (his eleventh local win out of the last dozen races), while Justine Johnson led the Berwick area women in 1:01.26.

VII
The Berwick Hat Tricks
87th Run for the Diamonds, November 29, 1996

Scoring three goals in ice hockey or soccer is commonly referred to as a hat trick—admittedly a difficult achievement. Coming into the 87th Run for the Diamonds, both Jason Bodnar and Wendy Nelson-Barrett were in position to capture their third Berwick crown.

Bodnar, who had missed the 1995 race because it took him some time to recover from his bout with pneumonia and its aftereffects, was ready to rock around the Briar Creek Hills again. But he was also going to face some fierce competition in the way of Berwick newcomer and former Auburn University star Chris Fox (who had finished 7th in the 1992 US Olympic Marathon trials), Mike Mykytok, Randy Haas, Budd Coates, and others.

Fox and Bodnar got down to it on "the Hill" and gained some ground on the pack, but apparently at quite a price to their reserves. Soon after halfway, Fox dropped way back in the field. In a recent interview, Bodnar was quick to admit that "I really was fit enough to run fast . . . But we went so hard on the Hill that I was hurtin' the second half of the race."

But Bodnar fought through the pain and ran 44 minutes, 27 seconds for his third Berwick victory—exactly matching his PR on the course from his 1993 debut. However, he didn't have that much time to savor the win on Market Street because Mykytok charged home with a solid runner-up race a mere 7 seconds behind. Haas also put together a great race, cracking 5-minute-per-mile pace for third in 44:50.

The fourth through seventh slots were also fast. Former Eastern Michigan star Mark Dailey—a world-class performer on the track at 800 and 1500 meters—captured fourth (45:02) in his one and only Berwick. Fifth place went to Canadian runner Alain Boucher (45:45), while Lehigh Valley training partners Budd Coates and Todd Fach essentially came into together for sixth and seventh, both clocked in 45:51. Dave Shaffer hammered out a 47:35 to clinch the men's Masters title.

"That race was just *loaded* with talent," recalls Fach, who snagged the last diamond in his Berwick debut. "But for me, it was really good experience and I got to know the course."

Meanwhile, Wendy Nelson-Barrett rolled to her third—and, to date, unprecedented—Run for the Diamonds crown. She clocked 51 minutes, 31 seconds—placing her nearly 2 minutes ahead of runner-up Kristy Johnston (53:24). Johnston was a world-class runner who in 1996 had finished 5th in the women's US Olympic Marathon trials and placed second at the Chicago Marathon (2:31) just a few weeks before Berwick. Third place went to Debbie Grossman of Shavertown, Pennsylvania, who set a new women's Masters record in 53:38.

Wendy on the Wing: Nelson-Barrett flew to her third Diamond win, a feat unmatched in the women's race history.

Michigan's Laurel Park (4th, 54:40), Connie Buckwalter (5th, 54:55), Tina Bartholomew (6th, 56:03) and Michelle Wolyniec (7th, 56:27) rounded out the top female finishers.

The victory also vaulted Bodnar into special company in terms of Berwick race history, as he joined the likes of Tewanima, Kolehmainen, Gregory, and Pflaging as a three-time winner.

Finish Lines: Jason Bodnar recovered enough to make the US cross-country team in 1998, competing against the world's best in Marrakech, Morocco. Ten years later, Bodnar is still fairly fit. Despite the rigors of a dental practice near Ashville, North Carolina, the 36-year-old Bodnar found time to train for the Boston Marathon. He finished the 2008 run from Hopkinton to Back Bay in 2:33:58 and placed 68th overall.

VIII
Minnesota Fach Runs Table
88th Run for the Diamonds, November 27, 1997

Todd Fach isn't from Minnesota actually; he's originally from Ohio and moved to Pennsylvania's Lehigh Valley sometime after graduating from Wooster College (where he won the conference cross-country title three times). But like Minnesota Fats, Todd Fach—when he wasn't running or playing golf—was known to shoot a game of eight-ball or two. (Hannes Kolehmainen, the Flying Finn, would have approved; pool was how the Olympian relaxed in Berwick before he was called upon to race.)

"My father taught me how to play," Fach recalls, "and when it came to that point in the game when somebody had to take control, he'd announce: 'Okay, it's time to go to school, kid!' . . . And then he would run the table."

The 88th running of the Berwick classic—sans three-time winner Jason Bodnar—started out fairly tactical. Nobody blasted away up Summer Hill and, in fact, a good half a dozen runners were still in contention at the halfway mark—steady west wind perhaps the culprit.

But Fach—as he had seen only too well the year before—knew the fifth to sixth mile, the roller-coaster ride through Kachinka's Hollow—was bound to be fast.

Jamie Hibell—Fach's training partner on occasions—was running his first Berwick, and Fach felt a slight obligation to let him know that the pace was going to heat up in a hurry.

"After we made that hard left and went up that first hill, I turned to Jamie and said: 'It's time to go to school, kid . . .' . . . It sounds a lot worse than the way I meant it," says Fach. "What I meant was: 'Get ready! This is when the race *really* begins . . .'

And Fach, who zipped the fifth mile in about 4:35, had a lot to do with the inevitable increase in speed. By the time they hit Martzville Road, Scranton's Matt Byrne was still on his shoulder, but Rich Stark and Hibell had fallen back a bit. Behind them, Randy Haas—always dangerous if he could reestablish contact for the stretch drive—was waiting in the wings.

Clay Shaw Photo

Don't Be Schooled: Todd Fach (wearing ball cap) is ready to drop his famous in-race line—and the hammer. He's in fast company with Matt Byrne, Rich Stark, and future winner Jamie Hibell on Kachinka's Hollow Road.

Fach, his eyes narrowed beneath his red Nike baseball cap and decked out in the Bethlehem's Aardvark Sports Shop racing gear, kept applying the pressure and eventually pulled away from Byrne. "With a few blocks to go, I was thinking, 'I can win this thing . . .' and I just kept working," remembers Fach.

Fach worked right through the line in 45 minutes, 39 seconds, while Stark rallied in the last mile to overtake Byrne (3rd, 45:59) and claim second in 45:53. Haas won yet another diamond (4th, 46:07), while Hibell placed fifth (46:15) in his Diamond debut. Dave McMillian of Hershey

(6th, 46:38) and Chambersburg's Tim Schuler (7th, 47:13) corralled the last two diamond awards. Jeff Foster, once a top runner for the Edinboro Fighting Scots, won the Masters crown in 48:04.

Tracy Wartman of Bethlehem had never taken on the Run for the Diamonds, but the former five-time NCAA D-3 All-American for Moravian College was up for the challenge. She handled the Foundryville climb fairly well; just up ahead she could see Bob Thear and Chris Lowthert (both of whom had run on the men's team when she was in college), so she guessed she was running fairly fast. A former 1500-meter national champ in college, her leg speed matched up well with some of the generous descents. She essentially went wire-to-wire, stopping the clock in 53 minutes, 30 seconds.

Tina Bartholomew (2nd, 54:53) of Danville turned in her career-high placing, just about a minute ahead of Michelle Wolyniec of Plains, Pennsylvania (3rd). Rounding out the diamond winners were Mariann Foster of Edinboro (4th, 56:45), former champ Sarah Raitter (5th, 57:04), western Pennsylvania runner Gina Pacitti (6th, 57:25), and Bloomsburg's Lora Learn (7th, 57:42), who finished just a few seconds ahead of Berwick's own Justine Johnson (8th, 57:49). Onnie O'Neill of Dunmore, Pennsylvania, won the women's Masters (1:03:55).

Finish Lines: "The 'Time to go to school . . . ' line is something we're always going to joke about," says Jamie Hibell. In addition to being the recipient of one of Berwick's great in-race lines, Hibell had a big day in other ways, too. He won his first Berwick diamond and also proposed to his wife, Melissa, in the finish-line area that day.

In addition to some diamond-winning races at Berwick, Matt Byrne has twice qualified for the men's US Olympic Marathon trials and twice won Scranton's Steamtown Marathon (2004 and 2006).

Tina Bartholomew went on to win the women's title at the 2002 Steamtown Marathon in 2:50.

IX
Demko's Diamond Double
89th Run for the Diamonds, November 26, 1998

Jamie Hibell was in fantastic shape when he arrived in Berwick for the 1998 race, and he also had his rookie ("Time to go to school . . .") run out of the way. Still, someone might have suggested double-knotting the laces on his racing flats.

"My shoelace came untied about a quarter mile into the race," Hibell remembers. "Bart Wasiolek said that I should stop and tie it . . . I did, and I think Todd [Fach] slowed up the pace so I could catch back up."

Hibell scrambled to get back with the leaders by the mile mark, while former Bloomsburg All-American Dan Pszeniczny—looking to improve just one place from his 1997 finish—pushed the pace at the front.

But as the hardest running began on the climb up to Summer Hill, the two teammates representing Aardvark Sports out of Bethlehem took over at the front, and it soon became a two-man race. When they reached the hard left turn and swung onto Kachinka's Hollow Road, Hibell couldn't resist a comment to Fach: "Well . . . Are you gonna say it?"

Presumably Fach (who had picked Hibell to win prior to the race) was running too hard to utter anything so profound and impromptu again. True to Fach's prediction, it was actually Hibell who took control of the race once the leaders reached Martzville Road, but Fach kept digging to stay close.

Once Hibell took the lead out on the Martzville Road he was running with some doubt. "I ran scared coming in," he says, "knowing I only had about 10 seconds on Todd and that a bad mile could erase all that . . . I was so happy to see the Fuzzy Grub [a hunting and fishing store in North Berwick]. It had become our tradition to jog out and touch the Fuzzy Grub on our warm-ups, so I knew I only had about a mile to go."

Hibell bolted past the Fuzzy Grub and churned on to victory in 45 minutes, 56 seconds. Fach stayed glued to the task and nailed down second (46:21), with Pzeniczny third (47:25) and Bob "Rads" Radzwich—former West Hazleton and Penn State runner—turning in his most sparkling Diamond run with a fourth-place effort (47:39).

Perhaps the closest race of the day was former Kutztown University steeplechase ace Wasiolek hammering home for fifth (47:51) just a second before James Hamilton (6th) and several more ticks of the clock ahead of Danville's Chris Miller (7th, 47:59).

Thomas Grant of New York was the top Master (22nd overall, 50:55), and Canadian Mike Sheridan was the first 50-plus guy. (57:34).

As if it were something of a testimonial to Berwick's historic lure, there were three (in addition to Fach) former Diamond Kings in the race: Brian Ferrari (18th), Tom Carter (41st), and Dave Northey (47th).

For Hibell, it was a good, solid win in a race that historically attracts some tough regional competition and—occasionally—a world-class-runner to-be. "For those first two Berwicks I was coached by Todd Lippin [former Lehigh University assistant aka "the Lip"] and he helped me prepare for the race."

Hibell had been a promising young runner at Southern Lehigh High School in Coopersburg, Pennsylvania, and (after starting at Pitt) eventually graduated from Allentown College (now DeSales) where he achieved D-3 All-American honors in the 5000 meters.

By the summer of 1998, Hibell was training a lot with Budd Coates, Todd Fach, and other assorted runners as he began the transition to the full marathon distance of 26-miles. As Fach notes, signing on to follow "the program" with Coates was not for the timid. "If the program had down 30 miles for the Sunday long run, you had to be ready to do it," says Fach. (There was no need to add that Coates' courses for those runs were notoriously hilly.)

By the summer of 1999, Coates was constructing Hibell's marathon workouts in an attempt to help Hibell qualify for the US Olympic trials (a sub-2:20). Hibell was the first American finisher in the 2000 Boston Marathon, running 2:22 despite a strong, cold headwind that certainly slowed down the field. After initially feeling frustrated, Hibell now looks back on that performance in inhospitable conditions as "probably my best race."

"My biggest regret in running, besides not making the trials in the marathon, was not winning a second Berwick," says Hibell. "I know the list of multiple winners is short."

Speaking of multiple winners, Misti Demko accomplished that feat when she won her second Berwick. Demko says she had little choice but to go out fast, because Wendy Nelson-Barrett scorched the first mile (in around 5:10) and neither runner was willing to let the other get that far ahead so early in the race. "I remember running past Mike [her husband] who was watching the race," says Demko. "I just sort of threw up my hands as if to say: 'What can I do?'"

After the race Demko acknowledged that she started out unreasonably hard, but she nevertheless held together up "the Hill" and was jousting with the second dozen men.

She maintained her fast pace through the Hollow, but by mile 8 her legs got the heavies . . . and any shot at a new record melted slowly away.

Nevertheless, her time of 51:24 was the third fastest time ever by a woman on the course and put her right on the heels of some accomplished male runners in the race such as former Bloomsburg standout Mark Jobes, Bill Bull, and former East Stroudsburg Road Warrior Seth Kuchar—all of whom were just a handful of seconds ahead of her.

Lisa Haas ran a personal best (53:27) on the Berwick course to place second behind Demko's aggressive attack from the front. Wendy Nelson-Barrett placed third (54:10). "For me it was pretty exciting to be up there running with Wendy," Haas recalled recently, "because she was such a talented runner."

Laurel Park of Ann Arbor, Michigan (Rich Stark's wife), captured another diamond (4th, 55:06). Rounding out the rest of the women's top seven were Jennifer Moyer Malavolta (5th, 56:24), Brenda Pennell (6th, 56:53), and Sherry Albin (7th, 57:23) of Maryland.

Laurie Knight of Lewisburg won the women's Masters, equaling the diamond her husband, Jim, won back in 1981.

X
The Hot Tub Kid Comes In
90th Run for the Diamonds, November 25, 1999

Imagine Jay Leno or David Letterman attempting to tour the Berwick beast and crack jokes at the same time. Either would most likely by tailed by a squad of nervous paramedics and require hits of oxygen between the one-liners.

Although his jokes perhaps didn't measure up to the late-night TV comedy giants, Carleton "Buck" Jones of Ohio blasted around the rain-slick Berwick course, won the 90th Run for the Diamonds, and even tossed out the occasional gem to the photographers and scribes on the press truck as he cruised along with a big lead on Kachinka's Hollow Road.

"Anybody got a hot tub?" the 33-year-old Jones quipped, dripping wet with cold rain and warm sweat.

Jones had driven about seven hours from Columbus, Ohio, just to run in his first Berwick, so you couldn't blame the guy for being a little bit goofy. Jones passed his last true rival—Bill Frawley—at the top of the mountain and then did something reminiscent of Tewanima and the Carlisle Indian era: He let out a spirited yell. But Jones's yell was less war whoop and more celebratory "whoo-hoo!"—as in, "I'm glad *that's* over with!" And then he proceeded to put more distance between himself and Frawley—a 2:17 marathoner who had competed in the 1996 Olympic Marathon trials.

However, not *everything* went perfectly for Jones. Having recently moved from Seattle to Ohio, Jones was in no danger of being called back by the Seahawks for an NFL tryout; he dropped a football tossed his way by a young boy who was watching the race. "It hit me in the hands," Jones later joked in the *Press-Enterprise*.

Despite the chilling rain, the start of the race blasted down Market at what would be for some of the front-runners a pace too hot to handle. Nearly a dozen men bolted through the mile at sub-5 or 5-flat per mile pace. Frawley did the bulk of the work on the climb to the Summer Hill churches, with Jones content to follow—but poised to countersurge once they reached the top.

"That's the make or break point," Jones told *The Runner's Gazette*. "The course was absolutely brutal, but definitely worth it."

Jones zoomed on to the victory in 44 minutes, 56 seconds—essentially averaging 5-flat per mile over the roller-coaster ride through the Briar Creek Hills. Frawley, however, certainly did not disappear; he launched a rally down Martzville Road, and Jones was forced to reboot his engines down Market. Frawley, who had finished 9th in 1993, sprinted in for a strong second in 45:18, though he was quick to admit it was too little, too late. "You could tell he [Jones] was having fun out there," Frawley told the *Press-Enterprise*.

After the top pair, Bart Wasiolek, former Kutztown star, snagged third (46:41), holding off Glen Mays (4th, 46:53). Rounding out the diamond winners were Chris Miller (5th, 47:19), and Rich Stark (6th, 47:29), and former Central Columbia High School standout Greg Remaly, a Kenyon College frosh, pounced on the last open diamond (7th, 47:41).

Greg Cauller was eighth (47:55)—usually the place that means you missed a diamond by one—but as first Master, he landed one anyway. Steve Ruckert (53:12) won the Senior (50-plus) diamond.

In the women's race, long-striding Kristina Laubenstein, the 24-year-old former West Chester University star, blitzed the field with a brisk 52 minutes, 21 seconds. By halfway, she had a comfortable lead and concentrated on racing the men around her. She placed 35th overall in a field of nearly 950 finishers. Julie Bowers, another former West Chester ace, ran 53:53

Clay Shaw Photo

The Master Plan: Greg Cauller (York, Pennsylvania) won his first 40-plus diamond in 1999. At last tally, his stash is at seven and counting.

for second—a time that sometimes is fast enough to win.

Behind Bowers there was more than a minute wait, but then five women charged the line in a space of just 22 seconds: former East Strouds-burg All-American middle-distance ace Jan Blake (3rd, 55:07), Patty Ful-ton of Maryland (4th, 55:11), former Moravian College All-American Kristie Reccek (5th, 55:13), Jen Moyer Malavolta (6th, 55:34) and Lisa Reilly (7th, 55:39) all landed diamond pendants. The Masters champ was Mimi Newcomer, while Debby Gebhardt (previously a three-time winner of the Masters at Berwick) secured the Veterans diamond.

Gebhardt's race was all the more satisfying since it showed how well her comeback was going. In 1996 she had been struck by a hit-and-run driver while on a training run.

"I had to learn how to walk again," recalls Gebhardt, who spent fifteen days in the hospital after the incident. "But I was determined to run again. My first goal was to run the Marine Corps Marathon. But since I'm from Hazleton, running Berwick has always been part of Thanksgiving for me."

The ninth woman finisher—just 23 seconds from a diamond-winning performance—was 31-year-old Laurie Corbin of New Jersey. Just a few months after racing at Berwick, Corbin (now Laurie Gordon) would show a lot of perseverance in the face of true adversity. Laurie's experience was eerily similar to Gebhardt's.

In late January 2000 the former Lehigh University runner was struck by a car while on a training run, suffering a fractured skull and a broken nose. The next day—despite her injuries—she checked herself out of the hospital and jogged on a high school track for eighteen minutes to keep her daily "running streak" alive. Not only that, but Laurie placed 77th (out of 141 finishers) in the women's US Olympic Marathon Trials in February 2000, clocking 2:56 over a hilly course in Columbia, South Carolina.

Finish Lines: Carleton Buck Jones placed 12th overall (out of 50,000-plus participants) and was the second American at the 2000 Bloomsday 12K staged in Spokane, Washington. Jones, competing against international runners from Kenya, Brazil, and Mexico, clocked 36:37 over the challenging route that includes the infamous "Doomsday Hill."

A former qualifier for the women's US Olympic trials in the 3000-meter steeplechase, Kris Laubenstein Hoey is now the head women's cross-country coach at Washington and Lee University in Lexington, Virginia.

27

Countdown to 100

With the new millennium well under way, some of the old-time runners (and the author includes himself in that motley crew) no doubt found themselves surprised that a hundred years of racing in Berwick was just around the bend. It is a bit like standing by one of those very long freight trains—hearing the whistle from far off—and then next thing you know, the box cars are creaking by . . . slow and steady at first . . . and suddenly rocking faster and faster . . .

It is enough to make you lose count! But then again, the Berwick Marathon Association diligently and enthusiastically reminds anyone reading its website that "the countdown continues!"

And so it does.

I
Barker's Basic Berwick Blast
91st Run for the Diamonds, November 23, 2000

A first-time Berwick participant, Jeff Barker—former Boyertown High School and Edinboro University star—decided to go back to basics. That is, the basic how-to-win-at-Berwick theory that said "He who hits the Hill first with the most (and doesn't die in the process) has a good shot at winning.

"Basically, I wanted to run uphill real hard," Barker told the *Press-Enterprise* after the race. "I figured I could recover on that downhill a little."

He figured correctly on both counts. The lanky, long-striding Barker was already pushing—with defending champ Carleton "Buck" Jones (who would eventually fall off to 24th) and 1998 champ Jamie Hibell in tow. But Barker hammered the climb up to the Summer Hill churches, grabbed a big lead, and then recovered enough on the downside of Hosler's Hill to re-stoke his engines for the second half of the race.

And nobody was coming to get him. At the spot of the hard left turn, just a few yards beyond the halfway mark on the road, a surprised fan exclaimed: "I've never seen this before . . . There's no one behind him!"

That wasn't *entirely* true; 960 other runners were coming, just not at the same speed. They chugged along in the cold, sunny weather.

Barker raced on by himself—the kind of loneliness that long-distance runners actually *like*—en route to a victory without a whole lot of worry. He arrived back on Market Street with only cheers and claps to follow him home, as he hit the tape in 45 minutes, 33 seconds.

A little less than a minute later, Hibell scooted in for second place (46:26), while Lancaster's Justin Krebs charged up to grab third (47:29), just ahead of mountain runner Bill Raitter (4th, 47:33) and Kenyon University (by way of the region's Central Columbia High School) athlete Greg Remaly—eating up yards with his 6-5 stride—capturing his first diamond with a solid fifth (47:35). Former Bucknell runner Dave Granger placed sixth (47:53), while Budd Coates—affectionately known as "the old man" by his training partners Jamie Hibell and Todd Fach—snagged yet another double diamond—one for seventh and one for top Master.

The eight through ten slots were taken by Jeremy Hoffman, Eric Reese, and former Dickinson College All-American Lowell Ladd. Steve Molnar nailed the Veterans diamond (50-plus).

In the women's race, one might say it was time for the sentimental favorite to make hay. Connie Buckwalter—who had a stellar high school career for Solanco High School then went on to race in college for Millersville—blasted through with her diamond victory run. Buckwalter—decked out in tights, long sleeves, gloves, and headband to ward off the cold—broke a Berwick streak of three fifth places en route to her 54 minute, 50 second triumph. Second went to Amy Pyles (55:49); and former Bloomsburg University runner Michelle Wolyniec placed third (56:12).

Rounding out the top seven were Jen (Moyer) Malavolta, former top runner at East Stroudsburg (4th), Mimi Newcomer (5th), Sarah Raitter (6th), and Kathleen Jobes of Bethlehem (7th). Newcomer successfully defended her Masters title, while Karen Mitchell put down her camera long enough to snare the Veterans (50-plus) diamond.

Finish Lines: Greg Remaly was a top cross-country/track runner at Kenyon College and also swam on NCAA D-3 championship teams for the Lords. In an obvious transition, Remaly is now a professional triathlon participant based in Incline Village, Nevada. On his website, Remaly proudly lists his accomplishments from Run for the Diamonds. In high school he placed 6th in the Pennsylvania cross-country championships.

II
Wagoner Rolls Downhill
92nd Run for the Diamonds, November 22, 2001

Prior to the 92nd Run for the Diamonds, Jeremy Hoffman—a well-known runner from the area and former Shippensburg University athlete—approached race director Margaret Livsey and requested a small favor. Could Hoffman's former teammate Matt Wagoner perhaps have a seeded number that would allow him to get on the front line?

The request was granted, and then Wagoner proceeded to justify the favor by delivering a very fine performance. However, that performance unfolded gradually.

When some of the Mid-Atlantic region's best runners—and occasional special guest stars from elsewhere—come dueling for diamonds, the tactics are typically more kamikaze than cautionary. Usually someone—or two or three guys—hit "the Hill" with about 95 percent of what they have and hope to open up a significant cushion of space on the chase pack, then hang on.

But the 2001 Berwick race—in a very rare occurrence—found half a dozen runners together even after climbing "the Hill" and moving in a pack through Summer Hill. If it were a game of cat-and-mouse one could have argued that the pace was more rodent-like than feline. Then again, the temperatures were slightly on the warm side.

But on the descent off of Hosler's Hill, one of the pack pounced—Wagoner got the race rolling with a 4:30 downhill mile. "I figured I would just let it go and see if I could pull it out," he was later quoted in the *Press-Enterprise.*

The pack was momentarily taken by surprise. Wagoner quickly carved out a lead of 5 or 6 seconds as he hit the hard left onto Kachinka's Hollow Road. The pack, meanwhile, regrouped and tried to hunt him down.

But once rolling, Wagoner had no intention of putting the brakes on. He held the lead back to North Berwick, got the crowd behind him on the homestretch, and—like many a Berwick leader before him—rode their infectious enthusiasm all the way through the tape.

"My goal was to come here and win a diamond," admitted Wagoner. "I thought I had an outside shot at winning, but I was really just hoping for a top-seven diamond."

And he did get a top-seven diamond—the first one, in fact, albeit in a modest time (by modern Berwick standards) of 47:08. Just behind him, one of the most ferocious battles for second in the history of the race took place—with three finishers within several seconds of each other. Former Berwick champ Todd Fach won out (2nd, 47:15), with Mike Craighead (3rd, 47:16) and mountain running specialist Bill Raitter (4th, 47:22) applying the pressure.

Not far behind the rush for runner-up laurels came Wagoner's former teammate Jeremy Hoffman (5th, 47:22) and accomplished Masters division ace Greg Cauller (6th, 47:27). Former Bucknell runner Rich Stark (7th, 47:57) charged for the final diamond.

The eight through fifteen slots included some big Berwick names of the past, including two-time winner Budd Coates (9th, 48:52) and road warrior Mark Amway (10th, 48:54).

Others in that bunch included Greg Remaly (8th, 48:36) of Kenyon College in Ohio, former Ursinus College runner Marty Owens (11th, 49:01), Tim Thomas (12th, 49:09), Justin Krebs (13th, 49:20), Mike "Stilts" Lehtonen (14th, 49:31), and Palmerton's Shane Anthony (15th, 49:49). Susquehanna University senior Lehtonen started the race conservatively because he had just competed in the NCAA D-3 cross-country nationals five days before, but he quickly got into the groove as he took on the climb.

In the women's race, Laurel Park—a former University of Michigan runner, where she once achieved All-Big Ten honors in the 10,000—led by nearly 200 yards through the 10K mark. But Sarah Raitter—an accomplished hill running and snowshoe racing specialist—was on the prowl and finally caught Park with about a mile to go. Raitter pushed even harder at that point, not wishing the race to come down to a late kick with the finish line in view. "I knew that Laurel has a good kick . . . so I really stepped on it," Raitter said afterward.

Raitter's winning time was 53 minutes, 29 seconds, with Park just 8 seconds back. Rounding out the top seven diamond winners were Amy Pyles (3rd, 54:20), former Moravian College All-American Kristie Reccek (4th, 55:28), Michele Wolyniec (5th, 55:31), former Berwick winner Connie Buckwalter (6th, 55:55), and Amy Aston-Rome (7th, 56:02). Ann Sick was the top Master and Barbara Zeske the first Veteran.

Wendy Blass blasted in as first local on the women's side. She clocked 58:30 (good for 8th overall in the women's event) and locked up her fourth straight local title. She was only 9 seconds off her course record for local women.

Berwick fans must have wondered who in the world kept asking for ice cream during the race. (They are used to mid-packers coming by and asking, "Hey! Is that turkey ready yet?") But the ice cream man was none other than devoted vegetarian Gary Fanelli—the Philadelphia-area runner and one of the true "free spirits" of the sport. Fanelli (coaxed up to Berwick as a guest speaker at the Wednesday-night pasta dinner) is infamous for his on-road shenanigans and various outfits—perhaps the most memorable being his Blues Brothers attire, though he has run as Michael Jackson and in a New York Mets uniform, too.

Lest we forget, Fanelli was (and still is) a fairly fast runner. In 1980 he led the US Olympic Marathon trials for 15-miles, displaying a racing shirt boldly proclaiming: THE ROAD TO MOSCOW ENDS HERE!" In 1988 Fanelli ran for American Samoa in the Seoul Olympic Games. Hard to figure how a guy from suburban Philly got to represent an island in the Pacific, but Fanelli placed 51st in that marathon—well in the top half of the starting Olympic field.

Fanelli enjoyed his Berwick experience. Bryan Stride (52:34)—a top-notch Canadian runner—won the Veterans diamond (first overall 50-plus runner), but Fanelli (53:28) placed high in the 50-54 age bracket. "I personally call it the Run for the Fossilized Coal," Fanelli quipped about the Diamond run. "Think about it."

III
The Second-Half Hammer
93rd Run for the Diamonds, November 28, 2002

If you put together a history of a 100-year-old tradition, sometimes you just have to bow to superior scene setting. This is how the Berwick Marathon Association article began its 2002 race story—a piece of writing with a triple byline from BMA stalwarts Margaret Livsey, Bev Bull, and Bill Bull:

Snow Makes for Interesting 93rd Run for the Diamonds

Berwick, PA—Excitement fills the air of every Diamonds race. Pre-race jitters abound. Anticipation of "The Hill" is in the minds of all runners, experienced and novice. A certain "electricity" is in the air. This is what the runners feel every year while driving into town, while warming up, while listening to "Rocky," while listening to Ed Livsey play the American and Canadian National Anthems on the clarinet, and while standing on the starting line waiting for the gun to go off. This year was the same. Then a strange calm filled the starting line. A snow squall hit Berwick just minutes before the start. Then the local newspaper, The Press-Enterprise, had a helicopter appear out of nowhere. This gave the whole starting area a surreal quality. Two-time winner Budd Coates commented: "Only in Berwick! I love this race!"

And then the gun went off!

It really was a pretty little snow, though admittedly more so if you were sipping a mug of great coffee in front of a pleasantly cracking fire and gazing out a large picture window—as opposed to, say, feeling that slip-slip of racing flats on top of a slightly slick glaze as you tried to climb up to Summer Hill. Still, it was nothing like 1909, 1938, or 1940—or, for that matter, 1971, when the race committee reluctantly pushed the event back to Saturday.

So . . . swirling flakes floated above the onslaught of runners. And it wasn't just *any* field of runners, but Berwick's first over the 1,000 mark as 1,006 would finish the 9-mile race up and down the Briar Creek Hills.

By the time the front-runners hit "the Hill,"—now frosted with enough white stuff that the runners searched out the occasional dry patches to run on—the contenders had whittled down to a gang of four. The leaders included Shippensburg coach and 1992 Olympian Steve Spence and Jamie Hibell (both former Berwick winners), plus former Bucknell runner Dave Bronfenbrenner—wearing the telltale navy and orange of the Lewisburg legions—and Steve Walsh of the Bryn Mawr Running Club.

Shortly after the halfway mark, Walsh pushed out to a 30-yard lead. But Bronfenbrenner began to reel him back in on the descents. "I'm a good downhill runner," he said afterward. "I knew if I kept it close, I would have a chance."

Bronfenbrenner's words were seconded by Hibell: "The way he runs down hills, nobody was going to bring 'Bronf' back in the second half of the race."

A 9:18 2-mile split between 5 and 7 miles didn't hurt Bronfenbrenner's chances either. Turning onto Market Street, he had carved out about a 60-

yard edge and rode the cheers of the crowd for the final mile. "If it weren't for the crowd," he said, echoing the words of many a Berwick leader, "it would have been really, really tough."

Walsh, a man with fairly consistent sub-4:10 mile speed on the track, was not to be taken lightly in the homestretch. But Bronfenbrenner's lead held up, as he stopped the clock in 46 minutes, 10 seconds. Walsh secured the runner-up spot 12 seconds later, while Hibell placed third in 46:40. Spence's fourth (47:28) was good for two diamonds—a top-seven gem, plus a second one for winning the Masters division.

Bill Raitter—an accomplished mountain running specialist and occasional snowshoe racer who probably enjoyed the slippery climb up to Summer Hill—nailed down a solid 5th (47:45). Finish-line fans were treated to a battle for sixth and seventh, as former Shippensburg All-American distance runner Randy Lowe (6th, 47:55) held off former Bloomsburg harrier Kip Hoffman by 1 second.

Rounding out the 8 through 15 places were Mike Craighead, Dan Pszeniczny, Budd Coates, Marty Owens, Jeff McCabe, Greg Remaly, Mike Styczynski, and Tim Schuler.

In the women's race, former Moravian College All-American Kim Jaick (now Kim Jaick Soden) came from fourth to first in the last mile to capture the first-place diamond pendant.

As the front-runners—Jaick's former Greyhound teammate Heidi Wolfsberger, Patty Fulton of Silver Springs, Maryland (the 1999 Steamtown Marathon champion), and former Bucknell star Carly Graytock—battled one another up to Summer Hill, Jaick stayed off a pace that seemed too hard, too soon. But then she rallied on the steep downhill and realized she had gained back some ground. She drew even closer through Kachinka's Hollow, and on the sweeping descent from Martzville Church down to the golf course, the diminutive Jaick zipped into first place.

There was only one strange thing about that move: Kim Jaick did not *know* she was in first place!

The always knowledgeable crowds at Berwick, however, were only too happy to let her in on the secret.

"Over the last 2 miles, people in the crowd kept yelling to me 'Way to go . . . You're the first woman!' she recalls. "But I didn't actually *believe* them! So I just kept running fast. Over the last mile, I tried to kick as hard as I could."

Jaick never did pass another female runner—and with good reason.

Clay Shaw Photo

You Better Believe It: Kim Jaick thought it was too good to be true when the Berwick fans yelled "First woman!"

The crowd was right. There were no other women to pass. She crossed the line on Market in 55 minutes, 46 seconds for the victory. "It wasn't until I actually finished that I fully believed I had won, because coming into the race my goal was just to try and win a diamond."

Graytock placed second (56:10), with Fulton (3rd, 56:11) and Wolfsberger (4th, 56:21) not far behind. Tina Bartholomew also cracked 57-minutes, securing fifth (56:52). Amy Rome (6th, 57:31) and former Bloomsburg runner Michele Wolyniec (7th, 58:10) rounded out the diamond pendant award winners.

Tony Lawson (51:30) and Wendy Blass (59:00, 9th woman) led the "Berwick Brigade" for top local honors.

Finish Lines: Third-place finisher Patty Fulton—originally from Drums, Pennsylvania—helped the University of Scranton Royals to an NCAA D-3 title in women's basketball in 1984-85. "I had my diamond mounted on a pendant and gave it to my mom," Bronfenbrenner said recently. "But I just got engaged, so I might have to come back and try to get another one."

Clay Shaw Photo

Just Coastin': Dave Bronfenbrenner (680) dueled with Steve Walsh at Berwick in 2002, winning in just over 46 minutes. In 2003 Bronfenbrenner took five months to run from the New Jersey shore to the Oregon Coast.

IV
Mykytok Makes His Move
94th Run for the Diamonds, November 27, 2003

We can only imagine what C. N. MacCrea, A. E. Domville, and James Sigman would have thought had they miraculously reappeared at the Market Street finish line in 2003 and heard hundreds of chirping "beeps." Berwick, despite its endearing time-warp charm, had finally succumbed to high tech. For the 2003 race, computer chips—over the same course on which the Carlisle Indians once raced in deerskin-leather moccasins—were attached to the shoes of more than a thousand runners.

So, computer chips were there.

The defending men's champion was *not* there, but Dave Bronfenbrenner had a good reason—in fact, *two* good reasons—for not defending his title.

The first reason was that Bronfenbrenner went for a long run during the summer. Well, actually, the run started in the spring and took about five months. This particular long run was across the United States of America.

Said Bronfenbrenner about this little jaunt (from Seabright, New Jersey, to Florence, Oregon), which he undertook with former Bison teammate Scott Sehon:

> "There is no way to comprehend how we will feel on that first day, as we stand with our feet in the Atlantic staring west. There is no way to know what the drudgery of covering 20 miles a day, every day, for five months will feel like. But I tell you what, of all the pain, repetition, or bad luck that could happen I am totally and completely ready for it."

And then, having run across the entire country, Bronfenbrenner flew back to the Lehigh Valley to his parents' home, threw his stuff in a car, and drove *back* across the country to UC-Berkeley for graduate school. (Our 2002 Berwick winner was working on a project at Berkeley described thusly: "Mr. Dave Bronfenbrenner is pursuing new synthesis methods to generate NiTi thin films that avoid the common amorphous-to-crystalline phase transformation required of conventional sputtering routines." (The author invites interpretations of just what exactly that might mean . . .)

So . . . the defending champion, with a run across the country and some deep-thinking research to be confronted, was out.

But Mike Mykytok—former Bound Brook, New Jersey, scholastic standout and University of Florida Gator—was in and that all but guaranteed that the 2003 Berwick race would be a fast one. It was his first time back in Berwick since his gutsy runner-up finish to Jason Bodnar in 1996. Although arguably Mykytok was a bit past his very best running years, he had accomplished some big goals in his sport since his '96 Berwick race. High up on the list was a US track championship at 10,000 meters in 1999 in which he led, was passed, and then came back to nip big kicker Reuben Reina in a hotly contested photo finish. Mykytok clocked 28:34 in that race.

Like Tom Carter, Mykytok was—and is—a full-fledged member of the "free spirit" running association. (One story has it that he once sat on a roof and read poetry to his Florida Gator teammates.) As Carter usually did, Mykytok preferred to blast away from the opening gun. When the 2003 event got the gun, that's exactly what Mykytok did—he attacked. He hammered down to Foundryville and then he diligently tucked into "the Hill." At the top, he had a big cushion.

Mark Stallings, former Millersville All-American, however, wasn't about to give up the chase. He cut away at the lead on the plunging descent from Hosler's Hill. Mykytok still led at 5 miles, but Stallings was within striking distance. The former Marauder reached down deeper, got a little closer . . .

Coming out of Martzville and down to the golf course, Stallings drew even. The two men battled for the next 2 miles. Back on Market Street, Mykytok—as he had in that track 10,000 in '99 against Reina—found that extra comeback gear. He pulled away ever-so-slightly to post a 3-second triumph in 45 minutes, 41 seconds.

Mykytok's win was nearly a minute slower—but one important place better!—than his 1996 race. "He had to exert a lot of energy to catch me," Mykytok said afterward. And it was an observation that Stallings

Pick Your Kicker: Mykytok (2) and Stallings (3) dig into the last 2 miles, poised for a fast finish.

admitted to—his courageous charge had given him a shot to win, but he lost the coin flip when Mykytok responded.

Third was more than two minutes behind, but Ed Schlichter of Chambersburg (47:53) held off Bethelehem's Phil Reutlinger (47:57) in the homestretch. Mountain specialist Bill Raitter of California (5th, 48:15), Dan Pseniczny (6th, 48:36), and Jeff McCabe (7th, 48:49) rounded out the diamond winners.

The eight through fifteen spots went to: Scott Lewandoski, Justin Krebs, Shane Anthony, former Penn State runner Jeff Dobias, Fred Joslyn, Dan Dragwa, Kip Hoffman, and Pete Lobianco.

In the women's race, 47-year-old Debbie Grossman (1st, 54:23) of Shavertown, Pennsylvania, and Heidi Wolfsberger (2nd, 55:08) of Moosic, Pennsylvania, raced each other through halfway, and into Kachinka's Hollow. Grossman gradually pulled away over the final 4 miles, posting a 45-second win. "I just kept my pace . . . It's what I always do," Grossman said. "It's what I always do. The day was perfect. The whole town was out to cheer . . . They push you to the finish."

Berwick racing fans were thrilled to see one of their own—Becki McClintock—running a strong third (55:58). Before going onto Messiah College, McClintock had done her scholastic running for Coach Bill Bull

Clay Shaw Photo

Master Blaster: A rare feat, Debbie Grossman won the overall and Masters honors.

at Berwick High School, so she was flooded with cheers as she raced home.

After McClintock came Amy Pyles (4th, 56:08), 2001 champion Sarah Raitter (5th, 56:46), Lindsey Keller (6th, 57:09), and Molly Sunderlin (7th, 57:23).

Grossman got to double-dip—she won the Masters diamond, too. Deborah Gebhardt, a former Hazleton resident now living in Maryland, captured the Veterans diamond (1:08:43.)

V
McClintock's Homecoming Hurrah
96th Run for the Diamonds, November 25, 2004

Berwick race fans—through the decades—have, of course, always craved the thought of a truly local winner.

Of course, they did have Harry Williams, the 1908 inaugural winner, when the race was only between Berwick residents. But even Williams had originally come from the Scranton area.

Certainly John Luther "Blondy" Romig was from the *surrounding* area; the Penn State star of the 1920s era was from across the Susquehanna and upriver a few miles in the tiny farming community of Wapwallopen. Romig's upset of Ville Ritola—the fast-rising Finnish star—guaranteed him some historical spotlight in the history of the race.

But you could argue that the first true Berwickian to win the race was Becki McClintock, the former Messiah College runner, who galloped home first in 2004 to sweep the women's first-place diamond. McClintock certainly had had lots of practice on the course—it was her eighth race as a runner. (As a child her parents had often taken her out to 14th and Market to watch the throngs of runners run out and—eventually—come back.)

Thanksgiving morning didn't start all that promising; it was one of those fairly typical Berwick race days that appears bad initially, but clears up suddenly for the actual race. (Well, okay, it doesn't *always* cooperate in that fashion . . .)

But by the time the runners assembled on Market Street for the 10:30 start, the rain had stopped, the winds (which were strong enough to topple some trees) had mostly subsided, and the sun's rays were stroking across the Briar Creek Hills as if they were petting a friendly kitten.

McClintock, who did her high school running for Berwick and Coach

Bill Bull, charged to the front on the ascent to the Summer Hill churches. It was on the steep climb that she gradually pulled away from former champion Lisa Haas and Heidi Wolfsberger, one of her collegiate rivals.

"I remember someone on the press truck telling me that I was the first woman," McClintock recalls, "which was hard to believe because I felt so good. I didn't even feel like I was racing."

Although she now lives in the Harrisburg area, McClintock was still highly recognizable by the local fans, and their cheers and encouragement helped stoke her race.

"The locals were—and still are—the best part of the race," McClintock remarks. "There are several families that live along the course that know my family. It was great to hear them cheering for me and to hear their excitement in telling me that I was the first woman."

As McClintock raced up and down the dips of Kachinka's Hollow Road, she spotted Roberta Carlin, her sixth-grade gymnastics teacher, and her husband Bryan, her dentist, cheering for her.

McClintock rode this wave of enthusiasm back to North Berwick. In the final quarter mile to the finish, her father was so excited that he ran along beside her. She crossed the line in 54 minutes, 18 seconds—raising her black-gloved hands slightly in celebration, with a smile that overrode any slight signs of fatigue on her face.

It was just one of those races that you dream about, and McClintock essentially did just that.

"Leading up to that specific race, I had run some of my best times in the summer and fall—all with the intention of running well at Berwick. Each night—probably for a month before the race—I pictured myself running and winning, and hoped that I could bring those dreams to fruition."

Clay Shaw Photo

Berwick Becki: Becki McClintock's victory had the local community all abuzz in 2004. For her, a dream come true.

Behind McClintock's dream run, Heidi Wolfsberger (2nd, 56:36) held off Lisa Haas (3rd, 56:46) down Market Street. The four through seven places were quite spread out: Hazleton's Maria Monks (4th, 57:16), Lori Kingsley (5th, 58:43), Aimee Shebest (6th, 59:31), and Aimee Baylor (7th, 1:00:07).

Joyce Stevens won the Masters (1:07:08), Dianna Golden captured the Veterans (1:03:23), and Joan Miller took the 60-plus title (1:25:30).

In the men's race, Mark Stallings—just 3 seconds off the win in 2003—took no prisoners. "I didn't want it to come down to a kick," he was later quoted in *The Runner's Gazette.*

With that thought etched on his mind, Stallings battled up the Foundryville Hill with former North Carolina-Charlotte runner Ed Schlichter and former Saint Joseph's ace Karl Savage, with Canadian Matt Kerr attempting to keep contact. But at the top of the hill, Stallings applied the pressure and established a lead that he continued to stretch out in the second half of the race. Stallings charged down Market Street for the victory in 45 minutes, 25 seconds.

Savage—who back in his collegiate days was the Atlantic 10's most valuable runner in both cross-country and track—captured second (46:12), while Schlichter (3rd, 46:42) out-dueled Kerr by 2 ticks. The fifth through seventh slots went to Matt Byrne (47:41), former Elizabethtown College All-American Dave Berdan (6th, 47:48) and C. Fred Joslyn (7th, 48:10) of SUNY Cortland.

Greg Cauller (14th overall in 49:55) won the men's Masters and Terry Permar (52:23) the men's 50-plus bracket, both familiar road warriors in Berwick.

But perhaps the most eye-opening age-group effort came from the game Canadian (by way of his native Great Britain) Ed Whitlock. The 73-year-old Whitlock cranked out 57 minutes, 45 seconds—a time that would have beaten the best in the 55 to 59 age group. Then again, Whitlock previously ran a world record for 73-year-olds with his 2:54:49 marathon earlier in the year, well under 7-minute-per-mile pace for 26 miles.

VI
Kerr Cruises and Wolfsberger Wins
96th Run for the Diamonds, November 24, 2005

Those who really know running will tell you not to put too much stock in what a runner has done in the past. After all, they say, that's why you run the race. Nevertheless, those lining up for the 96th Run for the Diamonds who *didn't* know a lot about Matthew Kerr's running résumé probably were better off. Coming from Winston-Salem, North Carolina—by way of Ontario, Canada, by way of Arkansas—perhaps Kerr flew under the pre-race hype radar. Besides, he had "only" finished fourth in his Berwick debut the year before.

However, running fanatics who were truly fine-tuned could have said things like this about Kerr: two-time NCAA steeplechase champion for John McDonald's Razorback herd (with a PR of 8:20 something), an All-American in cross-country, a 4:02 miler, two times on Team Canada's squad that competed in the World Track and Field Championships. Knowing that kind of background, you could assume he didn't come back to Berwick merely to place in the top seven again.

Kerr, who arguably had hit "the Hill" way too hard in 2004 and paid for it, also had a fine-tuned strategy. He wasn't going to fry himself with a blistering pace that might lead to yet another mountain meltdown. Instead, he keyed off others, and was content to keep contact with the front-runners as they labored up to Summer Hill in the chilly, winter-like conditions.

This time the end results matched Kerr's potential. He put the hammer down in the second half of the race en route to a zippy victory in 45 minutes, 13 seconds. Kerr crossed the line with his "number one" finger waving somewhat casually in the air, a comfortable winner.

Behind the Canadian ace, Chambersburg's Ed Schlichter ran a solid race to snag second (45:59)—just 1 second ahead of Scranton's Matt Byrne. Rounding out the top seven diamond award winners were C. Fred Joslyn (4th, 46:21), Ryan Bender (5th, 46:52), Ian Dickinson (6th, 48:12) and Peter Boyd (7th, 48:49).

In the women's race, Heidi Wolfsberger once again was knocking on the diamond door—she ran aggressively up to Summer Hill, grabbing a small lead over Vicki Boyer Cauller and the rest of the women's field. The former Moravian College star (a 12-time NCAA D-3 All-American) doesn't mind towering climbs—in fact, she often trains on the road leading to the top of the Montage ski resort near her home in Moosic, Pennsylvania.

"The thing people sometimes forget about Berwick, though," says Wolfsberger, "is that the downs can be tough, too. Sometimes I would get to the last few miles and get passed . . . I just didn't have much left."

Vicki Cauller, the former Saint Joseph's University ace, did pass Wolfsberger around the 7-mile mark. But the long-striding Wolfsberger rallied and surged back into the lead as the runners charged down Market Street. "I knew that I had less than a mile to go," Wolfsberger said, "so I gave it another push . . . and just held on."

Three's the Charm: After two straight seconds, Heidi Wolfsberger pushed through to clinch the first-place diamond in 2005.

Her last move held up and Wolfsberger—after two straight runner-up efforts at Berwick in 2003 and 2004—secured the first place diamond in a time of 54 minutes, 24 seconds. Vicki Cauller finished second in 54:39, while third went to Lisa Haas in 55:07.

The diamond pendant awards for the four through seven spots went to Kathleen Jobes (4th, 55:18), Amy Rome (5th, 58:14), Aimee Baylor (6th, 59:10), and Lynda DeBoer of Toronto (7th, 59:24), who also won the Masters diamond. The winner of the Veterans (50-plus) diamond was Dianna Golden (1:02:06), while Danville's Joan Miller won the Seniors (70-plus) diamond.

In a tight battle between men's Masters, Greg Cauller out-dueled Budd Coates by less than 10 seconds for the top 40-plus effort, clocking 50:59. Terry Permar of Perkasie, Pennsylvania, won the Veterans diamond in 52:25, while the incomparable Ed Whitlock of Canada won the Seniors diamond in 1:00.59.

The top locals (first Berwick finisher) were Tony Lawson (51:33) and Christa Johnson (1:07:24). Doug Alter wrestled the top local Masters spot from multi-time local champ Bill Bull.

Finish Lines: The 2005 race was dedicated to the memory of BMA member and longtime race announcer Rick Heller. Heller had passed away between the 2004 and 2005 races. Along with his family, Rick had been a longtime fixture on the flatbed truck situated at the finish for five decades. Reverend Reg Thomas (a frequent runner in the Berwick race) conducted a short memorial just prior to the starting gun.

Lynda DeBoer has pretty good bloodlines when it comes to running Berwick: Her dad was none other than Diamond's legend Wilmer "Whitey" Sheridan, and both her brothers (Mike and Dave) have been longtime racers of the event.

The 2004 women's champion (and hometown hero) Becki McClintock was conducting missionary work in Cambodia and missed the race. While in Asia, she ran several races, including one around the famous temple of Angkor Wat.

VII
Joslyn and Jobes Jump Up
97th Run for the Diamonds, November 23, 2006

C. Fred Joslyn, former Cortland State star and NCAA D-3 indoor 5000-meter champion, admits he is "not a strong uphill runner." Of course, that statement is relative; Joslyn proved strong enough to stay close to the leaders laboring up Foundryville Hill toward the Summer Hill churches. In a late reprieve, the rainy weather had subsided to actually provide nice racing conditions—overcast, calm, and just cool enough to wear racing gloves.

And then the descents followed, which Joslyn does run quite well, thank you. He saved his major move for the 6th mile—the long down past the golf course on Martzville Road—and zoomed to a 4:11 for that stretch. The surge broke him free from Scranton's Matt Byrne—the former Saint Joseph's runner and 2006 Steamtown Marathon champion—en route to the victory in 45 minutes, 51 seconds. Joslyn—wearing a singlet that read ALBANY RUNNING EXCHANGE—felt good enough to raise his right hand in the "number one" salute as he crossed the line.

It was a nice improvement for Joslyn. The Binghamton, New York, native had raced for the diamonds three other years, coming away with a fourth and a seventh, plus one 12th-place showing.

Byrne held on for second place, clocking 46:37, while Tristan Colangelo of Charlottesville, Virginia, thundered home third in 47:00. Former Elizabethtown College runner Greg Wetzel nailed down fourth (47:42), followed by Shawn Duffy (5th, 48:14) of Hazleton, former Messiah College star Bobby Dressler (6th, 48:21) and Kevin Stover (7th, 48:37) to wrap up the men's diamond awards. Greg Cauller, 14th overall, won the men's Masters in 50:10.

In the women's race, defending champion Heidi Wolfsberger hammered out a small lead up to Summer Hill, but Kathleen Jobes of Bethlehem stayed close enough to launch a second-half counterattack. Jobes grabbed the lead back around the 7-mile mark, then powered on for the win in 52 minutes, 39 seconds. Wolfsberger secured runner-up honors and a new personal best (53:01) time on the challenging course.

Good Job, Jobes: Kathleen Jobes came from behind to win the Run for the Diamonds, 2006 edition.

For the 35-year-old Jobes—who continues to improve her times even as she ages—the victory was a big one. "I'm excited about my win," she said. "Last year, when Heidi won, I finished fourth. I always wanted to win this race. This is my first time winning here in four attempts."

Vicki Cauller (3rd, 54:39), Amy Falk (4th, 55:34), Berwick's Becki Mc-Clintock (5th, 57:14), Lori Kingsley (6th, 57:45), and Sarah Muhlbredt (7th, 58:14) rounded out the women's diamond winners. Kingsley also won the Masters diamond award, while Dianna Golden was the top Veteran in 1:02.22.

Tony Lawson of Berwick was the top local finisher in 51:47, while Wendy Blass led the local ladies in 59:15.

Finish Lines: Kathleen Jobes and Heidi Wolfsberger are frequent rivals in Mid-Atlantic regional races. In 2008, they took it to another level as both runners qualified for the women's US Olympic Marathon trials held in Boston. Both athletes placed better than their seeded spots: Jobes (seeded 88th) placed 56th in 2 hours, 44 minutes, 57 seconds; Wolfsberger (seeded 66th) placed 28th in a personal best time of 2 hours, 41 minutes, 21.

C. Fred Joslyn is one of the newest members of the famed Hansons-Brooks racing team—the elite Olympic training group based in Michigan. His 10th place showing helped Hansons-Brooks win the team title at the 2008 US 25K championships held in Grand Rapids, Michigan.

Under the needs-further-investigation department is this fact: Under the section of "role models," Joslyn's Hansons-Brooks profile lists "Jesus and Tom Carter." . Like 1976 Berwick champ Carter, Joslyn originally resided in the Binghamton, New York, area.

VIII
On Celebration's Threshold
98th Run for the Diamonds, November 22, 2007

With some major celebrations—the 100th anniversary of the first race in 1908 and the actual 100th running—just around the corner, it stands to reason that the 2007 race might be slightly "low-key."

The size of the field, however, was anything but, with a new record of 1,123 runners streaming through the finish-line chutes on Market Street.

Weather was a factor, too, but not in the far more typical Berwick tradition of Thanksgiving Day snowflakes. Instead, runners stripped down to their racing vests and shorts, left their gloves in the car, and found the grind up to Summer Hill quite sweaty in the muggy, 70-degree temperatures.

The unseasonable temperatures affected the women's race, in that former Bucknell University runner Jennifer Stevens of Lacyville, Pennsylvania, led for more than 8 miles but, slowed by dehydration, gave way to the Hazleton area's Maria Monks. Monks, a sophomore on the MIT cross-country team, did not enter the race feeling she was truly fit to race a hard 9 miles, but she was able to switch gears well enough when the opportunity presented itself.

"When a fan yelled I was in second, I decided to push it and go for it," she said after her win in 57 minutes, 36 seconds. "But before that I wasn't going for the win. The leader had about 200 meters on me and I just kept getting closer and closer as we went on . . ."

Kelly Devine of Arlington, Virginia (57:52) also passed Stevens—who held on for a gutsy third in 58:17—in the last few blocks. Kingston, Pennsylvania's Kelly Ochreiter, who often competes in the sport of triathlon, placed fourth (58:45), while the remaining diamond award places went to Kate MacNamara of Dundas, Ontario (5th, 58:45), high school runner Shelby Pealer (6th, 59:08) of Naperville, Illinois, and Vicki McGrew of Factoryville, Pennsylvania (7th, in exactly 1 hour flat).

The age group diamond winners included Amy Snyder of Lansdale, Pennsylvania (40-plus, 1:07.18), repeat Veteran winner Dianna Golden of York, Pennsylvania (1:04:17) and Joan Miller (60-plus) in 1:27:19.

In the men's race, Tristan Colangelo of Charlottesville, Virginia (by way of Massachusetts, where he was a sub-4:10 miler and state cross-country champ in high school) was racing for another diamond, yes—but also a little redemption. Colangelo was less than happy with his third-place debut finish in 2006; in fact, to hear him tell it, you'd think he had a slice of humble pie, not pumpkin, for Thanksgiving dessert the previous year.

"I think I appreciate the win more, just because I didn't do well last year [note to readers: he was still third!]," Colangelo allowed after winning the 2007 race. "I really thought [in 2006] that I could come in and blow the field away. Then I lost by 2 minutes and it was a real eye opener."

Colangelo—a 2004 Princeton graduate with sub-9-minute steeplechase credentials—didn't cut loose from former St. Joe's Hawk stud Karl Savage until the Martzville Road, but then he moved out to a fairly comfortable victory in 46 minutes, 7 seconds. Savage still captured the runner-up slot in 46:49, while Canadian Matt Kerr (3rd, 47 flat) held off defending champ C. Fred Joslyn (4th, 47:06). A first-time Berwick runner, young Canadian Brendan Kenny, landed a diamond (5th, 47:20) in a virtual photo finish over rapidly improving Scranton area runner Kevin Borelli (6th, 47:20). The last open diamond went to Mike DiDio (7th, 47:42).

Chris Wadas (coach at Misericordia College in nearby Dallas) was recognized as the first finisher in the tricounty region (Luzerne, Columbia, and Wyoming) as he placed 14th overall in 49:59.

Richard Hellard of Ottawa, Canada, ran off with the Masters diamond in 51:49, while Budd Coates of Emmaus snagged the 50-plus diamond in 51:34. Yet another Canadian—Bill Horwich of Kitchener, Ontario—won the 60-plus diamond with 1:02:20.

Frequent Berwick participant Kim Gasper (formerly of Hazleton, now from Bellefonte, Pennsylvania) ran the race with a dislocated shoulder and her arm in a sling—merely to keep her Diamond streak, which spans several decades, alive.

THE LOCALS

In the beginning, there were the locals—in fact, *only* locals. Though it is often mentioned that Harry Williams, the 1908 winner, was a recent import from the Scranton area, he was a town resident at the time of the inaugural event. In fact, in the 1909 race program there is an advertisement for Williams' Café (H. L. Williams, Propr.) on Berwick's bustling Front Street. "Why not drop down to 'Hi's' for something refreshing after the race . . . ," the blurb implores. Even in its earliest days, merchants in the race program would often connect their message to the race itself in some manner.

The Pioneers

Williams was the first winner of the race, but the overall game changed abruptly when the Carlisle Indians—led by the Olympian Louis Tewanima—showed up for the second race in 1909. Don McQuaig, the first Canadian runner, appeared in 1909, too, so the race rapidly became an event that attracted serious runners from outside the region.

However, the first area runner was always of great interest to the townspeople and fans of those early Berwick Marathons—almost a race within the race. The first local finisher—almost from the event's inception—was an important result. (There is a lot of evidence, for example, that bets were made on who would be the first local finisher.)

The first dominant local runner in those early races was **Arthur Letteer**. Letteer won four local crowns (1914-15, 1917, 1920) and even broke 53 minutes—quite a feat in those early years.

Allen Parr from nearby Mifflinville was the next man to dominate the local scene. The former Bloomsburg Normal School runner pounded out five titles (1927 through 1931) and ran a personal best on the course of 51:47. Parr loved running on the unpaved layout around Berwick and actually retired once the new hard roads came on the scene because he said they hurt his feet.

In the years just before World War II, **Fitch Hons** was the local flier to be reckoned with. Hons won a trio of local titles (1935-37). Hons lost a leg in the war, but he remained very active in support of the Berwick

Photo courtesy of Berwick Marathon Association

Smooth Landing: Arthur Letteer appears to be performing "the airplane" as he heads for the finish and another local title in 1917.

Marathon; he often added a handsome cowhide briefcase to the list of race prizes.

Other three-time local Berwick winners include **Don Karnes** (Espy, Pennsylvania, 1938-1940), **Don Bedio** (1951-1953), and **Steve Fraind** (1954-55, 1958).

It would be impossible to cover the local angle of the race without a tip of the hat toward **Lanny Conner.** Conner won four crowns (1968, 1970, 1974 and 1976) and was the first local man to snap the 50-minute barrier with a course best of 49:31. The former Bloomsburg College cross-country coach also served the Berwick Marathon Association (BMA) in many capacities, including president.

If there is one area name that seems synonymous with the Berwick race, you would have to put the spotlight on **Bill Bull.** Bull's attention to detail may explain why he has raced so successfully over the years at Berwick—he has been known to actually sweep away some of the loose stones and gravel on Kachinka's Hollow Road after he fell there one year.

Regardless of the occasional mishap, Bull is the most dominant local runner in the history of the event. He won his first local crown in 1971 and—over the next several decades—collected an eye-opening 18 total titles (his most recent back in 1998). His personal best time of 46 minutes, 59 seconds is still the course record for locals and a mark that will not be easy to eclipse. In addition to years and years of dedicated service with the BMA, Bull also helped guide some of the area's best young runners in his capacity as Berwick High School cross-country coach. (Bill has also run the Boston Marathon 26 years in a row, but that's another story . . .)

Not surprisingly, the rest of the Bull family gets involved with Run for the Diamonds—wife Bev Bull is an important member of BMA, while in recent years daughters Alex and Abby have toed the starting line.

Bill Bull wasn't without competition during his reign—far from it. Some other outstanding local races came from **Steve "the Hare" Johnson**. He secured four titles (1975, 1977-78 and 1983) and, in 1983, posted a personal best of 48:08—relegating his friend and training partner Bull to

Clay Shaw Photo

Bullish on Berwick: Bill Bull charging to just one of his 18 local wins, this one in 1984. The next year Bull blasted his still-standing local mark of 46:59!

a rare second in a local battle royal.

One of the most eye-opening local performances ever came in 1980 when 16-year-old **Curt Whitmire** blasted 48:10—not only a new record on the course for Berwickians, but an effort that left both Bull and Johnson chasing the youngster (to no avail) down Market Street.

In recent years, **Tony Lawson** has been awesome on the area scene. Lawson has won 10 titles—nine straight from 1999 through 2007. His best time on the course has been a very respectable 50:40.

Although **Chris Aurand** and **Roger Davis** have never won top local honors, they both have big Berwick streaks to speak of. Aurand has run every race since 1973 when he was a senior at Berwick High. Davis has run every race since 1975—each and every one *under* an hour!

A consistent age-bracket winner over the decades has been Berwick's **Richard Hause**. In 2005, Hause was first in the men's 70-plus age group.

Clay Shaw Photo

Berwick Blass and Tough Tony: With eight local titles, Wendy Blass is the local diamond queen. Lawson has ten lifetime local wins to Bill Bull's eighteen notches.

The local women did not appear on the course until 1973, when **Debbie Focht** finished the course. But soon the local time to beat for the ladies was already under an hour, as **Carol May** clocked 59:47 and won the first of her three titles (1979, 1985-86).

May's mark stood until 1998 when **Wendy Blass** shattered the local women's record with 58:37, then broke again the next year in 58:21 (currently the time to beat for Berwickians). Blass has won more area crowns—a solid stash of eight—than any other local lass.

Justine Johnson (1991-1993 and 1995), who won the district cross-country title for Bill Bull when she ran for Berwick High School, has four local victories. Johnson also achieved NCAA D-3 All-American honors in cross-country for Moravian College.

Other local women with multiple wins in that division include **Kathy Pyles** (1996-97), **Christa Johnson** (2004-05), and **Betsy Shope-Thomas** (1977-78).

JJ Can Jet: Justine Johnson won four Berwick local crowns, coinciding with an outstanding collegiate career.

Running the Show

As **C. N. MacCrea** (who passed away in 1973) got on in years, the job of running the Berwick Marathon fell increasingly upon the able shoulders of **Bill Heller.** Heller did a great job promoting the race—both bringing in top runners from the Baltimore area, such as three-time winner Frank Pflaging, and writing about the Berwick Marathon in the local papers. A former Berwick High School cross-country coach, Heller also launched the first Schoolboy Race in 1959—an event that will soon celebrate its 50th anniversary. The Heller family also often hosted visiting runners, particularly the Canadian stalwart Whitey Sheridan.

Photo courtesy of Michael Sheridan

Berwick YMCA / Barry Lush / A.V. Smith / Whitey Sheridan / Jean & Bill Heller / Richard Heller

Berwick Bonds: The Hellers loved to host Canadian visitors (here runners Barry Lush and Whitey Sheridan, flanking Canadian coach A. V. Smith in the 1950s). That little guy—Rick—eventually announced many a runner at the Berwick finish line.

When Bill Heller died suddenly in 1970, his son **Rick Heller** immediately answered the call to take over the demands of running the race.

"That may well have been a critical time in the history of the race," says present race director **Margaret Livsey.** "If Rick Heller had not risen to the challenge and agreed to be race director, then it is possible the race might have ceased."

But the race continued to prosper under Rick Heller's leadership. Like his father, Rick continued to generate publicity and post-race articles about the race. He also never shied away from the small tasks—such as painting numbers on cloth back in the day! Rick Heller passed away suddenly in 2005.

Any list of crucial taskmasters in the Berwick Marathon/Run for the Diamonds operation over the years must also include **Karl Herr** (who did not run himself, but his son Bob Herr won the local title in 1965), who served as BMA president during the 1970s "boom" years; **Dr. Harold "Doc" Fisher** (who was an avid solicitor for advertising for the race program); and many, many others.

The present hierarchy of the Berwick Marathon Association includes **Margaret Livsey** (many years as race secretary and/or race director), **Bill Hower** (an officer in BMA for over 30 years), Bill Bull (a BMA member since 1977, presently president), and **Bob Eveland,** a former Bulldog football man who handles all the heavy work around the chutes—an increasingly tough jobs as the fields have topped 1,000 in recent years.

Ed Livsey (Margaret's husband) is recognizable to anyone who has waited for the gun to go off at Berwick. He is not the starter—he comes on *before* the guy with the gun. Ed is the guy with the clarinet. His renditions of both the Canadian and US national anthems gets everybody ready to rock-and-roll when it's time to "Run for the Diamonds."

It's a Berwick tradition that bolsters the running spirit before it goes forth and slams into "the Hill."

Making Notes: Ed Livsey reaches for the high notes—as Margaret lends a mike.

EPILOGUE

Historic Heartbeat

One hundred years . . . a century . . . ten decades . . . No matter how you compile it, a lot of time has passed by since the original 13 men lined up on Market Street. With both the ever-present Susquehanna River and the span across to Nescopeck so close at hand, the clichéd temptation, of course, is to compare all those passing years to water flowing beneath the bridge. Keep in mind that an ice jam early in the twentieth century—a few years before the first race—took out the bridge; it had to be replaced. There are no guarantees in this world in terms of "lasting."

The landmarks around Berwick have changed and continue to change, some faster than others.

For example, in 1908 the Berwick Hotel was still about fifteen years away from being built. It was "state of the art" in 1925. You could say that it passed through its heyday some decades back and now—sadly—has boards over some of its windows. Sometimes I want to shout at the building: "Do you know Johnny Kelley had his picture taken in your lobby?" But how blatantly *crazy* would that be?

Before the First World War, the St. Charles Hotel was considered one of the best in the county—and Pop Warner made sure his Indian runners roomed there (if under strict supervision) on their trips to Berwick. The St. Charles, in fact, had been built upon the foundation of what once had been Evan Owen's homestead. (Owen—a Quaker settler—was the original founder of Berwick, Pennsylvania, in 1786.) Some townspeople can tell you that the once cozy St. Charles burned to the ground in 1982.

In 1908, the YMCA stood on Market Street—the "new" one is now several blocks away. But for many years, the runners would emerge from the YMCA dressing rooms on Market and trot out to the line—accompanied by much fanfare and some brassy notes pouring forth from the Berwick cornet band—as they were announced to the crowd. Many fans, as we know—especially in those early races—had more than a passing interest in the outcome; they were betting on one fleet lad or another.

In 1908, Brit Seely followed the runners around the course on horseback and was able to verify that the race had been fairly contested. But it wasn't long before the first clumsy automobiles were lumbering around the race route and kicking up dust. In 1980, there was a thundering helicopter looming above Pete Pfitzinger when he made his major move—the thunk-thunk-thunk of its blades obliterating any chance that Pfitzinger might hear the footsteps of would-be pursuers.

As we can document, what the runners wear has greatly changed, too. The racing shoes are lighter, faster, more cushioned. Gone are the cumbersome cotton sweats (not to mention the full-length fur coat Yonkers runner Russell Springsteen wore to the starting line in the pre-World War I era), the cotton vest and shorts. The first numbers worn by the runners were actually hand-painted on cloth, progressing to those big, awkward cardboard numbers, and—finally—to the high-tech, lightweight versions of today. You could argue that with the emergence of the chip in recent years, the numbers serve only to identify the runners for the fans—so they know whom they might be cheering for—but not to track them for the purpose of final results.

In the 1980s, the Berwick Marathon Association changed the name of the race from the "Berwick Marathon" to the "Run for the Diamonds"— perhaps an obvious fix since the old event was not (in the technical 26-mile sense) a full marathon. Besides, the enticing diamonds probably deserved some kind of mention—luring runners to the infamous "Hill" as surely as the legendary Lorelei nymph lured sailors to the rocks of wreckage on the Rhine.

Interestingly, though, a number of the old runners—contacted decades after they last raced at Berwick—had some trouble remembering the actual distance. Horace Ashenfelter thought it might have been a half-marathon, and Doug Kyle (who snapped Browning Ross's seven-straight streak in 1957) thought it was 15 miles. (In their defense, both men only ran Berwick once.) When I mentioned to Kyle that the race was really "only" 9 miles, there was a slight pause on the other end of the line in western Canada and then Kyle rebounded nicely with: "Well, it certainly *felt* like 15 miles!"

The question that most begs asking, of course, is not if the length and layout will remain the same, but whether the Run for the Diamonds will still "be" at the end of another hundred years.

"Hard roads and wide will run through . . . You will hunt it on the map and it won't be there," writes Ross Lockridge Jr. in *Raintree County*—his best-selling novel set in a mythical place in rural Indiana.

Berwick, of course, is a real place. The race is part of its reality, its historic heartbeat. If you listen closely to the history of the race, you can hear the twin heartbeat of the town. Without the race, Berwick might still be *called* Berwick, but I would argue that the town would be something less than its best.

I can picture them, then, a hundred years from now. They will gather on the bluff above the Susquehanna—these children of our running tribe—ready to wind through the Briar Creek Hills, ready to rage against all the loneliness, against their own fear . . . They will gather to run in our strange race ritual . . . this celebration of camaraderie, this celebration of courage. And their heartbeats will sound a little bit like . . . history.

Of course, we can only guess if this scenario will actually come to be. But isn't it nice to think so?

BERWICK MEN'S CHAMPIONS

Date	Winner	Time	Weather
1908—Harry Williams		59:37	Cloudy, mild, breezy
1909—Louis Tewanima		54:16*	Snow, sleet, calm
1910—Louis Tewanima		49:56*	Clear, warm, breezy
1911—Louis Tewanima		49:34*	Fair, cool, calm
1912—Harry Smith		49:26*	Clear, cool, muddy
1913—Willie Kramer		48:33*	Cloudy, snow, breezy
1914—George Holden		50:29	Fair, mild, calm
1915—Hannes Kolehmainen		49:03	Mild, clear, muddy
1916—Hannes Kolehmainen		49:22	Fair, mild, breezy
1917—Hannes Kolehmainen		49:15	Fair, clear, calm
1918-1919	No Race (World War I)		
1920—John "Blondy" Romig		50:51	Rain, sleet, cold
1921—Ville Ritola		49:24	Rainy, windy, mild
1922—Ville Ritola		47:56*	Mild, clear, calm
1923—Jimmy Henigan		48:39	Clear, mild, breezy
1924—Jimmy Henigan		48:43	Clear, cool, breezy
1925—Fred Wachsmuth		49:54	Clear, cool, windy
1926—Cliff Bricker		49:05	Cloudy, cool, breezy
1927—Cliff Bricker		48:22	Rain, cool, breezy
1928—Phil Silverman		49:30	Cloudy, mild, calm
1929—Gus Moore		49:42	Cold, windy, cloudy
1930—Dick Detwiler		50:15	Cold, windy, cloudy
1931—Lou Gregory		48:01	Mild, clear, calm
1932—Wilf McCluskey		49:09	Fair, cool, breezy
1933—Robert "Scotty" Rankine		48:35	Fair, high winds
1934—Robert "Scotty" Rankine		48:08	Rain, cool, breezy
1935—Robert "Scotty" Rankine		47:35*	Rain, mild, calm
1936—Robert "Scotty" Rankine		47:35	Cold, wind, flurries
1937—Robert "Scotty" Rankine		47:16*	Clear, cool, calm
1938—Pete Olexy		51:25	Snow, windy, cold
1939—Lou Gregory		47:40	Clear, cool, calm
1940—Ellison "Tarzan" Brown		50:35	Sleet, cold, windy
1941—Lou Gregory		48:25	Clear, cool, calm
1942—Johnny Kelley		48:55	Cloudy, mild, breezy
1943—Johnny Kelley		48:47	Clear, mild, breezy
1944—Johnny Kelley		49:20	Windy, cloudy, cold
1945—Johnny Kelley		49:16	Clear, cold, calm
1946—H. Browning Ross		48:35	Clear, cold, breezy
1947—H. Browning Ross		48:37	Clear, cold, breezy
1948—H. Browning Ross		48:24	Clear, cool, windy
1949—Curt Stone		47:19	Clear, cold, breezy
1950—H. Browning Ross		46:50*	Clear, cold, calm
1951—H. Browning Ross		46:41*	Cloudy, cold, breezy
1952—H. Browning Ross		46:40*	Cloudy, cold, calm
1953—H. Browning Ross		46:38*	Cloudy, cool, calm
1954—H. Browning Ross		47:15	Cloudy, cool, windy
1955—H. Browning Ross		46:43	Cloudy, cool, windy
1956—H. Browning Ross		46:39	Clear, cold, windy
1957—Doug Kyle		46:40	Cloudy, warm, breezy
1958—Bob Carman		47:33	Clear, cold, windy

1959—Jim Green	46:54	Clear, cool, breezy
1960—Vic Zwolak	46:25*	Cloudy, mild, calm
1961—Dick Shirey	47:38	Cloudy, drizzle, cold
1962—Kevin Quinn	47:35	Rain, cold, windy
1963—Frank Pflaging	46:50	Clear, cold, breezy
1964—Frank Pflaging	46:46	Cloudy, rain, cool
1965—Frank Pflaging	45:57*	Cloudy, mild, calm
1966—Charlie Messenger	45:36*	Cloudy, cold, breezy
1967—Bob Scharf	46:11	Cloudy, cool, calm
1968—Patrick McMahon	45:19*	Cloudy, mild, breezy
1969—Herb Lorenz	45:18*	Clear, cool, calm
1970—Jerry Richey	45:29	Clear, mild, breezy
1971—Dave Northey	44:55*	Rainy, mild, calm
1972—Jeff Bradley	46:03	Cloudy, cold, calm
1973—Tim Cook	45:39	Clear, cool, breezy
1974—Lou Calvano	45:39	Cloudy, cool, windy
1975—Rob Legge	45:08	Cloudy, cool, breezy
1976—Tom Carter	44:16*	Clear, cool, calm
1977—Ed "Bo" Brennan	45:12	Cloudy, cool, breezy
1978—Dave Northey	44:03*	Clear, cool, breezy
1979—Dave Patterson	44:29	Cloudy, cool, calm
1980—PETE PFITZINGER	43:21*	Clear, cold, breezy
1981—Pete Pfitzinger	44:05	Clear, mild, calm
1982—John Doub	44:19	Rain, cold, windy
1983—Rob Earl	43:47	Rain, cool, windy
1984—Budd Coates	44:06	Fair, cold, breezy
1985—Bill Reifsnyder	44:19	Rain, cold, windy
1986—Brian Ferrari	44:43	Clear, cool, breezy
1987—Steve Spence	44:20	Cloudy, cool, breezy
1988—Kevin Ruch	44:41	Clear, mild, breezy
1989—Craig Thompson	45:52	Clear, cool, breezy
1990—Jeff Martin	46:01	Clear, warm, calm
1991—Budd Coates	45:11	Cloudy, cool, calm
1992—Randy Haas	44:39	Rainy, mild, calm
1993—Jason Bodnar	44:27	Clear, cool, calm
1994—Jason Bodnar	45:17	Sunny, cold, windy
1995—Randy Haas	45:29	Cloudy, cool, calm
1996—Jason Bodnar	44:27	Cloudy, cold, windy
1997—Todd Fach	45:39	Clear, cool, windy
1998—Jamie Hibell	45:56	Cool, damp, calm
1999—Carleton "Buck" Jones	44:56	Rainy, cold, calm
2000—Jeff Barker	45:33	Sunny, cold, calm
2001—Matt Wagoner	47:08	Warm, breezy
2002—Dave Bronfenbrenner	46:10	Snow flurries, cold, breezy
2003—Mike Mykytok	45:41	Sunny, cool
2004—Mark Stallings	45:25	Cool, partly sunny
2005—Matt Kerr	45:13	Cold, blustery
2006—C. Fred Joslyn	45:51	Cloudy, cool, calm
2007—Tristan Colangelo	46:07	Warm, muggy

*Course Record
Note: From 1946 through 1954, the race finished at Crispin Field. All other races finished on Market Street.

BERWICK WOMEN'S CHAMPIONS

1972—Laurie Ruggieri	1:06:52
1973—Debbie Focht	1:24:09
1974—No entries	
1975—Laurie Griffith	1:20:40
1976—Sharon Jarrey	59:58*
1977—Karin Von Berg	57:58*
1978—Beth Guerin	55:03*
1979—Karen Warlow	58:55
1980—Kathy Warlow	55:04
1981—Katy Schilly	50:54*
1982—Laura deWald	53:23
1983—Barb Swan	55:23
1984—Muffi McLeod	51:50
1985—Tammy Donnelly	52:33
1986—Chris Skarvelis	55:25
1987—Lori Adams	54:12
1988—Eileen Thompson	53:45
1989—Tammy Slusser	53:10
1990—Kirsten Harteis	54:19
1991—Molly Mitke	53:33
1992—Misti Demko	51:00
1993—Wendy Nelson-Barrett	51:38
1994—Lisa Reilly	53:31
1995—Wendy Nelson-Barrett	52:50
1996—Wendy Nelson-Barrett	51:31
1997—Tracy Wartman	53:30
1998—Misti Demko	51:24
1999—Kristina Laubenstein	52:21
2000—Connie Buckwalter	54:50
2001—Sarah Raitter	53:29
2002—Kim Jaick	55:46
2003—Debbie Grossman	54:23
2004—Becki McClintock	54:18
2005—Heidi Wolfsberger	54:24
2006—Kathleen Jobes	52:39
2007—Maria Monks	57:36